Constructing Democratic Governance
in Latin America

Constructing Democratic Governance in Latin America

Fourth Edition

EDITED BY

Jorge I. Domínguez
and
Michael Shifter

The Johns Hopkins University Press
Baltimore

9 8 7 6 5 4 3 2 1

The Johns Hopkins University Press
2715 North Charles Street
Baltimore, Maryland 21218-4363
www.press.jhu.edu

Library of Congress Cataloging-in-Publication Data

Constructing democratic governance in Latin America / edited by
Jorge I. Domínguez and Michael Shifter. — Fourth edition.
        pages cm
    Includes bibliographical references and index.
    "An Inter-American Dialogue Book."
    ISBN 978-1-4214-0979-5 (pbk. : alk. paper) — ISBN 978-1-4214-0980-1
(electronic) — ISBN 1-4214-0979-8 (pbk. : alk. paper) — ISBN 1-4214-0980-1
(electronic)
    1. Latin America—Politics and government—1980–   2. Democracy—
Latin America.   I. Domínguez, Jorge I., 1945–   II. Shifter, Michael.
    JL966.C677 2013
    320.98—dc23   2012041079

A catalog record for this book is available from the British Library.

*Special discounts are available for bulk purchases of this book. For more
information, please contact Special Sales at 410-516-6936 or
specialsales@press.jhu.edu.*

The Johns Hopkins University Press uses environmentally friendly book
materials, including recycled text paper that is composed of at least
30 percent post-consumer waste, whenever possible.

To the memory of Carlos Iván Degregori (1945–2011), a dear friend and colleague whose rare intellect and commitment to democracy remain an inspiration

Contents

Preface

It is fitting that this fourth edition of *Constructing Democratic Governance in Latin America* coincides with the Inter-American Dialogue's 30th anniversary. In 1982, when authoritarian governments largely dominated the region, the Dialogue convened its first conference. From the outset, democracy was a fundamental, animating concern that has shaped the organization's programming and policy efforts over the subsequent three decades. With the transition to civilian, constitutional rule in the early 1990s, the focus of the Dialogue's work has shifted to improving the quality of democratic governance.

The centerpiece of the Dialogue's work in this area has been a series of systematic exercises aimed at tracking the progress of democracy throughout the Americas. The idea has been straightforward: to engage topflight analysts from Latin America, the United States, and Europe to appraise the advances and setbacks in democratic governance in the Americas, as well as to examine the impact of highly pertinent, cross-cutting regional themes related to the topic. The chapters would not only adhere to the highest academic standards, but would also have practical value. The products were intended for scholars, for use in the classroom, and for key decision makers in the policy community.

This fourth edition takes on the measure of the quality of democracy over roughly the last five years since the third edition came out in 2008. The first was published in 1996 and the second in 2003. We hope this edition, as previous ones, offers valuable baselines and reference points against which to judge democratic performance in countries and particular issues while shedding light on the complexities and nuances that should inform assessments of democratic performance in these countries. Although we have sought to achieve some continuity in the themes and countries covered—and in the authors commissioned to write them— each edition contains a distinct mix of the two. This volume contains eight country studies and four on crosscutting themes. The chapters are necessarily selective—some key countries and issues are not included—but they are at least in part representative of the evolving priorities in the study of democratic governance.

In each edition we have used terms of reference that seemed most pertinent. Since the first edition we have asked authors to consider critical dimensions of democratic governance such as the performance of political parties, civilian control over the armed forces, the protection of human rights, emphasis on social inclusion and equity, productive relations between the executive and the legislature, and harmony between democratic practices and state reforms. These dimensions have been integrated, as warranted, into the individual country chapters on Argentina, Bolivia, Brazil, Chile, Colombia, Mexico, Peru, and Venezuela. The thematic chapters focus, respectively, on the effects of constitutional rewriting, commodity booms, the spread of criminal violence, and the changing role of the media on the quality of democratic governance.

In all four editions we have profited enormously from the magnificent intellectual direction and leadership provided by Jorge I. Domínguez, Antonio Madero Professor for the Study of Mexico and vice provost for international affairs at Harvard University. Domínguez, a prodigious and indefatigable scholar and founding member of the Inter-American Dialogue, contributed to this exercise in immeasurable ways. No one is more experienced and skilled in conceptualizing and producing a volume of this kind. It has been an immense delight to collaborate and coedit this edition, as the previous two, with him. Domínguez thanks the Weatherhead Center for International Affairs and the David Rockefeller Center for Latin American Studies for general support, and in particular Kathleen Hoover for her superb assistance.

The chapters went through several drafts and benefited a great deal from vigorous discussions among the authors at a workshop in Washington, DC, in October 2011. The constructive feedback on the original drafts considerably enriched the final product. Participants in that workshop included Peter Hakim, Dialogue president emeritus, and Abraham F. Lowenthal, the Dialogue's founding director and coeditor of the 1996 edition, who provided acute and helpful comments on the drafts.

In keeping with previous attempts to give this project a policy focus, we were honored and pleased that Bill Richardson—former New Mexico governor, cabinet official, Organization of American States envoy, and Dialogue member—addressed a dinner gathering of the Washington policy community at the Carnegie Endowment for International Peace. Governor Richardson's thoughtful remarks on US policy challenges in Latin America, which explored ways of helping to foster democratic practices and institutions in the region, offered a valuable backdrop to the following day's discussion. We were also delighted that Lázaro Cárdenas, former Michoacán governor and Dialogue member, agreed to share some opening remarks and introduce Richardson.

At the Johns Hopkins University Press, we are deeply grateful to Suzanne Flinchbaugh for her steadfast support, exemplary professionalism, and unfailing patience in shepherding this edition through. We note with sadness the passing of Henry Tom in 2011. Tom worked closely in the production of the first three editions at the Press and was a strong advocate for this project.

At the Dialogue, we are indebted to several staff members. We particularly express our thanks to Alexis Arthur and Cameron Combs for their outstanding management and coordination of the effort as well as excellent editing. Adam Siegel helped organize the project during its initial phase, and Rachel Schwartz ably edited several chapters. We also appreciate the valuable contributions made by Dialogue interns Sarah Cardona, Mariel Aramburu, Laura Zaccagnino, and Tim Heine.

The Inter-American Dialogue is profoundly grateful to the Vidanta Foundation, whose generous support made this effort possible. Roberto Russell, the Foundation's president, was an active participant in the authors' workshop and source of enormous encouragement. We also thank Daniel Chávez Morán, the president of the Vidanta Group, for believing in this project.

Michael Shifter
President
Inter-American Dialogue

Contributors

Ángel E. Álvarez is the director of the Institute for Political Studies at the Universidad Central de Venezuela (UCV). He has authored several books and articles on Venezuelan politics, including *El sistema político venezolano: Crisis y transformaciones* (UCV, 1996), *Los dineros de la política* (UCV, 1997), and, coedited with José Enrique Molina, *Los partidos políticos venezolanoas en el siglo XXI* (Vadell Hermanos, 2004).

Taylor C. Boas is assistant professor of political science at Boston University, where his research and teaching focus on comparative politics, Latin American politics, methodology, political communication, electoral campaigns, and political behavior. His publications include articles in *American Journal of Political Science, World Politics, Studies in Comparative International Development, Journal of Theoretical Politics,* and *Latin American Research Review.* He is also coauthor of *Open Networks, Closed Regimes: The Impact of the Internet on Authoritarian Rule* (Carnegie Endowment for International Peace, 2003).

Ernesto Calvo is associate professor of political science in the Department of Government and Politics at the University of Maryland. His research focuses on the comparative study of electoral and legislative institutions, patronage and cosponsorship networks, and representation. His work has been published in the *American Journal of Political Science, World Politics, Comparative Political Studies, British Journal of Political Science,* and *Electoral Studies.*

Javier Corrales is professor of political science at Amherst College in Amherst, Massachusetts. His recent research spans Venezuela, politics of sexuality, and constitutional reforms. He is the coauthor of *Dragon in the Tropics: Hugo Chávez and the Political Economy of Revolution in Venezuela* (Brookings Institution Press, 2011), the coeditor of *The Politics of Sexuality in Latin America: A Reader on GLBT Rights* (University of Pittsburgh Press, 2010), and author of *Presidents Without*

Parties: The Politics of Economic Reform in Argentina and Venezuela in the 1990s (Pennsylvania State University Press, 2002).

Lucía Dammert is an associate professor at Universidad de Santiago de Chile. Her most recent books are *Maras* (coedited with Thomas Bruneau, University of Texas Press, 2011), and *Crime and Fear in Latin America* (Routledge, forthcoming). She has consulted for the Inter-American Development Bank, the World Bank, the United Nations Development Programme, and the European Commission, in countries such as Peru, Bolivia, Argentina, Dominican Republic, El Salvador, Honduras, and Costa Rica.

Jorge I. Domínguez is the Antonio Madero Professor for the Study of Mexico in the Department of Government and vice provost for international affairs at Harvard University. His recent work addresses US-Latin American relations and the Cuban revolution, among others. He has been coeditor for all four editions of *Constructing Democratic Governance in Latin America* and is a founding member of the Inter-American Dialogue.

Steven Levitsky is professor of government at Harvard University. His research interests include political parties, authoritarianism and democratization, and weak and informal institutions, with a focus on Latin America. He is author of *Transforming Labor-Based Parties in Latin America: Argentine Peronism in Comparative Perspective* (Cambridge University Press, 2003), coauthor of *Competitive Authoritarianism: Hybrid Regimes after the Cold War* (Cambridge University Press, 2010), and coeditor of *Argentine Democracy: The Politics of Institutional Weakness* (Pennsylvania State University Press, 2005), *Informal Institutions and Democracy: Lessons from Latin America* (Johns Hopkins University Press, 2006), and *The Resurgence of the Latin American Left in Latin America* (Johns Hopkins University Press, 2011). He is currently engaged in research on the durability of revolutionary regimes, the causes and consequences of party collapse in Peru, and the challenges of party-building in contemporary Latin America.

Sebastián Mazzuca studied political science (PhD) and economics (MA) at UC Berkeley, and was a post-doctoral fellow at Harvard University (WCFIA Academy Post-doc). His work focuses on the origins and transformations of states and political regimes, and their coevolution with economic development. His most recent articles have been published in *Comparative Politics*, *Hispanic American Historical Review*, *Studies in International Comparative Development*, and *The Oxford Handbook of Political Science*. He taught comparative politics, political economy, and institutional analysis at the Universities of Harvard, Salamanca (Spain), de los Andes (Colombia), and Di Tella (Argentina). He is a research fellow at CIAS and a visiting professor at UNSAM (Buenos Aires).

George Gray Molina is a Bolivian economist and political scientist. He is coeditor of *Tensiones irresueltas: Bolivia pasado y presente* with Laurence Whitehead and John Crabtree (Plural, 2010), *La otra frontera* (UNDP, 2009), *El estado del estado* (UNDP, 2007), *La economía más allá del gás* (UNDP, 2005), and author of a number of articles on politics, economics, and development. He also cofounded a think tank on green development, Instituto Alternativo. He currently works at the United Nations Development Programme, based in New York.

María Victoria Murillo is a professor at Columbia University's School of International and Public Affairs. Her work covers distributive politics and political parties in Latin America. She is the author of *Labor Unions, Partisan Coalitions, and Market Reforms in Latin America* (Cambridge University Press, 2001), and *Political Competition, Partisanship, and Policymaking in Latin American Public Utilities* (Cambridge University Press, 2009).

Shannon O'Neil is Senior Fellow for Latin America Studies at the Council on Foreign Relations (CFR). Her expertise includes US-Latin American relations, energy policy, trade, political and economic reforms, and immigration. She is the author of the forthcoming book, *Two Nations Indivisible: Mexico, the United States, and the Road Ahead*, which analyzes the political, economic, and social transformations Mexico has undergone over the last three decades and their significance for US-Mexico relations. She is a frequent commentator on major television and radio programs, and her work has appeared in *Foreign Affairs*, *Foreign Affairs Latinoamérica*, *Americas Quarterly*, *Política Exterior*, *Foreign Policy*, the *Washington Post*, and the *Los Angeles Times*, among others.

Eduardo Posada-Carbó is a departmental lecturer at Oxford University's Latin American Centre and research fellow at St Antony's College. His research interests include the history of elections and democracy, the role of ideas and intellectuals in national history, the history of the press during the nineteenth century, and corruption and party politics. He is the author of *La nación soñada: Violencia, liberalismo y democracia en Colombia* (Norma, 2006), and *El desafío de las ideas: Ensayos de historia intelectual y política de Colombia* (Universidad EAFIT, 2003). He has also published essays in several edited collections and international academic journals, including the *Historical Journal*, *Latin*

American Research Review, Journal of Latin American Studies, Hispanic American Historical Review, Caravelle, and *Revista de Occidente.*

David Samuels is Distinguished McKnight University Professor of Political Science. His research and teaching interests include Brazilian and Latin American politics, US-Latin American relations, and democratization. He is the author of *Presidents, Parties, and Prime Ministers* (with Matthew Shugart) (Cambridge University Press, 2010), *Ambition, Federalism, and Legislative Politics in Brazil* (Cambridge University Press, 2003), and the coeditor of *Decentralization and Democracy in Latin America* (University of Notre Dame Press, 2004).

Michael Shifter is president of the Inter-American Dialogue. He is the author of numerous articles and reports on US-Latin American relations, democratic governance, and the politics of hemispheric affairs, and has been coeditor of the last three editions of *Constructing Democratic Governance in Latin America.* He is adjunct professor at Georgetown University's School of Foreign Service, where he teaches Latin American politics.

Peter M. Siavelis is professor of political science and director of the Latin American and Latino Studies program at Wake Forest University. His research focuses on Latin American electoral and legislative politics, particularly as it pertains to the Southern Cone region. He has published *Getting Immigration Right: What Every American Needs to Know,* an edited volume with David Coates (Potomac Books, 2009), *Pathways to Power: Political Recruitment and Candidate Selection in Latin America,* edited volume with Scott Morgenstern (Pennsylvania State University Press, 2008), and *The President and Congress in Post-Authoritarian Chile: Institutional Constraints to Democratic Consolidation* (Pennsylvania State University Press, 2000).

Acronyms and Abbreviations

General

ACP	African, Caribbean, and Pacific
BTU	British Thermal Units
CCT	conditional cash transfers
CSO	civil society organizations
FDI	foreign direct investment
GDP	gross domestic product
HDI	Human Development Index
HHI	Herfindahl-Hirschman Index
IFI	international financial institution
ISI	import substitution industrialization
LAC	Latin America and the Caribbean
LGBT	lesbian, gay, bisexual, and transgender
NAFTA	North American Free Trade Agreement
NC	national conferences
NGO	nongovernmental organizations
NTO	nontraditional opposition force
PR	proportional representation
TCO	transnational criminal organization
VAT	value added tax
WWII	World War II

International Organizations

ALBA	Alianza Bolivariana para los Pueblos de Nuestra América (Bolivarian Alliance for the Americas)
CEDAW	Convention on the Elimination of All Forms of Discrimination against Women
EU	European Union

GATT	General Agreement on Tariffs and Trade
IDB	Inter-American Development Bank
IMF	International Monetary Fund
Mercosur/Mercosul	Common Market of the South
OAS	Organization of American States
OECD	Organisation for Economic Co-operation and Development
SIP	Inter-American Press Society
UN	United Nations
UNASUR/UNASUL	Union of South American Nations
UNIFEM	United Nations Development Fund for Women

Argentina

APR	Acción por la República (Action for the Republic)
CGT	Confederación General del Trabajo (General Labor Confederation)
CONADEP	Comisión Nacional sobre la Desaparición de Personas (National Commission on the Disappearance of Persons)
DNU	Decreto de Necesidad y Urgencia (Need and Urgency Decree)
FREPASO	Frente País Solidario (Front for a Country in Solidarity)
INDEC	Instituto Nacional de Estadística y Censos (National Institute of Statistics and the Census)
MTD-Evita	Movement of Unemployed Workers-Evita
PJ	Partido Justicialista (Judicialist Party, Peronist)
PRO	Propuesta Republicana (Republican Proposal)
Telefe	Televisión Federal (Federal Television)
UCEDÉ	Unión del Centro Democrático (Center Democratic Union)
UCR	Unión Cívica Radical (Radical Civic Union)

Bolivia

| ABC | Administradora Bolviana de Caminos (Bolivian Administrator of Roads) |
| ADN | Acción Democrática Nacionalista (Nationalist Democratic Action) |

CIDOB	Confederación de Pueblos Indígenas de Bolivia (Confederation of Indigenous Peoples of Bolivia)
CONAMAQ	Consejo Nacional de Ayllus y Markas del Qullasusyu (National Council of Ayllus and Markas of Qullasusyu)
CONDEPA	Conciencia de Patria (Fatherland Consciousness)
CSUTCB	Confederación Sindical Única de Trabajadores (Unified Syndical Confederation of Rural Workers)
MAS	Movimiento al Socialismo (Movement toward Socialism)
MIP	Pachakutik Indigenous Movement
MIR	Movimiento de la Izquierda Revolucionaria (Leftist Revolutionary Movement)
MNR	Movimiento Nacional Revolucionario (Nationalist Revolutionary Movement)
TIPNIS	Territorio Indígena y Parque Nacional Isiboro-Secure (Isiboro Secure National Park and Indigenous Territory)
UCS	Unidad Cívica Solidaridad (Civic Unity of Solidarity)
UN	National Unity
YPFB	Yacimientos Petrolíferos Fiscales Bolivianos (National Oil Fields of Bolivia)

Brazil

CLT	Consolidação das Leis do Trabalho (Consolidated Labor Law)
CUT	Central Única dos Trabalhadores (Unified Worker's Central)
DEM	Democratas (Democrats)
PL	Partido Liberal (Liberal Party)
PMDB	Partido do Movimento Democrático Brasileiro (Brazilian Democratic Movement Party)
PSDB	Partido da Social Democracia Brasileira (Brazilian Social Democracy Party)
PT	Partido dos Trabalhadores (Workers' Party)
PTB	Partido Trabalhista Brasileiro (Brazilian Labor Party)

Chile

AFP	Administradora de Fondos de Pensiones (Pension Fund Administrators)
AUGE	Plan de Acceso Universal con Garantías Explícitas (Universal Access Plan with Explicit Guarantees)
CODELCO	Corporación Nacional del Cobre (National Copper Corporation)
PDC	Partido Democrático Cristiano (Christian Democratic Party)
PEM	Programa de Empleo Mínimo (Minimum Employment Program)
RN	Renovación Nacional (National Renovation)
UDI	Unión Democrática Independiente (Independent Democratic Union)

Colombia

ANDI	Asociación Nacional de Industriales (National Association of Industrialists)
AUC	Autodefensas Unidas de Colombia (United Self-Defense Forces of Colombia)
CC	Corte Constitucional (Constitutional Court)
CR	Cambio Radical (Radical Change)
CRIC	Regional Indigenous Commission of Cauca
DAS	Departamento Administrativo de Seguridad (Administrative Security Department)
ELN	Ejército de Liberación Nacional (National Liberation Army)
FARC	Fuerzas Armadas Revolucionarias de Colombia (Revolutionary Armed Forces of Colombia)
PC	Partido Conservador (Conservative Party)
PDA	Polo Democrático Alternativo (Alternative Democratic Pole)
PL	Partido Liberal (Liberal Party)
PU	Partido de la Unidad, Partido de la U (Unity Party)
PV	Partido Verde (Green Party)
RCN	Radio Cadena Nacional

Costa Rica

PLN   National Liberation Party

Ecuador

CONAIE   Confederación de Nacionalidades Indígenas del Ecuador (Confederation of Indigenous Nationalities of Ecuador)

El Salvador

ARENA   Alianza Republicana Nacionalista (Nationalist Republic Alliance)

FMLN   Frente Farabundo Martí para la Liberación Nacional (Farabundo Martí National Liberation Front)

Mexico

AFI   Agencia Federal de Investigación (Federal Investigative Agency)

AMLO   Andrés Manuel López Obrador

ASF   Auditoría Superior de la Federación (Superior Auditory Agency)

IFAI   Instituto Federal de Acceso a la Información Pública (Federal Institute for Access to Public Information)

IFE   Instituto Federal Electoral (Federal Electoral Institute)

PAN   Partido Acción Nacional (National Action Party)

PFP   Policía Federal Preventiva (Federal Preventive Police)

PGR   Procurador General de la República (Attorney General)

PJF   Policía Judicial Federal (Federal Judicial Police)

PRD   Partido de la Revolución Democrática (Party of the Democratic Revolution)

PRI   Partido Revolucionario Institucional (Revolutionary Institutional Party)

SNSP   Sistema Nacional de Seguridad Pública (National System of Public Security)

SSP   Secretaría de Seguridad Pública (Secretary of Public Security)

Nicaragua

FSLN	Frente Sandinista de Liberación Nacional (Sandinista Front for National Liberation)

Peru

AP	Acción Popular (Popular Action)
APP	Alianza para el Progreso (Alliance for Progress)
APRA	Alianza Popular Revolucionaria Americana (American Popular Revolutionary Alliance)
CODE	Democratic Coordinator
CONAPA	National Commission on Andean, Amazonian, and Afro-Peruvian Peoples
ESAN	School of Business Administration
FIM	Independent Moralizing Front
IU	Izquierda Unida (United Left)
PPK	Pedro Pablo Kuczynski
PP	Perú Posible (Possible Peru)
PPC	Partido Popular Cristiano (Popular Christian Party)
SIN	Servicio de Inteligencia Nacional (National Intelligence Service)
UN	Unidad Nacional (National Unity)
UPP	Unión por el Perú (Union for Peru)

United States

ATPA	Andean Trade Preference Act
CALEA	Commission on Accreditation for Law Enforcement Agencies
CIA	Central Intelligence Agency
DEA	Drug Enforcement Agency
FBI	Federal Bureau of Investigation

Venezuela

AD	Acción Democrática (Democratic Action)
BR	Bandera Roja (Red Flag)
Causa R	Causa Radical (Radical Cause)
CD	Coordinadora Democrática (Democratic Coordinator)

CESAP	Centro al Servicio de la Acción Popular (Center at the Service of Popular Action)
CNE	Consejo Nacional Electoral (National Electoral Council)
COPEI	Comité de Organización Política Electoral Independiente or Partido Social Cristiano de Venezuela (Social Christian Party of Venezuela)
CTV	Confederación de Trabajadores de Venezuela (Venezuelan Confederation of Workers)
MAS	Movimiento al Socialismo (Movement toward Socialism)
MEP	Movimiento Electoral Popular (Popular Electoral Movement)
MIGATO	Movimiento Independiente Ganamos Todos (Independent Movement We All Win)
MPJ	Primero Justicia (Justice First)
MRT	Movimiento Revolucionario Tupamaro (Revolutionary Tupamaro Movement)
MUD	Mesa de la Unidad Democrática (Democratic Unity Platform)
MVR	Movimiento V República (Fifth Republic Movement)
PCV	Partido Comunista de Venezuela (Communist Party of Venezuela)
PDVSA	Petróleos de Venezuela (National Petroleum Corporation of Venezuela)
PODEMOS	Por la Democracia Social (For Social Democracy)
PPT	Patria para Todos (Fatherland for All)
PROVE	Proyecto Venezolano (Venezuela Project)
PSUV	Partido Socialista Unido de Venezuela (Unified Socialist Party of Venezuela)
PURS	Unified Party of the Socialist Revolution
RCTV	Radio Caracas Televisión (Radio Caracas Television)
UNT	Un Nuevo Tiempo (A New Time)
UPV	Unidad Popular Venezolana (Popular Venezuelan Unity)
URD	Democratic Republican Union
VTV	Corporación Venezolana de Televisión (Venezuelan Television Corporation)

Constructing Democratic Governance
in Latin America

Introduction

New Issues in Democratic Governance

Michael Shifter

A More Prosperous Region

In recent years, the state of democratic governance in Latin America has been decidedly mixed. Discussion has turned away from elections and the leftward swings in several countries. Electoral contests are increasingly a matter of routine, and ideology has become notably less salient. As this fourth edition of *Constructing Democratic Governance in Latin America* makes clear, the debate now centers on how leaders and institutions confront the complicated tasks of managing their economic and social affairs while representing heterogeneous societies with heightened demands and expectations.

It is striking that while a bulk of the region's governments have taken markedly different directions, most of them have performed reasonably well. They have benefited from a mostly favorable economic environment over the last decade as well as social policies that have succeeded in reducing poverty and even, in a number of countries, inequality (López-Calva and Lustig 2010). The wide disparity between the region's rich and poor has long been—and arguably still remains—Latin America's Achilles' heel. Yet for the first time since this effort was launched in the early 1990s—and in contrast to the analyses in the three previous volumes—there is considerable progress to report on the social front.

Brazil's notable success is a significant piece of the regional picture. As David Samuels elucidates in this volume, under the effective leadership of Luiz Inácio "Lula" da Silva and the Workers' Party, Brazil has registered remarkable social gains. Bolsa Família largely accounts for this success, lifting some 20 million out of poverty through prudent macroeconomic management and the cash transfer program. Brazil's strides have been accompanied by persistently high levels of corruption and profound challenges in undertaking thoroughgoing institutional reforms of the political and justice systems. But Brazil's regional and global rise would have been unimaginable without a solid foundation of economic and social development and effective democratic governance.

The Brazilian case also underlines a phenomenon that increasingly characterizes much of the region—an expanding middle class. Though there are debates about what precisely constitutes a middle class, few dispute that as Latin America deepens and multiplies its global ties, the number of its citizens with access to consumer goods and higher levels of education is growing considerably. A recent study by the World Bank estimates that Latin America's middle class expanded by 50 percent between 2003 and 2009, from 103 million to 152 million people ("Class" 2012). Indeed, in several countries the middle class constitutes roughly half of the total population. The implications for the region's politics and the quality of its democratic governance are immense (Fukuyama 2012). In fundamental respects, the expanding middle class is a salutary development that gives citizens a more substantial stake in their political systems, but its strength increases pressures on governments that, in many cases, have scant capacity to respond and deliver the public services demanded. Depending on how such expectations are managed, this could well be a recipe for public frustration and political uncertainty.

In Mexico, too, such a trend is evident (which in part explains why migration to the US has sharply declined and is now a net zero). This factor is, however, frequently eclipsed by reports of spreading criminal violence. But Shannon O'Neil's chapter on Mexico counters the dominant media portrayals of a country utterly overwhelmed by unrelenting drug-fueled chaos. The appraisal instead showcases the economic and social advances as well as the strengthening of democratic institutions. The country's 2012 elections, for example, revealed a highly competitive political party system and a vibrant press. Profound problems in democratic governance remain. These focus in particular on building the rule of law and constructing an effective justice system and police forces. Fiscal, energy, and labor reforms will also be required for Mexico to achieve and sustain high growth rates and to pursue more vigorous antipoverty policies. Nevertheless, observers remain largely optimistic about the possibility of coalitional responses to these challenges.

Deficit of Stable Political Parties

In his treatment of Colombia, Eduardo Posada-Carbó is similarly sanguine and highlights the country's rich democratic and institutional strengths, in particular, the progress made in recent years that defied the dire predictions of a decade ago. The "transition" from the more personalized leadership represented by President Álvaro Uribe (2002–2010) to the more institutional, consensus-building approach favored by his successor Juan Manuel Santos is quite remarkable. Despite such political stability and the laudable performance of key institutions such as the Constitutional Court, the country's political party system remains in considerable flux, serious security issues persist, and the social agenda is formidable. Colombia is still the only Latin American country with an ongoing armed conflict and continuing political violence. Whether Santos will be able to achieve the durable peace that has eluded his predecessors is a major question.

Colombia's evolving parties still remain preferable to the Peruvian case. Steve Levitsky points out in his chapter that Peru's democratic system is virtually devoid of coherent political parties. Since the collapse of the political party system in the late 1980s, personalistic instruments and ad-hoc movements as electoral vehicles largely predominate. Without doubt, Peru stands out for its performance not only in sustaining impressively high levels of growth but also in substantially reducing poverty—from more than 50 percent to just 34 percent over a decade—and even modestly narrowing the gap between the rich and the poor.

Yet paradoxically, such positive economic and social gains have not been accompanied by institutional reforms and a more consolidated democratic system. Indeed, as outlined in the Peru chapter, the Latinobarómetro comparative survey indicates some of the region's lowest levels of trust in political institutions and politicians. Despite its leftist roots and promises of radical change, the government led by Ollanta Humala, elected in 2011, largely represents continuity with its more conservative predecessors, Alan García (2006–2011) and Alejandro Toledo (2001–2006), deepening disenchantment among Humala's original supporters.

Even in Chile, arguably the region's best economic performer over the last several decades, there is growing dissatisfaction with political parties and leaders, who for many seem removed and indifferent to ordinary concerns. In his chapter on Chile, Peter Siavelis considers—albeit with some qualifications—the term "partidocracia," previously employed to describe ossified political structures in Peru (1990) and then Venezuela (1998), for a country frequently touted for its democratic success and institutional progress. The nation's continued economic advance is not at risk, though in the political realm there are growing calls—particularly by a vigorous student movement and youth in general—for political reform and renewal, more than two decades after the end of the Pinochet dictatorship.

Political party challenges are also a major theme in the country chapters focused on Argentina, Bolivia, and Venezuela. María Victoria Murillo and Ernesto Calvo amplify the notion of "dealignment" of the Argentine political party system, juxtaposing Argentina's impressive growth rates in recent years with profound institutional weaknesses and rampant factionalism and infighting within the dominant Peronist Party. On Bolivia, George Gray Molina asserts that the government headed by Evo Morales since 2003 appears increasingly stuck and stagnant. Opposition comes not from the remnants of the traditional party system or the local leaders from eastern Bolivia but rather from splinter groups within Morales's own Movimiento al Socialismo (MAS; Movement toward Socialism) coalition. The grandiose dreams of a sweeping transformation in the country have not been realized and have now mostly receded. Nonetheless, the chapter argues that, while difficulties have mounted, the Morales experiment has signified much higher levels of social inclusion and participation of previously marginalized groups—especially the country's majority indigenous population.

Mounting Security Concerns

In Venezuela, governance depended for more than a dozen years on the "one-man rule" exercised by the late President Hugo Chávez who, Ángel Álvarez makes clear, was himself the beneficiary of an implosion of the traditional political parties in the late 1990s. An army lieutenant colonel, Chávez gave his government a decidedly military cast and governed autocratically, through confrontation and conflict. He controlled key institutions, including the justice system and electoral council. Though Chávez retained a strong emotional and sentimental connection with many Venezuelans, governance was dismal by most measures, crime and violence have skyrocketed, and the economy remains deeply troubled (in addition to shortages of basic goods, Venezuela's inflation rates are the region's highest). While the opposition over the last dozen years has been highly fragmented, and in many instances inept, it has recently shown a stronger capacity to unify and develop leadership and a clear-headed political strategy.

Venezuela's grave internal security crisis—clearly the most acute in South America—illustrates a broader regional trend that poses perhaps the greatest risk to democratic governance in most countries. According to all reliable polls, including Latinobarómetro and AmericasBarometer, citizen security is the principal concern among most Latin Americans, even more so than unemployment. Citing these statistics, Lucía Dammert systematically dissects this challenge and points to its many complexities and varied manifestations throughout Latin America. The situation in the "Northern Triangle" of Central America—Guatemala, Honduras, and El Salvador—is especially dire and threatens the very integrity of the state. (According to the United Nations, in 2011 Honduras and El Salvador had the highest homicide rates in the world, and Guatemala was not far behind.) In countries in the Southern Cone, in sharp contrast, the chief concern is one of "victimization," of crime against patrimony such as robbery instead of homicide.

Dammert goes beyond a straightforward analysis of the security challenges facing the region and explores the complex relationship between violent crime and democracy. Why is it that democratic consolidation has not reduced violence in Latin America and, in fact, in many cases has been accompanied by a rise in citizen insecurity? Some experts assume that weak institutions created a space for illegality and organized crime, as reflected in such cases as Mexico and Central America. But other countries characterized by weak political systems do not exhibit comparable levels of violence. The chapter attempts to chart a strategy by which important processes in democratic governance can help, not hinder, efforts to reduce citizen insecurity in the region.

Media, Constitutionalism, and Commodities

Taylor Boas explores the role of the media in Latin America and its relationship with democratic governance. The media have performed a variety of constructive functions in the region, enhancing accountability, exposing wrongdoing and, as a "fourth power," providing a further check on executive, legislative, and judicial branches of government. The media can, however, be quite problematic in terms of building more effective democratic governance. In some countries the media have become a tool for the consolidation of power, sometimes through intimidation and censorship. And journalists in some countries—Honduras stands out— are in physical danger because of their work.

The remaining thematic chapters in this volume—which deal with constitutionalism, resource nationalism, and commodity price booms—generate important comparative insights on a set of crucial issues. The region's various experiments with constitutionalism, Javier Corrales argues, have not fared well of late, resulting in greater concentration of power in the executive, with scant constraints or checks. Revamped constitutions can, however, yield more positive outcomes in countries with robust institutions and longstanding democratic traditions. Sebastián Mazzuca provides an illuminating chapter on the political and democratic governance implications of the worldwide commodities boom in several South American countries and the possible consequences of another global economic downturn. The politics and various regime types associated with both the natural resource blessings and curses are likely to mark much of the continent in coming years.

In discussing the nexus of commodity booms and democratic governance, a critical turning point for the region may have been in 2009 when, as Alejandro Foxley has argued, the dire predictions made by many economists proved wrong (Foxley 2009). Rebutting bearish forecasts, the crisis that emerged in the United States—not Latin America—was weathered remarkably well by most of the region (with the notable exception of Mexico, mainly because of close economic links to its northern neighbor). To be sure, the decade's prevailing economic order—especially China's huge appetite for the region's commodities—was a critical contributing factor to Latin America's economic success and resiliency to crisis. Yet the region's improved policymaking (using lessons learned from previous decades) and effective social programs also help account for its sound performance.

Convergent Challenges?

For many Latin Americans, the 2008 crisis exposed as never before the weaknesses of fiscal management and democratic governance in the United States. Indeed, this volume—surely more so than the previous ones—suggests a growing convergence between the chief democratic governance challenges facing Latin America and those faced by the United States. This is particularly evident in the surveys highlighting the declining levels of trust in public institutions and confidence in democratic leaders across the Americas.

Levels of trust in political parties and institutions such as Congress, for example, are at rock bottom in the United States. A 2012 Pew Research Center study found that approval for the US federal government had fallen to 33 percent, down from 64 percent a decade ago. Approval of Congress is even lower, with a mere 6 percent of Americans having "a great deal" of confidence in the institution. The lack of popular support for Congress is unsurprising given the increasingly dysfunctional nature of the decision-making process, with less and less room for compromise and consensus. US citizens also feel increasingly distant from their elected representatives, dissatisfied with how democracy works—or rather fails to work—in the nation. For some observers, the paralysis in US decision making is affecting progress in the country and also limits the United States' ability to participate effectively in global affairs.

As the United States slowly emerges from the recession, further negative consequences are becoming clear. Americans have long accepted higher levels of income inequality than other developed countries on the assumption that the US offered greater opportunities for social mobility. Recent studies, however, show these opportunities to be far lower than commonly assumed. Indeed, those born poor are much more likely to remain so when compared to their European counterparts (*The Economist* 2010). Despite steady economic growth in the 1980s and 1990s, 80 percent of income gains in the last thirty years have gone to the top one percent of US citizens (Hacker and Pierson 2010). As Latin Americans well know, the widening gap between the rich and poor in the United States poses a fundamental problem for democratic governance.

Washington's prescriptions for Latin America's woes are a not-too-distant memory and serve as a stark contrast to the current situation. The causes for common problems such as inequality and political dysfunction are anything but uniform. The hyperpartisan environment of the United States stands out as a notable difference to the overall lack of functioning parties in the Americas. Nonetheless, it is hard to overstate the fact that the United States is no longer seen as the hemisphere's economic and political exemplar.

A Laboratory of Democracy

This edition of *Constructing Democratic Governance* marks a dynamic and exciting time for the subject. The convergence of several forces—a decrease in US power, an increase in viable choices for development models coming from Asia and Europe, and a commitment to democracy by Latin Americans—has made the region fertile ground for experiments in democratic governance. This has been facilitated by generally good economic growth, which in some cases has greatly expanded the capacity of governments to pursue the pressing challenges they face.

The issue of illegal drugs and trafficking is a salient example in which Latin American leaders have directly defied the United States while pushing for a wider array of options to combat issues of violence and public health. The bold positions taken not only by several former Latin American presidents, but also by acting heads of state in Colombia, Mexico, Guatemala, Uruguay, and other countries exemplify an unmistakable trend toward increased autonomy and policy innovation and experimentation. Washington's drug policy remains on automatic pilot, though public opinion—at least in some states—is at odds with federal law. US policymakers may well want to follow and assess the efficacy of initiatives coming from a region searching for practical solutions to common problems.

This phenomenon has been played out in the realm of social policy as well, upsetting long-held perceptions of a set of socially conservative peoples. In the arena of gay rights, for instance, some Latin American countries have even moved faster than the United States, often defying public opinion by passing antidiscrimination legislation, providing constitutional recognition for LGBT citizens, and even legalizing same-sex marriage on the national level. The hemisphere's proponents of equality are not limited to the examples provided by a handful of US states, when pressuring their lawmakers: they may draw from the experience of Argentina, Brazil, and Mexico City. Furthermore, it is hard not to be struck by the increasing prominence of women's leadership in Latin America's political life. This trend is dramatically reflected by former and sitting female presidents in Brazil, Argentina, Costa Rica, Chile, and Panama, as well as several highly competitive women candidates in many countries in the region. In this respect, both the United States and the global community can learn much from Latin America's progress. The same is true when speaking of approaches to poverty alleviation, indigenous rights, and energy development.

The Americas have, in short, become a veritable laboratory for democratic government. As the hemisphere struggles with myriad issues—some country-specific, others regional—the successes and failures provide compelling insight when examined both individually and collectively. As such, both the thematic and country chapters of this volume reflect the acumen, innovation, and contributions of specific countries to expanding the repertoire of global leaders.

Much Remains to Be Done

Nonetheless, despite Latin America's impressive social performance in recent years, there are grounds for caution. It is by no means clear the conditions that have propelled growth and the policies that have led to a greater redistribution of resources will necessarily be sustained. There is a risk of complacency and failure to adopt necessary and difficult reforms in areas such as infrastructure, health, justice, and education, which are vital for yielding higher levels of productivity and competitiveness. The successful cash transfer programs that have been such a positive factor in Brazil, Mexico, and other countries may well have run their course. More developed social insurance programs—for example, pensions and unemployment protections—are critical. Yet the politics of making progress on these reforms will not be easy.

Although some progress in reducing poverty and even inequality in certain countries is undeniable, the fruits of such progress have not been evenly distributed. The most marginalized sectors—including indigenous and Afro-descendant populations—still perform well below national and regional averages. Such groups also have significantly lower levels of educational attainment and health indicators. Should the macroeconomic outlook darken—perhaps because of a crisis in the Eurozone, continuing problems in China, or other developments in the global economy—Latin America may be less equipped to weather the storm as well as it did in 2008. The ensuing consequences could be very serious for the quality of democratic governance in the region.

Even though the overall assessment of democratic governance in the region is, on balance, positive, a number of this volume's scholars reflect on citizen malaise regarding the state of politics. The economic and even social outlook may be upbeat, but the political realm remains more problematic. Such issues as corruption and citizen security—though repeatedly the subject of political discourse—essentially remain unaddressed. Although positive legislation reforming justice systems and political parties has been passed, meaningful change is hard to discern. As a result, disenchantment sets in.

Latin America's relative success in the globalized economy has led to improved well-being for many of the region's citizens. But it has also generated unprecedented demands and expectations for more effective, democratic governance. As the chapters in this volume make clear, some of the region's political institutions and leaders are better prepared to respond to such claims than others. Those divergence responses account for the separate paths being pursued throughout the region. The authors of this volume provide perceptive and rigorous analyses that shed considerable light on the complicated journeys involved in constructing democratic governance in Latin America.

REFERENCES

"Class in Latin America: The Expanding Middle." 2012. *The Economist*, November 10.
"A Family Affair: Intergenerational Social Mobility across OECD Countries." 2010. Paris: Organization for Economic Co-operation and Development.
Foxley, Alejandro. 2009. "Recovery: The Global Financial Crisis and Middle-Income Countries." Washington, DC: Carnegie Endowment for International Peace. www.oecd.org/tax/publicfinanceandfiscalpolicy/45002641.pdf.

Fukuyama, Francis. 2012. "The Politics of Latin America's New Middle Class." Washington, DC: Inter-American Dialogue.

Hacker, Jacob S., and Paul Pierson. 2010. *Winner Take-All Politics: How Washington Made the Rich Richer—and Turned Its Back on the Middle Class*. New York: Simon & Schuster.

López-Calva, Luis F., and Nora Lustig. 2010. "Explaining the Decline in Inequality in Latin America: Technological Change, Educational Upgrading, and Democracy." In *Declining Inequality in Latin America: A Decade of Progress?*, edited by Luis F. López-Calva and Nora Lustig, 1–24. Washington, DC: Brookings Institution Press.

PART I / Themes

CHAPTER ONE

Constitutional Rewrites in Latin America, 1987–2009

Javier Corrales

This chapter addresses two questions that are central to comparativists in general and Latin Americanists in particular. First, what are the origins of institutions, and specifically, constitutions? Significant research exists on the effects of different types of institutions, even constitutions (Reynolds 2002; Persson and Tabellini 2003), but less is known about their origins.[1] Second, what are the origins of different forms of presidential powers in new constitutions? Research has shown that democratic constitutions vary in how much power they grant to the executive branch (Shugart and Carey 1992). But less is known about the conditions that give rise to such variation.

This chapter answers these two questions by looking at developments in Latin America since the 1980s. Latin America is known worldwide as the land of presidentialism. It should also be known as the land of constitutional rewrite. Since the transition to democracy in the late 1970s, the region has seen ten cases of major constitutional rewrite:[2] Nicaragua (1987), Brazil (1988), Paraguay (1992), Colombia (1991), Peru (1993), Argentina (1994), Ecuador (1998), Venezuela (1999), Ecuador (2008), and Bolivia (2009).[3] All these post-transition rewrites occurred through highly participatory processes, that is, through constituent assemblies composed of elected delegates, rather than by negotiations among a restricted circle of elites.[4]

None of these assemblies abolished presidentialism, but the resulting documents affected presidential powers in different directions. Some assemblies expanded presidential powers; others hardly changed presidential powers; still others reduced presidential powers. This variation in outcomes thus provide an opportunity to study the factors that give rise to constitutions, and within each constitution, levels of power concentration, while controlling for historical era and region.

I will argue that this variation in presidential powers is mostly the result of power asymmetries between incumbent (I) and opposition (O) forces. I define power asymmetry as the power differential between these actors, measured, as we will see, through various indicators of vote share. At the most basic level, cases can display three forms of asymmetry: I and O can have comparable levels of power (reduced asymmetry); I can be far stronger than O (large pro-I asymmetry); or O can be far stronger than I (negative, or pro-O asymmetry).

My argument is that conditions of reduced asymmetry yield constitutions that lessen presidential powers. Large asymmetry, in contrast, yields constitutions that expand presidential powers, and negative asymmetry increases the chances of I aborting constitutional rewrites. These propositions are based on the premise that, in the politics of constitutional change, Is prefer expanding presidential powers, while Os prefer instead to expand the powers of nonexecutive branches. The power differential explains whose preference prevails.

This power asymmetry argument has implications for theories of institution making and democratization. Regarding institution making, my main point is that institutions originate as a result of the bargaining leverage between state holders and their rivals. Other factors typically invoked to explain institutional change, namely, economic conditions and the ideological preferences of the constitution makers, are secondary. No doubt, economics and ideology play a role. But they explain mostly the decision to launch a rewrite more so than the final output. What best determines the outcome is the bargaining leverage of the players, which in turn has to do with power differentials that are actually measurable.

Regarding democratization, my argument is that prospects for it do not improve when one major force overwhelms the other politically. The balance of forces between I and O helps to explain both the constitution and whether the constitution will offer new opportunities and new restraints on I. Following Kantor (1977), Geddes (1994), Colomer (1995, 74–85), Bermeo (1997, 305–22), Negretto (1999, 2001, 2002), Hartlyn and Luna (2009), I posit that under conditions of reduced asymmetry (e.g., where I and O are both strong), constitutional negotiations will impose limits on I's preferences. As Olson argues, democracy emerges when there is a "broadly equal dispersion of power that makes it imprudent for any leader or group to attempt to overpower the other" (Olson 2000, 31). Under large asymmetry, however, *I* has no incentive to offer guarantees to *O* because it does not fear it, and *O* is not strong enough to compel *I* to yield.

Constitutions as Bargaining Outcomes

A constitution can be defined as the "codes of norms which aspire to regulate the allocation of powers, functions, and duties among the various agencies and officers of government, and to define the relationship between these and the public" (Finer, Bogdanor, and Rugden 1995, 1). In many ways, constitutions are similar to political pacts. First, constitutions typically emerge, just as pacts do, as a result of negotiations among actors with different bargaining power. Also like pacts, democratic constitutions are quintessential functional institutions: actors draft and sign them hoping to restrain their counterparts and mitigate their own political insecurity. Many times, actors offer constitutional rewrites as possible antidotes to polarization and mutual suspicion, just as they often think of political pacts as mechanisms to ameliorate tensions and offer mutual guarantees (O'Donnell and Schmitter 1986; Di Palma 1990; Karl 1990, 1–23; Karl and Schmitter 1991, 269–84; Przeworski 1991; Reynolds 2002). They are also a mechanism through which actors offer concessions to their opponents in return for some gains (Acemoglu and Robinson 2006).

What determines whether these negotiations will in fact offer solutions to political insecurity? Constitutions can take multiple forms and occur in diverse political settings. Yet, there is one simple distinction in the negotiating process that shapes the key contours of the outcome: the balance of forces among signatories. If the balance of power among signatories is deeply asymmetrical, the constitution either does not get rewritten, or if changed, becomes intensely biased toward *I*'s preference.

So who are typically the signatories? Because most of constitutional rewrites, by definition, occur within the context of an established government in office (as opposed to constitutions that occur prior to the establishment of a nation, regime, or administration), constitutional rewrites invariably get drafted by political bodies that reflect the fundamental *I* versus *O* cleavage that is present in all democracies. Constitutional rewrites are thus the outputs of negotiations between *I* and *O*.

This *I* versus *O* divide also helps explain some of the starting preferences of the signatories. Each actor will want to expand the powers of the institutions that they control. Thus, *I*'s in presidential democracies typically have a monopoly over the executive branch (and must share power in other branches of government such as the legislature and subnational offices). Thus *I* forces will prefer to maximize the powers of the executive branch. There are exceptions. Sometimes, for instance, *I*s will accept relaxing some presidential powers in order to gain other victories. But my main point is that how much they accept relaxation of presidential powers depends on the bargaining leverage of their counterparts.

In contrast, *O* forces will want to maximize the powers of the other branches of government that they control. There are of course variations. Often some opposition forces might be interested in weakening other opposition forces, and this might lead them to side with *I* if this gives them a chance to undermine their rivals. But where this inter-*O* split does not occur, it is safe to assume that *O* will be less interested in maximizing presidential powers than *I* forces.

Which of these two actors has the greater chance of prevailing? The central proposition of this chapter is that the stronger the power of *O*, the least likely it is for *I* to maximize its preference (of expanding presidential powers).

For this reason, high pro-*I* asymmetry is fatal for a balanced outcome (see Arato 2005, 17). In this environment, *O* will lack the necessary bargaining leverage to extract favorable concessions from *I*. *O* needs bargaining leverage because it has a particularly ambitious agenda, perhaps more so than *I* (Horowitz 2002, 27). *O* needs the constitution to offer protection (or minimum guarantees), and also provisions that make it easier for it to leave its opposition status (Lijphart 1991, 72–84; Lijphart 1992). This is the paradox of constitution making: *O* needs the most out of this bargain; yet, it often faces the risk of being the weaker party in the negotiation.

Pivotal Issues: Taming or Expanding Presidential Powers

The politics of constitutional change engages a multitude of issues that vary across countries and times. In Latin America, especially since the 1980s, some important areas have included granting new rights to new groups and individuals, delimiting the economic and social functions of the state, and setting the country's development priorities. However, one issue seems common in constitutional rewrites in all democracies, not just Latin American cases, not just in the contemporary period: how much to tame or expand presidential powers.

Armony and Schamis argue that *all* majority-based democracies are susceptible to presidents who "strive for greater autonomy . . . circumvent congressional and judicial oversight . . . and ultimately thwart the principle of separation of powers" (Armony and Schamis 2005, 116–17). If all democracies face a "perpetual tension" between the impulse of executives to expand their powers and the countervailing tendency of groups (in office or in society) to control and oversee the executive branch, these tensions are even more conspicuous during constitutional processes. As Elkins, Ginsburg, and Blount (2009) argue, actors will want to maximize the power of the office they hold (what they call "self-dealing").[5] This means pro-*I* forces typically push for presidential powers, what Hartlyn and Luna (2009) refer to as "power concentration," while opponents seek power diffusion. Furthermore, *I*'s own party will tend to support *I*'s preference. As Samuels and Shugart argue, in presidential systems (as opposed to parliamentary systems) parties tend to also become "presidentialized," granting far greater "discretion" to the leader that they select (Samuels and Shugart 2010). For the most part, therefore, *I*s face a lesser probability of defection during the constituent assembly.

This analysis could be criticized for positing excessive myopia on the part of actors. Surely, *I* can imagine a time in which it will be out of office, and *O*, conversely, a time in which it might capture the executive branch. Shouldn't one expect more forward-looking *I*s and *O*s to be less fixated in maximizing the power of the office they hold in the present? My answer is that actors prefer to focus on the instruments that they hold. *I*s may end up in the opposition, but they often conclude that the best way to avoid ending there is precisely to enhance the power of the office that they hold, since they estimate that such an office is the best instrument at their disposal to exert influence. Likewise, *O* often concludes that agreeing to more powers for *I* in the short term will weaken their chances of ever becoming *I*. Even by positing the idea of a more forward-looking *I* and *O*, actors would still prefer to enhance the office that they currently control.

The above is of course a theoretical proposition, subject to testing. I offer this chapter as proof. As we will see, the sectors that most strongly resisted power concentration on the presidency were the organized political parties in the opposition holding seats in Congress. They were cognizant that hyperpresidentialism, in the short term, hurts opposition parties the most. They thus approached the politics of constitution making with a strong preference to lessen power concentration and expand instead the powers of nonexecutive branch institutions (where they have a presence).

Having said that, there are times when *I*'s preferences for maximizing the power of the executive branch will yield. *I*s often discover that it might make sense to negotiate some concessions toward *O* in exchange for some gains for *I*. Likewise, *O* might reach the same conclusion at times. Sometimes *O* might split, with some sectors siding with *I* against *O*s. When this occurs, no doubt, the negotiation is different, as we will see in the Ecuador 2008 case. But my argument is that this propensity to negotiate on the part of *I* is not necessarily accidental or fortuitous, but bargain-dependent.

Furthermore, the propensity of *O* to split, in turn, has to do with a more complicated actor: the relative strength of up-and-coming, nontraditional opposition forces (*NTOs*). By definition, *NTOs* are those sectors of *O* that are not currently holding state office in large numbers (legislatures, governorships). They may not have an interest in defending the powers of the more established *O*s. What to do with these newcomers, in Latin America at least, was the next most important pivotal theme in constitution making.

Opening Opportunities for Nontraditional Opposition Forces

The second major issue in the politics of constitutional change in Latin America since the 1980s has been the creation of new political opportunities for nontraditional opposition forces (*NTOs*) (Van Cott 2000). Between the 1970s and early 1990s, almost every country in Latin America experienced a boom in *NTOs*. This included a wide array of new or previously marginal forces, social movements, civic groups, women's rights groups, and citizens' groups.

Initially, these new groups were too weak and fragmented to sustain any national-level political movement or government (Roberts 1998). But by the 1990s, *NTOs* were central actors in politics, sometimes supplanting parties, and became vital lobbyists for change in economic, social, and human rights policies.

The rise of *NTOs* starting in the 1970s is arguably the most significant political transformation at the societal level in Latin America since the eruption, in the 1930s, of industrial labor groups and the middle classes. These mid-twentieth-century corporatist groups (together with the colonial-era groups of the church, the military, and landed elites) dominated Latin American politics until the 1980s (Collier and Collier 1991; Wiarda and Kline 2000). But the combination of dictatorship, economic contraction, and deindustrialization reduced the power of these groups, making room for and even encouraging the rise of new *NTOs* (see Hochstetler 2012, 241). In the 1970s, these groups were often aided financially by transnational actors, which further bolstered their political power (Keck and Sikkink 1998). These new small political forces all sought to either expand the power of previously unrepresented constituents (including women, ethnic groups, informal workers, landless peasants, human rights victims, children) or lobby on behalf of new issues (including abortion rights, gender and ethnic quotas, transparency in public administration, decentralization, and protection of the environment) (Eckstein and Wickham-Crowley 2003). Even gay groups, a closeted actor in Latin American politics until the 2000s, played a role in campaigning to elect delegates to the constituent assembly in Ecuador in 2007.[6]

What is distinctive about these groups is not that they emerged (that's expected in a democratizing context) but that so many of them turned so anti-party. In Hellman's words, these new forces shared a "fundamental distrust of" and sometimes outright hostility toward traditional parties, even on the Left (Hellman 1992, 53). NTOs often felt shunned or exploited by traditional parties. Despite their gains in strength since the 1980s, these new forces did not feel exactly as active participants in "pacting" the transitions to democracy in the 1980s or deciding the economic reform in the 1990s, processes that were kept mostly in the hands of traditional Os (Avritzer 2002). For this reason, many civil society actors felt particularly excluded in the 1980s and 1990s. They became the most vocal critics of what Carothers's denominated "feckless pluralism": democracies in which freedoms exist, but the whole class of political elites, "though plural and competitive, are profoundly cut off from the citizenry" (Carothers 2002, 11).

The bigger the gap in representation left by parties, the more likely it was for these groups to take center stage (Hochstetler and Friedman 2008). Their key political demand became "participatory democracy." They demanded the opportunity, not just to watch and vote for political elites, but also to participate in decision making. They proclaimed themselves to be the preeminent political outsiders. They wanted to "institutionalize their access to political power, and not necessarily in ways that strengthened political representation" (Hochstetler and Friedman 2008, 11). They wanted in, and constitutional rewriting came to be seen as the entryway. It was no longer enough to discuss and ratify policy. They now wanted a chance to legislate change and be recognized.

NTOs thus emerged in the 1980s and 1990s as loud demanders of constitutional change in the direction of "local democratization" and "decentralization" (Falleti 2006). In essence, NTOs wanted to create more institutional opportunities and lower barriers to entry into the political world, even if that meant closing opportunities for the already participating actors, namely traditional Os. In some instances, they worked as "insiders," supporting and complementing party activity and institutional politics. Many other times they behaved as "outsiders," directly challenging and hoping to replace existing institutions (Smith and Korzeniewicz 2007). They demanded new rights mostly for new societal actors, but they did not necessarily become defenders of rights of traditional Os.

In many occasions, their anti-O sentiment reached a level of hostility that led them to support punitive policies toward traditional Os (see Schedler 1996). For instance, in the 1999 Venezuelan constituent assembly, the majority of civil society groups essentially formed a tacit alliance with I against traditional Os. Civil society representatives supported I's desire to create a constitutional ban on public funding for political parties, in return for numerous constitutional provisions that benefited civil society groups: state funding of civil society organizations, requiring state-level legislatures to consult with civil society, and empowering civil society groups to nominate three members of the National Electoral Council (Salamanca 2004). In Ecuador in 2008, likewise, previously unrepresented civil society groups such as feminists and environmentalists initially supported I's drive to arrogate power from traditional political parties in return for concessions such as pregnancy, child-rearing, and social security benefits for the former, and ecological rights for the latter. Little did they know that a serious dispute would emerge with the government about who belonged to this "civil society." But the main point is that pacts between I and $NTOs$ against traditional Os are quite conceivable in this procivil-society era in the history of democracy promotion.

Hypotheses and Case Justification

Having identified the key actors (I, O, $NTOs$) and factors (power asymmetries) shaping constitutional contents, as well as a pivotal issue of negotiations (presidential powers), I can now formulate a set of hypotheses:

H1: Under conditions of expanded asymmetry, assemblies will yield constitutions that increase power concentration (i.e., expansion of presidential powers).

H2: Under conditions of reduced asymmetry, assemblies will yield constitutions that diffuse power (reduction in presidential powers), especially if the status quo constitution was too biased toward executive powers.

H3: Under conditions of reduced asymmetry, assemblies will not reduce presidential powers significantly, if the status quo constitution was not too biased toward power concentration.

Before examining these hypotheses against the evidence, a word on methodology: My study focuses on medium-n, i.e., a selection of cases that is neither too small nor too large. Specifically, I focus on the ten cases of constitutional rewrite through constituent assemblies plus a few aborted cases. Medium-n studies offers some advantages over the more traditional single-case study or large-n studies. The merit of single-case studies is that the researcher can draw from a variety of authoritative sources to understand subtleties and trace cause-and-effect mechanisms. The disadvantage is uncertainty about generalizability across other cases. The virtue of large-n studies is, of course, the opposite. Propositions can be generalized because they can be tested across cases and time spans. However, large-n studies have the disadvantage of being somewhat blind to the context of constitutions, that is, to pivotal issues and how those issues get resolved, which is key to whether constitutions become acceptable or not. Furthermore, many large-n studies of constitutional change do not test situations of aborted constitutions, and thus, they can never offer a complete theory about the rise of constitutional change.

By focusing on multiple cases exclusively in one region (Latin America) during only one historical era, I can control for factors known to affect constitutions such as regional variables, historical eras, and cultural heritage. I can also be more sensitive to pivotal issues, in this case, presidential powers, and thus understand better the short-term response of actors. And as shown at the end of the article, I can also study instances of aborted change, offering a variation of outcomes that should allow for a more thorough review of hypotheses.

Measuring Presidential Powers

My first task is to rank the degree of presidential powers across cases. I developed an index that expands on Shugart and Carey's (1992) seminal work on presidential powers. Shugart and Carey organize their scores of presidential powers into two broad categories: legislative powers and nonlegislative powers. Since then, other authors have identified additional presidential powers, within and outside Shugart and Carey's categories. My index draws from these authors, especially Hartlyn and Luna (2009), Lutz (2006), Alberts (2006), and Bejarano (2006). In addition, I added my own categories, based on my reading of key items that emerged in the new Latin American constitutions. Country codings are available from the author.

The scorecard produced a raw score for each constitution, which was then converted into an index ranging from 0 (no presidential powers) to 1.0 (full presidential powers). In a democracy, values approaching 0 and 1 are untenable, by definition: all democracies rely on an executive branch, which makes 0 impossible, and on limited government, which makes 1 also impossible. Thus, in my index of presidential powers, democracies are expected to vary within a narrow range that never comes close to either 0 or 1.

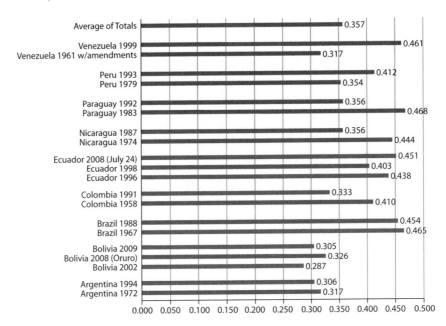

Figure 1.1. Index of Levels of Presidential Powers

Figure 1.1 shows the before and after scores for each Latin American case of constitutional rewrite. The outcomes vary starkly. But first, a comment about the index's reliability: the index is very clear about two of the most studied cases of constitutional change in the 1990s, Alberto Fujimori's constitution in Peru (1993), which expanded presidential powers, and César Gaviria's constitution in Colombia (1991), which curtailed presidential powers. These index scores are perfectly consistent with what the qualitative literature on these cases has concluded—presidential powers expanded in Peru and shrank in Colombia. That my index reflects well what the qualitative literature documents supports its reliability.

Nevertheless, this index is not perfect, on at least two counts. First, it measures presidential powers mostly in terms of the relationship between the executive branch and the other branches of government, while ignoring other dimensions of power, such as the electoral system and party regulations. The index also offers rather basic measurements of the state's role in the economy and variations in subnational powers. Second, the index assigns equal weight to every category, when in reality, some categories may be far more important than others in general, or across countries, or across time. The literature does not offer consensus on how to assign those weights, and so, I opted not to do that.

Given these imperfections, it is better to use the index less as a way to rank countries among each other, as a way to gauge change within countries, how a given country moved from one constitution to the new one. That is how this chapter uses the index.

Measuring Power Asymmetries

I propose two ways of measuring power asymmetries. The first is "institutional asymmetry": the distance between I and O within any given political institution such as Congress, governorships, party votes, or more simply, a nationwide electoral process.[7] The other is what could be called "table asymmetry": the distance between I and O at the negotiating table itself (the constituent assembly), measured by share of seats held by each.

In some cases, institutional and table asymmetries will not be perfectly aligned: the power differential at the negotiating table might differ significantly from the power differential throughout the political system as a whole. For instance, O can end up with more power (shares of seats) in the constituent assembly than it obtained in the most recent electoral contest or in Congress, and vice versa.

To determine whether constitutional negotiations will take place or not, we need to rely on institutional asymmetries; table asymmetries do not exist yet since no constituent assembly has been invoked. But to study constitutional outcomes, I will argue, the best indicator of power differential is table asymmetry, since it measures the bargaining differentials between I and O at the moment of negotiation.

Explaining the Origins of Constituent Assemblies

My first test is whether reduced asymmetry explains the *rise* of constituent assemblies. Table 1.1, column A, lists one measure of power asymmetries for all the Latin American countries that held constitutional assemblies since the 1980s: the difference between I and O in the distribution of seats in the House of Representatives, or the legislature as a whole, if the legislature is unicameral. Column A shows that most constitutional assemblies occurred in a context of preexisting pro-I asymmetry or low negative asymmetry (measured by the results of the previous legislative elections). This is consistent with my argument about the conditions that lead to constitution change. The only cases of large negative asymmetry (Ecuador, Peru, and Venezuela) exhibited exceptional circumstances or exogenous pressures.

However, there is too much variation in power asymmetries, ranging from 33.5 for Paraguay to −2.72 for Argentina, to conclude that asymmetries play the main

Table 1.1.   Power Asymmetries and Changes in Presidential Powers

Country	A Institutional Asymmetry[1]	B Table Asymmetry[2]	C Net Change in Presidential Powers	D Hypothesis Confirmed
Colombia[3]	20.00 (1990)	−42.20 (1991)	Reduction	H2
Ecuador 97[4]	−34.14 (1996)	−40.00 (1997)	Reduction	H2
Argentina[5]	−2.72 (1993)	−24.20 (1994)	Slight Reduction	H3
Brazil[6]	6.52 (1986)	6.00 (1988)	Imperceptible	?
Nicaragua[7]	25.80 (1984)	9.00 (1987)	Reduction	H2
Peru[8]	−31.20 (1990)	10.00 (1993)	Expansion	H1
Paraguay[9]	33.34 (1989)	16.00 (1991)	Reduction	H2
Venezuela[10]	−40.00 (1998)	86.26 (1999)	Expansion	H1
Bolivia I (Sucre)[11]	10.8 (2005)	7.4 (2006)	No Agreement	—
Bolivia II (Oruro)		84.9 (2007)	Expansion	H1
Bolivia III (2009)		−20 (2009)	Reduction	H2/H3
Ecuador 08	−100 (2006)	22.0 (2007)	Expansion	H1

Sources: Political Database of the Americas 2007; for Colombia 1991: Cepeda 1992; Ecuador 1996: Payne, Zovatto, et al. 2002; Ecuador 1997: CNN Election Watch 2007; Argentina 1993: CDP 2007a; Argentina 1994: Tow 2007; Argentina 1995: CNE 2007b; Nicaragua 1984, 1987: Reding 1987; Jonas and Stein 1990; Nicaragua 1990: CDP 2007b; IDEA 2007; Paraguay 1989: Payne et al. 2002; Paraguay 1991: Facts on File World News Digest 1991; Payne et al. 2002; Venezuela 1998, 1999: CDP 2007c; CNE 2007a; Bolivia 2005: Europa World Year Book 2006; Bolivia 2006: Latin American Regional Report: Andean Group 2006.

[1] Difference in number of seats between *I* and *O* in the lower chamber of Congress (or the entire congress if the legislature is unicameral). For Argentina 1994 and 1995, Colombia 1991, and Nicaragua 1984, percentage of vote, rather than seats, was used.

[2] Difference in number of seats between *I* and *O* at the negotiating table, i.e., the constitutional assembly (year).

[3] *I* = Liberal Party, 1990, 1991, 1994.

[4] *I* = Social Christian Party, 1996, 1997. Democracia Popular, 1998.

[5] *I* = Justicialista (or Peronist) Party, 1993, 1994, 1995.

[6] *I* = Brazilian Democratic Movement Party, 1986, 1988, 1990.

[7] *I* = FSLN, 1984, 1987; National Opposition Union, 1990.

[8] *I* = Fredemo, 1990; New Majority Alliance—Cambio 90, 1993, 1995.

[9] *I* = National Republican Association, 1989, 1991, 1993.

[10] *I* = AD 1998; MVR-MAS-PPT, 1999, 2000.

[11] *I* = MAS, 2005 and 2006.

role in triggering constitutional assemblies. What else might explain the origins of constitutional assemblies?

Bruce Ackerman (2002) provides vital clues (see also Ginsburg, Elkins, and Melton 2007). He discusses conditions under which most constitutions arise: "catastrophic defeat scenario" (when a nation suffers some type of crisis), "triumphalist scenarios" (when a political or revolutionary movement achieves a "decisive breakthrough of collective meaning" and a new constitution is devised to prevent collective backsliding), and the "maximal leader problem" (when a leader emerges who in the eyes of the masses is "the" symbolic representative of the movement's yearning for political definition). From Ackerman's list, the following triggering factors can be posited:

1. Compelling exogenous factors: These are structural pressures, or crises, that are so destabilizing that I becomes persuaded, often grudgingly, that a constituent assembly is the best political instrument to placate political agitation. These exogenous pressures include serious economic crises or generalized political instability (see Van Cott 2000, 27). They are equivalent to Ackerman's catastrophic defeat scenarios.

2. Regime Transition: The collapse of an authoritarian regime triggers a desire to carry out a constitutional assembly (see Nolte 2009). It is a time of enormous momentum for democratic forces, which are eager to lock in their gains. This is equivalent to Ackerman's triumphalist scenarios.

3. Rising I Popularity: When political asymmetry is considerably pro-I or the executive is persuaded that his or her popularity is rising (i.e., I anticipates large asymmetry) (Van Cott 2000; Salazar Elena 2007), I will be tempted to launch a constitutional assembly as a way to acquire more prerogatives in relation to other branches of government. This is equivalent to Ackerman's maximalist leader problem.

4. Strengthened O, which compels I to negotiate (Negretto 2009; Nolte 2009). O's strength can rise in two ways: overwhelming street mobilizations producing instability or through institutional means (i.e., what this chapter has labeled reduced power asymmetry).

Table 1.2 shows which of these factors played a major role in triggering constituent assemblies in Latin America. Severe economic crises (especially high inflation, recession, and exchange-rate crises) triggered or at least closely preceded assemblies in Brazil, Ecuador in 1997, Nicaragua, and Venezuela. Constitutional crises (premature presidential eviction from office) triggered assemblies in Bolivia, and Ecuador in 1997 and 2007, and transitions to democracy triggered the assemblies in Brazil and Paraguay.

Situations of I's rising popularity (relative to previous recent predecessors) preceded the constitutional assemblies in Argentina, Bolivia, Peru, Venezuela, and Ecuador 2007. In all these cases, I felt that it had gained far more power in its brief time in office than was reflected in the most recent elections. The key issue for Is

Table 1.2.   Constituent Assemblies Triggering Factors

	Arg 1993	Bra 1988	Bol 2006	Col 1991	Ecu 1997	Ecu 2007	Nic 1987	Par 1991	Per 1992	Ven 1999
Compelling Exceptional Circumstances										
Severe economic crisis		✓			✓		✓			✓
Recent presidential crises (e.g., resignations) or transition to democracy		✓	✓		✓	✓		✓		
Rising power of *I*										
I anticipates large asymmetry at constitutional assembly	✓		✓	✓		✓	✓	✓	✓	✓
Heightened Power of *O*										
Violent street conflicts or armed insurrection			✓	✓	✓		✓		✓	
Low or negative asymmetry in Congress	✓	✓	✓		✓					✓

Source: Author's estimation

was public opinion polls. If the president's approval ratings were high and rising, *Is* would feel more inclined to call for a constituent assembly in the expectation that this rise in popularity would grant greater bargaining leverage at the assembly. In Peru, for instance, President Alberto Fujimori offered the constitutional assembly after carrying out a self-coup in 1992, which raised his approval ratings. In Venezuela, Hugo Chávez rushed the constitution during his honeymoon, amid signs of quickly rising popularity. In both Peru and Venezuela, presidents estimated that their level of popularity far exceeded the asymmetries in Congress, and hence their eagerness to launch a constitution process. In Ecuador 2007, president Rafael Correa was elected in a second round with 56.7 of the vote (the largest margin of any Ecuadoran president since the early 1990s), yet he had zero representation in Congress. Days prior to the election, Correa's minister of government, Gustavo Larrea, argued that the government expected to win between 66 and 72 seats in the 130-seat assembly (*Latinnews Daily*, September 28, 2007). These expectations convinced *I* that a constituent assembly would pay off.

And as expected, the government scored a major victory in the elections for the constituent assembly: 80 of 130 seats.

Finally, there are situations of strengthened Os (low asymmetries): Brazil, Bolivia, and Nicaragua. It is worth noticing that Os and Is can gain strength simultaneously: the incumbent can accumulate more votes than predecessors and the opposition can become less fragmented. President Evo Morales, for instance, was the first president in Bolivia since 1982 to win more than 50 percent of the vote (strengthened *I*), while at the same time the opposition developed new organizational and ideological assets, such as unity and a coherent autonomy-oriented message.

The more idiosyncratic case is perhaps Ecuador 1997. It exhibits enormous negative asymmetry prior to the constituent assembly, and the president was not all that popular, conditions that, according to my argument, should lead to no constituent assembly. Yet, a constituent assembly did take place. Interim president Fabián Alarcón had to call for a constitutional assembly to placate the turmoil generated by economic and political crisis that followed the impeachment of President Abadalá Bucaram. He used the constituent assembly to avoid addressing economic issues.

Table 1.2 also makes clear that, except for Peru, none of the factors above was sufficient alone to trigger constituent assemblies. Two combinations prevail. First, compelling structural conditions (exceptional circumstances) triggered constitutional assemblies only in combination with the rise of *O* (through mobilizations, low asymmetry, or even negative asymmetry). Under these conditions, *I* had no option but to yield to pressures for constitutional change. Second, a strong desire by *I* to seek new powers also triggered constituent assemblies. This happens when *I* anticipates a large asymmetry. In short, reduced power asymmetry is not a sufficient condition for constitutional reforms, but neither is any other factor.

Explaining Resulting Presidential Powers

Overall, the index reveals three clusters of outcomes (fig. 1.1): Peru, Venezuela, and Ecuador 2008 expanded presidential powers. Nicaragua, Paraguay, Ecuador 1998, and Colombia reduced presidential powers. Argentina and Brazil show small movements, while Bolivia goes back and forth.

To what extent do power asymmetries explain these outcomes? Table 1.1 shows my two measures of power asymmetry. The first is a measure of *institutional* power asymmetry, the distance between *I* and *O* according to the most recent election prior to the formation of the constituent assembly. The other measure is *table* asymmetries: the exact difference in number of seats between *I* and *O* at the negotiating body.

Despite the variety of triggering circumstances, most *Is* confronted (to their surprise) significantly reduced table asymmetries at the constituent assemblies. This was true even in Argentina, Peru, and Bolivia, where presidents Menem, Fujimori, and Morales expected large table asymmetries given their high approval ratings in public opinion polls and yet received constituent assemblies that had less than favorable table asymmetries (Kay 1996; Calvert 2002; Gamarra 2007). The sole exceptions were Venezuela 1999 and Ecuador 2008, where table asymmetries were greater than *I* anticipated or enjoyed previously.

Table 1.1 shows the hypotheses confirmed by each case. Pro-*O* and reduced table asymmetries are associated with reduced presidential powers: Nicaragua, Colombia, Ecuador 2008, Argentina, and Bolivia 2009. Large table asymmetries are associated with expanded presidential powers: Ecuador 2008, Peru, Venezuela, and Bolivia 2008.

Figure 1.2 illustrates this relationship more clearly. It compares table asymmetries (vertical axis) with percent change in the index between the status quo ante and the new constitution. As table asymmetry moves from negative to positive values, presidential powers rise.

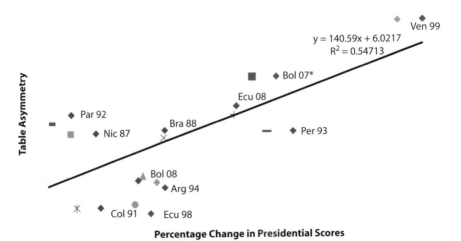

Figure 1.2. Table Asymmetries and Changes in Presidential Powers. For Bol 07, the reported table asymmetry is the average between the Sucre meeting (where negotiations began) and the Oruro meeting (where a draft was approved).

Paraguay and Nicaragua specifically support H2. The status quo ante had excessive power concentration (constitutions from the authoritarian era), and table asymmetry was far lower than institutional asymmetry in both cases. The result was a reduction in presidential powers, as is expected of cases undergoing transitions to democracy.

In all cases of reduced table asymmetry, O forces obtained crucial victories, including curtailment of executive branch powers, empowerment of nonpresidential institutions, and deepening of decentralization. Small and nontraditional forces obtained more access to political resources such as state funding. In Argentina and Peru, presidents obtained one of their most significant preferences (consecutive reelection, expanded decree authority, and, in Peru, a smaller unicameral Congress), but they had to concede to O more than they had planned (Jones 1997, 290–98; Schmidt 2000; Llanos 2003, 37–42).

In Argentina mutual victories were clearer, confirming H3. As Calvert (2002) argues, Menem "had to pay a high price" for his right to seek reelection: a reduction in the presidential mandate from six to four years, delegation of some presidential powers to a chief of cabinet who can be removed by the legislature, a run-off election, the creation of an autonomous government in Buenos Aires, and an increase in the number of senators. In addition, the new constitution regulates the president's leeway to regulate by decree.

The one seemingly inconsistent case is Brazil: despite reduced asymmetry, the constitution did not change presidential powers significantly (Alston et al. 2005), which seems to challenge H2. Yet, seen from the point of view of realized intentions, the case is still consistent with my argument. Despite his broad popularity, the incumbent José Sarney was unable to increase presidential powers as he had intended. Sarney was anxious for greater powers because he was engaged in a losing battle against runaway inflation. With two severe adjustment plans failing,[8] Sarney argued for greater powers to control fiscal spending. Instead, the 1988 constitution increased the national state's financial commitments to various sectors of society and transferred portions of federal tax revenues to subnational governments, without requiring them to provide additional services.

Power Asymmetry versus Ideology

An important rival argument to explain the origin of institutions is ideology and partisanship (see Pérez-Liñan and Castañeda 2012). Does the expansion of presidential powers reflect the ideological orientation and party affiliation of Is? My cases reveal that the answer is no: ideology and partisanship are not better at predicting movements in presidential powers. This can be seen by comparing several clusters of cases.

Different Ideologies, Similar Outcomes: Colombia and Nicaragua

Colombia and Nicaragua are two clear cases of pro-O asymmetries, each occurring under Is with divergent ideological proclivities. If ideology were decisive, we should observe huge differences in resulting presidential powers between Colombia and Nicaragua. And yet, the constitutional assemblies produce similar changes, all in the direction of reducing presidential powers.

For Nicaragua, constitutional change occurred under the auspices of a revolutionary-leftist I, President Daniel Ortega of the Frente Sandinista de Liberación Nacional (FSLN; Sandinista Front for National Liberation). In the 1984 legislative elections—billed as the preamble to a constituent assembly—the FSLN won a comfortable power advantage (see table 1.1). Yet, the FSLN decided to carry out the constitutional rewrite through a mechanism that favored O: The FSLN-dominated legislature appointed a commission composed of twelve members from the FSLN and ten members from other parties. Essentially, I agreed to a smaller proportion of seats than it held in the legislature (Reding 1987), thereby reducing asymmetry from 26.5 in the legislature to 9.0 at the negotiating table (Jonas and Stein 1990). While right-wing parties were excluded (United States Department of State 1991 [1987]), the key point is that table asymmetry became misaligned from institutional asymmetry in the direction of O.

The result was a reduction in presidential powers. This is clear in comparison to two benchmarks. The first is the last Somoza constitution of 1974 (see fig. 1.1), which, although considered "bogus" (Mijeski 1991, 5) because Somoza ruled by fiat, did contain some "advanced elements" (Escovar Fornos 2000, 134), including separation of power, a prohibition on reelection, and a wide array of social rights. A second benchmark is the "Fundamental Statutes of the Republic," the short document that served as the de facto Sandinista constitution between 1979 and 1987 and which justified FSLN rule by fiat (Azicri 1991; Prevost 1997). Relative to either benchmark, the 1987 constitution reduced presidential powers in general and during states of emergency (Jonas and Stein 1990). It included "liberal" elements such as four separate branches of government and the multiparty system (McConnell 1997). The resulting power diffusion partly explains why so many O delegates (74 percent) agreed to sign the 1987 constitution, why the ruling party had to resort to govern by decree after the signing (it felt in need of far more formal powers than the constitution granted in order to advance its revolutionary agenda), and why O was able to capture the presidency in 1990 (previously unavailable channels of contestation were opened).

In contrast, the president in Colombia during the constitution, César Gaviria, could easily be seen as ideological opposite to Ortega, i.e., more committed to a liberal market-oriented democracy. Yet, like Ortega, Gaviria adopted a selection rule for electing delegates to the constituent assembly that was very favorable to O, yielding a dramatic reversal from pro-I institutional asymmetry to a pro-O table symmetry, with no single political bloc dominating.

Consequently, the 1991 Colombian constitution, like the Nicaraguan constitution, also curtailed presidential powers. It introduced the election of governors, gave governors more resources, reduced the presidential powers in many policy areas, limited the president's decree powers, increased the power of the legislature to overrule presidential veto, and introduced an automatic system of revenue transfer from the national budget to departments and municipalities (Archer and Shugart 1997; Cepeda Ulloa 2003; Cárdenas, Junguito, and Pachón 2004).

These pro-O table asymmetries in Nicaragua and Colombia were the result of pressure. In Nicaragua, sectors of O were well armed (the Contras), and foreign actors (the United States, the Contadora group) pressed I for accommodation (Pastor 2002). In Colombia, the pressure came mostly from within. As in Nicaragua, a sector of Colombia's O was armed (the M-19), but also, the nonarmed sectors (especially the media and the student movement) pressured hard for a pro-O election rule (Van Cott 2000, 54–60), leading to reduced table asymmetry and subsequently to reduction in presidential powers.

In short, the bargaining leverage of the opposition, more so than the ideology of the president, is responsible for levels of presidentialism.

Similar Ideologies, Different Outcomes: Venezuela and Bolivia

Another approach is to compare the outcomes of two ideologically similar cases: Venezuela and Bolivia. Chávez and Morales are probably the two most ideologically similar presidents in this pool. They both share a "radical" commitment to socialism, disdain for traditional parties, resource nationalism, alternative forms of democracy, and anti-imperialism. Morales directly sought technical (not just financial) assistance from Chávez when organizing his constituent assembly. And yet, despite this close ideological alignment, the results of the constituent processes in terms of presidential powers were completely different.

At inauguration time in early 1999, Hugo Chávez was overwhelmingly popular, but he faced negative asymmetry in the legislature. His popularity encouraged him to pursue constitutional rewrite; his negative asymmetry in Congress encouraged him to avoid the congressional route, as mandated by the existing constitution. He proposed a constituent assembly with a selection rule that was deliberately designed to minimize the electoral success of *O* forces. The result was a constituent assembly that had the most extreme, pro-*I* table asymmetry in the history of democratic Venezuela and Latin America—88.6 points.[9]

The president obtained almost every one of his wishes. By September 1999, the constituent assembly, with the help of Chavista supporters in the streets, deactivated Congress and penalized federal judges who expressed reservations about the assembly's extraordinary powers. The president of the Supreme Court, Cecilia Sosa, resigned, arguing that the courts preferred to "commit suicide" than to suffer assassination (Sosa Gómez n.d.). In November, the directorate of the assembly approved a decree restricting the extent of the debate, in order to rush the signing of the constitution. In December, a week after the electorate approved the new constitution, the constituent assembly decreed the "Public Power Transition Regime," whereby the existing Congress, the state legislatures, the authorities in the Supreme Court of Justice, attorney general, the national comptroller, and the National Electoral Council were disbanded. The assembly proceeded to appoint "provisional authorities" for these posts, including a twenty-one-person provisional legislature (the *Congresillo*) (see Combellas 2007; Viciano Pastor and Martínez Dalmau 2001). These acts shared the same logic—abolishing all institutions in which Chávez could potentially face reduced asymmetry, all done in a completely "closed process," to quote Martha Harnecker, one of Chávez's most renowned supporters (Chávez, Harnecker, and Boudin 2005, 48–50).

The result of extreme table asymmetry in Venezuela was an extraordinary expansion of presidential powers in both relative and absolute terms relative to the status quo ante. No doubt, the new constitution conferred new rights on citizens. It is written in gender-inclusive language, creates the mechanism of popular referenda, and raises traditional social rights (e.g., to education and health) and less traditional rights (e.g., environmental protection, motherhood, indigenous rights) to the same levels as political rights (Wilpert 2003). Furthermore, the president did not obtain the power to rule by decree in some areas, as in Argentina, Brazil, Ecuador, Paraguay, and Peru. These limitations on presidential powers are important because they mean that presidents still required "partisan powers" (congressional majorities, disciplined ruling party) to rule unencumbered. However, there is no question that the biggest winner—in terms of net powers—was the executive branch.[10] In a significantly large number of areas, the president expanded its powers.

More clearly than in Venezuela, Bolivia had reduced institutional asymmetries at the start of the process. *I* was majoritarian in some regions: La Paz, Oruro, Potosí, and Chuquisaca, whereas *O* was majoritarian elsewhere: Santa Cruz, Beni, Tarija, and Pando (Gustafson 2006; Eaton 2007; Gamarra 2007; Gray-Molina 2008; Lehoucq 2008). Furthermore, table asymmetry at the constituent assembly was a mere 7.4, with *I* failing to replicate the overwhelming majority that Chávez gained in 1999. In addition, rather than fragment as in Venezuela, *O* forces in Bolivia coalesced into a more unified political party, Poder Democrático y Social (PODEMOS; Democratic and Social Power). In short, *I* was strong, but *O* had widespread support (especially in the east), institutional presence (majority in the Senate, control of crucial governorships and mayoralties), and a cohesive organization (PODEMOS).

Yet, *I* spent 2006 through 2008 disregarding this reduced institutional asymmetry. For instance, *I* insisted on approving articles by simple majority rather than supermajorities, hardly conceded any opposition demand, relied on street mobilizations to harass pro-*O* forces, held plebiscites while negotiations were still underway to flaunt the president's national popularity, and moved the location of the meeting three times (first, to the suburb of Sucre, then to Lauca Ñ, and finally to Oruro) to maximize *O*'s absence rates. At the Oruro meeting—a stronghold of pro-*I* support—a draft of the constitution was approved without a single member of PODEMOS in attendance.

As in Venezuela, this pro-*I* table asymmetry generated two predictable consequences. First, the constitutional draft approved in the city of Oruro (extreme table asymmetry, see table 1.1) expanded presidential powers (see fig. 1.1). The second effect was to galvanize the opposition. Essentially, *O* forces began to emulate some of *I*'s intransigent tactics. By 2007, *O* forces were also mobilizing social movements, inciting violence, carrying out unauthorized plebiscites (on departmental autonomy), calling for civil disobedience, seizing government buildings, and of course, rejecting every draft generated. By September 2008, Bolivia was close to the brink of war.

Only when *I* agreed to negotiate with *O*—i.e., to align table asymmetry with institutional asymmetry—was a truce possible. As in Nicaragua, this agreement ultimately came about due to both *O* and international pressures. Following a massacre between pro-*O* and pro-*I* social movements in the department of Pando in

September 2008, the members of UNASUR (Union of South American Nations), a diplomatic block of Latin American countries, held a meeting to address the Bolivia issue. They offered full support for Morales, but demanded a compromise.

Morales budged. First, he agreed to move the negotiations to Congress, where O had a strong presence in the lower chamber and a majority in the Senate. He also agreed to create a special commission to revise the Oruro draft, comprising an equal number of Movimiento al Socialismo (MAS; Movement toward Socialism) and PODEMOS representatives, plus seats for two other opposition parties. Table asymmetry thus became −20. Under this negative table asymmetry, presidentialism was lessened relative to the Oruro draft (fig. 1.1). Morales agreed to a series of concessions: not to seek reelection, abandoning the idea of reducing the size of the lower chamber and abolishing the Senate, and accepting that future amendment would require two-thirds of total votes in Congress rather than a simple majority. Moreover, 105 of the 411 articles of the Oruro draft were amended. A significant amendment involved expanding departmental autonomy. The constitutional draft was approved by O delegates and by 61.4 percent of the electorate; civil strife subsided shortly thereafter.

In sum, power asymmetry—and thus bargaining—seems a stronger prediction of institutional formation than ideology and partisanship. Pro-O asymmetries result in constitutions that lower presidential powers relative to the status quo, while pro-I asymmetries result in constitutions that expand presidential powers.

Splits among O: Ecuador 2008

Thus far, I have discussed the politics of constitutional reform as a bilateral bargain between I and O. However, very often, O forces are split, converting the process into a trilateral affair. The split allows I to negotiate with one sector of O to the detriment of the other. Ecuador 2008 illustrates this scenario.

In terms of power asymmetries, the Ecuador 2008 case exhibits similarities and differences from the Venezuelan 1999 experience. As in Venezuela, pro-I asymmetry was large (president Correa won the presidency with a majority), and the president's supporters were ideologically on the Left, virulently antiparty, and very "trusting" of the presidency.[11]

However, there were two important differences. First, although Ecuador's O forces were weak, deinstitutionalized, and volatile (Conaghan 2007), they were not as weak as in Venezuela 1999, where the process of party collapse was more advanced. Ecuadorean parties still retained regional roots and could act as veto players (Mejía Acosta et al. 2008). Second, there existed a more autonomous and vigorous *NTO* sector: more movement-oriented organizations, namely, the indigenous movements, Confederación de Nacionalidades Indígenas del Ecuador (CONAIE; Confederation of Indigenous Nationalities of Ecuador), the feminist movement, environmental organizations, and a variety of civic organizations. These forces did not align themselves with traditional parties, but they did not align unconditionally with *I* either (unlike Venezuela). These *NTOs* thus played a third, relatively independent role during the constituent assembly.[12]

Essentially, *I* and the NTOs struck a bargain. NTOs acceded to Correa's plan to centralize a bit of power for the sake of weakening traditional *Os* (whom these groups also viewed as political villains), but *I* had to agree to a series of concessions demanded by these forces (e.g., feminist groups obtained a multitude of rights).[13]

Nevertheless, *I* did not feel compelled to negotiate indefinitely, in part because Correa's political power expanded as the negotiations proceeded, based on his soaring approval rates (and declining approval rates for CONAIE). This expansion of power asymmetry encouraged Correa to end the negotiations abruptly: in the fall of 2008, he fired the assembly's president, Alberto Acosta, for yielding too much to social movements, and shortly thereafter finalized the draft.[14]

Ecuador 2008 can thus be explained by power asymmetries *and* splits among *O*. Because *I* was stronger than any previous president in the last twenty years, the 2008 constitution expanded presidential powers relative to the status quo. Because initially *I* needed to negotiate with the nonparty side of *O*—which was not as weak as in Venezuela—the expansion of presidential powers did not match that of Venezuela 1999.

Once again, these cases confirm my power asymmetry argument while also challenging the ideology hypothesis. There is agreement that of all *Is* in Latin America in the 1990s, the *Is* in Ecuador, Bolivia, and Venezuela shared the most ideological affinity and even resources to help each other out. Yet, the constitutional outcomes varied sharply across these cases. Variations in power asymmetries—more so than other variables—explain this variation.

Negative Asymmetry and Aborted Rewrites

A more complete test of power asymmetry would consider the effects of the third variation of asymmetry: situations where *O* forces are stronger than *I*. For these cases, my argument predicts aborted constitutional change. Unable to muster the bargaining leverage to prevail in negotiations, the probability of ending in *I*'s rejection zone increases. *I* thus has every incentive to use the power of office-holding to shelve the constitutional project entirely, or if *O* pressure is too strong, to consent only to a watered-down reform, such as changing just a few articles in the constitution (the amendment process), rather than carrying out constitutional replacement. In short, presidents who are facing or anticipate declining powers will avoid constitutional rewrite.

Nine of the ten cases in table 1.1 partially confirm this hypothesis. In the majority of cases, *I* either enjoyed large power asymmetries prior to calling a constituent assembly (Argentina, Brazil, Nicaragua, Paraguay, Colombia) or anticipated a large table asymmetry (e.g., Bolivia, Ecuador 2008, Peru, Venezuela). The sole exception is Ecuador 1998: *I* was an interim president with minimal powers, and the country was undergoing unrest. *I* launched a constituent assembly, despite his weakness, as a last-ditch effort to pacify the country.

Nevertheless, a more convincing approach would be to consider actual "negative" cases, i.e., those where major constitutional rewrite efforts were actually aborted by *Is*.[15] In the social sciences, it is difficult to identify nonoccurring cases, but it is not impossible. One route is to follow Stokes (2001) and study policy switches: individuals who make a promise as candidates renege once in office. In Latin America, several presidential candidates since the 1990s made constitutional rewrite a key campaign issue and faltered on their promises once elected. While comparing platform and policy betrayal may never produce an exhaustive list of all possible negative cases, it can identify enough cases to do an initial probe of the negative asymmetry hypothesis.

Table 1.3 offers a list of cases of betrayed promises, drawing exclusively from the countries discussed in this chapter. All *Is* in table 1.3 campaigned strongly on behalf of constitutional change (source provided). In some cases, they even began formal preparations for major constitutional rewrite once in office. All of them, however, ultimately changed their mind, either avoiding constituent assemblies altogether or agreeing to small-scale amendments.

Table 1.3 also provides evidence of negative asymmetry for each case: minority status in Congress for *I*, low approval ratings for *I*, outbreak of a political scandal involving *I*, splits and defections in the ruling party, or a combination of each. Negative asymmetry was a salient factor in all these cases.

Finally, there are cases of presidents who did not campaign on behalf of constitutional change, but did spend energy in office orchestrating a major constitutional change, only to see their plans frustrated. This too was due to sudden negative political asymmetry. Carlos Menem in Argentina 1997–1999 and Nicanor Duarte in Paraguay 2007, for instance, abandoned efforts to change the constitution to allow for reelection, due to splits in their parties and declining approval ratings.

Table 1.3.   Negative Power Asymmetry and Nonoccurring Constituent Assemblies

Country	I	Evidence that *I* campaigned for office in support of constitutional rewrite	Evidence of negative power asymmetry	Outcome
Bolivia	Jaime Paz Zamora	Van Cott 2005	Minority president	No constitutional assembly
	Gonzalo Sánchez de Lozada	Van Cott 2000, 2005	Minority president	No constitutional assembly; reform by legislative negotiation
Colombia	Ernesto Samper	Restrepo 1996	Corruption scandal; defections from ruling party	No constitutional assembly
	Andrés Pastrana	Cepeda Ulloa 2006	Minority president	No constitutional assembly
Ecuador	Alfredo Palacios	Latin American Regional Report: Andean Group 2005, 6.	Interim president; low approval ratings; impeachment threats	No constitutional change
Nicaragua	Violeta Chamorro	McConnell 1997; Esgueva Gómez 2003	Divisions within the ruling coalition	Watered-down amendment rather than a constituent assembly
Venezuela	Rafael Caldera	Álvarez 1998; Combellas 1998	Minority president; low approval ratings	No constitutional change

Ernesto Pérez Balladares in Panama 1999 lost a referendum to change the constitution to allow for his reelection, following a drop in approval ratings. Carlos Mesa in Bolivia in 2005 resisted calls for a constituent assembly, and agreed only to watered-down constitutional reforms, mostly because he was an interim president associated with a collapsed administration. Manuel Zelaya in Honduras was removed from office in June 2009 for trying to go forward with an electoral "consultation" on whether to proceed with a referendum on whether to have a constituent assembly most likely to secure reelection. Zelaya, however, faced growing negative asymmetry: his own party, the entire Congress, the Supreme Court, and most media deemed the "electoral consultation" illegal (as well as other acts by the president). These powers used the military to remove the president from office, with few signs of popular disagreement.

Many factors might have caused each of these aborted cases, but it is hard to deny the role of pro-O asymmetry. Pro-O asymmetry matters because it compels I to change his or her mind in expectation of low bargaining leverage, or renders O strong enough to block Is efforts to expand presidential powers. The evidence is not (and might never be) definitive, but it is plentiful.

Conclusion: Implications for Theories on Democratic Renewal

Constitutional rewrite occurs under many circumstances and covers many topics, as Ackerman (2002) explained, but in democracies, the distance between I and O is crucial for understanding both the incidence of change and the resulting levels of presidential powers. In Latin America since the 1980s, economic crises (in the form of runaway inflation, exchange rate instability, and unsustainable debt), political crises (in the form of either regime transitions or political instability), and the expansion of civil society as a result of more open democratic systems raised the demand for new constitutions, as is typical of worldwide cases of constitutional rewrite (Elkins, Ginsburg, and Blount 2009). But the distance between I and O is a powerful variable to explain how this demand for change was met. If I felt far stronger than O (large asymmetry), he promoted constitutional replacement as a way to secure more presidential powers.

Complications for I occurred if the distance between I and O was small or even negative. Under low asymmetry—when I is stronger than O but only slightly—O could still pressure I to carry out a constitutional assembly with an outcome that was far more advantageous to O, and thus, more power diffusing. In this context, almost all forces gained something and all forces, especially I, ended up compromising. If, however, O was far stronger than I (negative asymmetry), the result was often aborted constitutional replacement. Aware of their declining bargaining leverage, Is simply avoided entering into negotiations, even if this meant betraying a campaign promise.

My selection of cases allowed me to control for a number of alternative explanations, including the idea that I's ideology is an important determinant of constitutional outcomes. Four presidents with similar ideologies (preference for centralism, economic statism, rhetorical embrace of "participatory" democracy, and disdain for traditional parties) yielded different constitutions: Nicaragua 1987 reduced presidential powers, Ecuador 2008 expanded presidential powers but to a lesser degree than Venezuela 1999, and Bolivia 2007–2009 expanded presidential powers at first, generating much violence, until a new draft was renegotiated, which lowered presidential powers and violence. I's ideology—similar across cases—cannot explain these various outcomes. My power asymmetry argument fared better.

The finding about the independent effect of power asymmetry has implications that go beyond mere constitution making. First, my argument contributes to the literature on institutionalism by positing a theory about the origins of institutions, in this case, constitutions, and within constitutions, presidential powers. Second, the theory advanced is parsimonious: it focuses on a single variable (power asymmetry), affecting mostly a few key actors (I, O, and sometimes $NTOs$). Third, it heeds Snyder and Mahoney's (1999) advice on the need to be clear about how institutions affect the actor's preference, in this case, the institutional position of the negotiating party (either in control of the Executive branch, or not) shapes preferences toward constitutional outcomes.

And fourth, my argument has implications for theories on democratization. Specifically, my findings depart from some well-established structuralist arguments about the proper route toward democratization. Structuralists tend to see democratization as contingent on maximizing the power of any given country's democratizing class. They disagree on which group constitutes the key democratizing force: the modern bourgeoisie (Moore 1966), organized labor (Collier 1999; Rueschmeyer et al. 1992), the middle classes (Luebbert 1991), or the nonelite citizenry in general (Tilly 1992; Acemoglu and Robinson 2006). Yet, they all agree that democratization requires a "transfer," to use Acemoglu and Robinson's word (2006, 27), of formal powers from the traditional elite classes to the democratizing class and its allies. Once these democratizing classes get complete hold of the state (and displace old elites), democracy can happen.

My argument disagrees with both the protagonists and the storyline in these structural accounts. Total victory of one actor over another may not be the route to democratic renewal because, in constitution making, it leads to an expansion of presidential powers relative to the status quo, which translates into an increase in the stakes of power-holding. As North et al. (2000) and Weingast (2004) argue, increasing the stakes of powerholding can be destabilizing because it infuriates the opposition and lessens the chance of loyalty. It also encourages I to subsequently arrogate even more powers, which conspires against the notion of limited government, the sine qua non of democratic governance. A more reliable route to enduring democracy, this chapter suggests, is to reduce rather than expand the power differential between political majorities and minorities at the moment of constitutional foundation.

NOTES

I am especially grateful to my students and various research assistants at Amherst College, especially Sam Grausz, who have assisted my work over the years. I am also grateful to John Carey, Zachary Elkins, Jonathan Hartlyn, and the contributors to this volume for helpful comments.

    1. Research on the origins of constitutions is in its infancy. For Latin America, see Negretto 2009, Nolte 2009, and Hartlyn and Luna 2009.

    2. Constitutional change occurs through two mechanisms: complete rewrites (replacement) and amendments (reform). This chapter looks at rewrites only, although change through amendment has been significant. Nolte, for instance, counts 312 amendments in Latin America between 1978 and 2008. In some cases (Chile and Mexico) the amendments created significant transformations in civil-military relations (Chile), the effectiveness of electoral institutions (Mexico), and the relationship between the president and the legislators (both Chile and Mexico). However, for this chapter I decided not to look at the amendment process since it seems to respond "to a different logic" than the one I identify for rewrites. Amendments are narrower in scope, are approved by a smaller number of actors (usually, the executive branch in conjunction with a few parliamentarians), and tend to be mostly about policy-related matters (see Nolte 2009, 8; see also Hartlyn and Luna 2009).

    3. The 1983 El Salvador and 1985 Guatemala constitutional rewrites are not included because they were enacted under authoritarian settings (a nonelected government).

    4. On the different ways in which constitutions can change, especially the distinction among legislature-based, constituent assembly-based, and president-based changes, see Elkins, Ginsburg, and Blount 2009.

    5. On how I's demand for more presidential powers rose in Latin America since the 1980s, see O'Donnell's (1994) famous essay on "delegative democracy," which is both a summary and a normative lamentation of this heightened demand.

    6. The Guayaquil-based gay group, Lista 85, conducted a powerful parade (*Latin-news*, September 28, 2007).

    7. Amorim Neto (2002) applies a similar argument to executive-legislative relations under fragmented political party systems, what he calls "cabinet coalescence."

    8. Plan Cruzado of 1986 and Plan Bresser of 1987.

    9. Although the total votes obtained by opposition and independent candidates reached approximately 30 percent, only six made it into the constitutional assembly. For an explanation of how the electoral system and electoral strategies led to this underrepresentation, see Penfold 1999; Maingón, Pérez Baralt, and Sonntag 2000; Crisp and Johnson 2001; and Coppedge 2003.

    10. For qualitative assessments reaching the same conclusions, see Álvarez Díaz 1999; Virtuoso 1999; Maingón, Pérez Baralt, and Sonntag, 2000; Blanco 2003, 250–54.

    11. See Freidenberg 2008. The antiparty sentiment was strong across the political system, not just within the Correa's party. Only 33.7 percent of assembly delegates ex-

pressed agreement with the view that "democracy cannot exist without parties," down from 85.7 among legislators in 1996. Furthermore, almost 80 percent of Correa's delegates at the constituent assembly had never belonged to a party, and 71.7 percent of expressed having "a lot of trust" in the presidency. See Freidenberg 2008.

12. On how civil society groups gravitated toward Chávez in 1998–1999, see Álvarez 2006.

13. In Ecuador, as elsewhere in Latin America, these nonparty organizations wanted to lower barriers to entry into the political world, even if that meant closing opportunities traditional parties. On this divide between parties and nonparty representative organizations, see Hochstetler and Friedman 2008; and Hellman 1992.

14. Interview, Quito, January 2009.

15. On the methodological merit of negative cases, see Ragin 2004.

REFERENCES

Acemoglu, Daren, and James A. Robinson. 2006. *Economic Origins of Dictatorship and Democracy.* New York: Cambridge University Press.

Ackerman, Bruce. 2002. "The Rise of World Constitutionalism." *Virginia Law Review* 83 (4): 771–97.

Alberts, Susan. 2006. "Subjecting Power to Rules: Constitutionalism and Democratic Survival in Latin America." Unpublished paper presented at the American Political Science Association, Philadelphia.

Alston, Lee J., Marco Melo, Bernardo Mueller, and Carlos Pereira. 2005. "Political Institutions, Policymaking Processes and Policy Outcomes in Brazil." *Latin American Research Network Working Paper No. R-509.* Washington, DC: Inter-American Development Bank.

Álvarez, Ángel E. 2006. "Social Cleavages, Political Polarization and Democratic Breakdown in Venezuela." *Stockholm Review of Latin American Studies* 1:18–28.

Álvarez, Tulio A. 1998. *La constituyente: Todo lo que usted necesita saber* [The constituent assembly: Everything you need to know]. Caracas: Editorial CEC, Libros de El Nacional.

Álvarez Díaz, Ángel. 1999. "La constitución: Realismo político e ilusión democratizadora." *Revista SIC,* no. 620 (December): 465–67.

Amorim Neto, Octavio. 2002. "Presidential Cabinets, Electoral Cycles, and Coalition Discipline in Brazil." In *Legislative Politics in Latin America,* edited by Scott Morgenstern and Benito Nacif. New York: Cambridge University Press.

Arato, Andrew. 2005. "Constitutional Learning." *Theoria.*

Archer, Ronald P., and Matthew Soberg Shugart. 1997. "The Unrealized Potential of Presidential Dominance in Colombia." In *Presidentialism and Democracy in Latin America,* edited by Scott Mainwaring and Matthew Soberg Shugart. New York: Cambridge University Press.

Armony, Ariel C., and Héctor E. Schamis. 2005. "Babel in Democratization Studies." *Journal of Democracy* 16 (4): 116–17.

Avritzer, L. 2002. *Democracy and the Public Space.* Princeton: Princeton University Press.

Azicri, Max. 1991. "Examining Some Relevant Political and Constitutional Issues of the 1987 Nicaraguan Constitution." In *The Nicaraguan Constitution of 1987: English Translation and Commentary*, edited by Kenneth J. Mijeski. Athens, OH: Ohio University Monographs in International Studies no. 17: 179–218.

Bejarano, Ana María. 2006. "Placing the Constitution of 1991 in Time: Colombia's Long Road to Democratization." Unpublished paper presented to the American Political Science Association, Philadelphia, August 30–September 2.

Bermeo, Nancy. 1997. "Myths of Moderation: Confrontation and Conflict during Democratic Transitions." *Comparative Politics* 29:305–22.

Blanco, Carlos. 2003. *Revolución y desilusión: La Venezuela de Hugo Chávez* [Revolution and disappointment: Hugo Chávez's Venezuela]. Madrid: Catarata.

Calvert, Peter. 2002. "Argentina: The Crisis of Confidence." Unpublished paper presented at the Annual Conference of the UK Political Science Association.

Cárdenas, Mauricio, Roberto Junguito, and Mónica Pachón. 2004. "Political Institutions and Policy Outcomes in Colombia: The Effects of the 1991 Constitution." Washington, DC: Inter-American Development Bank, Research Department.

Carothers, Thomas. 2002. "The End of the Transition Paradigm." *Journal of Democracy* 13 (1): 5–21.

CDP. 2007a. "Argentina 1993 Legislative Elections." Center on Democratic Performance, Electoral Results Archive.

———. 2007b. "Nicaragua 1990 Legislative Elections." Center on Democratic Performance, Elections Results Archive.

———. 2007c. "Venezuela 1998 Legislative Elections." Center on Democratic Performance, Election Results Archive.

Cepeda, Manuel José. 1992. *La constitución de 1991 ante nuestra realidad: Respuesta a algunas críticas*. Bogotá: Folletos Esap.

———. 1993. *Introducción a la constitución de 1991*. Bogotá: Imprenta Nacional.

Cepeda Ulloa, Fernando. 2008. "Colombia: The Governability Crisis." In *Constructing Democratic Governance in Latin America*, edited by Jorge I. Domínguez and Michael Shifter, 209–41. 3rd ed. Baltimore: Johns Hopkins University Press.

Chávez, Hugo, Martha Harnecker, and Chesa Boudin. 2005. *Understanding the Venezuelan Revolution: Hugo Chávez Talks to Marta Harnecker*. New York: Monthly Review Press.

CNE. 2007a. "Elecciones, República Bolivariana de Venezuela." Consejo Nacional Electoral.

———. 2007b. "Resultados de Elecciones Presidenciales Anteriores."

CNN Election Watch. 2007. "Ecuador (National Assembly)." CNN.com.

Collier, Ruth Berins. 1999. *Paths toward Democracy: The Working Class and Elites in Western Europe and South America*. New York: Cambridge University Press.

Collier, Ruth, and David Collier. 1991. *Shaping the Political Arena: Critical Junctures, the Labor Movement, and Regime Dynamics in Latin America*. Princeton: Princeton University Press.

Colomer, Josep Maria. 1995. "Strategies and Outcomes in Eastern Europe." *Journal of Democracy* 6:74–85.

Combellas, Ricardo. 1998. "Introducción." In *Constituyente: Aportes al debate*, edited by Ricardo Combellas. Caracas: Fundación Konrad Adenauer, COPRE.

———. 2007. "El proceso constituyente y la Constitución de 1999." In *Venezuela en retrospectiva: Los pasos hacia el régimen chavista*, edited by Günther Maihold, 47–76. Madrid and Frankfurt am Main: Iberoamericana and Vervuert Verlag.

Conaghan, Catherine M. 2007. "Notes on Recent Elections: The 2006 Presidential and Congressional Elections in Ecuador." *Electoral Studies* 26 (4): 823–28.

Coppedge, Michael. 2003. "Venezuela: Popular Sovereignty versus Liberal Democracy." In *Constructing Democratic Governance in Latin America*, edited by Jorge I. Domínguez and Michael Shifter, 165–92. 2nd ed. Baltimore: Johns Hopkins University Press.

Crisp, Brian, and Gregg Johnson. 2001. "De instituciones que restringen a instituciones ausentes" [From restricting institutions to missing institutions]. In *Venezuela en transición: Elecciones y democracia, 1998–2000*, edited by José Vicente Carrasquero, Thaís Maingón, and Friedrich Welsch. Caracas: Red Universitaria de Estudios Políticos de Venezuela, CDB Publicaciones.

Di Palma, Giuseppe. 1990. *To Craft Democracies: An Essay on Democratic Transitions*. Berkeley: University of California Press.

Eaton, Kent. 2007. "Backlash in Bolivia: Regional Autonomy as a Reaction against Indigenous Mobilization." *Politics and Society* 35 (1): 71–102.

Eckstein, S., and T. P. Wickham-Crowley, eds. 2003. *Struggles for Social Rights in Latin America*. New York: Routledge.

Elkins, Zachary, Tom Ginsburg, and Justin Blount. 2009. "Can We Trust Legislators to Write Constitutions?" Unpublished paper presented at the Latin American Studies Association Congress, Rio de Janeiro.

Escovar Fornos, Iván. 2000. *El constitucionalismo nicaragüense* [Nicaraguan constitutionalism]. Vol. 2. Managua: Editorial Hispamer.

Esgueva Gómez, Antonio. 2003. *Historia Constitucional de Nicaragua* [Constitutional history of Nicaragua]. Managua: Lea Grupo Editorial.

Europa World Year Book. 2006. "Bolivia." London: Europa Publications.

Facts on File World News Digest. 1991. "Constitutional Assembly Elected: Paraguay." Facts on File.

Falleti, Tulia. 2006. Review of Kathleen O'Neill, "Decentralizing the State: Elections, Parties and Local Power in the Andes." *Latin American Politics and Society* 48 (3): 208–11.

Finer, S. E., Vernon Bogdanor, and Bernard Rugden. 1995. *Comparing Constitutions*. Oxford: Oxford University Press.

Freidenberg, Flavia. 2008. "¿Renovación o continuismo? Actitudes, valores y trayectoria de la clase política ecuatoriana" [Renewal or continuity? Attitudes, values and career paths across Ecuador's political class]. Salamanca: Instituto de Iberoamérica, Universidad de Salamanca.

Gamarra, Eduardo A. 2007. "Bolivia on the Brink." New York: Council on Foreign Relations, Center for Preventive Action.

Geddes, Barbara. 1994. *Politicians' Dilemma*. Berkeley: University of California Press.

Ginsburg, Tom, Zachary Elkins, and James Melton. 2007. "The Lifespan of Written Constitutions." *American Law and Economics Association Annual Meetings*. Berkeley: Electronic Press.

Gray Molina, George. 2010. "The Challenge of Progressive Change under Evo Morales." In *Leftist Governments in Latin America: Successes and Shortcomings*, edited by Kurt Weyland, Raúl L. Madrid, and Wendy Hunter, 57–76. New York: Cambridge University Press.

Gustafson, Bret. 2006. "Spectacles of Autonomy and Crisis: Or, What Bulls and Beauty Queens Have to Do with Regionalism in Eastern Bolivia." *Journal of Latin American Anthropology* 11 (2): 351–79.

Hartlyn, Jonathan, and Juan Pablo Luna. 2009. "Constitutional Reform in Latin America: A Framework for Analysis." Unpublished paper presented at the Latin American Studies Association Congress, Rio de Janeiro, Brazil.

Hellman, Judith Adler. 1992. "The Study of New Social Movements in Latin America and the Question of Autonomy." In *The Making of Social Movements in Latin America*, edited by Arturo Escobar and Sonia E. Alvarez, 52–61. Boulder, CO: Westview Press.

Hochstetler, Kathryn, and Elisabeth Jay Friedman. 2008. "Can Civil Society Organizations Solve the Crisis of Partisan Representation in Latin America?" *Latin American Politics and Society* 50 (2): 1–26.

Horowitz, Donald. 2002. "Constitutional Design: Proposals versus Processes." In *The Architecture of Democracy: Constitutional Design, Conflict Management, and Democracy*, edited by Andrew Reynolds, 15–36. Oxford: Oxford University Press.

IDEA. 2007. "Voter Turnout: Nicaragua." International Institute for Democracy and Electoral Assistance. www.idea.int/vt/countryview.cfm?id=169.

Jonas, Susanne, and Nancy Stein. 1990. "The Construction of Democracy in Nicaragua." *Latin American Perspectives* 17 (3): 10–37.

Jones, Mark P. 1997. "Evaluating Argentina's Presidential Democracy." In *Presidentialism and Democracy in Latin America*, edited by Scott Mainwaring and Matthew Soberg Shugart, 290–98. Cambridge: Cambridge University Press.

Kantor, Harry. 1977. "Efforts Made by Various Latin American Countries to Limit the Power of the President." In *Presidential Power in Latin American Politics*, edited by Thomas V. DiBacco. New York: Praeger.

Karl, Terry Lynn. 1990. "Dilemmas of Democratization in Latin America." *Comparative Politics* 23:1–23.

Karl, Terry Lynn, and Phillipe Schmitter. 1991. "Modes of Transition in Southern and Eastern Europe and South and Central America." *International Social Science Journal* 128:269–84.

Kay, Bruce H. 1996. "'Fujipopulism' and the Liberal State in Peru, 1990–1995." *Journal of Interamerican Studies and World Affairs* 38 (4): 55–98.

Latin American Regional Report: Andean Group. 2006. "Rows as Constituent Assembly Looms." *Latinnews*. www.latinnews.com.

Lehoucq, Fabrice. 2008. "Bolivia's Constitutional Breakdown." *Journal of Democracy* 19 (4): 110–24.

Lijphart, Arend. 1991. "Constitutional Choices for New Democracies." *Journal of Democracy* 2 (1): 72–84.

———. 1992. "Introduction." In *Parliamentary Versus Presidential Government*, edited by Arend Lijphart. New York: Oxford University Press.

Llanos, Mariana. 2003. *Privatization and Democracy in Argentina: An Analysis of President-Congress Relations*. Hampshire: Palgrave Macmillan.

Luebbert, Gregory M. 1991. *Liberalism, Fascism, or Social Democracy: Social Classes and the Political Origins of Regimes*. New York: Oxford University Press.

Lutz, Donald S. 2006. *Principles of Constitutional Design*. New York: Cambridge University Press.

Maingón, Thaís, Carmen Pérez Baralt, and Heinz R. Sonntag. 2000. "La batalla por una nueva Constitución para Venezuela." *Revista Mexicana de Sociología* 62:91–124.

McConnell, Shelley. 1997. "Institutional Development." In *Nicaragua without Illusions: Regime Transition and Structural Adjustment in the 1990s*, edited by Thomas W. Walker, 45–63. Wilmington: SR Books.

Mejía Acosta, Andrés, María Caridad Araujo, Aníbal Pérez-Liñán, and Sebastián Saiegh. 2008. "Veto Players, Fickle Institutions, and Low-Quality Policies: The Policymaking Process in Ecuador." In *Policymaking in Latin America: How Politics Shapes Policies*, edited by Ernesto Stein, Mariano Tommasi, Carlos Scartascini, and Pablo Spiller, 243–85. Cambridge, MA: Harvard University Press.

Mijeski, Kenneth J. 1991. "Introduction." In *The Nicaraguan Constitution of 1987*, edited by Kenneth J. Mijeski, 1–22. Athens, OH: Ohio University Center for International Studies.

Moore, Barrington. 1966. *Social Origins of Dictatorship and Democracy: Lord and Peasant in the Making of the Modern World*. Boston: Beacon Press.

Negretto, Gabriel. 1999 "Constitution-Making and Institutional Design: The Transformations of Presidentialism in Argentina." *Journal of European Sociology* 2 (Fall): 193–233.

———. 2001. "Negociando los poderes del presidente: Reforma y cambio constitucional en la Argentina." *Desarrollo Económico* 163 (41): 411–44.

———. 2002. "Gobierna solo el presidente? Poderes de decreto y diseño institucional en Brasil y Argentina." *Desarrollo Económico* 167 (42): 377–404.

———. 2009. "Political Parties and Institutional Design: Explaining Constitutional Choice in Latin America." *British Journal of Political Science* 39:117–39.

Nolte, Detlef. 2009. "Constitutional Change in Latin America from a Comparative Perspective." Unpublished paper presented at the Meeting of the Latin American Studies Association. Rio de Janeiro, Brazil, June.

North, Douglass C., William Summerhill, and Barry R. Weingast. 2000. "Order, Disorder, and Economic Change: Latin America versus North America." In *Governing for Prosperity*, edited by Bruce Bueno de Mesquita and Hilton L. Root, 23–29. New Haven: Yale University Press.

O'Donnell, Guillermo. 1994. "Delegative Democracy." *Journal of Democracy* 5 (1): 55–69.

O'Donnell, Guillermo, and Phillipe Schmitter. 1986. *Transitions from Authoritarian Rule: Tentative Conclusions about Uncertain Democracies*. Baltimore: Johns Hopkins University Press.

Olson, Mancur. 2000. *Power and Prosperity*. New York: Basic Books.

Pastor, Robert A. 2002. *Not Condemned to Repetition: The United States and Nicaragua.* 2nd ed. Boulder, CO: Westview Press.

Payne, J. Mark, Daniel G. Zovatto, Ferando Carrillo Flórez, and Andrés Allamand Zavala. 2002. *Democracies in Development: Politics and Reform in Latin America.* Washington, DC: Inter-American Development Bank.

Penfold, Michael. 1999. "Constituent Assembly in Venezuela: First Report." Atlanta: Carter Center.

Pérez-Liñán, Aníbal, and Néstor Castañeda Angarita. 2012. "Institutionalism." In *Routledge Handbook of Latin American Politics,* edited by Peter Kingstone and Deborah Yashar, 395–406. New York: Routledge.

Persson, Torsten, and Guido Tabellini. 2003. *Economic Effects of Constitutions.* Cambridge, MA: MIT Press.

Political Database of the Americas. 2007. "Electoral Data." Georgetown University and Organization of the American States.

Prevost, Gary. 1997. "The FSLN." In *Nicaragua without Illusions: Regime Transition and Structural Adjustment in the 1990s,* edited by Thomas W. Walker, 149–64. Wilmington: SR Books.

Przeworski, Adam. 1991. *Democracy and the Market: Political and Economic Reforms in Eastern Europe and Latin America.* New York: Cambridge University Press.

Ragin, Charles C. 2004. "Turning the Tables: How Case-Oriented Research Challenges Variable-Oriented Research." In *Rethinking Social Inquiry: Diverse Tools, Shared Standards,* edited by Henry E. Brady and David Collier, 123–38. Lanham, MD: Rowman and Littlefield.

Reding, Andrew. 1987. "Nicaragua's New Constitution: A Close Reading." *World Policy Journal* 4 (2): 257–94.

Restrepo M., Luis Alberto. 1996. "El Ejecutivo en la crisis: Dimensiones, antecedentes y perspectivas." In *Tras las huellas de la crisis política,* edited by Francisco Leal Buitrago. Bogotá: Tercer Mundo Editores/Fescol/IEPRI.

Reynolds, Andrew, ed. 2002. *The Architecture of Democracy: Constitutional Design, Conflict Management, and Democracy.* Oxford: Oxford University Press.

Roberts, Kenneth M. 1998. *Deepening Democracy? The Modern Left and Social Movements in Chile and Peru.* Stanford: Stanford University Press.

Rueschemeyer, Dietrich, Evelyne Huber, and John D. Stephens. 1992. *Capitalist Development and Democracy.* Chicago: University of Chicago Press.

Salamanca, L. 2004. "Civil Society: Late Bloomers." In *The Unraveling of Representative Democracy in Venezuela,* edited by J. L. McCoy and D. Myers, 93–114. Baltimore: Johns Hopkins University Press.

Samuels, David J., and Matthew S. Shugart. 2010. *Presidents, Parties, and Prime Ministers: How the Separation of Powers Affects Party Organization and Behavior.* Cambridge: Cambridge University Press.

Schedler, Andreas. 1996. "Anti-Political-Establishment Parties." *Party Politics* 2 (3): 291–312.

Schmidt, Gregory D. 2000. "Delegative Democracy in Peru? Fujimori's 1995 Landslide and the Prospects for 2000." *Journal of Interamerican Studies and World Affairs* 42 (1): 99–132.

Shugart, Matthew Soberg, and John M. Carey. 1992. *Presidents and Assemblies: Constitutional Design and Electoral Dynamics*. Cambridge: Cambridge University Press.

Smith, William. C., and R. P. Korzeniewicz. 2007. "Insiders, Outsiders, and the Transnational Politics of Civil Society." In *Governing the Americas: Assessing Multilateral Institutions*, edited by G. Mace, J.-P. Thérien, and P. Haslam, 151–72. Boulder, CO: Lynne Rienner.

Snyder, Richard, and James Mahoney. 1999. "The Missing Variable: Institutions and the Study of Regime Change: Review Article." *Comparative Politics* 32 (1): 103–22.

Sosa Gómez, Cecilia. n.d. "Renuncia a la presidencia de la Corte Suprema de Justicia, palabras de Cecilia Sosa Gómez." Analítica.com. www.analitica.com/bitblioteca/csj/renuncia.asp.

Stokes, Susan. 2001. *Mandates and Democracy: Neoliberalism by Surprise*. New York: Cambridge University Press.

Tilly, Charles. 1992. *Coercion, Capital, and European States, AD 990–1992*. Cambridge, MA: Blackwell.

Tow, Andy. 2007. *Electoral Atlas*. http://towsa.com.andy.totalpais/.

United States Department of State. 1991 [1987]. "The Sandinista Constitution." In *The Nicaraguan Constitution of 1987*, edited by Kenneth J. Mijeski. Athens, OH: Ohio University Monographs in International Studies.

Van Cott, Donna Lee. 2000. *The Friendly Liquidation of the Past: The Politics of Diversity in Latin America*. Pittsburgh: University of Pittsburgh Press.

———. 2005. *From Movements to Parties in Latin America: The Evolution of Ethnic Politics*. New York: Cambridge University Press.

Viciano Pastor, Roberto, and Rubén Martínez Dalmau. 2001. *Cambio político y proceso constituyente en Venezuela, 1998–2000* [Political change and constituent process in Venezuela]. Caracas: Vadell Hermanos.

Virtuoso, José. 1999. "Una oportunidad perdida." *Revista SIC* 620: 462–64.

Weingast, Barry R. 2004. "Constructing Self-Enforcing Democracy in Spain." In *Politics from Anarchy to Democracy: Rational Choice in Political Science*, edited by Erwin L. Morris, Joe A. Oppenheimer, and Karol Edward Soltan. Stanford: Stanford University Press.

Wiarda, Howard J., and Harvey F. Kline. 2000. "The Latin America Tradition and Process of Development." In *Latin American Politics and Development*, edited by Howard J. Wiarda and Harvey F. Kline. 5th ed. Boulder, CO: Westview Press.

Wilpert, Gregory. 2003. *Venezuela's New Constitution*. www.venezuelanalisis.com.

CHAPTER TWO

Mass Media and Politics in Latin America

Taylor C. Boas

I n Latin America, the mass media are sometimes referred to as a *cuarto poder*, or "fourth power," to denote their potentially crucial role in safeguarding and deepening democracy.[1] By reporting on wrongdoings and malfeasance as well as achievements and good governance, the media can hold politicians accountable and help citizens make informed decisions about their choice of leaders. By giving voice to individuals, social movements, political parties, and interest groups, the media help determine who gets to participate in public discourse and influence the political agenda. Through their own decisions about what to cover and how to cover it, the media can also play a crucial independent role in shaping that agenda. Following Waisbord (2008), we can refer to these three prodemocratic actions of the mass media as their watchdog, gate-keeping, and agenda-setting functions.

This chapter explores politics and the mass media in the eight countries covered in detail in this volume, examining the degree to which they contribute to, or hinder, healthy democratic governance. The first section examines media concentration and ownership structures and their implications for the media's gate-keeping function. Historical patterns of market concentration and ownership have changed little for Latin America's mass media; a few media sources in each country boast a majority of viewers or listeners, and these outlets are typically controlled by wealthy families or individuals with conservative political leanings. Politicians themselves often become owners of the media, working the system to gain broadcasting concessions and then using them as political mouth-pieces. The proliferation of low-power community media offers the possibility that new voices might gain access to the airwaves, but all too often, these broadcasters also fall under the sway of powerful politicians. On the whole, concentration of audience and ownership means that the Latin American mass media should continue to give voice primarily to those with political and economic power.

The second part of the chapter examines factors that influence the media's role as watchdog of democracy. Historically, patterns of media ownership, combined with conservative governments in many countries, meant that the media often colluded with politically like-minded presidents. More recently, the rise of a "new Left" in Latin America has brought to power several populist presidents who routinely clash with their countries' media owners. Where the media might have been complicit in prior abuses of executive power, they now aggressively denounce them. Yet the polarized political climate in these countries complicates the media's watchdog function—journalists are unlikely to investigate malfeasance on their own side of the political divide, and retaliation by authorities may silence some critical voices. Elsewhere, conflict between politicians and the press is rampant at the local level, where political bosses can eliminate potential watchdogs through their manipulation of the judicial system or control over local security forces. In such countries, media with national scope may exercise all the functions of a fourth power, but local media remain weak, intimidated, and subject to political control.

The final section of the chapter addresses the media's agenda-setting role by examining coverage of candidates in recent presidential elections. Historically, the media in Latin America were often markedly biased against left-wing candidates and openly favored conservative politicians. In Brazil, Mexico, and Chile, which had some of the most notorious patterns of bias in the past, electoral coverage of major left- and right-wing candidates is now quite even-handed. In countries with more polarized politics, however, substantial biases against left-wing politicians remain. Where populists have gained power, as in Venezuela and Bolivia, they have been able to level the playing field only by countering their negative portrayal in commercial media with an even more one-sided positive coverage in media outlets controlled by the state. Extreme polarization of this sort means that the media, first and foremost, engage in partisan battles; informing the public is relegated to a secondary plane.

The focus of this chapter is on broadcast media, primarily television, which remains the most politically influential medium in the region. As shown in table 2.1,

Table 2.1.   Media Penetration and Use as an Information Source (in percentages)

Country	Penetration			Information Source		
	Television	Radio	Newspaper	Television	Radio	Newspaper
Argentina	98.0	76.0	5.0	72.8	8.0	6.3
Bolivia	67.3	82.4	2.5	78.9	15.6	3.1
Brazil	94.0	91.4	6.2	73.8	2.4	10.4
Chile	99.8	95.0	5.9	78.5	2.3	6.5
Colombia	99.3	71.0	4.8	88.0	5.6	1.2
Mexico	98.0	57.0	6.8	82.4	4.6	5.2
Peru	75.0	82.0		78.3	11.0	6.4
Venezuela	98.0	66.0	10.5	64.3	1.0	26.5

Note: Penetration figures for television and radio are percent of homes owning the device, from *Mídia Dados Brasil* 2010 and Bolivia 2009. Newspaper penetration figures are average circulation per hundred adults, from World Association of Newspapers 2010. Information source figures, from the 2010 wave of the AmericasBarometer, reflects responses to the question "what is your main source of information about the country's situation?"

television is present in more than 95 percent of homes in most countries, and it is the citizens' primary source of information about current events by a wide margin. Radio plays an important secondary role in some countries, particularly in Bolivia and Peru, where its penetration rates are somewhat greater. Newspapers also matter for political information—especially in Venezuela, where their circulation rates are relatively high—and in some countries they play particularly important roles in breaking scandals and setting the political agenda. Where relevant, therefore, the chapter also examines trends in newspaper and radio.

Media Concentration and Ownership Structures

Historically, a major impediment to the mass media acting as a force for democracy in Latin America was that relatively few voices were represented. In countries such as Argentina, Brazil, Colombia, Mexico, and Venezuela, control of multiple media outlets by a handful of conglomerates meant politicians only had to collude with a few major players to ensure overwhelmingly favorable coverage. Oligopolistic market structures limited competitive pressures, so media owners could safely hue to the wishes of politicians without fear of losing readers, listeners, or viewers. Concentrated media markets also boosted the media's influence on public opinion. Where citizens across the political spectrum can choose from media espousing a variety of different perspectives, exposure tends to reinforce existing opinions. Where options are limited, media exposure is more likely to shift attitudes in one direction or another (Boas 2005; Lawson and McCann 2005).

Audience Share

Latin America's media markets have become less concentrated since the 1980s, when Mexico's Televisa and Brazil's TV Globo boasted more than 80 percent of the national television audience during prime time (Lima 1990; Lawson 2002), though they remain at least moderately concentrated in comparative perspective. Table 2.2 lists the major broadcast television networks and average share of viewers in seven of the eight countries covered in this volume, as well as in the United States and Canada.[2] For each country, audience data are used to compute the Herfindahl-Hirschman Index (HHI), a measure of industry concentration that is obtained by squaring and summing the percentage share of each firm in a particular market. The HHI approaches zero at the low end and would be 10,000 for a perfect monopoly.

Compared to the United States and Canada, Latin American broadcast television markets range from moderately to highly concentrated. Chile's market structure is most similar to those of the US and Canada; in each country, the leading network claims about a quarter of viewers. Elsewhere, the industry leader boasts a third to more than a half of all viewers and is typically well ahead of its closest competitor. In both Colombia and Mexico, broadcast television is essentially a duopoly; the third most popular network has less than a 5 percent audience share. However, broadcast television markets in most countries have become less concentrated in recent years. Compared to the figures calculated by Hughes and Lawson (2005) using data from 2002, the HHIs of Mexico and Brazil have declined by 1,419 and 667 points, respectively. These changes reflect the declining dominance of Televisa and TV Globo, though each network still comfortably leads its closest competitor by about 30 percentage points.

National markets for radio and newspapers are generally less concentrated, in part because there are lower barriers to entry (Waisbord 2008). Using data from 2004, Becerra and Mastrini (2009) found that radio was more competitive than broadcast television in each of these eight countries—sometimes quite significantly. In Mexico City, the HHI for radio in 2010 was approximately 2,900, or two-thirds of the national figure for broadcast television.[3] Newspaper markets are also less concentrated than television in most countries, though Chile stands as an important exception; the latter is essentially a duopoly dominated by the El Mercurio and COPESA groups (Becerra and Mastrini 2009).

Table 2.2.   Audience Share and Ownership of Broadcast Television in the Americas

Network (Parent)	Audience (%)	Majority traded	Politician owned	Foreign owned
Argentina: HHI 2502				
Canal 13 (Grupo Clarín)	32			
Telefe (Telefónica)	32	✓		✓
Canal 9 (Albavisión)	18			✓
América TV	12	✓		
Canal 7 (State)	7			
Bolivia				
ATB				
Unitel (Grupo Monasterio)			✓	
Red Uno (Grupo Kujlis)			✓	
Bolivisión (Albavisión)				✓
Red PAT				
Brazil: HHI 2904				
TV Globo	47			
TV Record	18			
SBT (Grupo Silvio Santos)	14			
Bandeirantes	6			
Chile: HHI 2067				
Televisión Nacional (State)	25			
Megavisión (Grupo Claro)	24			
Chilevisión (Time Warner)	23	✓		✓
Canal 13 (Grupo Luksic / Universidad Católica)	18			
La Red (Albavisión)	6			✓
Colombia: HHI 3898				
RCN (Grupo Ardila Lülle)	45			
Caracol (Grupo Santo Domingo)	44			

Network (Parent)	Audience (%)	Majority traded	Politician owned	Foreign owned
Mexico: HHI 4253				
Televisa	57	✓		
TV Azteca	28			
Peru: HHI 2350				
América (Plural TV)	37			
ATV (Albavisión)	23			✓
Frecuencia Latina	19			
Global (Albavisión)	8			✓
Panamericana (Telespectra)	7			
Venezuela: HHI 2835				
Venevisión (Grupo Cisneros)	47			
Televén (Camero Comunic.)	22			
VTV (State)	7			
Globovisión	6			
United States: HHI 1745				
CBS (Nat'l Amusements)	25			
Fox (News Corporation)	19	✓		✓
ABC (Disney)	19	✓		
NBC (Comcast/GE)	16	✓		
Univisión (Broadcasting Media Partners)	7			
Canada: HHI 1700				
CTV (Bell Canada)	26	✓		
TVA (Quebecor)	17	✓		
Global (Shaw Comm.)	15	✓		
CBC (State)	13			
Radio Canada (State)	9			

Note: HHI = Herfindahl-Hirschman Index. Networks with more than 5% audience share are listed, but shares for all available networks were used to calculate the HHI. "Majority traded" means that the parent corporation is listed on a public stock exchange, and insiders do not own more than 50% of all shares or all voting shares. Ownership data are based on annual reports, public disclosure data, and Internet research. See text for audience share data sources.

The greater competitiveness of radio and newspaper markets in Latin America is mitigated by several factors. First, these media serve as much less important sources of political information. In many countries, a competitive radio market essentially means multiple music options rather than different news perspectives. Second, cross-media ownership means that the major players in television are often represented in radio and newspapers, and vice versa. Several dominant television networks, such as Mexico's Televisa and Colombia's RCN, started as radio broadcasters and still maintain significant holdings in this market. Other conglomerates, such as Globo in Brazil and Clarín in Argentina, began as newspapers before diversifying into both radio and television. Finally, in some countries, television plays an important agenda-setting role for other media, so that the topics covered by a small number of dominant networks tend to be reflected in the coverage of many more newspapers and radio stations (Lawson 2008).

Ownership

The small number of networks dominating broadcast television in Latin America is only half of the concentration story; the ownership of these firms is also highly concentrated, with control typically exercised by a single family or individual. The predominant ownership pattern for broadcast television in Canada and the United States, in which the network's parent is a publicly traded corporation with no insider holding a controlling share, is uncommon in Latin America. As shown in table 2.2, only three networks fall into this category. Of these, Mexico's Televisa has an ownership structure most similar to that of North American networks; its shares trade on its country's stock exchange (as well as in New York), and only a minority is controlled by the family of its president.[4] The other two networks, Chilevisión and Argentina's Telefe, are owned by conglomerates that trade only on foreign exchanges, which effectively limits the weight of any home-country concerns in corporate governance. Several other parent companies (Argentina's Grupo Clarín and Mexico's Azteca Holdings) list a minority of shares on their countries' exchanges, though their founders or directors hold controlling stakes.

The vast majority of Latin America's broadcast television networks are subsidiaries of privately held rather than publicly traded corporations, which are often wholly owned by a single family or individual. These include Brazil's TV Globo, RCN and Caracol in Colombia, and Venevisión in Venezuela, all of which belong to family-owned conglomerates. Albavisión, property of Mexico's Ángel González, owns major television networks in Argentina, Bolivia, Chile, and Peru, as well as Ecuador, Paraguay, Central America, and several Mexican states. Privately held corporations such as these ensure that only a single voice is heard in corporate governance and, presumably, editorial decisions. González has openly admitted to using his media outlets to favor certain politicians, and journalists from his local stations in Mexico routinely toe the line (Hughes and Lawson 2004, 92–93). In addition, media conglomerates not traded on public exchanges are subject to few if any disclosure requirements, reducing transparency and making even basic information about their operations difficult to obtain. The owners of such firms also feel none of the market pressures that come from watching a share price plummet in response to media scandals. Most of Latin America's media moguls can act with an impunity that Rupert Murdoch would envy.

State-owned networks have a relatively minor presence in Latin America's television markets. Chile's Televisión Nacional, the country's most popular television network in 2010, is the major exception. Its strong audience share may be because it operates in the same fashion as its privately owned competitors, producing similar content and funding itself entirely through advertising revenues (González-Rodríguez 2008). State-owned television networks exist in each of the other countries, but only in Argentina and Venezuela do they have more than 5 percent market share. Rather than functioning according to a "public service" model, with educational objectives and a mandate for impartial journalism, state networks in Argentina, Bolivia, and Venezuela have been turned into partisan weapons in their presidents' repeated clashes with the private media (Hawkins 2003; Becerra and Mastrini 2010; Torrico and Sandoval 2011). In Mexico, television stations owned by state governments have similarly become mouthpieces for whoever inhabits the governor's office (Hughes and Lawson 2004).

Several Latin America's media moguls are politicians as well as businessmen. The partners in Argentina's América TV include Francisco de Narváez, a Peronist deputy, and José Luís Manzano, a former Peronist deputy and Minister of the Interior. In Bolivia, Unitel belongs to the family of Osvaldo Monasterio Añez, a former senator, while Red Uno is property of Ivo Kuljis Fuchtner, a vice presidential candidate in 1993, 1997, and 2002. The group of politician-owners was even larger in the recent past. Former Bolivian president Carlos Mesa Gisbert was the founder and a part owner of Red PAT until 2007, including his years in executive office. Mesa's media ownership preceded his political ambitions, but the same cannot be said of Chilean President Sebastián Piñera, who acquired Chilevisión in April 2005, just before his first run for the presidency, and sold it only in October 2010, seven months after his inauguration. Media ownership by prominent politicians does not guarantee that they will use their influence improperly, but it certainly creates a strong temptation to do so.

At the regional and local level, politicians may be even more prominently represented among owners of the mass media, especially in large federal countries. In Brazil, commercial broadcasting licenses were routinely awarded free of charge to politicians and their families until competitive auctions began to be required in 1995 (Lima and Lopes 2007). As a result, at least 271 Brazilian politicians are partners or directors of state or local broadcast media (Donos da Mídia 2008). Among them are Fernando Collor, a senator and former president, and Roseana Sarney, a governor, former senator, and daughter of senator and former president José Sarney. The Collor and Sarney family conglomerates own radio stations, major newspapers, and the local affiliate networks of TV Globo in the states of Alagoas and Maranhão, respectively. In 2009, Brazilian police recorded a conversation between José Sarney and his son in which they discussed using their television network and newspaper to attack one of Roseana's political opponents (Souza and Seligman 2009).

Community Media

A positive media ownership trend in many Latin American countries has been the proliferation of community broadcasting. Beginning in the 1990s and early 2000s, countries such as Colombia, Brazil, Venezuela, and Bolivia established legal frameworks to regulate community radio and television (Murillo 2003; Lima and Lopes 2007; Lloreda 2007; Martín 2010). Stations are usually licensed to local civic associations and required to operate as nonprofit entities, with advertising restricted or prohibited entirely. Broadcasting range is typically limited to the municipal or even neighborhood level. Community media have proliferated quite rapidly in some countries. There were 400 community radio and thirty-four community television stations in Venezuela as of 2008, and 2,328 community radio stations in Brazil as of June 2009 (Moen 2009; Boas and Hidalgo 2011).

Community radio and television stations have a small but potentially important role to play in countering the domination of Latin American broadcasting by commercial interests. They can give voice to individuals, groups, and social and political agendas that would be unlikely to find space in mainstream broadcasting. They can also play an important role in informing citizens about local politics, which, outside of major cities, is unlikely to be covered by commercial media. In Brazil's primarily rural Northeast, for instance, local radio stations—many of them licensed as community broadcasters—are the principal source of information about the doings of mayors and city council members, who might otherwise govern with much less public scrutiny (Lauría and González Rodríguez 2006).

Unfortunately, community broadcasters often fall under the sway of local or national politicians, functioning more as political mouthpieces than as authentic civic voices. In Brazil, half of all community radio stations licensed from 1999 to 2005 had a local politician or major campaign donor among their directors (Lima and Lopes 2007). Local governing officials often leverage their connections to help get radio licenses approved. Boas and Hidalgo (2011) found that proposed community radio stations with ties to incumbent city council members are approved at twice the rate of those whose political sponsors lost the last election. Once a politically controlled community radio station is up and running, it becomes a useful campaign tool. In Brazil's 2004 and 2008 municipal elections, city council candidates with ties to licensed community radio stations could expect a 17 percent higher vote share and 28 percent greater probability of winning (Boas and Hidalgo 2011).

In several other countries, community broadcast media tend to have ties to national governments. In Bolivia, community radio stations have received strong state support under the government of Evo Morales, calling into question whether they represent independent community voices. The vast majority of licensed Bolivian community radio stations are part of the *Red Nacional de Radios de los Pueblos Originarios* (National Network of Indigenous Radio Stations), which was developed in partnership with the state. The Bolivian government grants broadcasting licenses to the community but loans them the necessary equipment and trains each station's lead reporters. Stations essentially function as affiliates of the state-run Radio Patria Nueva; they are required to broadcast Patria Nueva newscasts at certain times and also send local dispatches to the national radio network (Martín 2010).

The government of Venezuela's Hugo Chávez also took an active interest in promoting community media. Though state support was less formalized than in Bolivia, the government donated equipment and headquarters to some stations and also favored them by purchasing advertising time. From 2006 onward, funds in the national budget were specifically allocated for promoting community broadcasting. Stations are required to broadcast 70 percent locally produced content, but they are also allowed to rebroadcast material from state media, and many of them spent a lot of time airing Chávez's speeches (Hawkins 2003; Lloreda 2007; Dinatale and Gallo 2009; Leary 2009; Moen 2009). More research is necessary to determine if political criteria are used to award community broadcasting licenses in Venezuela, or if the progovernment tilt of these stations reflects its use of leverage, rather than simply the strong public support Chávez had in poor communities. At the very least, it is clear that governing officials in multiple countries, from city council members to the president, make a serious effort to get even low-power community broadcasting outlets on their side.

In sum, concentration of the mass media in Latin America suggests that they will continue to give voice primarily to powerful politicians and leading economic interests rather than a wide range of actors in civil society. Broadcast television markets are highly concentrated, approaching duopolies in some countries. Concentration has lessened during the first decade of the 2000s, but those networks gaining market share are mostly similar in profile to the industry leaders that have ceded ground. Few parent corporations are publicly traded; most are owned outright by one or a few wealthy investors. Politicians have significant stakes in several national television networks and may be even more dominant at the local level. Latin America's commercial media, therefore, seem likely to represent the economic and political interests of a few wealthy, largely conservative owners. Community and state-owned broadcasters may fall outside of the media moguls' sway, yet here too, there are signs that power and politics prevail. In particular, leftist presidents like Chávez and Morales have enlisted these outlets in their struggle against hostile commercial media.

Press-State Relations, "Left Turns," and the Rule of Law

Patterns of media concentration may have changed little during the first decade of the 2000s, but Latin American politics has undoubtedly shifted in ways that should have implications for the traditionally cozy relationship between state authorities and the press. In the past, conservatively inclined commercial media often coincided with conservative governments, facilitating collusion between the two. More recently, the "left turn" in Latin American politics has seen left-of-center presidents come to power in six of the eight countries covered in this volume—Argentina, Bolivia, Brazil, Chile, Peru, and Venezuela (Cameron and Hershberg 2010; Weyland, Madrid, and Hunter 2010; Levitsky and Roberts 2011). Some of these presidents—most prominently, Chávez and Morales—have not only championed economic policies that challenge media owners' class interests, but have also aimed to exert greater state control over the media themselves. In such countries, politicized journalism in the commercial media seems likely to produce conflict with national governments rather than collusion.

A second trend of relevance for press-state relations in Latin America is a general improvement in the rule of law at the national level, combined with ongoing weaknesses in "brown areas"—primarily rural zones where local political bosses exert undue influence over security forces and the judiciary (O'Donnell 1993). In present-day Latin America, it seems unlikely that a national government would resort to a systematic, extralegal campaign against independent media, such as the bribery, surveillance, and intimidation of journalists carried out by Peru's Servicio de Inteligencia Nacional (SIN; National Intelligence Service) under Alberto Fujimori in the 1990s (Conaghan 2005).[5] Though isolated incidents may occur, use of the legal system is a more likely weapon for presidents who want to silence critical media. In areas with weak rule of law dominated by local political bosses, however, outspoken journalists and media owners may be much more at risk of extralegal retribution by governments and security forces, as well as to abuses of the legal system via influence over local courts.

To examine recent trends in press-state relations in these eight Latin American countries, I catalogued and coded all separate, specific instances of government actions against the press mentioned in the annual Human Rights Report from the US Department of State, Freedom of the Press survey from Freedom House, and Attacks on the Press survey from the Committee to Protect Journalists. The coding scheme assigned each incident a score from 1 to 5, according to the degree to which it would likely silence critical media; police detaining a reporter on assignment would merit a 1, whereas permanently shutting down a media outlet would be a 5. I also distinguished whether the incident involved government officials and security forces at the national level versus the local level. After classifying each incident, I summed the individual scores to generate a "national" and "local" total for each country in each year.

Results from this analysis are presented in figure 2.1, which graphs the scores for each country over the 2001–2009 period. Several trends are notable. Venezuela stands out in terms of the overall severity of government actions against the press, especially those taken by the national government. Countries also differ in terms of the level of government that most often clashes with the press. In Bolivia and Venezuela, national authorities take more severe action against the media; in Argentina, Brazil, Mexico, and Peru, it is local governments that do so. To some extent, this contrast is a product of government structure and country size: Bolivia has no subnational security forces, whereas Argentina, Brazil, and Mexico are all large federal systems with numerous subnational jurisdictions. Yet the high incidence of local government actions against the

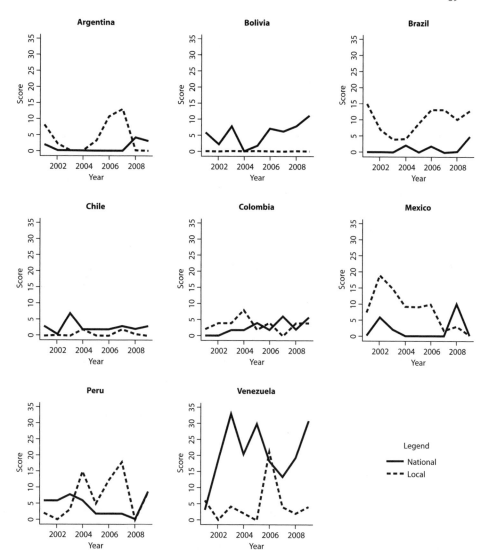

Figure 2.1. Government Actions against the Media in Latin America

press also reflects significant weaknesses in the rule of law in the "brown areas" of these four countries.

Populists versus Media Moguls

In Latin American countries that have seen a more radical Left come to power, relations between populist presidents and the commercial mass media have been highly conflictual.[6] While left-wing leaders have occasionally cultivated friendly relations with certain media outlets and their owners, the more common pattern is all-out war between the two. Many commercial media outlets have abandoned all pretense of neutrality and openly taken the side of the political opposition, especially where right wing and other opposition parties remain weak and incapable of mounting a serious electoral challenge. In return, populist presidents have targeted the media with a series of weapons. The first is use, and abuse, of the legal system. Regulatory agencies, backed up by a pliant judiciary, can charge media outlets with everything from tax evasion to airing prohibited content. New laws, such as Venezuela's 2004 Law of Social Responsibility in Radio and Television, allow media to be shut down for offenses such as showing "disrespect toward legitimate institutions and authorities." Even if rarely invoked, such laws can have a strong deterrent effect. Strategic allocation of state advertising, police action targeting critical journalists, and inflammatory rhetoric (carried by state broadcasters) against media owners and reporters are additional weapons that populist presidents have used in their battles against the commercial media.

Conflict between a president and major private media outlets has been most intense in Venezuela. In the early 2000s, all major commercial television stations actively supported the political opposition to Hugo Chávez, who fought back with an array of questionable legal proceedings. In April 2002, commercial television networks gave extensive and often biased coverage to antigovernment protests that preceded the unsuccessful coup attempt; Venevisión went so far as to broadcast edited footage falsely suggesting that Chávez supporters shot unarmed demonstrators. At the height of the crisis, Chávez responded by shutting down the signals of all four leading broadcasters. Commercial television stations continued their open support for the opposition over the next several years—for example, broadcasting public service messages urging people to join a general strike against the government in 2002–2003. In return, the leading networks were hit with a litany of charges, including nonpayment of taxes, transmitting prohibited content, and broadcasting on illegal frequencies. When an appeals court ruled in favor of Globovisión on the latter case, the court was shut down and its judges suspended (Hawkins 2003; Wilpert 2007; Dinatale and Gallo 2009).

In more recent years, Chávez's approach to the commercial media discriminated between those that supported the opposition and those willing to adopt a more neutral stance. After Venevisión owner Gustavo Cisneros struck a truce with Chávez in 2004, the network eliminated its critical news and opinion shows, as did Televén between 2004 and 2005 (Dinatale and Gallo 2009). From

2004 onward, no government actions against either network occurred. Instead, Chávez intensified his campaign against the two major networks that remained loyal to the opposition. In 2007, the government refused to renew the broadcasting license of Radio Caracas Televisión (RCTV), the leading network at the time. RCTV was forced to move to cable, and it was shut down entirely in 2010. For its part, Globovisión has been charged repeatedly with inciting violence against the government for such offenses as airing footage of the 1981 assassination attempt on Pope John Paul II. The government also moved to obtain a 20 percent ownership stake in Globovisión by confiscating the shares of an investor, Nelson Mezerhane, whose bank had been taken over by authorities.

Bolivia has also witnessed conflict between the government and critical media during the presidency of Evo Morales, though antipress actions have stopped short of shutting down broadcasters or newspapers. Some moves against the press have involved use of the judicial system. In March 2009, for instance, the government sued newspaper *La Prensa* for slander after it implicated Morales and one of his ministers in a plan to smuggle contraband goods into Brazil. More common have been actions by security forces, especially against television network Unitel, whose owner Morales once declared an "enemy of the government." Police intelligence agents have spied on Unitel's news director, and an army officer bombed a local Unitel television station in June 2008. In September 2009, police attacked and fired upon a Unitel reporter and cameraman while they were covering the arrest of a farm owner. Reporters from Red PAT, also critical of Morales, were assaulted by police and shot at while reporting on a kidnapping in November 2009.

Argentina's Cristina Fernández de Kirchner has also taken action against critical commercial media, primarily those owned by the Clarín group. During the presidency of her husband Néstor Kirchner, relations with Clarín were quite friendly, and coverage of the government was generally positive. The relationship deteriorated after Fernández de Kirchner took office and announced increased taxes on soy exports in 2008, sparking a "farm war" that involved a producers' strike and massive demonstrations. Fernández claimed that Clarín's coverage favored the farmers, and she began to lash out against the newspaper, going so far as to organize an anti-Clarín rally. In September 2009, tax agents conducted a raid of Clarín's offices, later claiming that the action was a mistake (Waisbord 2010). Other media also came under attack: Radio Continental, which had criticized the government during the farm war, saw its FM broadcasting license suspended. Though government actions against the press did not reach the severity of those in Venezuela or Bolivia, the atmosphere of polarization was similar.

While not reflected in figure 2.1, the principal tool used by both Néstor Kirchner and Cristina Fernández de Kirchner to punish critical media and reward friendly media is the allocation of advertising revenues. State spending on advertising increased from $5 million in 2002, the year before Kirchner took office, to $47 million in 2006 and $52 million in the first half of 2008 alone (Freedom House 2007, 2010). Critical media received a smaller allocation of this budget than would be suggested by their circulation or audience share, while friendly media benefited. In 2006, the progovernment *Página/12* (circulation 51,000 per day) received $4.5 million in state advertising, while *La Nación* (circulation 187,000) received only $2.8 million (Dinatale and Gallo 2009; Fernández 2007).

Apart from incidents in which Venezuelan, Bolivian, and Argentine officials targeted the press with concrete actions, rhetorical battles between presidents and the commercial media have created a climate in which government supporters frequently attack media installations or individual journalists, while authorities do little to intervene. In the State Department, Freedom House, and Committee to Protect Journalist reports, violent actions by mobs of protestors, or assaults and even murders for which a suspect was never charged, were more common than actions that could be attributed to state security forces or government officials. Frequently, such attacks followed specific presidential invectives against the media, sometimes naming individual journalists or owners.

Populist attacks on critical media are not limited to left-wing presidents, as Peru's Alberto Fujimori amply demonstrated during the 1990s. Colombia's Álvaro Uribe has employed some of the same tactics as his leftist counterparts in an effort to silence critical journalists. During his presidency, Uribe referred to Gonzalo Guillén, Bogotá correspondent for Miami's *El Nuevo Herald*, as "a person who has persisted in trying to harm me," and he denounced Hollman Morris, invited by the Fuerzas Armadas Revolucionarias de Colombia (FARC; Revolutionary Armed Forces of Colombia) to interview hostages, as an "accomplice to terror." Both received anonymous threats in the aftermath and had to leave the country for their safety. In 2010, an investigation revealed that agents from the state Departamento Administrativo de Seguridad (DAS; Administrative Department of Security) had been ordered to follow Morris and Daniel Coronell, another critical journalist, because Uribe was upset about their reporting.

A climate of conflict between populist presidents and the commercial media complicates their ability to serve as effective watchdogs of democracy. Some media will be intimidated by legal sanctions or actions taken by state security forces and will self-censor or abandon investigative and critical reporting entirely. Others may choose to remain silent because they have struck deals with populist governments and been spared the harassment directed at their competitors. Those that take up the mantle of opposition politics will pursue a watchdog function with vigor, but only in battles against a government they seek to defeat. Politicized watchdog journalism is unlikely to be credible to those who do not already support the opposition, and its practitioners will probably avoid investigating wrongdoings on their own side of the political divide.

Political Bosses versus the Press

In several countries where relations between presidents and major commercial media have been more harmonious, conflict still abounds at the local level, where powerful political bosses use their influence over the judiciary and security forces to intimidate and silence critical journalists and media outlets. One of the most common weapons consists of laws against defamation, slander, and libel. Thanks to statutes with roots in military regimes or even the colonial period, insulting the honor of public officials is a criminal offense in many countries (Lawson and Hughes 2005). Cases against journalists are prosecuted most frequently in local courts, where powerful mayors or governors may be able to ensure convictions, silencing investigations into their own malfeasance. State-sponsored violence against critical journalists and media owners, including murder and abduction, is also disturbingly common at the local level. Lethal violence perpetrated by nonstate actors such as drug traffickers and criminal gangs (quite possibly with the complicity of local authorities) is an even more frequent occurrence where states fail to exert authority throughout their national territory.

In Brazil, judges routinely employ prior censorship to prevent the publication or airing of information that would defame public officials, typically in response to petitions from politicians with influence over local courts. In May 2010, for example, a São Paulo state court forced the *Diário do Grande ABC* to stop reporting on mismanagement of public school supplies after a complaint from the mayor of São Bernardo do Campo. Sometimes judges abuse the law to protect their own colleagues: in July 2009, the newspaper *A Tarde* in Salvador, Bahia, was barred from reporting on allegations that an appeals court judge had sold sentences. Many examples of prior censorship target local or regional media, but some of Brazil's most prominent national publications are also affected. In July 2001, a Rio de Janeiro judge banned *O Globo*, the city's leading newspaper, from printing the transcript of a phone conversation in which state governor Anthony Garotinho authorized a bribe.

Prior censorship is common only in Brazil, but defamation laws are used in many countries to punish journalists and media outlets after their stories are printed or aired. In November 2006, a court in the Brazilian state of Mato Grosso do Sul sentenced the editor of newspaper *Correio do Estado* to ten months in prison for accusing the governor-elect of corruption during his previous term as mayor. In Mexico, after journalist Lydia Cacho published a book in 2005 that implicated a wealthy businessman in a child prostitution ring, he conspired with the governor of the state of Puebla to have her arrested and harassed by police. In January 2010, the editor of the newspaper *Nor Oriente*, based in Bagua, Peru, was sentenced to a year in prison for defamation after writing several articles on corruption in a local public school. As with prior censorship, abuse of defamation laws is not limited to smaller, regional media. In 2001 and 2002, defamation charges were filed against the president and publisher of *Reforma*, one of Mexico's City's leading newspapers, for reporting on city and state government corruption.

Most troubling are cases in which critical journalists have been killed or abducted in crimes linked to local government officials or security forces. Such events are most common in Brazil. In 2003 and 2004, politically outspoken radio hosts were murdered in Limoeiro do Norte, Ceará, and Coronel Sapucaia, Mato Grosso do Sul; local mayors were later charged with both crimes. In May 2008, journalists from the Rio de Janeiro newspaper *O Dia* were kidnapped and tortured by a local police officer and accomplices after reporting on the control of local politics by criminal gangs in a Rio slum. Similar crimes have taken place in other countries. In 2004, Peruvian mayors in the towns of Yungay and Pucallpa were implicated in the murders of radio journalists who had been investigating local corruption and government ties to drug traffickers. In 2003, a radio journalist in Barrancabermeja, Colombia, was killed following his reports on local corruption; the city's mayor was eventually convicted of ordering the assassination. These murders and abductions come on top of numerous incidents in which reporters were assaulted by local security forces when attempting to cover politically sensitive issues or events.

In Colombia and Mexico, acts in which government officials are implicated are only a minority of cases in which lethal violence is used against local media. In parts of northern Mexico along the US border, and in large swathes of the Colombian jungle, state security forces have little effective control over drug traffickers, paramilitaries, guerrillas, or criminal gangs. Journalists investigating the activities of these groups are routinely murdered in retaliation. Though their involve-ment rarely comes to light, it is likely that corrupt local authorities are complicit in many of these killings, especially when the topic of investigative reporting was government ties to armed nonstate actors.

While most local government assaults on the media do not seem to follow any partisan logic, those in Argentina have primarily involved Peronists, mirroring the conflict at the national level. In 2001, after printing an insulting headline, newspaper *El Liberal* in Santiago del Estero province was subject to espionage by the Peronist-controlled provincial government, a lawsuit by the women's branch of the Peronist Party, and nonpayment of government advertising debts. In 2006, the Peronist mayor of Quilmes convinced federal regulators to revoke the li-censes of two local radio stations. In September 2007, a court in Salta gave jour-nalist Sergio Poma a suspended sentence for slander and barred him from re-porting for one year after he called the province's Peronist governor "a crook of the worst kind." These and other incidents reflect the dominance of Peronist political machines in many parts of the country; they also suggest that conflict between politicians and the media in Argentina cannot simply be attributed to the confrontational personality and governing style of president Cristina Fernán-dez de Kirchner.

Assaults on the press by regional and local governments are likely to have an even more chilling effect on watchdog journalism than conflict between populist presidents and prominent national media. The small local media that are most often targeted by political bosses have many fewer resources than national tele-vision networks based in major cities and owned by wealthy media moguls, so they are much less able to defend themselves. Moreover, they tend to be targeted precisely because of their investigations of local corruption, rather than ideologi-cally driven criticism of the government and its policies. Murders of local jour-nalists and criminal defamation suits almost certainly have a strong deterrent effect on watchdog journalism, extending their impact well beyond those who were actually targeted.

Media Coverage of Recent Election Campaigns

If concentrated ownership makes it unlikely that the media will give voice to new actors, and conflict between governments and the press complicates or inhibits its watchdog function, what about the media's role in setting the political agenda and influencing citizens' choices about who should govern them? Historically, biased political coverage was the norm among Latin America's most influential mass media. The now-deceased former heads of Globo and Televisa, Roberto Marinho and Emilio Azcárraga, famously proclaimed that they had no qualms about using their media empires to influence their countries' politics in ways that they saw fit (Miguel 2000, 69; Lawson 2002, 30). Yet generational changes in leadership, increased competition, the growing professionalization of journalism, and political democratization have all combined to create strong incentives for more balanced political reporting by these and other media conglomerates in Latin America (Lawson 2002; Porto 2012). At the same time, bitter conflict with leftist presidents in Venezuela, Bolivia, and Argentina has encouraged the commercial media to defend their economic interests and also take up the mantle of opposition politics where right-wing political parties have been particularly weak.

Given these conflicting incentives, how has the media's coverage of politics evolved in Latin America during the first decade of the 2000s? This section draws on the results of content analyses of newspaper, radio, and television news coverage of selected presidential election campaigns (plus Venezuela's 2004 presidential recall and 2009 constitutional amendment referenda) in seven of the eight countries covered in this volume.[7] Electoral coverage is an attractive focus because there is a relatively clear standard by which one can assess bias versus balance. Ideally, mass media should not tilt heavily one way or the other in their coverage of competing candidates for office. If strong editorial preferences do end up influencing the content of reporting, it is better that major outlets lean in different directions so that no single candidate is systematically disadvantaged by the media as a whole.

Table 2.3 presents a summary measure of the tone of coverage—positive versus negative—of major candidates in recent elections for which content analysis data are available. For most elections, "Net Positive Differential" is defined as the difference in percent net positive coverage (positive coverage minus negative coverage divided by total coverage) between the leading right- and left-wing candidates. A score greater than zero thus indicates bias in the direction that, knowing nothing else about the election, we would expect commercial media to lean. For Mexico's 2000 election and the two Argentine elections, net positive differential is the difference between the second-place candidate and the winner, with the latter less likely to receive positive coverage. Where disaggregated data are available, the table also presents the standard deviation of net positive differential, a measure of the degree to which bias differed across major media outlets.

In several of the countries that historically had some of the most biased media coverage, reporting on major contenders in recent elections has been remarkably

Table 2.3.   Media Bias in Latin American Elections

Country	Year	Type of Media	Net Positive Differential	Standard Deviation
Brazil	2002	TV	−5.6	6.5
Brazil	2002	newspaper	−10.7	15.0
Brazil	2006	newspaper	13.6	19.0
Brazil	2010	newspaper	8.2	0.5
Mexico	2000	TV	2.0	23.3
Mexico	2006	radio	6.8	
Mexico	2006	TV	3.3	
Chile	2006	newspaper	−25.3	
Chile	2006	radio	−8.1	
Chile	2006	TV	5.0	
Venezuela	2004	newspaper	13.7	110.9
Venezuela	2004	radio	−20.8	104.2
Venezuela	2004	TV	20.0	62.0
Venezuela	2009	newspaper	−4.0	105.3
Venezuela	2009	TV	14.0	96.0
Bolivia	2005	newspaper	−3.0	
Bolivia	2005	radio	30.5	
Bolivia	2005	TV	164.0	
Argentina	2007	newspaper	0.0	
Argentina	2011	newspaper	−20.1	66.1
Peru	2011	newspaper	16.8	
Peru	2011	radio	18.0	
Peru	2011	TV	20.3	

Sources: Figures are author's calculations based on data sources cited in the main text. Venezuelan data score percentage of news sources that are pro-government, pro-opposition, or unaffiliated; partisan sources are assumed to speak 100% positively about their own side and 100% negatively about the other, while unaffiliated sources are assumed to be neutral. Data cover news content only, except Bolivia 2005, which also includes opinion programs and editorials. Local/regional media are excluded.

Note: Net Positive Differential = (%positive$_A$ − %negative$_A$) − (%positive$_B$ − %negative$_B$). This is a weighted mean (by quantity of coverage) across stations; the standard deviation is based on the unweighted mean.

balanced. In Brazil, candidates of the left-wing Partido dos Trabalhadores (PT; Workers' Party)—including Luiz Inácio "Lula" da Silva, a favorite bête noir of the commercial media in the 1980s and 1990s—have received even-handed treatment in the 2000s. In 2002, the evening newscasts of TV Globo and TV Record both gave slightly more favorable coverage to Lula than to his right-wing opponent (Quenehen 2003). Four major newspapers leaned in somewhat different directions, but on balance, their coverage was also slightly more positive toward Lula (Doxa 2002). In 2006 and 2010, newspaper coverage tended to benefit the right-wing challenger rather than the PT candidate, but by similarly small margins (Doxa 2006; Massuchin, Tavares, and Nava 2011). More negative coverage of the PT—the party of the incumbent in both elections—likely reflected reporting on political scandals that came to light during each campaign rather than any systematic effort to hurt the Left's electoral chances.

In Mexico and Chile, similar transformations have taken place. Biases in Mexican television were legendary during the 1980s; Televisa once displayed images of Benito Mussolini and Fidel Castro next to videos of the ruling party's right- and left-wing opponents giving campaign speeches (Lawson 2002, 53). In the 2000 election, the two major television networks leaned in different directions from one another, but on average their individual biases canceled out, as indicated by a net positive differential of nearly zero (Lawson and McCann 2005). Likewise, in 2006, campaign coverage on both radio and television did not strongly favor one side of the political spectrum, despite bitter ideological polarization between the two leading candidates in this election (IFE 2006). In Chile, the commercial media were strong supporters of the Pinochet regime in the 1980s and favored the dictator in their coverage of the 1988 plebiscite (Hirmas 1993; Tironi and Sunkel 2000). In the 2005–2006 presidential election, however, biases were either negligible or in the opposite direction of what one would expect. Newspaper and radio coverage of candidates in the second round of the election favored center-left candidate Michelle Bachelet over Piñera. Only television leaned toward Piñera, and by a negligible margin (COMUNICAN 2006).

While Brazil, Mexico, and Chile all illustrate positive trends in the media's reporting on presidential elections, countries with more ideologically polarized politics tell a different story. In Venezuela, the conflict between Chávez and the commercial media was borne out in electoral coverage during the 2000s. On their own, the net positive differential figures presented in table 2.3 do not suggest extremely biased coverage of Venezuela's 2004 recall referendum and 2009 constitutional amendment referendum—some types of media tended to favor the opposition, while others leaned toward the Chávez government. However, these scores are relatively close to zero only because the extreme progovernment slant of state media countered moderate pro-opposition bias in major commercial media. Net positive differentials for individual media outlets are as large as 98 for newspaper *El Universal* in 2004 and 96 for Globovisión in 2009. But these are offset by even more extreme scores for government-owned media such as *Diario Vea* (−160 in 2009) and VTV (−132 in 2009). The standard deviation of scores for different media outlets, much larger than in Mexico or Brazil, testifies to the polarized coverage of each of these elections (Observatorio Global de Medios 2004, 2009).

The most extreme case of anti-Left bias is Bolivia. By the time of his second run for the presidency, Evo Morales had already earned the ire of commercial media, but he did not yet control any state-owned outlets. Television news coverage was thus overwhelmingly biased against him; only 1 percent of his coverage was positive, and only 2 percent of that devoted to his major opponent, Jorge "Tuto" Quiroga, was negative. Radio coverage was somewhat more balanced, but still favored Quiroga. Only newspapers, a relatively unimportant source of information for the mass public, treated the candidates in a roughly equal fashion (COMUNICAN 2005). In the 2009 election, evidence suggests a pattern similar to that of Venezuela: critical coverage of the Left in commercial media, along with an overwhelmingly positive treatment in the state-owned outlets that Morales's government now controls.[8] In television reporting, for instance, Unitel's news broadcasts most often cited sources from the party of challenger Manfred Reyes Villa, while state-owned Bolivia TV cited sources from Morales's party 51 percent of the time, and Radio Patria Nueva did so 80 percent of the time (ONADEM 2010).

To a lesser degree, Argentina presents evidence of the same sort of media biases as in Venezuela and Bolivia. In the 2007 election, major newspapers were, on average, completely evenhanded in their treatment of Cristina Fernández de Kirchner and her major opponent Elisa Carrió (Pontificia Universidad Católica Argentina 2007). Néstor Kirchner's strategy of cultivating a friendly relationship with major commercial media appears to have paid off during his wife's first campaign. A different pattern was evident in coverage of the 2011 election, after the government-media relationship became politically polarized during Fernández de Kirchner's first term. On balance, newspaper coverage leaned in her favor, but only because of overwhelmingly positive coverage in two progovernment dailies, *Página/12* and *Tiempo Argentino* (Pontificia Universidad Católica Argentina 2011). The standard deviation of coverage across different newspapers, similar to that of Venezuelan television in 2004, testifies to this relatively high degree of polarization.

Peru also shows evidence of ideological bias in campaign coverage, though less severe than in Venezuela or Bolivia. On average, major newspapers, radio stations, and television stations all favored right-wing candidate Keiko Fujimori over leftist Ollanta Humala during the first round of the 2011 presidential election (Transparencia 2011a, 2011b, 2011c). Bias may well have been even more severe during the bitterly fought second round, though comparable data are not available. Humala presented himself as a moderate social democrat in 2011, but in the 2006 election, he had run as a radical populist in the mold of Chávez or Morales, with frequent denunciations of the commercial mass media. Negative coverage of his candidacy thus reflects a similar polarization dynamic as in Venezuela and Bolivia.

What conclusions can one draw from these diverse cases of media coverage of recent presidential elections in Latin America? On the one hand, Brazil, Mexico, and Chile show that the mass media can be relatively balanced in their treatment of major candidates, even in countries where strong proestablishment biases existed in the past. Political democratization, changes in media leadership, and increased competition and professionalism in journalism have all contributed to these outcomes, but so has the more moderate nature of the Left, at least in Chile and Brazil. Where left-wing candidates present little credible threat to the business interests of commercial media and the class interests of their owners, there are fewer incentives for biased coverage. The case of Mexico shows that more radical populist candidates, such as Andrés Manuel López Obrador in 2006, can also sometimes find fair treatment in Latin America's commercial media.[9] These results are good news for the media's agenda-setting function and its implications for democracy in Latin America.

However, in countries with a recent history of more ideologically polarized politics, including Venezuela, Bolivia, Argentina, and Peru, commercial media have not treated left- and right-wing candidates equally during presidential elections. At the extreme, in Bolivia's 2005 election, television coverage of Evo Morales was almost entirely negative. More radical left-wing candidates thus face significant barriers in winning elections in an era in which most voters follow politics through broadcast media. Those that succeed despite the odds, as Morales did in 2005, are likely to enter the presidency with a vendetta against the commercial broadcasters who discriminated against them during the campaign. Once in office, they may be able to level the mass media playing field, but only by turning state-owned outlets (or private media heavily dependent on state advertising) into political mouthpieces that are even more biased in their favor. In these cases, media coverage of elections reflects only partisan agendas rather than civic ones.

Conclusion

The analysis presented in this chapter underscores that collusion between national executives and the mass media in Latin America is largely a thing of the past. The concentration of media markets and media ownership have not changed significantly, but the political scenario underlying these cozy relations has definitely been transformed. Democratization has eliminated the military regimes that collaborated closely with conservative media in previous decades. In Brazil and Mexico, voters have elected and reelected parties that were historically the targets of biased reporting. In Colombia, the presidencies of Álvaro Uribe and Juan Manuel Santos have ended the domination of the Liberal and Conservative parties, to which the two leading media groups had extensive ties. In Bolivia and Venezuela, the rise of radical populists has largely quashed any prospects of friendly relations between the government and the commercial media. Some collusion still occurs, as demonstrated by the Kirchners' use of state advertising to cultivate media allies in Argentina, but it seems to be the exception rather than the rule.

Yet the decline of outright collusion between presidents and the press does not mean that the media have taken on the role of a fourth power that contributes to democratic governance. Continued concentration of media markets and ownership, along with the politicization of state-owned media in many countries, mean that the media are most likely to give voice to those segments of society that currently hold economic or political power. The rise of community media offers the prospect of a counter-trend, but frequently even these small-scale broadcasters fall under the sway of powerful local or national politicians. In countries governed by the more radical of the "new Left" presidents, ongoing conflicts between authorities and commercial mass media are likely to deter some media outlets from exercising a watchdog function and encourage others to do so only when it serves their partisan interests. In countries with weak rule of law at the local level, political bosses' crackdowns on critical media should have an even more chilling effect on watchdog journalism.

News coverage of recent Latin American elections offers a partial silver lining to this assessment of the media's contribution to democracy in Latin America. The largely balanced treatment of major candidates in Brazil, Chile, and Mexico shows that the commercial media do not necessarily set the political agenda in a fashion that discriminates against the Left. Yet elsewhere, significant biases remain. In Venezuela and Bolivia, most commercial media have essentially become partisan supporters of the opposition, and populist presidents have abandoned any public service pretensions with state media, dragging them into the fray as well. Argentina and Peru may also be in danger of falling into this vicious cycle of polarization between a left-leaning president and the privately owned press.

The best hope for the future of democratic media in Latin America seems to lie in greater competition as well as greater scrutiny. The concentration of media markets has lessened in recent years as competitors have gained ground against historical industry leaders like TV Globo and Televisa. In Mexico and elsewhere, greater competition has played a key role in the decline of biased reporting (Tironi and Sunkel 2000; Lawson 2002). The slow but steady penetration of cable television is another positive development, especially since it carries international networks with less of a stake in domestic politics, such as CNN en Español. Greater scrutiny of the press also ensures that collusion and politicized reporting are more likely to be noticed, and denounced, than in the past. Mexico's Instituto Federal Electoral (IFE; Federal Electoral Institute) has commissioned monitoring of news coverage of recent elections, and local nongovernmental organizations or teams of foreign electoral observers regularly do the same in other countries. International organizations such as the Committee to Protect Journalists and Reporters without Borders help to publicize and denounce government actions against the press, especially those occurring far from national capitals that might otherwise remain unnoticed. Hopefully these trends will continue to play a role in transforming Latin America's mass media into true defenders of democracy.

NOTES

For helpful comments on previous drafts, I am grateful to Jorge Domínguez, Shannon O'Neil, Mauro Porto, and participants in the Constructing Democratic Governance Workshop. Thanks to Dominic Zarecki for research assistance.

1. The more typical English rendering is "fourth estate," a phrase attributed to Edmund Burke.

2. Audience share data are from Nielsen (US), AGB Nielsen (Venezuela), BBM (Canada), and IBOPE (all others), as cited in *Mídia Dados Brasil 2011*; G2Mi 2011; Fuenzalida and Julio 2011; IBOPE Colombia 2008; AGB Nielsen 2010; Initiative 2009; Media Life 2011; and Television Bureau of Canada 2011. Audience share measurement via set-top boxes is not done in Bolivia. Bolivian networks listed in table 2.2 are those mentioned as the most-watched network by more than 5 percent of La Paz respondents in Radio Fides's (2011) survey.

3. Calculated based on data in Grupo Radio Centro 2011, 24. National data for radio are not available.

4. The Azcárraga Trust owns 30 percent of voting shares (classes A and B) in Televisa, and 15.5 percent of all shares. www.televisa.com/inversionistas-espanol/preguntas-frecuen tes/160420/preguntas-frecuentes-televisa-inversionistas-espanol, accessed August 16, 2011.

5. The SIN's extralegal actions include bombing a local television station, wiretapping journalists, and most notoriously, paying massive bribes to media owners in ex-

change for editorial control over political content. The legal system was also used, e.g., by stripping a critical television station owner of his Peruvian citizenship in order to divest him of his shares.

6. In this section, I refer to Hugo Chávez, Evo Morales, and Cristina Fernández de Kirchner as populists based primarily on their rhetoric and political tactics. Typological schemes that focus on political organization tend to place them in different categories (e.g., Levitsky and Roberts 2011).

7. Comparisons among these individual studies should be taken with the caveat that they were conducted by a variety of scholars and monitoring organizations and employ different methodologies and samples of news content.

8. Data from the 2009 content analysis were not complete enough to compute the net positive differential.

9. Compared to his postelection political stance, López Obrador was much more moderate during the 2006 campaign, so in that sense he fits with the Chilean and Brazilian left-wing candidates.

REFERENCES

AGB Nielsen. 2010. "Habitos y tendencias televisivas Venezuela 2009." Accessed August 22, 2011. www.agbnielsen.com.ve/libro2009/.

Becerra, Martín, and Guillermo Mastrini. 2009. *Los dueños de la palabra: Acceso, estructura y concentración de los medios en la América Latina del siglo XXI.* Buenos Aires: Prometeo Libros.

———. 2010. "Crisis. What Crisis? Argentine Media in View of the 2008 International Financial Crisis." *International Journal of Communication* 4:611–29.

Boas, Taylor C. 2005. "Television and Neopopulism in Latin America: Media Effects in Brazil and Peru." *Latin American Research Review* 40 (2): 27–49.

Boas, Taylor C., and F. Daniel Hidalgo. 2011. "Controlling the Airwaves: Incumbency Advantage and Community Radio in Brazil." *American Journal of Political Science* 55 (4): 869–85.

Bolivia. Comite Técnico—Consejo Nacional de Alimentación y Nutrición. 2009. *Estudio Linea de Base D-Cero.* La Paz.

Cameron, Maxwell A., and Eric Hershberg, eds. 2010. *Latin America's Left Turns: Politics, Policies, and Trajectories of Change.* Boulder, CO: Lynne Rienner.

Committee to Protect Journalists. 2002–2010. *Attacks on the Press.* New York: Committee to Protect Journalists.

COMUNICAN. 2005. "Observatorio de medios de comunicación social: Elecciones presidenciales; Bolivia 2005." Accessed August 22, 2011. www.observatoriodemedios.org.ve/docs/investigacion_bolivia.doc.

———. 2006. "Monitoreo de los principales medios de comunicación social de alcance nacional: Chile; Elección presidencial 2006, segunda votación." www.observatoriodemedios.org.ve/docs/elecciones_2006.doc.

Conaghan, Catherine M. 2005. *Fujimori's Peru: Deception in the Public Sphere.* Pittsburgh: University of Pittsburgh Press.

Dinatale, Martín, and Alejandra Gallo. 2009. *Luz, cámara . . . ¡gobiernen! Nuevos paradigmas de la comunicación presidencial en América Latina.* Buenos Aires: Konrad Adenauer Stiftung.

Donos da Mídia. 2008. "Comunicação e politicos." Accessed August 22, 2011. donos damidia.com.br/levantamento/politicos.

Doxa. 2002. "Eleições 2002." Accessed January 1, 2012. doxa.iesp.uerj.br/eleicoes2002 .htm.

————. 2006. "Eleições 2006." Accessed January 1, 2012. doxa.iesp.uerj.br/eleicoes2006 .htm.

Fernández, Hernán. 2007. "¿Quién lee cuál?" *InfoBrand,* February 6. Accessed August 18, 2011. www.infobrand.com.ar/notas/8556-%BFQui%E9n-lee-cu%E1l%3F.

Freedom House. 2002–2010. *Freedom of the Press.* New York: Freedom House.

Fuenzalida, Valerio, and Pablo Julio, eds. 2011. *Quinto informe obitel Chile.* Santiago: Facultad de Comunicaciones, Pontificia Universidad Católica de Chile.

G2Mi. 2011. "Media Sector Data." London: Heernet Ventures.

González-Rodríguez, Gustavo. 2008. "The Media in Chile: The Restoration of Democracy and the Subsequent Concentration of Media Ownership." In *The Media in Latin America,* edited by Jairo Lugo-Ocando, 61–77. New York: Open University Press.

Grupo Radio Centro. 2011. *Reporte Anual.* Accessed August 22, 2011. radiocentro.com .mx/grc/grccorp.nsf/9206A7A3646FE97C862578B600600BE1/$File/RepAnual GRC2010.zip.

Hawkins, Eliza Tanner. 2003. "Conflict and the Mass Media in Chávez's Venezuela." Unpublished paper presented at the International Congress of the Latin American Studies Association, Dallas, March 27–29.

Hirmas, María Eugenia. 1993. "The Chilean Case: Television in the 1988 Plebiscite." In *Television, Politics, and the Transition to Democracy in Latin America,* edited by Thomas E. Skidmore, 82–96. Washington, DC, and Baltimore: Woodrow Wilson Center Press, Johns Hopkins University Press.

Hughes, Sallie, and Chappell Lawson. 2004. "Propaganda and Crony Capitalism: Partisan Bias in Mexican Television News." *Latin American Research Review* 3 (3): 81–105.

————. 2005. "The Barriers to Media Opening in Latin America." *Political Communication* 22:9–25.

IBOPE Colombia. 2008. "Rating y share canales." Accessed November 21, 2008. www .ibope.com.co/ibope/ratingshare.htm.

IFE (Instituto Federal Electoral). 2006. "Análisis general de los resultados del monitoreo de noticias." Accessed August 22, 2011. www.ife.org.mx/documentos/proceso _2005-2006/docs/monitoreo_noticiarios.pdf.

Initiative. 2009. "Evolución Rating Canales Televisión." Newsletter 10 (April–July). Accessed August 22, 2011. www.initiative.com.uy/newsletter/mailing/e10/img/pu/g5.gif.

Lauría, Carlos, and Sauro González Rodríguez. 2006. "Radio Rage in Brazil." Report, Committee to Protect Journalists.

Lawson, Chappell. 2002. *Building the Fourth Estate: Democratization and the Rise of a Free Press in Mexico.* Berkeley: University of California Press.

————. 2008. "Election Coverage in Mexico: Regulation Meets Crony Capitalism." In *The Handbook of Election News Coverage around the World*, edited by Jesper Strömbäck and Lynda Lee Kaid, 370–84. New York: Routledge.

Lawson, Chappell, and Sallie Hughes. 2005. "Latin America's Post-Authoritarian Media." In *(Un)civil Societies: Human Rights and Democratic Transitions in Eastern Europe and Latin America*, edited by Rachel A. May and Andrew K. Milton, 163–96. Lanham, MD: Lexington Books.

Lawson, Chappell, and James A. McCann. 2005. "Television News, Mexico's 2000 Elections and Media Effects in Emerging Democracies." *British Journal of Political Science* 35:1–30.

Leary, John Patrick. 2009. "TV Urgente: Urban Exclusion, Civil Society, and the Politics of Television in Venezuela." *Social Text* 99 (2): 25–53.

Levitsky, Steven, and Kenneth M. Roberts, eds. 2011. *The Resurgence of the Latin American Left*. Baltimore: Johns Hopkins University Press.

Lima, Venício A. de. 1990. "Televisão e política: Hipótese sobre a eleição presidencial de 1989." *Comunicação e Política* 9 (11): 29–54.

Lima, Venício A. de, and Cristiano Aguiar Lopes. 2007. *Coronelismo eletrônico de novo tipo (1999–2004)*. Brasília: Observatório da Imprensa/ProJor.

Lloreda, Oscar. 2007. "Televisión comunitaria en Venezuela: Una mirada en perspectiva." *Temas de comunicación* 14:125–42.

Martín, Juan Ramos. 2010. "De viejos y nuevos actores: Cambios en la estructura 'alterradiodifusora' boliviana." MA thesis, Instituto de Iberoamérica, Universidad de Salamanca.

Massuchin, Michele Goulart, Camila Quesada Tavares, and Mariane Nava. 2011. "Produção jornalística em período eleitoral: O posicionamento da Folha de S. Paulo e Estado de São Paulo em 2010." Unpublished paper presented at GT–Impresso, VII Ciclo de Debates sobre Jornalismo, Curitiba, PR, Brazil, November 9–11.

Media Life. 2011. "This Week's Broadcast Ratings." Accessed August 9, 2011. www .medialifemagazine.com/artman2/publish/mediaByTheNumbers/This_week_s _broadcast_ratings.asp.

Mídia Dados Brasil 2010. São Paulo: Grupo de Mídia São Paulo.

Mídia Dados Brasil 2011. São Paulo: Grupo de Mídia São Paulo.

Miguel, Luis Felipe. 2000. "The Globo Television Network and the Election of 1998." *Latin American Perspectives* 27 (6): 65–84.

Moen, Darrell Gene. 2009. "Public Access to Alternative/Critical Analysis: Community Media in Venezuela." *Hitotsubashi Journal of Social Studies* 41:1–12.

Murillo, Mario Alfonso. 2003. "Community Radio in Colombia: Civil Conflict, Popular Media and the Construction of a Public Sphere." *Journal of Radio Studies* 10 (1): 120–40.

Observatorio Global de Medios. 2004. "La información política en los principales medios de comunicación social de Caracas: Referéndum Presidencial 2004." Accessed August 22, 2011. www.observatoriodemedios.org.ve/docs/informe_i.doc.

————. 2009. "Los contenidos de opinión e información electoral en medios de comunicación social nacionales y regionales: Referendum enmienda constitucional,

Venezuela 2009." Accessed August 22, 2011. www.observatoriodemedios.org.ve /docs/Informa_FINAL_percent2o2dapercent2oversion.pdf.

O'Donnell, Guillermo. 1993. "On the State, Democratization and Some Conceptual Problems: A Latin American View with Glances at Some Postcommunist Countries." *World Development* 21 (8): 1255–369.

ONADEM. 2010. *Cobertura informativa de las elecciones generales 2009: ¿Campañas propagandístas o propuestas programáticas?* [La Paz, Bolivia]: Fundación UNIR.

Pontificia Universidad Católica Argentina. Instituto de Comunicación Social. 2007. "Elecciones a Presidente de la Nación, 28 de Octubre de 2007." Accessed October 20, 2007. www.diariosobrediarios.com.ar/observatorio07-final/index.htm.

———. 2011. "Observatorio Electoral 2011." Accessed December 31, 2011. www.uca.edu .ar/uca/common/grupo82/files/nov_2011_ICOS-REPORTE-CAMPANA-PEN-2011-1 .pdf.

Porto, Mauro. 2012. *Media Power and Democratization in Brazil: TV Globo and the Dilemmas of Political Accountability.* New York: Routledge.

Quenehen, Romulo. 2003. "A cobetura do JN e do JR durante as eleições 2002." Thesis, Universidade Tuiuti do Paraná.

Radio Fides. 2011. "ATB Y UNITEL las redes televisivas preferidas en La Paz y El Alto." *Periódico Digital* radiofides.com, April 14.

Souza, Leonardo, and Felipe Seligman. 2009. "Grampo da PF indica que Sarney usou jornal e TV para atacar grupo de Lago." *Folha de São Paulo*, February 9.

Television Bureau of Canada. 2011. "TV Basics 2010–2011." Accessed August 22, 2011. www.tvb.ca/page_files/pdf/InfoCentre/TVBasics.pdf.

Tironi, Eugenio, and Guillermo Sunkel. 2000. "The Modernization of Communications: The Media in the Transition to Democracy in Chile." In *Democracy and the Media: A Comparative Perspective*, edited by Richard Gunther and Anthony Mughan, 165–94. New York: Cambridge University Press.

Torrico, Erick, and Vania Sandoval. 2011. "Cómo elegir con los medios o qué medio elegir: Los medios en la política y las elecciones bolivianas." In *Medios y elecciones en América Latina 2009–2011*, 97–118. Bogotá, Colombia: Centro de Competencia en Comunicación para América Latina, Friedrich Ebert Stiftung.

Transparencia. 2011a. "¿De qué se ocupó la prensa escrita durante dos meses de campaña?" *Datos Electorales* 8 (April 19).

———. 2011b. "¿De qué se ocupó la radio limeña en dos meses de campaña?" *Datos Electorales* 10 (May 30).

———. 2011c. "¿De qué se ocupó la televisión de señal abierta en dos meses de campaña?" *Datos Electorales* 9 (May 25).

United States, Department of State. 2002–2010. *Country Reports on Human Rights Practices.* Washington, DC: Government Printing Office.

Waisbord, Silvio. 2008. "Press and the Public Sphere in Contemporary Latin America." Unpublished paper presented at the Harvard-World Bank Workshop, Cambridge, MA, May 29–31.

———. 2010. "All-Out Media War: It's *Clarín* vs. the Kirchners, and Journalism Will Be the Loser." *Columbia Journalism Review* (September/October).

Weyland, Kurt, Raúl L. Madrid, and Wendy Hunter, eds. 2010. *Leftist Governments in Latin America: Successes and Shortcomings*. New York: Cambridge University Press.

Wilpert, Gregory. 2007. "RCTV and Freedom of Speech in Venezuela." Znet. www.zcommunications.org/rctv-and-freedom-of-speech-in-venezuela-by-gregory-wilpert.

World Association of Newspapers. 2010. *World Press Trends*. Paris: International Federation of Newspaper Publishers.

CHAPTER THREE

Security Challenges for Latin American Democratic Governance

Lucía Dammert

Democracy in Latin America has not provided a response to violence and crime. Indeed, as many Latin American countries have undergone a democratic transition in recent decades, homicide rates and general crime have actually increased. The securitization of political agendas has become more prevalent, just as Latin America's citizens cite insecurity as their main concern.

Has crime and insecurity left democracy in jeopardy? Multiple public policies, debates, and international cooperation initiatives revolve around this question, but there is no clear answer. Nevertheless, there are indications that developments linked to rising insecurity in the region are undermining democratic processes and values. The lack of political transparency, fragile state of most political parties, and deficit of effective public policies that would tackle insecurity are key elements in the Latin American scenario. Concentrating on traditional security elements such as the quality of the police service or the importance of recidivism is insufficient to fully explain the profound roots of this insecurity.

This chapter outlines the main characteristics of insecurity in the region, highlighting elements that have not traditionally formed part of the analysis. These new factors have played an important role in the development of a more critical view of the way in which governments tackle insecurity.

The main challenge for democracy in Latin America is to enhance security by reforming political structures, strengthening the means to limit corruption, and increasing effective crime prevention and control. Fragile political systems open the door for a culture of illegality to permeate the state. In some situations, weak boundaries between illegal and informal practices allow for greater diffusion of organized crime. A lack of regulation for campaign funding, especially at the local government level, for instance, is considered one of the reasons why organized crime penetrated so many territories in Mexico. But this is not just a Mexican story; the problems of fragile states and weak governments can be found throughout Latin America.

The complex elements of the institutions linked to criminal justice in Latin America could play an important role in undermining the quality of new democracies. Legitimacy of democratic values and institutions could also be weakened due to rising public fears and general perceptions of insecurity. The worst-case scenario is an elected, democratic government that has been financed by organized crime and penetrated by corruption that creates the conditions for further inefficiencies. Unfortunately, in some countries this scenario is not inconceivable, and initiatives should be developed to prevent it. This chapter opens a door for a multidimensional analysis of insecurity and a deeper debate on the challenges for democratic governance in Latin America.

Violence and Crime in the Americas

At the end of the 1990s, Latin America was considered the second most violent region of the world (Krug 2002). More recent data shows that ten out of the twenty countries with the highest homicide rates in the world are from Latin America (UNODC 2011). A lack of reliable information and integrated data systems precludes a more detailed analysis of crime trends. The absence of strong diagnostics leaves analysts with few indicators to describe the security situation in the Americas. Figure 3.1, based on data collected during different years from official sources, shows the regional variation of homicide rates in Latin America. Based on this data, an average six people a day are murdered in Honduras, eight in El Salvador, and fourteen in Guatemala. The world average is less than half that of Latin America.

The sources of such high levels of crime vary even within countries. Some countries are heavily influenced by organized crime, especially drug trafficking, such as Honduras, El Salvador, and Jamaica, while others face different problems. Venezuela is a case that requires further analysis as increasing levels of violence cannot be explained by organized crime alone.

Young people have felt the brunt of the region's rising levels of crime and insecurity over the last decade, both as perpetrators and victims. Based on World

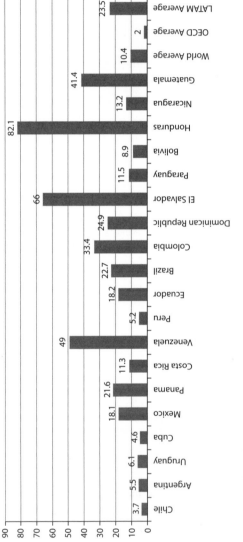

Figure 3.1. Homicide Rates per 100,000 in Latin America, 2010. *Source:* UNODC 2011

Health Organization estimates, homicide rates among young males in Colombia and El Salvador are among the highest in the world with 84.4 and 50.2 homicides per 100,000 inhabitants respectively. The situation is aggravated by growing drug and alcohol consumption, even among minors, which increases violence in all types of crime.

Homicides are only one facet of a complex phenomenon. Available information depicts a context in which overall victimization has increased in the last decade. Data from Latinobarómetro 2011 found that 33 percent of those interviewed were victims of a crime. In some cases, countries previously considered "safe" based on homicides rates have become increasingly insecure in other ways. Figure 3.2 shows the magnitude of the problem regionally. These figures speak to the rising number of Latin Americans who believe that crime is the main problem their country faces. The problem with the data presented in the figure 3.2, however, is that it paints an aggregated picture of crime, treating minor and aggravated cases equally. The severity of crimes range, but the general figure of victimization illustrates that countries such as Peru, Costa Rica, and Bolivia are facing a complex phenomenon of insecurity mostly linked to street crime.

Several hypotheses link political development and institutional arrangements to insecurity. Although the numbers are not conclusive, it seems that political development—consolidation of democracy or previous periods of internal

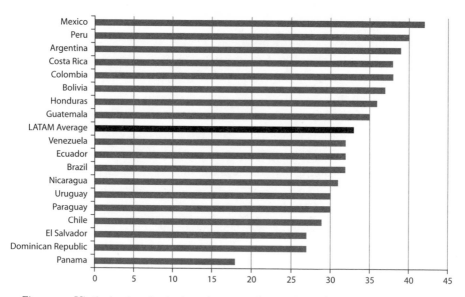

Figure 3.2. Victimization, Latin America 2010. *Source:* Latinobarómetro 2011

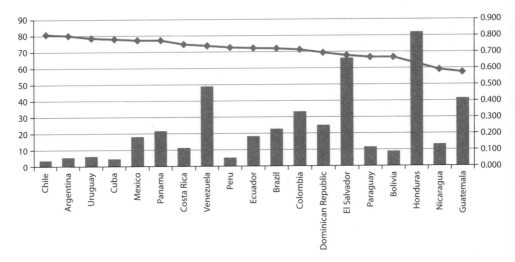

Figure 3.3. Homicide Rates and Human Development Index, Latin America, 2011.
Sources: UNODC 2011; UNDP 2011

violence—cannot be used as predictors of crime trends in the region. The Human Development Index (HDI) also does not show a clear pattern or correlation with crime indicators. For instance, countries with high HDIs such as Venezuela and Mexico report higher crime rates, while Nicaragua and Bolivia show the opposite trend (fig. 3.3).

Levels of economic development do not seem to play a decisive role in understanding insecurity, which plays out similarly in the poorest and richest countries in the region (Alda and Beliz 2007). Both results highlight that more analysis must be done to assess prominent theories generally developed in the US and Europe. Research on security issues is scant, and absent for some countries. The number of researchers interested in violence as a social phenomenon is growing but there is little basic research being done in the region. The lack of empirical evidence prevents better understanding of the problem and its links to social and political trends.

Multiple Types of Violence

Violence is a multidimensional phenomenon. Although it relates to specific crimes, it is also a cultural element in society. The key is to recognize that violence has become a facet of everyday life. A growing problem is the use of violence to resolve everyday conflicts, resulting in brawls and street fights. The latest analysis by the World Health Organization showed that the rates of deaths caused by injuries in the Americas are around 27.7 percent, that is, 40.6 percent of total deaths. In many cases, those injuries are products of street violence and in some cases household violence not related to crime; there is a need for specific public policies aimed at general violence. This problem has a clear socioeconomic component, as deaths caused by injuries in the upper socioeconomic groups were 17.2 per 100,000 inhabitants versus 34 deaths per 100,000 inhabitants in the low and middle groups (Krug 2002).

School violence is also an urgent problem affecting students and teachers alike. A survey conducted in fourteen state capitals in Brazil showed that 45 percent of students said that they were unable to concentrate, 32 percent felt uncomfortable, and 31 percent lost interest in school because of violence (Abramovay 2005).

In addition, Latin America and the Caribbean have some of the highest rates of family violence in the world. The scant information shows a clear problem. In a comparative report, the main conclusion was that "surveys from various countries indicate that an estimated 10 to 50 percent of women report being physically assaulted by their male partner."[1] The same source compiles data from different research that, at the end of the 1990s, showed alarming levels of physical violence: Chile (60 percent), Ecuador (60 percent), Colombia (41 percent), and Guatemala (39 percent). It has been estimated that more than six million children suffer abuse and more than 80,000 die each year as result (Knaul 2005).

In addition to interpersonal violence and common crime, most countries face the growing problem of organized crime, linked to the trafficking of drugs, arms, and people. In some countries, areas are considered "bastions of impunity," in which the rule of law is weak and the presence of the state minimal.

The presence of organized crime has been analyzed in Colombia and more recently in Mexico and Central America's "Northern Triangle"—comprised of Guatemala, El Salvador, and Honduras. For many decades, organized crime was tied almost entirely to drug trafficking, but the connection to gun trafficking and illegal migration has become more visible.

An actual crime "industry" has emerged, with networks in several countries. The permanent expansion of transnational organized crime is another form of violence that affects the economies of these countries, quality of life of their citizens, processes of privatization of security, militarization of the police, and ensuing corruption.

Violence affects mainly young men in the region (ages 15 to 29), with a homicide rate of 83.2 per 100,000 inhabitants. The death ratio exceeds 100 per 100,000 in cases of young men from the middle and lower socioeconomic strata and is the highest among all the regions of the world. The emergence of some juvenile gangs with varying degrees of organization is another element of this complex panorama. In Central America, where some groups are called *maras* (Lara 2006), gangs have become one of the most worrying contemporary phenomena, and have expanded into Mexico, Ecuador, Peru, and even Spain. This problem has also appeared in the English-speaking Caribbean countries and in Haiti, with destabilizing effects on government. Despite limited information, there has been an increase in gang activity in Jamaica, the result of social decay marked by poverty, urban marginalization and migration, as well as deportations from the US. Gangs are particularly related to microtrafficking, drug shipment protection, and human trafficking, all of which have become an important source of their funding (Bruneau and Dammert Maras 2011).

Another element is institutional violence. Although it has decreased with democratization, the use of violence by governmental institutions, particularly by the police, is still common. Lack of information on police activities has limited the development of civilian leadership in these institutions. Most excessive use of violence or human right abuses by the police go unpunished, increasing levels of insecurity and the sense of impunity.

All these elements combine to create a context marked by the increasing use of violence, the presence of highly developed criminal organizations, and limited capabilities among state institutions. These challenges should be tackled urgently to avoid further violence, societal fragmentation, and weaker state institutions.

Fear of Crime

Fear is a significant public policy issue (Bannister and Fyfe 2000), with evidence that much of the world's population experiences high levels of crime-related anxiety. Latin America is no exception, as many fear becoming a crime victim. The perceptions of risk and insecurity as well as the feeling of threat are sometimes of the criminal reality. Increasing perceptions of victimization are caused by media coverage of security issues, overexposure of unusually violent events, and the appearance of new media specializing in crime coverage. In addition, an important explanation for this growing fear is direct or indirect victimization. A criminal event sets off an information chain between relatives and acquaintances, which feel vulnerable and consequently become afraid. It is striking that petty crimes like the theft of auto parts when nobody is in the car have a similar or even higher impact on feelings of being at risk than other types of crime.

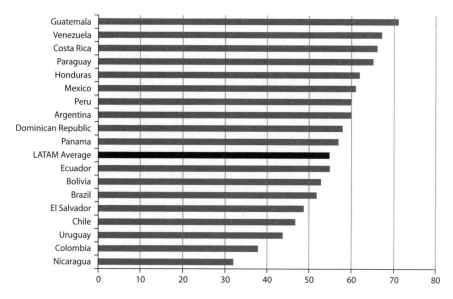

Figure 3.4. Insecurity, Latin America, 2011. *Source:* Latinobarómetro 2011

Reported crime is not a direct reflection of the criminal reality. In Chile and Argentina, where there is evidence of a slowdown in victimization levels, there are no noticeable changes in the levels of public insecurity. This suggests a "fear inertia," which implies that fear dissipates slowly. The reduction of victimization calls for strong sustainable policies that would increase citizens' sense of security.

Cruz concludes that economic certainties matter for fears of crime and the consequences that they bring to social relationships in the region. In the same study, focused on Central America, he explains that effectiveness and transparency of institutions shape levels of fear (2009).

The indicators used to quantify fear vary. The literature identifies the "affective" feeling of insecurity, which generates fear when criminal or dangerous situations arise. This fear is measured through a question about how safe respondents feel when walking alone at night in their own neighborhood. In a comparative analysis based on Latinobarómetro data for 2011, 34 percent of Latin Americans felt insecure walking at night in their neighborhood.

The perception that insecurity is higher than before is widespread across Latin America. On average 55 percent of all respondents feel that their country is more insecure than before (fig. 3.4). In Guatemala, Venezuela, and Costa Rica, although facing very different crime situations, there is no doubt about the increasing levels of insecurity.

In 2010, more than 40 percent of all Latin Americans believed that their neighborhoods were getting more insecure. The numbers are higher in countries such as Bolivia (49 percent), Ecuador (47 percent), Peru (47 percent), and Venezuela (66 percent) (Barómetro de las Américas 2011). Those countries that show decreasing levels of fear during 2000–2011 do not reflect lower crime rates. Fear of crime should be analyzed as a social problem that needs specific public policies and interventions.

The perception of fear relates to trust in the police. Judgment of the criminal justice system is negative when people feel that neither the police nor the law is effectively carrying out its duty to control crime. This directly affects the quality of life, increasing feelings of fear, threat, and helplessness in the face of what is considered a permanent state of victimization.

Fear has an impact at different levels. At the regional level, insecurity has serious consequences for a country's development rates and represents a substantial economic and social cost that some estimates say exceeds regional GDP by ten points (Londoño 2000). At the individual level, it has triggered multiple responses from the public. For instance, there have been requests for increased police presence, greater expenditure on criminal justice, and exemplary punishment for wrongdoers. There has also been an increase in individual protection strategies, varying from participatory initiatives to self-protection mechanisms.

Buying firearms is another typical, yet dangerous, response. In recent years there have been political proposals on the need for self-defense against criminal threats, including, in some cases, carrying firearms. This reality has led to the rather perverse and growing role played by private security companies, a development that emphasizes the lack of state response and need to install alternative systems. Fragile regulatory frameworks for private security companies have undermined the states' monopoly on the use of force, because all countries in the region have double or triple the number private security agents relative to police officers. In countries such as Guatemala, Honduras, Colombia, Peru, and Mexico, the threat of parapolice institutions is not far from becoming a reality. Heavily armed bodyguards are permitted and in some cases not regulated. All of these elements compound, and increase the general sensation of insecurity.

The Political Game: Penal Populism

How much crime is a society willing to put up with? Citizens and politicians tend to forget that conflict and crime are parts of society and that proposals for their elimination have little possibility of success. The role of the state is to keep crime at bay and prevent it from becoming a threat to authority and to citizens. Crime control is a central issue of public safety and criminal justice policy. Still, there is a gap between reality and expectations. The offender is rarely identified; conviction is even rarer. If the gap widens, the sense of insecurity increases. In cases of property crime (burglary, robbery, and theft), arriving at a sentence is unlikely due to lack of evidence. Since most crimes are not solved, the criminal justice system is perceived to be ineffectual.

The social demand for increased punishment is based on the perception that offenses are on the rise, combined with the feeling that the social order is being threatened. Thus, punishment and control reappear as the solutions likely to preserve the social order. These solutions place the onus of responsibility on the criminal justice institutions.

There are different cultural, social, political and even psychological explanations about the subjects' need for protection. Even in countries where distrust of the police is high, the population clamors for increased police presence. Data from the Latinobarómetro 2011 show that 61 percent of all Latin Americans believe that the state can solve the problem of crime. Cross-national figures range from 74 percent in Brazil and Venezuela to 27 percent in Guatemala. Even acknowledging that prisons operate more as schools of crime than as places for rehabilitation, the population demands increased punishments involving incarceration, even for minor offenses. The demand for increased control is a key factor in the development of strategies to manage uncertainty and fear in Latin America.

The criminal justice system is different from other sectors of the state. As suggested by Bottoms (1995), there are three crucial aspects to how it operates. The first is the tension between fair punishment and human rights. These concepts may show asymmetries due to their very definitions, as the characterization of what society considers fair punishment has varied significantly in the last few decades. Changes in the severity of the punishments in Latin America show how human rights—as principles of the rule of law—are permanently invoked and are the object of analysis in a region marked by their constant violation.

Second is the emphasis on management and administration in the criminal justice system, resulting in reduced attention on justice and increased focus on public expenditures or the results of the administration of cases. This provides incentives to improve achievement indicators, even when they may not go hand in hand with an increase in justice.

Third is the development of clientelism and the influence of citizen opinion in the criminal justice process. The media play an important role, portraying specific cases and, in some instances, even demanding punishment. In some countries the accused is judged and sentenced by the media before facing the justice system. These three aspects have played an especially important role in the definition and implementation of state measures in most countries.

Public myths posit links between the political sphere and criminal sanction. First is the perception that an increased punishment results in reduced crime, mainly due to the dissuasive effects of offenders being incarcerated. Second, strong sanctions are believed to strengthen the moral consensus against acts that violate the law, especially related to the moral panic that ensues in the case of sex- or drug-related crimes or crimes that subvert the public order. Politicians benefit when appearing strong against crime, as confirmed by Garland when he analyzed several national contexts: "The populist tendency in contemporary criminal policy is, to some extent, a political posture or tactic adapted to attain short term electoral advantages. As such, this can be rapidly reversed if the 'popular' initiatives no longer coincide with the calculations of political benefit" (2001, 282). In Latin America the populist tendency has been effective. During the last presidential elections in Chile and Peru, the main strength of the elected presidents Piñera and Humala respectively was crime. In this area, both candidates proposed increasing punishment and police presence.

Public anxiety and political opportunism explain the emphasis on punishment, as anything redolent of permissiveness is immediately rejected. The consequences of policy initiatives based on public opinion can be varied. They are positive when the expected objectives are attained, although they may cost a lot. They are negative when policies are not effective or generate unwanted externalities. Populist security policies tend to lead to an increase in public spending, even if there is a decline in effectiveness or, what is worse, a lack of information about initiatives on criminal activity. Some popular policies, such as the increasing presence of police officers, respond to an evident need, but do not necessarily solve public anxiety over crime. It seems that crime is only an issue when there is a crime scene on the news or when crime is evoked in the political debate. Thus, there is a lack of civil society engagement in monitoring crime policies, let alone evaluating them. The media are the main factor, since many reforms have been developed due to scandals of corruption and abuse, such as legal reforms after kidnappings in Argentina and Mexico or police reform initiatives after corruption scandals in Peru, Ecuador, and Honduras. Feelings of injustice and impunity emerged as public opinion witnessed the indulgent application of penalties and the increase in offenses. The citizenry started clamoring for changes and reforms to the criminal justice system on the basis of perceived safety needs. Citizens became more and more interested in an area that had traditionally been reserved for experts and demanded more severe punishments. Penal policies had to respond to these demands with more severe punishments for a series of offenses. In these cases, the policies were not necessarily associated with control but with the public visibility acquired by supporters of the approach. In some countries, an extreme case of violence followed by a clear lack of public response led to civil movements that were supposed to represent the "perspective of the victim." In Argentina, for example, Juan Carlos Blumberg rose to prominence following the 2004 murder of his son in Buenos Aires. He organized a movement that asked for legislators to harden crime laws and increase jail sentences, especially for drug related crimes. More recently, Mexican poet Javier Sicilia, whose son was killed by a drug gang in Cuernavaca, confronted the national government with a peace movement, which shows the limits of state power and the problems of drug violence. The latter revives some of the left-wing rhetoric regarding crime policies; it is unique in that realm, as most civil movements are conservative because they are based on victims' requests for more punishment and the general request for justice.

The whole idea that the state defends the criminal instead of the victim erodes the basic rule of law. Still, many Latin Americans feel that this is the norm. Data from the Barómetro de las Américas show that there is an inverse relationship between perception of insecurity and system support. The higher the insecurity the lower the percentages of system support.[2]

There are many characteristics that define the nature of penal populism. The first is the exclusion of the elite from the development of crime policy. The specialists and scholars that played a key role in previous decades now carry less weight. It is now the victims and those who feel vulnerable that play the most active role in promoting security as a fundamental civil right. Subjectivity is thus at the center of shaping the public policy agenda, because knowledge of crime does not necessarily include the direct experience of victimization. Second is the construction of a misinformed democracy. On the one hand, the limited information of the public about criminal justice combines with scant knowledge of the complexity of crime. On the other hand, at the political level, gauging people's opinion of crime may produce misinformation—for instance, the media focus on frustration, which may mislead decision makers.

In Latin America, public security is an object of political confrontation and public scrutiny, with limited success of policies in the short term. As a result, political strategies are designed to tell people what they want to hear (new laws, increased police staff, and exemplary punishments) but not necessarily what is technically feasible. The political security game takes eye-catching albeit superficial short-term measures aimed at winning elections. Thus, candidates embrace "super iron-fist" policies in Central America, death penalty for rapists in Peru, military intervention in Mexico, and the "first-and-last-time" policy in Chile. Concern about crime was among the three main issues in most of the presidential elections in recent years. A May 2010 public opinion poll in Peru showed that crime was the first concern among Lima respondents.[3]

Security becomes an item on the public agenda during election campaigns or when there is an event that causes public outcry—a homicide, kidnapping, or other crime that is covered extensively by the media and leads to public complaints.[4] With few exceptions, elections are characterized by debates on curbing crime. Policy proposals in general ignore prevention measures, as prevention is considered a "loser" in terms of media coverage. Politics enters the public security arena, and contending forces exploit fears and magnify the problem.

Such is the case in Central American countries, where it is assumed that most criminals are members of the *maras*. In Brazil, there is a stigma attached to those who live in the *favelas* (shanty towns) of the main cities. Such views are found throughout the region.

Defining the struggle against crime as a war leads to repressive policies such as the lowering of the age of penal responsibility throughout Latin America. The direct consequence of this decision will be the incarceration of juveniles in appalling conditions, with the aggravation of prison overcrowding and with minimal chances of social reintegration. Other examples are the many laws to increase penalties for offenses such as aggravated robbery. When a person is arrested and subsequently convicted, he or she risks a long sentence. However, the percentage of criminal cases that lead to a conviction does not exceed 5 percent (Dammert and Bailey 2005). Thus, these stiffer penalties have little impact. In most countries, investigative procedures are weak, and the crimes solved are the ones in which an offender was captured at the scene.

Where Is the State?

In Latin America, criminal justice systems are complex networks of institutions with little cooperative practices. In many countries, the institutional response to the state of affairs described above is generally compartmentalized because of a lack of coordination, absence of compatible and shared records, and competition between sectors. There are no information systems that liaise between the police and the legal and prison systems. There is no common strategy to prioritize the most salient security concerns. Paradoxically, the institutions directly concerned with public security face a two-pronged dilemma: first, they have failed to attain legitimacy with the public, and second, there are institutional barriers that restrict their effectiveness in crime control and prevention.

Although Latin American countries differ, the fragile situation of the criminal justice sector is widespread, and even countries with the strongest institutions, such as Colombia and Chile, face similar challenges. The countries that are facing more complex crime situations are those in which institutions are the weakest, such as Honduras and Guatemala. The question that arises is what happened first, increasing levels of crime or state fragility. Is there a vicious cycle that reinforces both processes? If so, how do authorities increase state presence and effectiveness while fighting organized crime? There are no clear answers, but in most contexts state fragility plays an important role allowing transnational organized crime organizations to flourish.

Mexico and Brazil face even more delicate situations since local and state governments are particularly weak. The actions of the state on crime control can be depicted as fragile.[5] The police, justice, and prison systems all share difficulties in the implementation of sound policies and initiatives. In the next sections, the role of the police and justice sector are discussed in detail. As for the prison system, there is evidence that Latin America is facing a crisis linked to overcrowding and the precarious quality of life of inmates. And there are allegations of human rights abuses in the prisons of countries such as Honduras, Mexico, and Chile.[6] Most prisons have turned into territories of "impunity" since crime gangs are de facto in charge of governing the daily routines of inmates (Salla et al. 2009).

The Police

Police institutions are undergoing a crisis of legitimacy. There are many types of police, depending on the work they do (prevention, investigation) or on their territorial deployment (national, state, or local), yet many of them share a lack of social prestige, due to inefficiency and corruption.[7]

The different institutions do not have the capabilities to deal with modern crime. In many cases, the gap between the technological capability of organized crime and that of the police is enormous, with the former having the upper hand. In Mexico and the Northern Triangle of Central America, organized crime has the capacity to deploy highly trained personnel and integrate crime organizations. Moreover, levels of corruption in the police are endemic. Only a decade ago, police institutions in Latin America were penetrated by corrupt practices and suffered a lack of professional officers. Also, working conditions were inadequate, with low salaries and limited social security, which further diminished professionalism in the forces.

Social security for the police force is a pending task in most countries. In Mexico, for instance, the retirement pensions of police officers do not even reach one-third of the salary they received while in active service (García Luna 2006). In many cases, police officers do not have insurance to provide financial stability to their families in case of death or injury. This generates a culture in which police membership is associated with a "police family" more than with professional merit.

All this has repercussions on the quality of police work. Often police in areas marked by insecurity establish a direct connection with people in the crime business, not only due to their limited professionalization but also because in some countries officers are allowed to work as private guards in their free time, which takes a toll on their effectiveness for crime prevention in their regular duties. In many countries, police officers may do private work when they go off duty, and frequently are permitted to wear their uniform and carry a gun while doing so. Those practices have debilitated the capacities of the police.

In many countries, the police are subordinate to ministries whose main tasks are political strategies rather than crime control strategies. It is not unusual for government ministries to assign the police a wide range of tasks that exceeds their proper duties.

Reforms to address these problems have had little or no success. The political power held by the police, their autonomy, and the need to keep the internal order, make it almost impossible to carry out long overdue reforms. These reforms range from improving the quality of police pre- and in-service training to the strengthening of internal and external control mechanisms.

Democratic consolidation in the region is badly in need of these reforms, intended to train police forces to apply the rule of law. These initiatives call for support from the highest levels of the government, since they may affect different interests. Failure to do so will enhance the militarization of public security being developed in several countries. After the experience of the 1970s and 1980s, it was necessary to keep the armed forces out of domestic politics, but this view is losing strength. The spread of firearms and the technologic power of organized crime has left whole areas where the presence of the state is almost non-existent in countries like Brazil, Colombia, Guatemala, Mexico, and Paraguay. The power of the *maras* in Central America has led to an even greater involvement of the armed forces in internal security, as they are asked to back up overburdened police forces.

This call for military participation speaks to the impotence of police forces to deal with crime, and the confidence in the military's purported effectiveness. Because the military is not trained to control crime but rather to "eliminate the enemy," its involvement may bring unintended consequences, such as human right abuses and increasing levels of corruption.

Justice

Latin Americans see the justice system as slow, corrupt, and inefficient. The prevailing notion is that the rich can literally get away with murder. The metaphor of the "revolving door" is a central public image referring to the limited capability of the criminal justice system to convict criminals. Public perception is that laws are not tough enough, few criminals are prosecuted, and too many are found not guilty.

Over the last decade, most Latin American states have introduced changes to their criminal justice systems. Previously, Latin America had frail, politically precarious, and ineffective judicial institutions. Criminal codes were antiquated, courts were poorly organized and underfunded, and in general, police, judges, and judicial officers were poorly trained and poorly compensated. The reforms to facilitate a more transparent process had the goal of guaranteeing citizen security by strengthening criminal investigations to obtain effective, timely, legitimate evidence.

In new criminal justice procedures, the judge—whose duty in the old system was to investigate, judge, and sentence—hears cases and hands down verdicts and sentences, but does not investigate. Investigating is the role of the police, and they perform this task under the supervision of the public prosecutor's office, the agency responsible for criminal prosecutions. This new institution must supervise the investigative work of the police and introduce the necessary flexibility and dynamism to investigation to ensure the efficiency of justice. Laws in some countries such as Chile, Peru, and Argentina have also given prosecutors some discretionary faculties aimed at simplifying proceedings and shortened procedures (De Shazo and Vargas 2006).

Despite the legislative reforms, problems have been detected in the practical application of these codes. Most have arisen between the public prosecutor's office and the police, as the latter have found it difficult to adapt to the supervising role of the investigative process assigned to the public prosecutor.

In turn, public prosecutor offices, which are ultimately responsible for criminal investigation, in some countries are afraid that police investigations may result in information leaks that compromise criminal prosecution. Because of this, they prefer to have control of the information and, in some cases, conduct the investigation themselves.

While this fear may be justified and explains why some countries have created specialized investigative units within the public prosecutor's office, the investigative role should not be taken away from the police. In addition, police institutions should be restructured and police agents selected and trained to enable them—or a specialized group within the institution—to perform honestly and efficiently the role they were assigned in the new criminal justice system. Efforts to coordinate operations between the public prosecutor's office and the police must continue if we want to confront the challenges of new, complex, and increasingly powerful crime organizations.

Although it is too early to confirm whether these reforms have had the desired impact on citizen security and perceptions, in countries where they have been fully implemented, the efficiency of the system has substantially increased, and the duration of the proceedings has been reduced. For instance, in Peru the Ministry of Justice stated that the average duration of the process has gone from twenty-eight to twenty-three months with the implementation of the new procedure.[8] For many, the reform is considered *garantista* (respectful of civil liberties), since criminals not only receive legal aid but are also given opportunities to avoid punishment. In some countries, a revision of the reform followed the first months of implementation, allowing more time for preventive imprisonment and increased police powers to seize and detain suspected criminals.

Citizens' Perceptions

Trust is a central pillar of life in society. Its absence brings about authoritarianism, fragmentation, and violence, as citizens lose interest in relating to their peers and in being represented by their institutions. Trust makes it possible for us to go safely about our daily activities, because there is a moral authority that states in a clear way the rules of the coexistence game. Social problems like crime and fear of crime have roots in political issues directly related to the type of society in which individuals hope to live and the processes that erode the norms and values underpinning this ideal model.

At present trust is undergoing a two-fold crisis. The first aspect refers to citizens' views on their neighborhoods and social cohesion. The lack of interpersonal trust makes it more difficult to undertake joint projects, look for solutions to social shortcomings, and consolidate an integrated society. Second is trust in institutions, which reveals the gap between people and the state. This negatively impacts the possibility to consolidate and develop the rule of law and democratic institutions. The authority of the state must be recognized by the people so that it can carry out the complex task of ordering social life.

The intrinsic difficulties involved in the difference between these two sides of the crisis are evident. In a society in which the citizens do not generate bonds of mutual trust, it is unlikely that trust in institutions will be strong.

Interpersonal Trust

Putnam (1993, 217) described social trust as an essential component of social capital and a key factor in the high economic dynamism and performance of government institutions. Furthermore, interpersonal trust is an important element of the sense of security in most communities.

Many scholars assert that political institutions relate to the rules of democracy that govern collective decision making as a mechanism to reach agreements. In contrast, for Putnam (1993, 9) institutions are not just agreements but also incorporate mechanisms to achieve political purposes through public policies (programs, projects, services) intended to meet the needs and demands of the public.

Several recent opinion polls have been carried out in Latin America to understand diluted trust. According to Latinobarómetro, from 1996 to 2010 an average of 20 percent of respondents agreed that, generally speaking, most people can be trusted. Data from a different question, on levels of trust in neighbors, show a clear element of distance within society. In most countries, the percentage of people who have little or no trust in their neighbors is around 50 percent (fig. 3.5).

Yet the findings reveal contradictory results. Most respondents from the countries that are more insecure show higher levels of interpersonal trust (Honduras, El Salvador, and Venezuela), while relatively safer regions have lower levels (Chile, Nicaragua). However, limited information and a lack of systematic analysis do not permit detailed conclusions on the relationship between victimization, fear, and interpersonal trust.

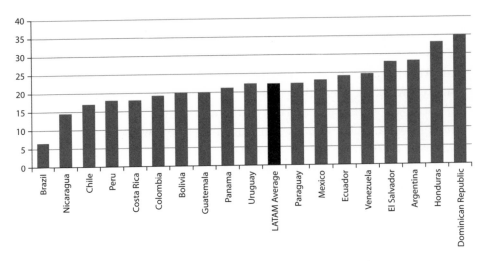

Figure 3.5. Interpersonal Trust, Latin America, 2011. *Source:* Latinobarómetro 2011

Institutional Trust

Citizen trust in public institutions is crucial for the functioning of democracy. The links between people and the institutions that represent them require trust as the cornerstone of the legitimacy of their acts.

Many studies have analyzed the processes of democratization in Latin America, taking this variable into account, based on the necessary legitimacy of the system, trust in institutions, and existing social capital in each context. Recent studies show the negative impact that crime has had on trust in government (Chanley, Rudolph, and Rahn 2000; Vlassis 2000). Empirical evidence shows that the perception of an increase in crime-related insecurity brings about a decline in trust in the political institutions in general, and particularly, in the institutions responsible for formal social control like the justice system and the police.

In Latin America, trust in government institutions is scant. Various sources of analysis such as Latinobarómetro and the Barómetro de las Américas show low levels of trust in the government and its principal institutions (fig. 3.6). This is related to general perceptions of inefficiency, corruption, neglect, and abuse by those who wield political power and to the growing gap between politics and the people.

An unanticipated phenomenon is that just a few decades after the return of democracy, most countries in the region face different processes and varying lev-

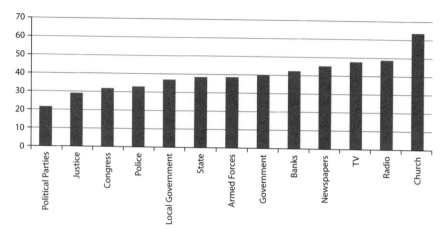

Figure 3.6. Institutional Trust, Latin America, 2011. *Source:* Latinobarómetro 2011

els of legitimacy of the state apparatus. Fear of crime along with distrust of political institutions may have a bearing on the chances of a return to authoritarian practices and discourses. This is shown by a recent survey in which more than 40 percent of the population in multiple countries justifies a military incursion into the government (Barómetro de las Américas 2008, 2010). This indicates the relationship between institutional distrust and the development of a popular authoritarian discourse.

The search for order and security seems to go hand in hand with fewer civil guarantees and an increased military presence. The high percentage of people who justify a coup in Mexico contrasts, for example, with relatively lower levels in Brazil and Colombia, if we consider that these countries have similarly high victimization rates. Apparently, the severity of crime does not explain the expression of an authoritarian discourse. In any case, it is likely that institutional distrust may play a key role in this trend.

In an effort to disentangle the multiple links between the perception of insecurity and the role of the state, Latinobarómetro included a question on whether democracy guarantees protection from crime. Only 30 percent in Latin America believe it does. In six countries, less than 25 percent, one in every four, believe that democracy can provide protection from crime, with the lowest level found in Argentina (fig. 3.7).

Focusing on institutions, levels of trust are even more problematic. There are high levels of dissatisfaction with the justice system and the police. The Barómetro

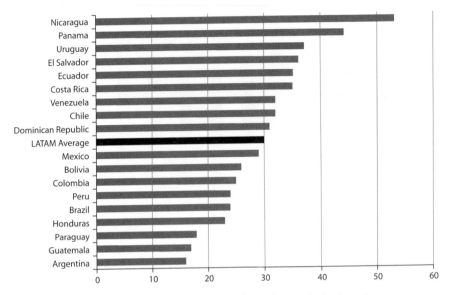

Figure 3.7. Democracy Warranties Protection from Crime, Latin America, 2011.
Source: Latinobarómetro 2011

de las Américas found that over 20 percent of respondents in Paraguay, Argentina, and Venezuela are dissatisfied with the justice system, and 34 percent in Guatemala are dissatisfied with the police. In Argentina, 32 percent of the population does not trust the police at all, while in Guatemala and Venezuela, the percentage was 34 and 29 percent respectively (Barómetro de las Américas 2011). Is it possible to trust institutions whose levels of corruption are high and who guarantee impunity for perpetrators? At the level of perception the police are seen as corrupt, and the reality does not contradict this perception. A survey conducted in several countries showed that in 2010 the percentage of the population who paid bribes to the police reached 20 percent in Bolivia, 25 percent in Mexico, and 15 percent in Peru (Barómetro de las Américas 2011). This situation confirms that the general perception is rooted in victimization and in a culture of illegality embedded in the daily activity of public institutions.

A Real Threat to Democracy?

There is an increasing concern over the impact of violence and crime on democracy in Latin America. Many experts thought democratic governments would end violence, but the reality has been different. Political violence, at a national level, is concentrated in a specific conflict in Colombia, but crime has grown everywhere in the region. The levels of violent crime have taken a tremendous toll on human lives, with many countries reporting homicide rates in excess of those experienced during civil wars and military dictatorships.

Three theoretical perspectives link democracy and crime. First, several authors have stated that democracy will bring long term declines in rates of violent crime, as the state will hold the legitimate monopoly over the means of violence. The hypothesis follows that private citizens will then demonstrate higher levels of self-control. The rapid demand for private security across Latin America, but particularly in violence-prone Central America, undermines the first argument, and there is no empirical evidence to support the second.

The second theoretical perspective focuses on the relationship between economic structures and crime rates. The theory posits that democratic governments will consolidate the economic structures of society, allowing market economies to flourish. However, these same elements have fomented discontent in the region, particularly in the last two decades, as neoliberal economic policies have dominated economic models. Instead of creating stability, the region has been marked by a growing economic inequality leading to widespread social conflict and political violence.

Third, modernization theory argues for a greater focus on the concept of social disorganization, as the effects of democratization on crime cannot be fully understood. It emphasizes that the democratization process introduces new values and norms without the benefit of an institutional framework.

Democracy in itself cannot limit violence. Democratic values introduced into a political system without an established framework of democratic institutions and practices could result in a "disjunctive democracy," which triggers high levels of violence (Caldeira and Holston 1999). Several theoretical approaches focus on the fact that the very institutions, practices, and democratic values desired are seen as encouraging violent crime. However, those perspectives also highlight the social and economic inequality that are a strong predictor of violence in all societies, including democratic ones.

Violence should not be analyzed as a failure of democracy but as an integral element in the configuration of democratic institutions. Most theoretical approaches to democracy fall short in understanding Latin America's complex democratic processes. The flexible manner in which Latin American democracies function requires an open mind when considering practices and values that are not traditionally included in definitions of democracy. Instead, these theories may not be suitable for fragile democracies, incapable of developing the types of public policy that are not even the norm in advanced democratic regimes (Bergman and Whitehead 2009, 10).

In Latin America, electoral democracy is not going to become a battleground of organized crime. Despite the increases in the technological and financial capabilities of criminal organizations, they have had limited interest in changing the political system. The main concern is that fragile democracies characterized by weak political parties and a lack of transparency and accountability at all levels of government will foster corruption.

Is it possible to have a narcostate in Latin America? Certainly, and it is also possible that a narcostate could develop within an electoral democracy in which deeper democratic values remain undeveloped. The lack of political reforms on issues such as campaign funding, political party representation, and democratic processes within parties opens a window for political parties funded by organized crime. As a result, the battle against crime must include political reforms in Latin America. The links that many political parties have with informal control groups in specific areas should be discussed and limited.

Democratic governance must include the development of public security policies with clear civil leadership that would limit corruption, increase transparency, and punish illegal political activities. A lack of trust in legitimate state institutions and a general perception that both the police and the justice system are corrupt or generally ineffective are problems that threaten to enhance an authoritarian discourse.

NOTES

1. For more information see www.prb.org/Articles/2001/DomesticViolenceAnOn goingThreattoWomeninLatinAmericaandtheCaribbean.aspx.

2. www.vanderbilt.edu/lapop/ab2010/2010-comparative-en-revised.pdf.

3. www.ipsos-apoyo.com.pe/opinion_publica?page=3.

4. The best-known case, the Blumberg kidnapping, took place in Argentina. It escalated into citizen demonstrations calling for more security measures and tougher punishments for offenders. Another initiative of this kind was the demonstration organized by "Mexico United against Crime," which took place in Mexico City.

5. It should be highlighted that the state has a special role in crime prevention initiatives that would impact insecurity and crime. However, those areas go beyond the scope of this chapter.

6. For more detail see www.hrw.org/americas.

7. There are a few exceptions in the region, namely, the national police forces in Chile and Colombia.

8. For further information see www.cejamericas.org/portal/index.php/es/biblioteca /biblioteca-virtual/doc_details/5456-informe-nacional-2006-2010-peru.

REFERENCES

Abramovay, M. 2005. Violencia en las escuelas: Un gran desafío. *Revista Iberoamericana de la educación* 38:53–66.

Alda, E., and G. Beliz, eds. 2007. *¿Cuál es la salida? La agenda inconclusa de la seguridad ciudadana.* Washington DC: Banco Interamericano de Desarrollo.

Bannister, J., and N. Fyfe. 2011. "Fear and the City." *Urban Studies* 38 (5–6): 807–13.

Barómetro de las Américas. 2008, 2010, 2011. www.LapopSurveys.org.

Bergman, Marcelo, and Laurence Whitehead, eds. 2009. *Criminality, Public Security, and the Challenge to Democracy in Latin America.* Notre Dame: University of Notre Dame Press.

Bottoms, A. 1995. "The Politics and Philosophy of Sentencing." In *The Politics of Sentencing Reform*, edited by C. Clarkson and R. Morgan, 17–49. Oxford: Clarendon Press.

Bureaus, Thomas, and Lucía Dammert Maras. 2011. *Gang Violence and Security in Central America.* Austin: University of Texas Press.

Caldeira, Teresa P. R., and James Holston. 1999. "Democracy and Violence in Brazil." *Comparative Studies in Society and History* 41:691–729.

Chanley, V., T. Rudolph, and W. Rahn. 2000. "The Origins and Consequences of Public Trust in Government: A Time Series Analysis." *Public Opinion Quarterly* 64 (3): 239–56.

Cruz, Jose Miguel. 2009. "Public Insecurity in Central America and Mexico." *AmericasBarometer Insights*, no. 28. Nashville: Vanderbilt University Press.

Dammert, Lucía, and John Bailey. 2005. *Seguridad y reforma policial en las Américas: Experiencias y desafíos.* Mexico City: Siglo XXI.

De Shazo, Peter, and Juan Enrique Vargas. 2006. "Judicial Reform in Latin America: An Assessment." *Policy Papers on the Americas* 17 (2). CSIS.

García Luna, Genaro. 2006. *¿Por qué 1,661 corporaciones de policía no bastan? Pasado, presente y futuro de la policía en México.* Mexico City.

Garland, David. 2001. *The Culture of Control: Crime and Social Order in Contemporary Society.* Chicago: University of Chicago Press.

Knaul, F. M. 2005. "Family Violence and Child Abuse in Latin America and the Caribbean: The Cases of Colombia and Mexico." Sustainable Development Department Technical Papers Series SOC-137. IADB.

Krug, E. G., et al., eds. 2002. "World Report on Violence and Health." Geneva: World Health Organization.

Lara, Martin. 2006. *Hoy te toca la muerte: El imperio de las maras visto desde dentro.* Barcelona: Planeta.

Londoño, Jose Luis. Asalto al Desarrollo. 2000. *Violencia en América Latina.* Washington DC: Banco Interamericano de Desarrollo.

Putnam, Robert. 1993. *Making Democracy Work: Civic Traditions in Modern Italy.* Princeton: Princeton University Press.

Salla, Fernando, et al. 2009. Democracy, Human Rights and Prison Conditions in South America. University of Sao Paulo. www.udhr60.ch/report/detention_salla0609.pdf.

UNODC. 2011. *Global Report on Homicide.* Vienna: UNODC.

CHAPTER FOUR

Natural Resources Boom and Institutional Curses in the New Political Economy of South America

Sebastián Mazzuca

Natural Resource Boom: A New Economy

As future economic history books will likely note, the twenty-first century in South America did not start in 2000, but in 2003. The delay, however, was more than compensated not only by the enormous growth in wealth that began in the second semester of 2002, but also by a better distribution of income. The first decade of the twenty-first century arrived late, but it was one of the best periods in history. Measured by income growth, it is similar to both the peak decades of export-led development of the last quarter of the nineteenth century and the most dynamic years of import-substitution industrialization after World War II, including the Brazilian "miracle." Contemporary South Americans can even claim that their decade is the best ever, with lower inequality than the 1880s and lower inflation than the 1960s. Sustained growth coupled with income redistribution and low inflation is a true novelty in 200 years of economic development. If it were not enough, the new economic development of South America has gone hand in hand with the consolidation of democracy throughout the region (fig. 4A.1).[1]

The timing of the "golden decade" could not have been better. Skepticism, if not disappointment, pervaded South America at the close of the twentieth century. After the lost decade of the 1980s, which in addition to negative growth was marked by sky-high levels of inflation, the hopes awakened by market reforms in the early 1990s evaporated only years later with the meltdown of 1998–2002, the "lost lustrum." Believing that neither the old statist model nor the new gamble on the free markets could provide a sustainable solution to the problems of economic growth, the resigned acceptance of underdevelopment became the dominant attitude among leaders, analysts, and the public. Precisely in that moment, China changed everything. Its rise as an industrial superpower and a voracious consumer of fuels, metals, and proteins presented South American economies with one of the biggest and easiest to capture opportunities for growth in history. In 2000, buying the most basic model of cellular phone required fifteen barrels of oil. In 2011, a barrel-and-a-half buys an iPhone. In 2002, one hundred metric tons of soybeans had the same value as a small Honda car. Ten years later, they are worth a convertible BMW. Raúl Prebisch died again.[2] To find equally favorable terms of trade for South American exports, historians have to go back to the last third of the nineteenth century, when world capitalism turned Argentina, Brazil, and Chile into the first emerging economies ever as suppliers of raw materials for the Industrial Revolution in the North Atlantic (fig. 4A.2).[3]

The new terms of trade are not news for economic analysts of Latin America. More importantly, lay citizens, from professionals in São Paulo to rural workers in the Bolivian Media Luna, can feel the effects in their pockets. The *political* repercussions of the boom are less obvious. But they are not less crucial. The boom is tightly connected with the two big political developments of the beginning of the twenty-first century: the general convergence on leftist governments and policies and the divergence between moderate-institutional and radical-hegemonic variants of the Left (Madrid, Hunter, and Weyland 2010; Levitsky and Roberts 2011a).

The Natural Sources of the Leftist Convergence and the Hegemonic Divergence

The "left turn" that swept across South America in the 2000s owes its consolidation, but not its origins, to the economic boom (Weyland 2009; Murillo, Oliveros, and Vaishnav 2011; Kaufman 2011). The origins of the turn lie in the demographic fact that the median voter of any Latin American country is poor, which means that median income is substantially lower than national GDP per capita. Consequently, political parties or movements that campaign on the promise of redistribution from rich to poor have, in principle, a considerable electoral advantage over conservative rivals (holding constant the effects of political "identities"). However, only fiscal latitude makes redistribution viable and allows leftist governments to stay in power. Without growth, fiscal surpluses evaporate. Without fiscal resources, leftist governments face a dilemma. Either they betray their electoral mandates and rule on the Right or they risk macroeconomic instability and plunge into potentially fatal governability problems. Colombia is the only exception to the left turn. While the median Colombian voter is also poor, the intensification of guerrilla warfare during the 1990s made security rather than redistribution the top concern (Posada-Carbó 2013).

Like the convergence on the Left, the radical-hegemonic divergence has separate causes for its origins and for its consolidation. The origins lie in the bankruptcy of traditional political parties caused by the exhaustion of their political capital after decades of governments that were too corrupt to supply a minimal level of public goods, too cartelized to allow for entry of new forces, or too impotent in the face of long periods of economic deterioration. Venezuela, Ecuador, and Bolivia are exemplary cases. The *consolidation* of radical hegemonies, however, is a repercussion of the economic boom. A fundamental intervening factor has been the rise of a social coalition that, on the basis of its source of funding and political components, can be called "rentier populism." The dominance of rentier populism has reshaped the political landscape in Venezuela, Bolivia, Ecuador, and to a lesser extent Argentina. In these four countries, rentier populism has created the conditions for the persistence of the radical variant of Left governments and, more importantly, of distinctly hegemonic forms of rule—political regimes in which the president dominates the policymaking process and is free from institutional oversight. Rentier populism reflects the type of natural resource that drives growth and the method the state uses to extract resource rents. In Argentina and the Andean countries except Peru and Colombia, the main economic beneficiary of the boom has not been a specific economic sector, a cluster of private firms, or a distinct social class. The big winner has been the government. The state is the main or sole owner of hydrocarbons in Venezuela, Ecuador, and Bolivia, the main producer of copper in Chile, and the largest recipient of soybean rents in Argentina. To different degrees, these countries have gravitated toward the so-called "rentier state," which derives its revenue from the exploitation of a single, government-owned natural resource (Karl 1987). By contrast, Peruvian gold and copper mines are privately owned, Brazilian and Uruguayan agricultural rents remain largely in private hands, and, given the legal structure of Petrobras, Brazilian oil rents are evenly divided between the state and a pool of minority shareholders around the world.

The methods and sources of fiscal extraction define what groups in society demand accountability. In the extreme case of the rentier state, the government does not owe anything to anybody and in principle has no incentive to make deals involving "taxation in exchange for representation," a canonical source of civil and political rights. Four of the five countries approaching the rentier state ideal type, Venezuela, Bolivia, Ecuador, and Argentina, in decreasing order of proximity, have experienced the rise of hegemonic forms of rule. At the same time, Chile—more of a rentier state than Argentina and Ecuador—has maintained, if not accelerated, its trajectory of institutional improvement. Chile could consolidate a hegemonic form of rule, but a strong party system prevents its emergence. Chile has additional immunity against radical hegemonies because, in contrast to other rentier states, copper was *already* owned by the state when the region received the first economic tailwinds in 2002. In Venezuela, Argentina, Bolivia, and Ecuador, the government fought with private firms for control of mineral and agricultural wealth. The fight exacerbated the level of political polarization that in general surrounds the emergence of radical hegemonies. For those governments that chose to fight, victory helped to consolidate power. Among nonrentier states, the effect of the natural resource boom is not as relevant in political terms. With the rise of the Partido dos Trabalhadores (PT; Workers' Party), a moderate, programmatic left-wing party, Brazil avoided radical hegemonies. Further, the election of Dilma Rousseff after Luiz Inácio "Lula" da Silva served two presidential terms appears to have started a transformation of the patrimonial institutions that have dominated politics since time immemorial. Uruguay, like Chile, replaced the old military dictatorship with a democracy that has improved itself through the very practice of representative government, and the victory of the Frente Amplio (Broad Front), another moderate and programmatic left-wing party, has only accelerated this trajectory.

While an economic blessing, abundant natural resources can be a curse for political institutions.[4] The risks of institutional poisoning are much higher for countries in which the physical structure of the economy allows rulers to build a rentier state without much effort. The modern state involves a fundamental political dilemma. On the one hand, the monopolistic control of the means of violence is a prerequisite for the protection of human lives and property, the most basic public good. On the other hand, the concentration of power, if it lacks strong boundaries or is captured by despots, can be the source of public evils like political oppression, economic predation, and underdevelopment traps. By strengthening the fiscal position of the state in all countries of South America, the boom of natural resources reinforced the power of national governments and made the dilemma of the modern state even more acute. The new power can contribute to the provision of the public goods still required for the economic and political development of the region—the boom as a blessing—but it also increases the risks of discretionary government and corruption, which would worsen the old accountability deficits of the new democracies—the boom as a curse. Only under special circumstances is a more powerful state a better state.

Chilean immunity against the type of poisoning that has affected other rentier countries, as well as the institutional improvements of Brazil, suggests that the physical structure of the economy and the methods of extraction are not the only causes behind divergence. Peru and Colombia, which are endowed with vast reserves of minerals and hydrocarbons but have avoided the creation of rentier states, also point to the need of extra explanatory factors. The obvious but crucial fact is that the economic boom has not worked its effects on countries as if they were blank canvasses. It hit countries at the same point in the calendar but at different junctures in their social and political trajectories. Different configurations of local conditions, *in addition* to the physical structure of the economy, refracted the shock into a variety of policy and institutional outcomes. Shared social and demographic conditions across South America processed the boom differently from commodity-abundant countries with high median incomes, like Norway, Canada, and Australia. Advanced economies have emphasized redistribution across generations, whereas South America spread the new torrent of wealth across social classes. At the same time, different conditions *within* Latin America, what Max Weber would call the "constellation" of political and economic forces, caused the commodity boom to improve the institutional quality of democracies in countries like Chile, Brazil, and Uruguay, and to dismantle the defenses against abuses of presidential power in Venezuela, Ecuador, Bolivia, and Argentina. The impact of the new economic abundance in South America has then been refracted by two types of prism, one shared by the entire region—the global features of the social structure—and one that creates divergence across countries, which, as we will see, includes a combination of constraints emerging from the structure of financial markets and the party system.

Convergence across South American countries resulted from the intersection of new international prices and persistent levels of economic inequality. This intersection produced a substantial change in the parameters that had dominated political activity during the last decades of the twentieth century. It made possible the economic incorporation of informal and marginalized sectors of the population, which expanded during the long period of economic stagnation that followed the debt crisis of 1982 and swelled as a consequence of the market reforms of the 1990s (Collier and Collier 1991). If the new commodity prices killed Prebisch's economy, they revived Gino Germani's political sociology with the creation of conditional cash transfers (CCTs), a scheme of economic redistribution that spread like wildfire among South American countries once fiscal conditions made it viable (Germani 1971).[5] Half a century after the original wave of "mass politics," the continent has embarked on the incorporation of the most vulnerable sectors in society. Like in the prior juncture, it is again the deliberate intervention of the state that extends protection from the risks that market economies present to those who did not accumulate a modicum of physical and human capital. In contrast to the past, however, the new welfare state is a minimalist one. It provides only a rudimentary safety net aimed at lifting people out of indigence, but not out of poverty. The incorporation of the structurally unemployed and informal sectors in the context of international free trade—a fundamental source of revenue for the minimalist welfare state—is another crucial contrast with the original incorporation wave, which generally resulted in the creation of formal jobs in state-protected industries and the unionization of workers. The new form of incorporation will not create new formal workers, new trade unions, or new labor parties. Incorporation through conditional cash transfers is not an invention of the new economic prosperity, but of the commodity boom that generated the revenue necessary to pursue CCTs as a systematic strategy, and spread the minimalist welfare state to the whole region. The boom consolidated the propagation of the new redistributive scheme.

Beyond the general outcome of informal sector incorporation, different sets of South American countries—depending on the structure of capital markets and party systems—experienced distinct coalitional dynamics, which in turn sent political regimes into contrasting trajectories of exercise of power and structures of political accountability.

Forms of Institutional Poisoning

Institutional poisoning has different manifestations, depending on whether it affects the state itself (poisoning as praetorianization[6]), the form of *access* to state power (autocratization), or the patterns of *exercise* of state power (hegemonization).

Praetorianization

Violent conflict is the curse par excellence of natural resources. The distribution of the new wealth created under booms almost always provokes dispute, and conflict may overflow legal channels of resolution. The consequence is Huntingtonean praetorianism: widespread noninstitutional mobilization. In South America, however, the commodity boom was a blessing for governability. Between 1996 and 2002, a period that roughly coincides with the lost economic lustrum, Argentina and Venezuela, two of the countries that would later benefit the most from the boom, experienced acute episodes of praetorianism, which included the twin events of general bankruptcy of traditional political parties and massive antiestablishment street protests. Bolivia, Ecuador, and Argentina became prominent examples of the syndrome of "interrupted presidencies," marked by the evaporation of presidential authority in the context of intense popular mobilization (Valenzuela 2004). Everything changed a few years later thanks to the first tangible fiscal repercussions of the commodity boom. The governments of Chávez, the Kirchner couple, Morales, and Correa restored presidential authority. After demobilizing the protest, they recovered governability and soon after were reelected or ratified with extraordinary levels of support. "We had to extinguish the fire," claims Alberto Fernández, the cabinet chief under the Néstor Kirchner government, "and the only way we could do it was by providing social assistance, and the only money we had to do it came from the taxes on [the exports of] soybeans."[7]

Autocratization

Dahlian democracy is another possible victim of the curse of natural resources (Dahl 1972). Autocratization occurs when access to power becomes less competitive because the opposition is boycotted or banned or less inclusive because substantial sections of the population are denied political rights. All countries in Latin America except for Cuba entered the new century with democratic regimes of access. In South America, according to a wide scholarly consensus, Venezuela has gradually lost democratic access due to a string of presidential blows against competition, although not against participation. The loss of competitiveness gained international attention in 2007 when Chávez closed Radio Caracas, an opposition television network, but it had already begun with the constitutional reform of 1999, which eliminated official financial support for political parties and created substantial asymmetries between government and opposition in terms of ability to campaign. Even though international agencies of regime analysis continue to classify Bolivia as a democracy, the government of Morales has also fostered, in an attenuated fashion, the autocratization of access. In contrast to Venezuela, the main victim in Bolivia has not been competition but participation, and not of voters but of opposition candidates, including the mayors of Sucre and Potosí, Jaime Barrón and René Joaquino, who have been harassed by judges controlled by the government. In Ecuador, shortly after taking office in 2007, President Correa set in motion a process that removed fifty-seven members of the opposition from Congress, which amounted to cancelling the verdict of the ballot box as a mechanism of access. Like clones of the Chávez government, the governments of Morales and Correa have engaged in high intensity rhetorical battles against established media. But only Correa went beyond words: the indirect control of the press under threat of intervention, which began with the expropriation of Gramavisión in mid-2009, became more systematic after the constitutional reform of May 2011 granted the president permanent powers of control.

Together with autocratization, however, the governments of Venezuela, Ecuador, and Bolivia have intensified the mechanisms of "vertical accountability" by means of an extraordinary expansion of the opportunities for voters to ratify or recall presidents. In addition to standard plebiscites, Chávez, Morales, and Correa subjected themselves to indirect popularity tests by calling for referendums on constitutional reform in which approval of reform and support for the president were tacitly but irreversibly linked (Corrales 2013). Displaying a level of convergence that cannot be coincidental, a few months after taking office, the three presidents called for referendums on constitutional reform and for elections of the constitutional assembly (1999, 2006, and 2007). In turn, once the work of the assemblies was finished, a new round of popular consultations took place for the approval of the new constitutional text (1999, 2009, and 2008). The reforms introduced presidential reelection in all three cases, and a new clock for the presidential term in Venezuela and Ecuador, which gave Chávez and Correa the opportunity to face an early test for renewing their mandates (2000 and 2009). Chávez and Morales, in addition, were subject to recall consultations (2004 and 2008) and, as the veteran of the trio, Chávez faced a second test for presidential reelection in 2006. Chávez and Correa also called for referendums for a second constitutional reform (2009 and 2011), which in the case of Venezuela resulted in the authorization for a third presidential term starting in 2013 (plus the portion of the term prior to the first constitutional reform). Between presidential elections, recall consultations, referendums for constitutional reform, and elections for constitutional assemblies, Chávez went to plebiscite on seven occasions, obtaining a mean support of almost 55 percent, Correa did it five times, an average of once a year, and Morales three times, once every two years. The average support for Correa and Morales has been 65 percent. Bolivia and Ecuador traded interrupted presidencies and massive social protests for strong presidents fortified by serial popular acclamation. In Argentina, which in contrast to the three Andean countries shows no signs of autocratization, the Kirchners have not called for any plebiscites. However, both government and opposition have increasingly equated midterm elections to popular consultations about presidential performance, providing Argentine democracy a functional substitute of the plebiscitarian pattern in the three Andean countries.

Hegemonization

Despite the visible signs of autocratization in Venezuela and the more tenuous ones in Bolivia and Ecuador, the main victim of the natural resource curse in South America has not been the form of access to power but the form of exercise. In Argentina, Bolivia, Ecuador, and especially Venezuela, presidents have dominated the state (Corrales 2010; Conaghan 2011; Madrid 2011).[8] They have concentrated policymaking power at the expense of the Congress, and their performance has been subject to only nominal scrutiny by legislatures, courts, and nonpartisan agencies of oversight. A plebiscitarian hegemonic presidency is the extreme case combining maximum decision-making power, minimum oversight, and indefinite reelection. Although no real case shows the three attributes in full degree, Chávez, Correa, the Kirchners, and Morales have come closer to the ideal type than any other elected president in the history of their countries. If recurrent plebiscitarian ratification furnished governments with a strong majoritarian tone, hegemonization has made them distinctly antiminoritarian. The conventional way of measuring hegemonization—the tallying of presidential decrees—supports the notion that presidents Chávez and Néstor Kirchner governed without the Congress given their exorbitantly high decree tallies. However, qualitative assessment of executive-legislative relations provides more valid measures of hegemonization. In Venezuela, Ecuador, and to a lesser extent Argentina, Congress has delegated the governance of the national economy to the president. The cause of power delegation has not been executive coercion against legislators, which would have actually involved the autocratization of the regime, as it occurred in Peru under Fujimori in 1992. The proximate sources of hegemonization have been varied: lack of interest on issues of national scope among members of the ruling party, inability of the opposition to solve collective action problems, and a general shortage of appropriate technical background.

   In Venezuela, delegation occurred through three Leyes Habilitantes (2000, 2001, and 2007) that allowed Chávez to decide on his own the nationalization of hundreds of economic assets and redefine a substantial number of budget allocations. Almost no important economic policy decision has been shared with the opposition. Year after year, the Argentine Congress has granted Néstor and Cristina Kirchner extraordinary powers despite the extinction of any indications of social or political emergency. In the preparation of the national budget, the keystone of Argentina's economic legislation, Congress has repeatedly approved presidential proposals with artificially low projections of economic growth and revenue. Similarly, Chávez sent barely credible estimates for the price of oil. Since the Congress cannot attach strings to revenues that exceed estimations, national budgets approved by the Argentine and Venezuelan legislatures leave the presidents ample room for discretionary spending. Between 2004 and 2009, the Argentine president allocated an average $18 billion a year without legislative oversight (about twice the size of the budget for the Ministry of Public Works). In Venezuela, such discretionary spending amounted to 20 percent of total revenues (Corrales 2010). The decision to use the Central Bank's international reserves to repay foreign debt, one of the three most important economic decisions of the Cristina Kirchner government, was made by presidential decree (December 2009). However, Argentina under the Kirchners is a case of moderate hegemony. For instance, the nationalization of pension funds in 2008, one of the other key decisions, was extensively debated in Congress and approved with support from the Socialist party. In debating the 2009 law creating the Universal Family Allowances, the Argentine CCT program, minority parties showed a capacity to participate in law making unparalleled in Chávez's Venezuela. In March 2008, President Cristina Kirchner's attempt to further raise export duties on soybeans by presidential decree provoked such resistance that she had to transform the decree into a legislative proposal. Congress rejected the proposal by one vote, handed a tough defeat to the government, and in the process discovered that it could limit presidential authority. The ultimate source of these limits was rooted in society, although the Congress's greater ability to echo social resistance is an indication of hegemonic moderation that sets Argentina apart from the three Andean cases.

Plebiscitarian Hegemony, Delegative Democracy, Classical Populism, and Neopopulism

Due to their regimes of access and exercise of power, Venezuela, Ecuador, Bolivia, and Argentina form a special group of countries in South America. They are, to different degrees, *plebiscitarian hegemonies*. In the polar type of plebiscitarian hegemony, mechanisms of vertical accountability—by which citizens ratify or revoke the presidential mandate—operate with maximum frequency, whereas horizontal controls—the oversight by legislatures, courts, and comptrollers—are suspended indefinitely. Plebiscitarian access and hegemonic exercise are "functionally" connected. From the perspective of the plebiscitarian presidents and their supporters, the continual acclamation of presidential performance has logical and political priority over any other form of accountability. The electorate is the ultimate political tribunal, and its ongoing support makes the judgments of other branches of government irrelevant. With seven plebiscitarian ratifications and almost complete presidential control over the economy, Chávez's regime in Venezuela was the closest to the polar type. Argentina under the Kirchners, who have relied on informal substitutes for plebiscites and gained control over only a portion of economic policymaking, is the most moderate case in the group. Ecuador under Correa and Bolivia under Morales are intermediate cases.

Despite obvious similarities to delegative democracies, plebiscitarian hegemonies are a different type of regime (O'Donnell 1992). Delegative democracies, which in Guillermo O'Donnell's original conceptualization were exemplified by the regimes of Menem in Argentina and Collor in Brazil, were above all *democracies*. Plebiscitarian hegemonies, by contrast, may not be democratic. In Venezuela, access to power became less competitive over time and has been classified as a case of electoral authoritarianism (Levitsky and Way 2010). The concept of plebiscitarian hegemony characterizes mainly a form of exercise of power and deliberately contains minimal information about the form of access, which refers only to the nature and intensity or frequency of presidential elections. That single attribute about access is included in the concept because, hypothetically, the plebiscitarian component is functionally linked to the hyperpresidential form of exercise that defines the hegemonic type. Both attributes, hegemony and plebiscitarianism, are either complementary or have a common cause. Regime competitiveness, by contrast, has a separate source. Delegative democracies, originally associated with large-scale market reforms, included two attributes that marked a strong contrast with classical populism: they *de*-mobilized popular sectors, and dismantled the redistributive schemes created in the state-led development era. Plebiscitarian hegemonies, by contrast, have strong empirical connections both with the *re*-mobilization of popular sectors and economic redistribution, especially of the wealth created by the commodity boom.[9] Precisely because delegative democracies lacked the attributes of classical populism, O'Donnell rejected the characterization of the Menem, Collor, and Fujimori regimes as "neopopulists" (O'Donnell 1995). Delegative democracies also included rule by technical experts. By contrast, the plebiscitarian hegemonies of Venezuela, Bolivia, Ecuador, and Argentina have militated against technocrats. A common denominator between these cases has been the gradual depletion of human capital and technical knowledge in finance ministers, statistical agencies, central banks, and state-owned firms, which is opposite to the trend in Chile and Brazil.

Two forms of conceptualizing populism have dominated the literature on Latin American politics. Accordingly, the relation between plebiscitarian hegemony and populism depends on the type of populism. "Classical populism" is a sociopolitical coalition, a set of economic policies, or a combination of both, whereas "neopopulism" refers almost exclusively to a type of political leadership (Barr 2009; Weyland 2001). Neither variant of populism is a regime type, whereas plebiscitarian hegemony is *only* a regime type. Despite the absence of analytical connections between plebiscitarian hegemony and populism, empirical relations are crucial. According to the definition of neopopulism, which centrally includes a political leader who mobilizes large-scale popular support from the top-down, Bolivia under Morales is clearly not a case of neopopulism. Most social movements that joined the Movimiento al Socialismo (MAS; Movement toward Socialism) had become active years before the emergence of Evo Morales. These movements autonomously coordinated the selection of common leaders and preserved their identities under the new leadership. The role of MAS's electoral base in the rise of Morales is much closer to that of active citizens than to passive followers. The other attribute of neopopulism, the use of a high-voltage antiestablishment rhetoric as a mobilization strategy, is in fact shared by all four empirical cases of plebiscitarian hegemony. From Correa's *pelucones* (bigwigs) and Chávez's *burguesía pro-yanqui* (pro-yankee bourgeoisie) to Morales's *oligarquías* (oligarchies) and the Kirchners' *grupos concentrados* (special interests), all plebiscitarian presidents give their audiences an enemy who is the source of the country's evils, leaves no room for negotiation, and has to be engaged in a fight to the end. Intense antiestablishment appeals are so systematic within each case and so common across cases that the possibility of random coincidence should be ruled out. However, in the context of the explanation that will be advanced in the following sections, neopopulist rhetoric is largely "superstructural." While interesting for its recurrence over time and repetition across cases, neopopulist rhetoric plays only an accessory role in the underlying political dynamics and can be placed at the very end of a long causal chain made of more fundamental factors.

No definitional connections exist between classical populism and plebiscitarian hegemonies, for the former is a type of coalition and economic policy and the latter is a form of political regime. They are phenomena of different orders. Precisely for that reason, it is possible to study causal relations between them and, in particular, to assess whether coalitions and policies similar to those of classical populism are the causes behind the rise and consolidation of plebiscitarian hegemonies. Classical populism was a state-sponsored coalition of the first generations of factory workers and national firms producing consumption goods. Redistributive policies, especially from rural to urban sectors, expansion of social rights, and tariff protection would create the conditions for semiautarchic development. Economic winners of the model would secure the political success of the populist leaders. The source of classical populism was the intersection of large social and economic processes, both national and international. The slow but steady deterioration of the terms of trade for Latin American exports, combined with demographic, industrial, and urbanization trends that reached politically critical thresholds, created new coalitional possibilities, including certainly the populist one.

Plebiscitarian hegemony is the political regime that reflects the emergence and domination of a new type of social coalition. Like classical populism, the new coalition pivots around a social sector that is the creature of a long accumulation of economic and social processes, the incorporation of which depends on an inflection point in export prices. However, the macroprocesses that came together to create the political room for new coalitions have very little in common with those of classical populism. Classical populism was an industrial coalition. The coalition behind plebiscitarian hegemonies is that of "rentier populism."

Rentier Populism: The Theory

In the extreme case of rentier populism, a caricature with no empirical instances in any place of the world or moment in history, only two actors form the ruling alliance: the government and the informal sectors. The government is the only owner of a natural resource that commands a high price on international markets. The government distributes the revenue from the natural resource to the informal sectors, which comprise a majority of the population. Exploiting the resource requires no substantial investments within the politically relevant time horizon. Either the necessary technology and physical capital are not expensive or they had been expropriated from a private investor. In exchange for redistribution, the informal sector provides votes to secure political victories and street mobilization to intimidate economic and political losers. The rentier populist coalition fully integrates itself into the international commodities market, but it refrains from participating in financial markets. It needs the former as much as it can dispense with the latter. Foreign trade is the fundamental source of rent, whereas international capital is an unnecessary source of conditionalities.

The economic and political bases of rentier populism define its structure of accountability. Vertical accountability is the most affordable way of staying in power because the informal sector vote is the least expensive to buy. The alternative to ignoring the majority and ruling through repression has higher costs with more uncertain political benefits. Like any other dominant coalition, rentier populism has no spontaneous reasons to set checks and balances on presidential authority. The groups most interested in horizontal accountability are those least likely to become partners in the dominant coalition and are most worried about discretionary use of political power. These include individuals who have made heavy investments in physical and human capital, require long maturation periods, and present the most appealing targets for expropriation. The effectiveness of groups demanding horizontal accountability is a function of their relevance within the political economy of the dominant coalition. When rentier populism rules, the effectiveness of demands for horizontal accountability is negligible. Rentier populist rulers do not need the minorities in the formal economy to sustain them, and the informal majority only requires the plebiscitarian mechanism to secure the uninterrupted flow of transfers. Plebiscitarian hegemony is a structure of accountability that is tailor made for rentier populism: complete deactivation of horizontal controls (the hegemonic component) and high frequency of vertical ratifications (the plebiscitarian component). The rentier populist coalition causes plebiscitarian hegemonies.

Rentier populism and plebiscitarian hegemonies appear undefeatable. So long as initial conditions hold, they result in high prices for the natural resource, low exploitation costs, and substantial size of the informal sectors. A small change in any of these conditions places a lot of pressure on the viability of the coalition and can provoke the collapse of the regime. If the international prices of the commodity fall below the threshold required for revenues to match the costs of the coalition, or the size of the informal sectors shrink so that they can no longer secure electoral success, it will be the end of the political regime. A new coalition replaces the old one, or the hegemonic president expands the coalition to sectors in the formal economy that demand institutional insurance against predation, for instance, effectiveness of legislatures in the economic policy process. Finally, if the costs of the technology for exploiting the natural resource become higher than the savings rate of the economy, rentier populism will be forced to end its isolation from international financial markets and, in exchange for fresh capital inflows, accept conditionalities that will curb the hegemonic features of the regime. Strong while the conditions for rentier populism last, plebiscitarian hegemonies are extremely fragile in the face of small variations in the parameters of its political economy.

Rentier Populism II: Comparative Political Origins

At the end of the twentieth century rentier populism was an unimaginable phenomenon in Latin America. One of its components, the informal sectors, was available, but the other, the rent from natural resources, was politically irrelevant. The commodity boom of the early twenty-first century contributed the remaining piece of the rentier populist alliance. However, only Venezuela, Bolivia, Ecuador, and Argentina built it. The reason for the divergence is that between the availability of the basic economic and demographic inputs and the effective construction of a new dominant alliance, a constellation of local economic and political conditions refracted the coalition-building process, preventing populism in some cases and encouraging it in others.

The critical political decision in the process of building a rentier-populist coalition is whether or not to expropriate the booming natural resource. In the ruler's cost-benefit analysis, the international price of the commodity, the scale of the national endowment, and the size of the informal sector define the potential reward. The costs, on the other hand, are determined by the damage to the country's reputation in international capital markets, and the resistance of national political forces that fear the risks rentier populism pose to their survival. These costs are shaped by financial markets and party systems, which are also structural constraints. These structures, however, are substantially more malleable and unstable than the ones that define the incentives, the rather fixed physical structure of the economy and the slow-moving social structure of the underlying population. Party system volatility in fact became endemic in the Andes and also Argentina by the turn of the century.

Financial reputation costs are especially high in countries with a long track record of receptiveness to foreign investment and debt repayment. All Andean countries are endowed with enough reserves of mineral wealth for expropriation to be a tempting political option in boom times. In Colombia, Peru, and especially Chile, the financial reputation costs have provided antipopulist immunization: flows of foreign investment are considerably higher than the expected gains of capture. This condition has been crucial in the Peruvian case, for in contrast to Colombia and Chile, it meets all the other requirements for the rise and consolidation of the plebiscitarian hegemonic variant of the Left. President Humala, who would otherwise be a natural architect of a rentier populist coalition, probably concluded that he had received too precious a legacy of financial reputation from the ortho-dox governments of Alejandro Toledo (2001–2006) and Alan García (2006–2011), which managed to achieve and keep investment grade status. In the opposite extreme, the physical structure of the Argentine economy is considerably less attractive for rentier political ventures. Nevertheless, by the time commodities started to boom, the financial reputation costs of capture had become negligible. In 2001, the Argentine government defaulted on a gigantic volume of foreign debt and doomed the country to years of abysmal credit ratings. For Néstor Kirchner, refraining from the rentier populist temptation would have only meant taking the first steps in a necessarily long process for rebuilding reputation, the divi-dends of which would have started to flow well beyond the politically relevant horizon. When Morales and Correa became presidents, credit ratings in Bolivia and Ecuador fell to all-time lows. For the fiscal needs of their coalitional proj-ects, expropriation was much more effective than patient reconstruction of their financial reputations.

Party systems, the other source of costs for the leader considering the construc-tion of rentier populism, prevent expropriation if the incumbent party has a solid constituency in the formal economy or the opposition parties have enough organi-zational strength (Levitsky and Roberts 2011b, 2011c; Madrid 2011; Flores-Macías 2010). The economic recession of 1998–2002 was a watershed moment for party systems in South America. The political parties that had implemented neoliberal reforms lost vital reserves of political capital. Only two established left-wing par-ties had remained in the opposition during the era of market reforms: the Brazilian PT and the Uruguayan Frente Amplio. Free from the blame for economic pains, they supplied a fresh but institutionalized post-neoliberal option to the public. In Chile, the economic crisis was mild (the recession was over by 2000), neoliberal reform did not cause disappointment, and, although they were partners in the ruling coalition, the Partido Socialista (Socialist Party) also became a credible post-neoliberal choice. Once the PT, the Frente Amplio, and the Chilean Socialists gained power, the price for the creation of a rentier populist alliance would have been the destruction of their historic ties with formal labor. A more profitable course of action was the gradual incorporation of the informal sectors as an extra layer to their established constituencies. In Venezuela, Bolivia, and Ecuador, when the economic slowdown began, party systems were already experiencing a deep and protracted crisis caused by cartelization and corruption. In Argentina, the representation crisis actually followed economic recession. In all four cases, however, party system volatility peaked and, with the exception of the Argentine Peronistas, stable political parties virtually disappeared (Coppedge 2007; Flores-Macías 2010, 423; Calvo and Murillo 2013). From that moment on, whoever became president would rule without organized opposition. Political barriers to the emergence of rentier populism vanished as parties lost the strength to resist expropriation. In Argentina, Bolivia, and Ecuador, the flip side of party deinstitutionalization under economic dislocation was mass praetorianism, especially informal sector mobilization. Massive street protests presented Kirchner, Morales, and Correa with a unique opportunity for moving beyond the strictly economic incorporation adopted in Brazil, Chile, and Uruguay, to try the *political* incorporation of the informal sectors. Informal sectors became key allies in the electoral coalition, providing the base for plebiscitarian ratifications, as well as in the government coalition, supplying control of the streets and intimidation of the opposition.

Cases and Mechanisms of Rentier Populism

In 2001 the Chávez government decided that the state-owned Petróleos de Venezuela (PDVSA; National Petroleum Corporation of Venezuela) should be the majority shareholder in all Venezuelan oil fields, which affected thirty-three multinational companies with operations in the Orinoco Basin. Two of them, Total and Eni, left the country. A year later, Chávez raised royalties on private oil companies from 1 percent to 30 percent and taxes from 34 percent to 50 percent. A presidential decree of 2007 raised the floor of PDVSA's share in exploitation joint ventures from 51 percent to 78 percent. Increased control over the flow of oil rents allowed for the creation of the Misiones Bolivarianas, Chávez's strategy of informal sector incorporation. In fact, PDVSA, rather than state ministries, has administered the missions. The programs created between 2003 and 2004 included Misión Robinson and Misión Ribas to target literacy and basic education, Misión Barrio Adentro to provide health services, and Misión Mercal to provide subsidized food.

In Bolivia, Morales nationalized the country's hydrocarbon resources four months after assuming the presidency. In a primarily symbolic action, he sent troops to occupy the Tarija gas fields, the second largest reserves in Latin America. Petrobras, the Brazilian oil giant, was the most affected firm, as its facilities came under the control of the Bolivian state company Yacimientos Petrolíferos Fiscales Bolivianos (YPFB; National Oil Fields of Bolivia). At the same time, Morales repurchased the remaining privately held shares of YPFB and transformed the various drilling projects from joint ventures, in which private firms received a proportion of profits, to service contracts based on flat fees. Taxes also rose from 18 percent to 82 percent, reversing the division of earnings between the state and private firms. In relative terms, no government benefited from nationalization and the commodity boom like Bolivia's. Revenues from mineral royalties grew 929 percent from 1997 to 2007 and hydrocarbon taxes 626 percent. The key political consideration behind hydrocarbon nationalization was the incorporation of the informal sector. Revenue from gas rents has financed the creation of the Bono Juancito Pinto, a family allowance of $29 for each child enrolled in primary school (October 2006), the Renta Dignidad, a payment of $340 to all seniors (April 2007), and the Bono Juana Azurduy, which gives $257 to pregnant women and mothers who undergo periodic medical checkups (May 2009). Despite the country's large oil deposits, the government of Ecuador was not dependent on mineral rents in the 1990s. Oil companies paid an average 20 percent of their revenues in taxes, which was far from enough to sustain a populist coalition. Yet, first as Finance Minister of Alfredo Palacio's transitional government (2005–2006) and later as president, Correa raised hydrocarbon taxes, which reached 50 percent in 2006 and 80 percent in 2007. As a result, Petrobras decided to gradually leave the country, and almost every other multinational firm stopped new investment. The new taxes strengthened the Correa administration's fiscal position and allowed it to launch the Bono de Desarrollo Humano, a redistribution program that covers 1.5 million households or 45 percent of the population.

With much smaller reserves, Bolivia and Ecuador cannot reach the degree of rentierism of Venezuela. With an economy that is more diversified than Venezuela's and larger than those of Bolivia and Ecuador, Argentina remains the least dependent on rents. Further, its resource, land, has natural barriers against state expropriation and exploitation. Yet the state can still extract massive rents by setting up a monopsony for agricultural products, as it did under Perón in the late 1940s, or by taxing exports. Although President Carlos Menem eliminated export taxes in the 1990s, transitional president Eduardo Duhalde reinstated them in March 2002 under the name *retenciones*. Originally set at 5 percent for processed soybeans and 10 percent for unprocessed, the *retenciones* quickly rose to 20 percent in order to fund unemployment benefits for almost two million people. President Néstor Kirchner maintained the tariff levels and the allocation of revenues almost until the end of his term. Ahead of the 2007 presidential elections, Kirchner raised duties to 24 percent for processed soybeans and 27 percent for unprocessed to subsidize consumption in low-income sectors. After his wife Cristina won the race in October, tariffs rose again to 32 percent and 34 percent to cover the debts incurred during the campaign. Soybean rents, which the central government has refused to share with the provinces, have brought Argentina closer to a rentier state than ever before.

No case perfectly fits the ideal type of rentier populism. During the commodity boom, however, Argentina, Bolivia, Ecuador, and Venezuela have moved closer to the ideal type, while Chile, Brazil, and Uruguay have moved away. Argentina, Bolivia, Ecuador, and Venezuela also differ among themselves in terms of proximity to the extreme case. The key point from the perspective of causal inference is that the degree of rentier populism in each case is concomitant with the extent of plebiscitarian hegemony. Venezuela, the case that best approximates rentier populism, is also the closest to plebiscitarian hegemony. Argentina is the case with the most tenuous attributes of both types, while Bolivia and Ecuador are intermediate cases. But correlation is not causation. Since the number of cases is too small for statistical analysis, it is crucial to find causal mechanisms, that is, processes that connect rentier populist coalitions to the generation of the institutional features of plebiscitarian hegemony.

Mechanisms that generate plebiscitarian hegemony can be distinguished into two types, depending on whether the rentier populist coalition is still fighting to control natural resources, or it has already consolidated as the dominant group. If rentier populism is in the formative process, rulers will treat institutions— legislatures, courts, laws—that block their path as an enemy threatening the coalition's viability. Although the Argentine constitution grants taxation power only to Congress, the two increases in export duties on soybeans in 2007 were decided by presidential decree. The economic crisis was over, but the financial needs of a plebiscitarian year persuaded the president to resort to emergency powers outlined in the Código Aduanero, a legacy of the military dictatorship. The construction of rentier populism requires hegemonic powers. Once rentier populism has consolidated in power, two mechanisms generate the features of plebiscitarian hegemony. The rising living standards of the informal sectors made possible by the boom and redistribution encourage presidents to intensify the use of plebiscites. In turn, popular ratification emboldens presidents to wrest remaining powers away from the other branches of government and portray resistances to hegemony as antidemocratic conspiracies. The string of ratifications dispels any doubt about the validity of the majority's verdict. Frequent plebiscitarian consultations extend a blank check for the use of hegemonic powers. The other mechanism is fiscal.

When prices are sufficiently high, rents from natural resources cover all the coalition's expenses. State ownership means the government has to negotiate with no one to secure the flow of revenue and grants rulers independence from any group, national or international, that might otherwise demand institutional quality in exchange for taxation. The relative simplicity of the rentier populist coalition and political economy explains the absence of demands for checks and balances on executive authority. The coalition of classical populism was a more heterogeneous construction, and its partners were more organized. Its political economy encouraged more sophistication of policies and institutions. The factory workers of classical populism were incorporated into unions that organized members along functional lines and on a permanent basis. The solidarity of the informal sectors is intermittent and, at most, territorially based. Organization provided industrial workers with tools, like strikes, that could inflict real damage on the political economy. The informal sectors can, at most, take to the streets, but not threaten the exploitation of natural resources or the fiscal position of the government. To maintain power, classical populist governments had to worry about productivity while balancing the interests of workers and national industrial firms. To survive, classical populism developed complex institutions—labor codes, collective bargaining mechanisms, technical institutes, and the expanded welfare state. In contrast, rentier populism relies only on plebiscites and the minimalist welfare state.

Venezuela, Bolivia, and Ecuador are more extreme cases of plebiscitarian hegemony than Argentina, precisely because of differences in the complexity of the underlying coalition and political economy. While Chávez and Morales have organized their supporters along territorial lines, the Kirchners revived collective bargaining between management and formal labor, thus enhancing institutional quality. While traditional political parties disappeared in the Andean countries, Peronism in Argentina survived the 2002 crisis and maintained its dominance. The crisis, however, marked the beginning of the party's incorporation of the informal sector as a central partner. Under Menem, the informal sector was a peripheral, purely electoral member of the coalition and incorporation was based on decentralized clientelism. Under the Kirchners, the party has become an amalgamation of classical and rentier populism. Due to the diversity of the economy and the strength of unions, Peronism has retained some of its industrial character, an antibody against extreme forms of plebiscitarian hegemony. Further, the fact that the natural resource in Argentina is land, which is privately held and very fragmented, has forced the Peronists to engage in battles over rents that the Andean rentier populists could avoid. With the stroke of a pen, Chávez and Morales gained full control of hydrocarbon rents by converting joint venture drilling contracts into service contracts with fixed payments. The functional equivalent in Argentina, the 2008 presidential decree raising export duties on soybeans, not only met with a level of resistance that the Kirchners could not overcome, but reinvigorated the Congress, which until then had been a rubber stamp for the executive by the admission of Peronist and opposition legislators alike.

Conclusions

The price boom of natural resources in the first decade of the twenty-first century has been a blessing for all South American economies. For some political regimes, however, it was an institutional curse. In Venezuela, Ecuador, Bolivia, and Argentina, the boom prompted the emergence of rentier populism, a new type of political coalition based on the economic and political incorporation of the informal sector and funded by windfall gains from commodity exports. Based on a new fiscal structure, rentier populism in turn fostered the intensification of plebiscitarian mechanisms of vertical accountability and neutralized constraints of horizontal accountability.

At the end of the twentieth century, Latin American countries faced the twin challenges of economic growth and poverty reduction. The left turn in South America has centered on the incorporation of informal sectors through minimalist welfare states based on conditional cash transfers. Incorporation marks the recovery of social rights that had been lost during long decades of crises and structural reform. The transfers of the minimalist welfare state partially address the problem of growth by incentivizing education and health, thus raising productivity. These improvements, however, are not sufficient to achieve sustained economic growth. Growth requires large investments in infrastructure, modern technology, and physical capital. In Brazil, Chile, and Uruguay, the left turn, in addition to minimalist welfare states, sponsored institutional improvements to attract the necessary investments. In contrast, in the cases of rentier populism, the commodity boom has enabled governments to ignore the complex task of institution building. Venezuela, Bolivia, Ecuador, and to a lesser extent Argentina, have constructed minimalist welfare states without addressing the problem of productivity. Barrels of oil and good harvests have postponed the agenda of sustainable growth. In the process, they shut off one of the most powerful sources of political accountability. Rentier populism also endangers the long-term prospects of social citizenship. Under rentier populism, social rights last only as long as the boom. And if economic history has taught anything, it is that no boom lasts forever.

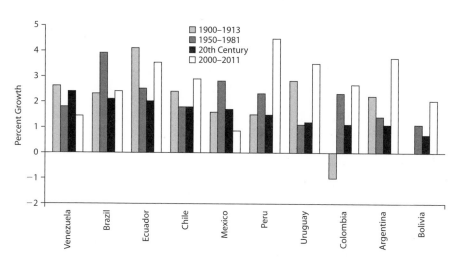

Figure 4A.1. Average Annual Per Capita GDP Growth, Selected Periods, 1900–2011. *Source:* Montevideo-Oxford Latin American Economic History Database, CEPAL

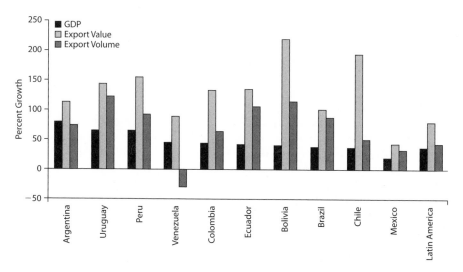

Figure 4A.2. GDP and Export Growth, 2002–2010. *Source:* CEPA

NOTES

For detailed comments to an earlier version of this piece I am especially grateful to Jorge Domínguez, Steve Levitsky, and María Victoria Murillo. I also benefited from comments by Natalio Botana, Gerry Munck, Juan Carlos Torre, and participants at the Constructing Democratic Governance in Latin America conference organized by the Inter-American Dialogue in Washington, DC, on October 6–7, 2011. Aaron Watanabe provided superb research assistance.

1. See figure 4A.1 for a comparison of economic growth across decades.

2. Raúl Prebisch (1901–1986) is the Argentine economist who put forward the notion that the terms of trade for Latin American primary products would deteriorate gradually but irreversibly over time, and founded the "structural" approach to economic analysis, a forerunner of dependency theory. His intellectual influence reached an almost hegemonic peak when he served as head of the Economic Commission for Latin America and the Caribbean (1948–1962) but it lasted until the debt crises of the 1980s and "lost decade" of the 1990s.

3. See figure 4A.2 in Appendix for growth of exports and income across countries in 2002–2010.

4. The statement should be qualified, for the "Dutch Disease" is an economic curse. This chapter will only focus on political repercussions.

5. CCTs are small payments to poor families in exchange for the commitment of school attendance and regular medical checkups.

6. Huntington 1968.

7. Author's interview, June 3, 2001.

8. For "hegemony" as used in this section, see Botana 2006.

9. These connections are strictly empirical and subject to test; they are not analytical because mobilization strategies and economic policy are not part of a purely institutional definition.

REFERENCES

Barr, Robert. 2009. "Populists, Outsiders and Anti-establishment Politics." *Party Politics* 15 (1): 29–58.

Botana, Natalio. 2006. *Poder y hegemonía: El régimen político después de la crisis.* Buenos Aires: Emecé.

Calvo, Ernesto, and María Victoria Murillo. 2013. "Argentina: Democratic Consolidation, Partisan Dealignment, and Institutional Weakness." In *Constructing Democratic Governance in Latin America*, edited by Jorge I. Domínguez and Michael Shifter. 4th ed. Baltimore: Johns Hopkins University Press.

Collier, Ruth Berins, and David Collier. 1991. *Shaping the Political Arena: Critical Junctures, the Labor Movement and Regime Dynamics in Latin America.* Princeton: Princeton University Press.

Conaghan, Catherine M. 2011. "Ecuador: Rafael Correa and the Citizens' Revolution." In *The Resurgence of the Latin American Left*, edited by Steven Levitsky and Kenneth M. Roberts, 260–82. Baltimore: Johns Hopkins University Press.

Coppedge, Michael. 2007. "Continuity and Change in Latin American Party Systems." *Taiwan Journal of Democracy* 3 (2): 119–49.

Corrales, Javier. 2010. "The Repeating Revolution: Chávez's New Politics and Old Economics." In *Leftist Governments in Latin America: Successes and Shortcomings*, edited by Kurt Weyland, Raúl L. Madrid, and Wendy Hunter, 28–56. Cambridge: Cambridge University Press.

———. 2013. "Constitutional Rewrites in Latin America, 1987–2009." In *Constructing Democratic Governance in Latin America*, edited by Jorge I. Domínguez and Michael Shifter. 4th ed. Baltimore: Johns Hopkins University Press.

Dahl, Robert. 1972. *Polyarchy: Participation and Opposition*. New Haven: Yale University Press.

Flores-Macías, Gustavo A. 2010. "Statist vs. Pro-Market: Explaining Leftist Governments' Economic Policies in Latin America." *Comparative Politics* 42 (4): 413–43.

Germani, Gino. 1971. *Política y sociedad en una época de transición: De la sociedad tradicional a la sociedad de masas*. 4th ed. Buenos Aires: Paidós.

Huntington, Samuel 1968. *Political Order in Changing Societies*. New Haven: Yale University Press.

Karl, Terry Lynn. 1987. "Petroleum and Political Pacts: The Transition to Democracy in Venezuela." *Latin American Research Review* 22 (1): 63–94.

Kaufman, Robert. 2011. "The Political Left, the Export Boom, and the Populist Temptation." In *The Resurgence of the Latin American Left*, edited by Steven Levitsky and Kenneth M. Roberts, 93–116. Baltimore: Johns Hopkins University Press.

Levitsky, Steven, and Kenneth M. Roberts. 2011a. "Democracy, Development, and the Left." In *The Resurgence of the Latin American Left*, edited by Steven Levitsky and Kenneth M. Roberts, 399–427. Baltimore: Johns Hopkins University Press.

———. 2011b. "Latin America's 'Left Turn': A Framework for Analysis." In *The Resurgence of the Latin American Left*, edited by Steven Levitsky and Kenneth M. Roberts, 1–28. Baltimore: Johns Hopkins University Press.

———. 2011c. "Conclusion: Democracy, Development and the Left." In *The Resurgence of the Latin American Left*, edited by Steven Levitsky and Kenneth M. Roberts, 399–427. Baltimore: Johns Hopkins University Press.

Levitsky, Steven, and Lucan Way. 2010. *Competitive Authoritarianism: Hybrid Regimes after the Cold War*. New York: Cambridge University Press.

Madrid, Raúl. 2011. "Bolivia: Origins and Policies of the Movimiento al Socialismo." In *The Resurgence of the Latin American Left*, edited by Steven Levitsky and Kenneth M. Roberts, 239–59. Baltimore: Johns Hopkins University Press.

Madrid, Raúl, Wendy Hunter, and Kurt Weyland. 2010. "The Politics and Performance of the Contestatory and Moderate Left." In *Leftist Governments in Latin America: Successes and Shortcomings*, edited by Kurt Weyland, Raúl L. Madrid, and Wendy Hunter. Cambridge: Cambridge University Press.

Murillo, María Victoria, Virginia Oliveros, and Milan Vaishnav. 2011. "Economic Constraints and Presidential Agency." In *The Resurgence of the Latin American Left*, edited by Steven Levitsky and Kenneth M. Roberts, 52–70. Baltimore: Johns Hopkins University Press.

O'Donnell, Guillermo. 1992. "¿Democracia Delegativa?" *Cuadernos del CLAEH* 17 (61): 25–40.

———. 1995. "Democracias y Exclusión." *Ágora: Cuaderno de Estudios Políticos* 2 (5): 180–85.

Posada-Carbó, Eduardo. 2013. "Colombia: Democratic Governance amidst an Armed Conflict." In *Constructing Democratic Governance in Latin America*, edited by Jorge I. Domínguez and Michael Shifter. 4th ed. Baltimore: Johns Hopkins University Press.

Valenzuela, Arturo. 2004. "Latin American Presidencies Interrupted." *Journal of Democracy* 15 (4): 5–19.

Weyland, Kurt. 2001. "Clarifying a Contested Concept: Populism in the Study of Latin American Politics." *Comparative Politics* 34 (1): 1–22.

———. 2009. "The Rise of Latin America's Two Lefts: Insights from Rentier State Theory." *Comparative Politics* 4 (2): 145–64.

Weyland, Kurt, Raúl L. Madrid, and Wendy Hunter, eds. 2010. *Leftist Governments in Latin America: Successes and Shortcomings*. Cambridge: Cambridge University Press.

PART II / Country Studies

CHAPTER FIVE

Argentina

Democratic Consolidation, Partisan Dealignment,
and Institutional Weakness

Ernesto Calvo and María Victoria Murillo

A month before the political and economic crisis of December 2001, trust in Argentina's political system was at an all-time low. According to the Gallup survey, 83 percent of respondents held negative or very negative views of political parties, 89 percent reported a lack of trust in the presidency, and 90 percent did not trust Congress. However, a majority of respondents still preferred democracy to any alternative form of government. The contrast became an object of much debate (Portantiero 2002; Torre 2003). How could Argentines identify democracy as the only game in town while those in charge of carrying out the democratic mandate—politicians and their parties—were consistently distrusted and held responsible for everything that went wrong with the country shortly thereafter? The Argentine public's support for democratic institutions was, in short, independent of the dismal perceptions of their efficacy.

This trend became even more apparent as the economic and political collapse unfolded into 2002; satisfaction with Argentina's governance fell further without damaging support for democracy as a concept. That year, Latinobarómetro found that 85 percent of Argentines supported democracy as a form of government, yet a paltry 8 percent were satisfied with their government. By 2010, this figure had increased to 50 percent. Throughout the decade, support for democracy in general remained high at 87 percent. This chapter seeks to describe how broad public support for democracy coexists with partisan dealignment—or a loss of voter-party identity—and institutional weakness, explaining the volatile satisfaction levels among Argentine voters.

Thirty years after transitioning from the latest military regime, there is neither an indication of a return to authoritarianism nor any credible threat to democratic stability in Argentina.[1] The military has been effectively extricated from the political system, and no former authoritarian elites remain embedded in the state bureaucracy or compete within Argentina's political parties. Leaders of the latest military administration have been prosecuted, and the economic and social policies of the regime quickly dismantled. Democratic consolidation has been accompanied by a decline in the partisan identification of Argentine voters as well as political elites. Over the last thirty years, traditional parties have lost much of their long-term constituencies, allowing elites to become more flexible and pragmatic in their search for viable electoral partners.

Two main parties have dominated Argentina's electoral arena for most of the twentieth century: the Radicals, Unión Cívica Radical (UCR; Radical Civic Union) and the Peronists, Partido Justicialista (PJ; Judicialist Party). The former, created in 1890, grew as a moderate political party representing the middle classes. The latter, created by President Juan Domingo Perón in 1947, grew into a multiclass party with strong labor support in the more developed provinces and a conservative constituency in the smaller, less developed ones. Yet competition between the Radicals and Peronists has since given way to a multiplicity of alliances and coalitions competing at both the provincial and federal levels. Partisan dealignment has been accompanied by the weakening of political allegiances among voters, who are now less likely to identify with major parties or readily distinguish the ideological location of candidates and are unable to anticipate the policy choices of party elites and government officials (table 5.1).

Political institutions remain weak (Levitsky and Murillo 2005) and prone to alteration at the first sign of trouble or in response to mood swings by the executive or state governors. Since democratization in 1983, the president has been elected under different electoral rules (or interpretation of those rules) in four out of the seven presidential elections.[2] Local constitutions and electoral processes have changed multiple times in every Argentine province, relaxing term limits, modifying the number of districts, redesigning municipal and departmental boundaries, as well as altering registration rules, nomination procedures, and electoral formulas (Calvo and Escolar 2005). The composition of the Supreme Court has been significantly altered three times, and new procedures are now in place for the appointment of local, federal, and Supreme Court justices (Iaryczower et al.

Table 5.1.   Estimates of Party Identification for the Peronist
and Radical Parties

Year	Sample Size	Party ID PJ (%)	Party ID UCR (%)
1985	1504	32.3	16.4
1994	2458	14.1	11.5
2001	401	11.0	4.0
2003	411	5.4	3.0
2010	1410	9.5	3.3

Sources: We thank Noam Lupu (2011) for the data. The 1985 data is from CID (national), the 1994 is from Sofres-Ibope (province of Buenos Aires), the 2001 and 2003 are from Fara y Asociados (Greater Buenos Aires), and the 2010 is from LAPOP (national).

2006; Leiras et al. 2011). Consequently, while support for democracy has increased, institutional stability has remained elusive.

These three disparate phenomena—democratic consolidation, partisan dealignment, and institutional weakness—jointly characterize politics in Argentina today. Consolidation has not been accomplished through programmatic party politics accompanied by robust governance institutions, as was expected in the early 1980s. When finally given the opportunity to compete in elections without fear of military intervention, political parties did not deepen their programmatic linkages to voters. Instead, thirty years of active local and national rivalry have weakened the Radical party. In the case of the Peronists, factionalism has been transformed into outright competition between alliances within the party. While democratic consolidation has halted the regime instability that characterized Argentina during most of the twentieth century, the coalitional conflicts that underpinned such volatility remain unresolved. Indeed, they have fostered the rapid creation and destruction of political institutions as well as the serial renewal of public policies. Nevertheless, despite these difficulties, democracy remains the only agreed-upon option.

Democracy, Breakdown, Democracy, Breakdown . . .

In *The Third Wave of Democratization*, Samuel Huntington noted that, rather than transitioning between democratic and authoritarian regimes, *continual alternation itself* characterized Argentina's political regime (1993). Indeed, for much of the twentieth century, Argentina experienced frequent vacillation between military regimes supported by traditional agro-based economic elites and democratic regimes headed by elected Radical or Peronist presidents.

The fifty years of political instability that eroded institutional capacity and defined the relationship between the military and the state began with the coup d'état against Unión Cívica Radical (UCR; Radical Civic Union) President Hipólito Irigoyen on September 6, 1930 (Spiller and Tommasi 2007; Scartascini et al. 2010). From the institutionalization of universal suffrage for adult males in 1912 until the democratic transition led by Raul Alfonsín (UCR, 1983–1989), Argentina had eleven presidents, five elected and six military, and a total of four democratization efforts.[3]

During democratic periods, party competition was dominated by two loosely organized political coalitions, the Peronists and the Radicals. The Peronist Justicialista Party (PJ) emerged in 1947 from a coalition of urban workers in the most developed areas of the country and local bosses in the most rural provinces.[4] The main opposition to Peronism throughout this period was the Radical Civic Union (UCR), a centrist party founded in the late nineteenth century that represented an urban constituency concentrated in the metropolitan provinces of Buenos Aires, Santa Fe, and Córdoba.[5] The UCR dominated the electoral arena from 1912 until 1946. Peronists, meanwhile, won all executive elections in which they were allowed to run from 1946 through to 1976.

While successful in overthrowing democratically elected elites, each military coup d'état failed to produce electorally viable, conservative alternatives capable of successfully competing with the two parties (Gibson 1996). With every new democratization effort, political and bureaucratic elites tied to the military were removed from government posts. Similarly, with each democratic breakdown, political and bureaucratic elites appointed by the Peronists and Radicals were deposed and their Supreme Court appointments revoked. The alternation between elected and authoritarian elites resulted in high rates of bureaucratic and judicial turnover, in addition to significant institutional instability at every level of the state apparatus. Such variability impaired economic performance, triggering stop-and-go cycles of economic growth, bursts of high inflation, and a political business cycle causing dramatic fluctuations in salaries and prices with every authoritarian reversal and democratic transition.[6]

. . . and Finally Democracy

The victory of UCR candidate Raul R. Alfonsín in 1983 signaled the first electoral defeat of the Peronist party and an end to the cycle of military coups, ushering in an unprecedented period of stable, democratic rule. The dramatic social, economic, and military failures of the last authoritarian regime[7] discredited the armed forces and helped foster broad public support for liberal democratic values (Catterberg 1991). The trials carried out during the Alfonsín administration were critical in exposing the human rights violations of the military junta. The trials led to the incarceration of former authoritarian rulers, while their crimes were publicized in the *"Nunca Más"* (Never Again) report drafted by the Comisión Nacional sobre la Desaparición de Personas (CONADEP; National Commission on the Disappearance of Persons).[8]

Despite several small-scale military rebellions in the 1980s as well as setbacks in pursuing lower level officials for crimes committed during the authoritarian period, these new democratic institutions proved surprisingly robust. Democracy survived the hyperinflation crisis of 1989, the resignation of two presidents, extensive economic policy reforms, and the political and economic meltdown of 2001–2002. The early years of democratization were also accompanied by significant social and policy changes, restoring basic social and political rights. Several important legislative changes also occurred during this same period, including the derogation of a military amnesty law and the establishment of antitorture legislation. Socially, the democratization process was accompanied by a renaissance of civil society and high levels of political activity (O'Donnell et al. 1986).

Economically, this period witnessed one of the most dramatic boom-and-bust cycles in Argentina's history. Argentina experienced a sharp economic downturn, triggered by the debt crisis in 1982; hyperinflation between 1989 and 1991; rapid economic growth between 1993 and 1997; a sharp recession and economic collapse in 2001; a debt default and the retraction of international credit; then six years of the fastest economic growth in a century. Each of these economic cycles contributed to the partisan dealignment and continued institutional weakness.

Party Politics after Democratization

The new democratic period was characterized by significant changes in party organization and competition. With the death of Juan Domingo Perón in 1974, the dominant Argentine political party of the postwar years initiated major organizational changes shaping its recruitment strategy, socioeconomic base, and political orientation. Similarly, the death of Ricardo Balbín in 1981 deprived the UCR of its most important historical leader of the postwar years and ensured the emergence of a new generation of Radical party leaders gravitating around the figure of President Raul R. Alfonsín.

The defeat of Peronist candidate Ítalo A. Lúder by Alfonsín (UCR) in 1983 ushered in expectations of a "third historical movement" among Radical party politicians and energized voters.[9] The electoral defeat also triggered the first significant realignment within the Peronist PJ, which in just two years would retire most of its old guard in favor of a new party faction (the self-denominated Renovadores). This new generation of Peronist leaders included Antonio Cafiero and José Manuel de la Sota, respectively of the wealthy provinces of Buenos Aires and Córdoba, and future president Carlos S. Menem, a pragmatic politician from the poor, northern province of La Rioja.

The congressional election of 1987 marked the return of Peronist electoral dominance, this time led by the rising Renovadores. Under the guidance of Antonio Cafiero, the PJ initiated a period of *aggiornamento*, displacing union members and party bureaucrats with an emerging class of professional politicians and territorial brokers (Levitsky 2003). As the Peronists regrouped around their new leaders, high inflation and low growth led to a sharp decline in the public's support for President Alfonsín. With inflation levels reaching three digits, food riots broke out in the largest cities during May 1989. Early presidential elections and the resignation of Raul Alfonsín then returned a Peronist presidency, this time under Carlos S. Menem.

Unlike the Peronist PJ, which saw electoral defeat as an opportunity to reinvigorate the party and energize its base, the early resignation of Raul Alfonsín failed to force equally significant realignments in the UCR. The defeat of 1989 signaled the beginning of a slow but steady decline in the political importance of this historical party, a process accelerated by the 2001 economic crisis.

Party Fragmentation and Voter Dealignment in the Democratic Period

With the election of Carlos S. Menem in 1989, the Renovadores faction consolidated their control of the PJ. Economically, President Menem quickly reversed his early campaign promises and implemented market-oriented economic reforms (Stokes 2001). Reforms included establishing a currency board that pegged the peso to the US dollar, dramatic trade liberalization, the privatization of most state-owned companies and social security, and measures to deregulate the economy and make labor markets more flexible. The economic right turn, however, faced significant resistance from Peronist constituencies in the metropolitan areas. To strengthen the reformist coalition, Menem sought the programmatic support of a rising conservative party, the Unión del Centro Democrático (UCeDé;

Union of the Democratic Center). Within the Peronist base, Menem sought to strengthen the importance of territorial leaders by granting them the distribution of workfare programs and providing resources to increase patronage in the poorest Argentine provinces. This came in conjunction with negotiations with Peronist labor unions to preserve collective labor laws while facilitating union participation in the privatization process (Gibson and Calvo 2000; Murillo 2001; Levitsky 2003).

The economic reforms of the 1990s successfully curbed inflation and increased domestic consumption, prompting high growth rates between 1993 and 1997. Strong economic performance allowed Menem to push his reelection bid, which required the approval of a new constitution in 1994. This reform shortened the presidential term from six to four years while allowing for a single consecutive reelection. It also provided for the direct presidential elections, eliminating the Electoral College, and added a third senator for each province allocated to the runner up.[10] These changes increased the electoral weight of the large metropolitan provinces—Buenos Aires, Córdoba, Santa Fe, and Mendoza—while compensating the Radicals' weakness in most other provinces.

Resistance to Carlos S. Menem's neoliberal policies within the Peronists led to the emergence of a new center-left faction ("Grupo de los 8" or Group of Eight). The faction was later consolidated outside the party as the Frente Grande (Great Front) and eventually launched as a separate party: the Frente País Solidario (FREPASO; Front for a Country in Solidarity). This new party, with Peronist origins and an electoral constituency composed of disaffected Radical voters, came second in the 1995 presidential elections.

The economic mismanagement of the late 1980s marked the beginning of the Radicals' decline. The median provincial vote for national representatives of the UCR fell from around 40 percent in the 1980s to approximately 30 percent in the 1990s, then close to 20 percent since the collapse of an UCR-FREPASO coalition known as Alianza in 2001 (fig. 5.1). The median provincial vote for national representatives of the Peronists remained around 40 percent.

The decline in the electoral importance of the UCR (fig. 5.1) was accompanied by the emergence of a multiplicity of electoral parties, some of which emerged from the ashes of the UCR, but most of which would quickly fade. On the right, the demise of the UCeDé after 1995 was followed by a short electoral burst by Acción por la República (APR; Action for the Republic); the party created by Menem Finance Minister Domingo Cavallo in 1999–2001; Recrear (Recreate) led by Radical economist Ricardo Lopez Murphy in 2003–2005; and more recently, the

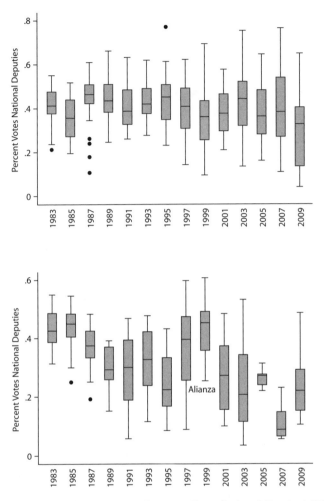

Figure 5.1. Boxplot Describing Provincial PJ Vote Share (*top*) and Provincial UCR Vote Share (*bottom*), 1983–2003. Line within the box describes the median provincial vote Share for each party. *Source:* Estimated using data from the Interior Ministry

party led by the conservative mayor of Buenos Aires, Mauricio Macri, Propuesta Republicana (PRO; Republican Proposal). On the center-left, the decline of the FREPASO in 2001 was followed with limited success by former Radical Elisa Carrió's Alternativa por una República de Iguales (Alternative for a Republic of Equals) and then Coalición Cívica (Civic Coalition) in 2003–2009, and more recently by the growing influence of former Socialist Governor Hermes Binner beyond his native Santa Fe.

From Menem to the Alianza

The final years of the Carlos S. Menem administration were dominated by three interrelated processes: an emergent recession, the decline of the UCR, and the rise of the Frente País Solidario (FREPASO; Front for a Country in Solidarity). The economic policies of the Menem administration had successfully curbed inflation, restored economic growth, and prompted a renaissance of domestic consumption. Yet, while political actors and the public wholeheartedly embraced the fixed currency policy implemented by Finance Minister Domingo Cavallo, differences in domestic and international inflation rates—particularly in the early years of the fixed currency program— resulted in high levels of currency appreciation that reduced competitiveness and generated external imbalances. The lack of monetary independence led to excessive borrowing, weakening fiscal accounts, and draining reserves to keep the fixed exchange rate. The Brazilian currency crisis of 1998–1999 and resulting devaluation also had a direct impact on Argentina. As the country's largest trading partner, its diminished import capacity led Argentina into a recession in 1998.

For most of his administration, Menem enjoyed high levels of public approval—largely a result of curbed inflation—allowing him significant discretion to implement economic policy. However, as the economy slowed down and the administration was marred by corruption scandals, the anticorruption discourse of the FREPASO was embraced by moderate voters who were moving away from the UCR. FREPASO quickly positioned itself as the most serious challenger to the administration. Leading the charge against corruption were Peronist Carlos "Chacho" Álvarez and human rights' activist Graciela Fernández Meijide. In the months preceding the 1997 midterm elections, leaders of both the UCR and the FREPASO initiated a rapprochement, knowing that neither would be able to defeat the PJ by themselves in the 1999 election. The success of their coalition in the 1997 elections, which denied Menem of majority in the House of Representatives, consolidated the new Alianza and set the stage for the presidential elections in 1999. After deciding the presidential ticket in open and competitive primaries, candidates Fernando de la Rúa (UCR) and Carlos "Chacho" Álvarez (FREPASO) ran a successful campaign, defeating Buenos Aires strongman Eduardo Duhalde by more than 10 points (48.3 percent to 38.2 percent). Key to the defeat of Duhalde was the lack of support from President Menem, already preoccupied with a 2003 presidential bid.

The Storm Arrives: The Rise and Demise of the *Alianza*

In December 2001, Fernando de la Rúa and "Chacho" Álvarez were formally sworn in as president and vice president of Argentina. High expectations, however, quickly gave way to widespread disappointment. As Argentina fell deeper into a recession, a run against the currency dried up credit markets and depleted international reserves. The financial crisis would prove the Alianza's undoing. To shield the fixed-exchange rate program from speculative attacks, the Alianza government sought to secure large credit lines from international lenders. Credit access, however, depended on the government's ability to demonstrate that tough reforms could be enacted by Congress. As a coalition government commanding only a plurality of seats in the House and facing a Peronist majority in the Senate, de la Rúa resorted to buying the votes of a few opposition senators on a critical bill to weaken the collective bargaining power of unions.

It would be hard to overstate the consequences of the Senate scandal that ensued. As evidence of side payments came to light, Vice President "Chacho" Álvarez publicly denounced President de la Rúa and resigned from his post, effectively ending the coalition experiment. Less than a year later, a lopsided electoral defeat prompted the government to impose strict limits on currency movements and deposit withdrawals in a desperate attempt to avert a currency run. Massive protests ensued, including looting, road blockages by unemployed groups (*piqueteros*), and middle class groups banging pots and pans (*cacerolazos*) to call for the resignation of de la Rúa and the whole political class, demanding "*que se vayan todos*" (throw everyone out). De la Rúa resigned at the end of 2001, leaving the economy in shambles. Despite the ensuing political vacuum, the military was not considered an option, and the government fell into the hands of the Peronist opposition.

With no party able to successfully absorb the disaffected UCR and FREPASO voters, Peronists quickly reasserted themselves as the only players in town. During two weeks of political jockeying, they first selected Adolfo Rodríguez Saá (a Peronist governor whose tenure lasted a week), and then Senator Eduardo Duhalde— with support from all the parties in Congress—as pro tempore presidents. Rodríguez Saá declared default on Argentine foreign debt, while Duhalde began a slow process of bringing the economy under control. Under Duhalde, Argentina abandoned its currency convertibility program, which had pegged the peso to the US dollar since 1991, and launched massive efforts to restart the economy. To cope with unemployment levels of almost 25 percent and poverty rates of 50 percent in 2002, Duhalde established a massive workfare program designed to reach 20 percent of households by 2003 (CENDA 2010). With the UCR and the FREPASO in disarray, the PJ became the only party option. Yet by 2003, factionalism had transformed into internal antagonism, with rival Peronist politicians seeking to broaden their coalitions to incorporate the middle class voters who had been "orphaned" by the Alianza's collapse during the crisis (Torre 2003).

It Is Hard to Be Peronist in a Peronist World

The end of the Alianza coalition led to a significant increase in the number of political parties. This was the result of Peronists holding on to their traditional voters while all other parties melted away. Electoral districts such as the City of Buenos Aires and the provinces of Córdoba and Santa Fe, which concentrated large numbers of middle class Alianza voters, saw a sharp increase in total and effective number of parties, with the latter accounting for relative party strength. The Peronists capitalized on the high levels of fragmentation in Congress to buttress their control. General increases in the effective number of parties did not result in similar increases in the effective number of legislative parties (tables 5.2 and 5.3). Instead, fragmentation allowed for the concentration of seats in the hands of Peronists, who enjoyed comfortable majorities in both chambers of Congress (tables 5.2 and 5.3).

Peronist legislative dominance was also subject to increased factionalism as different sectors sought to attract independent middle class voters in addition to the traditional constituencies. This dynamic was heightened by new rules for electing senators that allowed different Peronist lists to win majority and minority representation. As a result of this fragmentation, three of the top four presidential candidates in the election of 2003 were Peronists (Néstor Kirchner, Carlos S. Menem, and Adolfo Rodríguez Saá). Similarly, the most important race of the 2005 midterm election had Cristina Fernández de Kirchner and Hilda "Chiche" Duhalde, the Peronist wives of Néstor Kirchner and Eduardo Duhalde respectively, competing for the control of the Province of Buenos Aires—the largest electoral district in the country. The presidential election of 2007 faced off a coalition of Peronists and Radicals led by Cristina Fernández de Kirchner (Frente para la Victoria; FPV; Front for the Victory) against a coalition of former Radicals and Socialists led by Elisa Carrió (Coalición Cívica; CC; Civic Coalition) and another of Peronists and Radicals led by Roberto Lavagna (Una Nación Avanzada; UNA;

Table 5.2.   Seat Shares and Effective Number of Parties in the Argentine Lower Chamber, 1983–2007

POLITICAL PARTY	1983–1985	1985–1987	1987–1989	1989–1991	1991–1993	1993–1995
Partido Justicialista/FPV	43.7	37.8	38.6	47.2	45.1	49.4
Unión Cívica Radical	50.8	50.8	44.9	35.4	32.7	32.7
Unión del Centro Democrático	0.8	1.2	2.8	4.3	3.9	1.6
Frente País Solidario						
Acción por la República						
Afirmación para una República Igualitaria/ Coalicion Civica						
Propuesta Republicana						
Peronismo Disidente						
Provincial Parties	3.1	4.7	6.7	7.5	8.6	9.3
Others	1.6	5.5	7.1	5.5	9.7	7
TOTAL NUMBER OF SEATS	254	254	254	254	257	257
EFFECTIVE NUMBER OF LEGISLATIVE PARTIES	2.22	2.46	2.77	2.79	3.04	2.74

Source: Data from Jones, et al. 2009.
   Note: Dark grey indicates governing party or coalition controls more than 50 percent of the seats.
Light grey if governing coalition controls fewer than 50 percent of seats.

An Advanced Nation), minister of economy from 2002 to 2005. The 2011 presidential election highlighted a similar pattern, with Cristina Fernández de Kirchner running for reelection against Peronist candidates Eduardo Duhalde and Alberto Rodríguez Saá (brother of Adolfo) as well as Radical presidential hopeful Ricardo Alfonsín—son of president Raul Alfonsín—and Socialist candidate Hermes Binner.

Presidential Strength in a Booming Economy

In the context of party fragmentation that characterized the post-2001 period, Néstor Kirchner and his wife and successor Cristina Fernández de Kirchner were able to rebuild the authority of the president and craft a successful electoral coalition in the 2007 and 2011 presidential elections. The coalition included both

1995–1997	1997–1999	1999–2001	2001–2003	2003–2005	2005–2007	2007–2009	2009–2011
51	46.3	38.5	47.1	54.9	45.9	42.46	34.12
26.5	25.7	31.9	25.3	17.9	15.6	11.51	17.06
0.8	0.4	0.4	0.4	0.4			
8.6	14.8	14.4	2.7	1.2			
	1.2	4.3	1.6	0.4	0.4		
			6.2	4.3	5.1	5.95	7.54
				1.2	4.3	3.17	4.36
					13.6	10.31	13.45
8.6	10.5	9.7	8.6	7.4	8.2	7.94	9.92
4.7	1.2	0.8	8.2	12.3	6.9	18.66	13.49
257	257	257	257	257	257	257	257
2.88	3.19	3.55	3.28	2.81	3.84	4.96	5.76

traditional Peronist constituencies in the hinterland and the suburbs of Buenos Aires as well as important sections of the independent middle class, which had defected from the Alianza coalition. Their success, like Menem's before them, was intimately tied to the economic and consumption boom experienced in the post-2003 period. Argentina's export-led recovery was triggered by a sustained increase in the price of export commodities, reactivation of idle capacity, and lower real wages in the aftermath of the three-fold devaluation of the Argentinean peso.

Néstor Kirchner was elected president in 2003. Although Kirchner finished a close second in the first round of elections, with 23 percent of the vote, he received the endorsement of outgoing president, Eduardo Duhalde, boosting his run-off prospects. When his opponent, former president Menem, was confronted with what polls predicted would be a crushing defeat in the second round, he abandoned the

Table 5.3. Seat Shares and Effective Number of Parties in the Argentine Upper Chamber, 1983–2011

POLITICAL PARTY	1983–1985	1985–1987	1987–1989	1989–1991	1991–1993	1993–1995	1995–1997
Partido Justicialista/FPV (%)	45.65	45.65	45.65	60.87	60.87	60.87	54.17
Unión Cívica Radical (%)	39.13	43.48	43.48	26.09	21.74	21.74	27.78
Others (%)	15.22	10.87	10.87	13.04	17.39	17.39	18.06
TOTAL NUMBER OF SEATS	46	46	46	46	46	46	72
EFFECTIVE NUMBER OF LEGISLATIVE PARTIES	2.60	2.44	2.44	2.20	2.23	2.23	2.48

POLITICAL PARTY	1997–1999	1999–2001	2001–2003	2003–2005	2005–2007	2007–2009	2009–2011
Partido Justicialista/FPV (%)	54.17	54.17	55.56	56.94	58.33	62.50	47.22
Unión Cívica Radical (%)	27.78	27.78	31.94	25.00	23.61	13.89	31.94
Others (%)	18.06	18.06	12.50	18.06	18.06	23.61	20.83
TOTAL NUMBER OF SEATS	72	72	72	72	72	72	72
TOTAL NUMBER OF SEATS	2.48	2.48	2.35	2.38	2.33	2.15	2.71

Source: Secretaría de Información Parlamentaria.
Note: Dark grey indicates governing party or coalition controls more than 50 percent of the seats.
Light grey if governing coalition controls fewer than 50 percent of seats.

presidential race, blaming Duhalde's electoral maneuvering. Néstor Kirchner became president-elect by default. Four years later, Kirchner's wife, Cristina Fernández de Kirchner, succeeded with 45 percent of the vote and was comfortably reelected in October of 2011 with 54 percent of the vote.

This electoral success is explained both by a strong economy and by the Kirchners' political capabilities. Néstor began his presidency by introducing reforms to the Supreme Court, increasing its legitimacy through a more transparent process of judicial appointments. His predecessor, Menem, had been criticized for packing the court with political supporters. Néstor also replaced the heads of the armed forces and the police while pushing for the prosecution of former military officers for human rights violations during the last dictatorship. By contrast, Menem had pardoned generals prosecuted during the Alfonsín administration. More dramatically, Kirchner implemented a unilateral restructuring of the defaulted external debt through a public offering that was accepted by most bondholders.[11] This reduced its nominal value by 55 percent and avoided the payment of arrears on interest.

The Kirchners benefited greatly from the export boom of the 2000s (Mazzuca 2013). Indeed, Argentina experienced its highest growth rate in a century between 2003 and 2008. Unemployment declined almost 20 points, to 7.3 percent, while real salaries in the formal sector recovered to their precrisis levels in 2005 and (save a small decline in 2008) continued to grow until 2010 (CENDA 2010, 24–25). This trend also benefited from a resurgence of collective bargaining activity which, with the support of the government as well as tighter labor markets, reduced informality from 50 percent in 2003 to 35 percent in 2010 (Etchemendy and Collier 2007; Etchemendy 2011). Economic recovery was facilitated by heavy government spending on public works, a favorable exchange rate that boosted industrial production, and a battery of public subsidies covering energy, transportation, and food production. Indeed, economic activity in the industrial sector, which had declined by 61 percent between 1991 and 2001 due to trade liberalization and an appreciated exchange rate, bounced back approximately 16 percent between 2002 and 2008 (CENDA 2010, 184). Increases in production were accompanied by gains in industrial employment, which grew by almost 20 percent between 2003 and 2007 (CENDA 2010, 265).

The traditional Peronist coalition of industrialists and workers was back in place, thanks to the fiscal resources and economic activity generated by the commodity boom. Yet, as the economy began to overheat and inflation became a more prominent issue among voters, Néstor Kirchner resisted any increase in public utility prices (frozen by Duhalde). Instead, he adopted price controls and export restrictions on beef, gas, and other products, seeking to hold domestic prices down. He also put pressure on the national statistics office to modify the measures of inflation, undermining its autonomy.

Broadening an Electoral Coalition that Includes the (Elusive) Middle Class

The Kirchners, much like Menem, were able to hold together their traditional Peronist constituency—including organized labor—as well as the new set of organizations that represented informal and unemployed workers after the 2001 crisis. While the policies advanced by Néstor Kirchner and Cristina Fernández de Kirchner were dramatically different from those of Carlos Menem, the Kirchners were equally successful in garnering the support of middle class voters. High levels of public support allowed them to shrug off allegations of corruption and a protracted conflict with agro-producers over heightened export taxation. Furthermore, the rejection of the Menem labor reforms and favorable appointments allowed Néstor Kirchner to increase union support. Moreover, the government enacted real wage increases by decree to all workers in the formal sector and raised minimum wages, and the Ministry of Labor was generally favorable to union-led collective bargaining (Etchemendy 2011).

The reemergence of the unions was further supported by the mobilization of informal sector workers organizations and the unemployed (organized either by *piquetero* groups or by Peronist territorial brokers). These sectors benefited from a reform of the privatized social security system and the extension of family allowances to the children of informal or unemployed workers (Etchemendy and Garay 2010). Pension reform under Néstor Kirchner allowed individuals to return from the private to the public system, and extended coverage to informal workers. In 2009, Fernández de Kirchner nationalized privatized pension funds (gaining an important resource during growing fiscal pressures) and reached almost universal coverage (INDEC 2011). Family allowances, which had been tied to the salary of formal employees, were extended to low-income families in a noncontributory basis in 2009. In 2010, it was extended to pregnant mothers.

The middle class voters made available by the collapse of the Alianza were attracted to the Kirchners, because of the consumption boom and also by their human rights policies. With time, the electorate became more volatile as corruption scandals emerged, questioning electoral financing, the bidding for public works, clientelism, and the use of regulation to force the sale of privatized companies to friendly investors. Yet, because the Kirchners departed dramatically from Menem on human rights policies, they nevertheless gained the support of much of civil society. The couple, for instance, pushed for the annulment of two laws that limited prosecution of military personnel found guilty of human right violations and supported the reactivation of tribunals. The Kirchners converted one infamous detention and torture center into a human rights museum, cleaned up the top ranks of the armed forces, and brought human rights groups to the forefront of the political scene. Their progressive social stance also led Argentina to become the first Latin American country to legalize gay marriage.

In 2008, however, Fernández de Kirchner again faced tension with constituent groups. She had increased export taxes with a flexible rate to continue paying for government expenditures in the context of growing inflation and fiscal strain. Rural producers responded with a lockout and road blockades. When middle class protesters joined the rural producers, the government mobilized Peronist labor unions, allied unemployed organizations and party machines from the province of Buenos Aires while introducing a bill with the proposed tax increase to Congress. On July 5, 2008, the bill passed the Chamber of Deputies, but was defeated by a single vote in the Senate (that of the Radical Vice President Julio Cobos). Under pressure from rural mobilization, legislators representing the wealthy agricultural provinces broke ranks with the government. The conflict took a toll on President Fernández de Kirchner's popularity, which declined from 64 percent in January 2008 to 27 percent in June. As the economy slowed down in 2009 and suffered the effects of the global financial crisis, popular support for the president hovered around 35 percent (Poliarquia 2011).

The 2009 midterm election results reflected the volatility of a middle class facing an economic slowdown and the attempt to impose taxes without allowing for legislative discussion. The legislative candidates aligned with the government received 31.2 percent of the vote, closely followed by the 30.7 percent for the Acuerdo Civico y Social (Civic and Social Agreement, an alliance of the Radicals, the Socialists, and Coalición Cívica), and 18.7 percent for the dissident Peronists. The government's legislative delegation dwindled to less than 35 percent in the Lower House (see fig. 5.2), resulting from reductions in the large metropolitan provinces of Buenos Aires, Córdoba, Santa Fe, Mendoza, and Buenos Aires. The

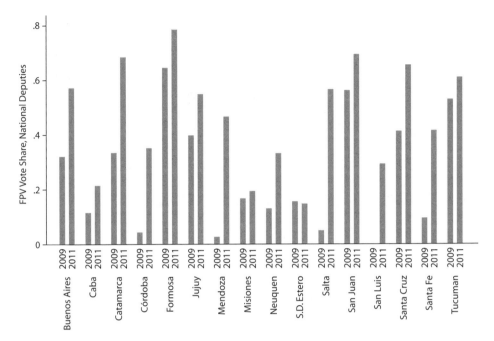

Figure 5.2. Vote Share for the Frente para la Victoria (FPV), National Deputy Elections, 2009–2011, Select Districts

government then broke its alliance with the major media conglomerate Grupo Clarín due to its coverage of the conflict. As a result, the government boosted a policy of unevenly distributing official advertising to progovernment outlets. The government also passed several media reforms, criticized for targeting critics (Boas 2013).[12]

The volatility of the middle classes to economic conditions became obvious when the economy recovered in 2010. By October, the president's popularity had reached 45 percent, though it jumped to 65 percent in November after the wave of sympathy generated by the sudden death of her husband (Poliarquía 2011). In the open primaries of August 2011, she commanded 50.7 percent of the vote while her nearest rivals received a paltry 12 percent. In the presidential election of October 2011, Fernández de Kirchner won all but one province, dominating the popular vote 54 percent to Hermes Binner's 17 percent.[13]

Both the popularity of Cristina and the weakness of opposition candidates explain her landslide win. Figure 5.2 compares the vote for national representatives in the 2009 and 2011 elections in select districts, revealing the return of middle class voters to the Kirchnerist legislative coalition. In short, in the context of electoral dealignment in the Argentine democracy, the capacity of the Kirchners to concentrate executive authority was crucial in building a successful electoral coalition. They maintained the traditional Peronist constituencies—labor and the poor—while adding the unstable support of the middle class, based on their human rights policies and, more importantly, Argentine economic performance. The weakening of the UCR without a clear successor for its organizational structure had left the opposition unable to make allegiances with those voters except as a protest vote against President Fernández de Kirchner in 2009.

Politics in Institutionally Weak Environments

In the aftermath of the Great Depression, Argentina followed a path characterized by institutional flux and the political incorporation of the working classes.[14] During decades of regime instability, the rules of the game were continually overturned, leading to the frequent collapse, suspension, or purging of institutions as important as the constitution, the presidency, the Congress, and the Supreme Court. Argentines, therefore, failed to develop expectations of durability. Formal rules remained short-lived or selectively enforced, despite democratic consolidation from the 1980s onward, promoting an endemic weakness in Argentina's institutions (Levitsky and Murillo 2005; Murillo 2011).

Institutional weakness has been associated with the concentration of executive authority permitted by periods of crisis (O'Donnell 1994). Responding to public opinion pressure, yet unconstrained by the separation of powers, presidents showed an enormous capacity for radical change that has hindered institutional durability. Dramatic policy swings in response to the economic booms-and-busts characteristic of the Argentine economy were implemented by powerful executives who, unlike military rulers, still largely respected civil liberties. In particular, both Menem and the Kirchners implemented dramatic policy responses, allowing them to win popular support for continuing with their mandates, while simultaneously attracting criticism for fostering institutional weakness.

The concentration of executive authority can be measured by the number of Need and Urgency Decrees (DNUs) issued by presidents (Ferreira Rubio and Goretti 1996). A mere twenty-five DNUs were issued before 1983. By contrast, President Raul Alfonsín issued ten DNUs between 1983 and 1989, and Menem issued 335 between 1989 and 1994 (Ferreira Rubio and Goretti 1996). Argentine democratic presidents have resorted to DNUs as a first rather than last resort. Both Kirchner and Menem used decrees to implement radical reforms to gain broad popular support.[15] Rapid unchecked policy change, however, further contributed to undermining the system of checks and balances, thus weakening governmental institutions.

Renovation by decree has been subject to change by successive waves of institutional reform. Menem's deregulation decree in 1991 removed regulation on the supply and pricing of goods and services, abolished numerous taxes and regulatory agencies, imported medicines and foods, and reformed the capital market and the health insurance system (Ferreira Rubio and Goretti 1996, 461–62). Similarly, Néstor Kirchner established export and import regulations by decree and in the same way reformed the social security system, undid Menem's pension privatization, and extended coverage to informal workers. President Cristina Fernández de Kirchner also used decrees for her extension of the family allowances to low income children and pregnant women. By implementing and dismantling major policies by decrees, successive presidents have contributed to policy volatility, which generates expectations of future policy change in the population.[16]

Decrees also prove crucial in the selective enforcement of rules; so while an institution may remain unchanged, its functionality becomes dramatically different. Such was the case of Argentina's Central Bank. President Menem's finance minister, Domingo Cavallo, pushed for a legal reform granting independence to the Central Bank in 1991. Then, as finance minister for President de la Rúa a decade later, Cavallo forced the resignation of Central Bank President Pedro Pou when he refused to subordinate to the president's will. President Fernández de Kirchner then issued a decree permitting the use of Central Bank reserves to pay for the interest on the public debt and, when the Central Bank president resisted, she announced another decree to have him dismissed. Although the law has remained unchanged since 1991, and formally the Argentine Central Bank maintains its independence, its enforcement has been selective.[17]

Both Menem and Kirchner also used decrees to regulate public utilities. When Menem privatized telecommunications, he created a regulatory agency subordinate to executive will by decree, thereby allowing him to modify the terms of the privatization following investors' pressure. When the board of the agency issued a ruling he disliked, he fired them. Similarly, under Kirchner, the lax enforcement of telecommunications regulations led to difficulties in promoting competition between providers. Indeed, even regulatory changes approved by President Kirchner and confirmed by Congress, such as the renegotiation of prices for the main electricity distribution companies, were never implemented and remained in legal limbo—at a high cost in subsidies to the Treasury (Murillo 2009).

Further evidence of the fragility of Argentina's institutions is found in the public dispute over official inflation figures. In January 2007, official inflation approached 10 percent, while food prices rose even faster, prompting the Kirchner government to request the resignation of the national statistics office's (Instituto Nacional de Estadística y Censos; INDEC; Nacional Institute of Statistics and the Census) chief of the price division.[18] After the officer was replaced, the INDEC modified its inflation formula, which sparked allegations of tampering to reduce official figures. INDEC's credibility plummeted as its inflation rate began to diverge dramatically from the assessments of private think tanks and provincial statistical agencies. Even Peronist labor unions claimed it could no longer be used as a reference in collective bargaining. Given the influence of prices for voting behavior and the sensitivity of voters to economic conditions, this case is particularly striking.

Finally, the evolution of the Supreme Court under the Kirchners suggests that understanding institutional enforcement requires observing not just a single institution, but also its complementarities. Supreme Court independence was rarely respected after 1930. When the Court appointed by Alfonsín during Argentina's democratic transition ruled against President Menem, he responded by expanding the number of its members from five to nine and packed the court with PJ loyalists. While de la Rúa kept the Menemist court, the institution became a target of citizen fury during the economic and political crisis of 2001–2002, resulting in impeachment charges for five judges. As Menemist justices were impeached or resigned, only two of Alfonsín's appointed judges and one appointed by President Duhalde remained. President Néstor Kirchner modified the appointment process by decree in 2003, increasing its transparency and public participation in response to demand by civil rights organizations. His successor, President Fernández de Kirchner, then overturned Menem's reform, resuming a five-member court with an interim period of seven justices (the number at the time of the reform).

These two measures limited the president's control over the court. Indeed, the court has ruled against the government on several important cases, such as the Perfíl case, in which the government was ordered to adopt a more even distribution of public advertising among media outlets; the Rosza case, which ordered the executive to fill the vacancies of the lower courts instead of appointing "temporary" judges; the CTA case, which asked the Ministry of Labor to recognize a union affiliated with the Argentine Central Workers' Union (CTA), thus challenging the monopoly of progovernment Central Confederation of Labor (CGT) unions; and the Riachuelo case, which mandated the government to enforce environmental regulations by fining the public officer in charge. Unlike Menem, the Kirchners accepted the rulings, boosting the independence of the Supreme Court. However, as noted by Gargarella (2011), the government has selectively enforced the rulings, thereby ignoring the Court despite tolerating its independence.

Concluding Remarks

The democratic transition of 1983 initiated an unparalleled period of democratic participation and party competition. In spite of significant economic and political turmoil, elections have been clean and their outcome accepted by voters and politicians alike. Since 1983, Argentines have voted seven times to elect presidents and fifteen times to select representatives to the House and Senate, resulting in five Peronist presidents and two Radicals.[19] Alternation was also observed in the Lower House and in a majority of provinces.

Democratic consolidation has also resulted in greater electoral competition and partisan dealignment. Argentina's federal system limited the Radical parties' ability to translate their electoral base in the richer, metropolitan provinces and more prosperous areas into national governance. This was partly due to Peronist dominance of key voter groups, including labor unions and the unemployed, which are crucial in terms of controlling "street" politics (Calvo and Murillo 2005). As a result, neither of the two Radical presidents finished their terms in office and, after the collapse of the de la Rúa administration, their traditional middle class voters defected.

The partisan realignment caused by the electoral decline of the Radical party and the volatility of the voters it "orphaned" resulted in the fragmentation of the party system. The alternatives to the UCR have failed to take root, whereas Peronist factionalism, which had been kept at bay by electoral threats from the Radicals, became increasingly pronounced. As a result, non-Peronist politicians allied with different Peronist factions to contest national and provincial elections. The growing independence of middle-class voters is crucial in explaining both the weakening of the UCR and the tensions within the Peronist party that is seeking to win their support.

Finally, the consolidation of Argentine democracy did not solve, only modified, the long-term problem of institutional weakness. Tensions arising from an economy dependent on commodity exports, yet which employs a majority of its citizens in the service sector, have been long-lasting. However, the frequent economic crises that had previously led to military coups now result in continuous attempts to change policies and institutions without abandoning the democratic regime. Indeed, voters seem to applaud executive concentration of power utilized to implement radical policy changes. The resulting reproduction of institutional weakness only makes it more difficult for institutions to take root as Argentine citizens get used to expecting future rounds of radical reforms.

APPENDIX

Table 5A.1. Argentine Political Parties and Coalitions

Peronists		Radicals		Other	
creation (disintegration)	Party/Coalition	creation (disintegration)	Party/Coalition	creation (disintegration)	Party/Coalition
1947	Partido Justicialista (PJ)	1890	Unión Cívica Radical (UCR)	1994 (2001)	Frente País Solidario (FREPASO) formed by Frente Grande, PAIS (Política Abierta para la Integridad Social), and Unidad Socialista, an alliance of socialist parties
1987	Renovadores (faction of the PJ led by Menem)	1987	Unión del Centro Democrático (UCeDé)	1997 (2001)	Alianza (alliance of UCR and FREPASO)
1989	Grupo de los 8 (PJ faction, later Frente Grande and then formed a party, Frente País Solidario, FREPASO)	1999	Acción por la República	2000	Alternativa para una República de Iguales (ARI) a coalition formed between the Popular Socialist Party, Socialist Democratic Party, and dissident sectors of the UCR, and FREPASO
2003	Frente para la Victoria	2002 (2009)	Recrear	2007	Coalición Cívica
		2005	Propuesta Republicana	2009	Acuerdo Cívico y Social (an alliance of Radicals, Socialists, and originally Coalición Cívica which left again in 2010)

Note: Frente País Solidario (FREPASO) formed a new party separate from the Peronists, coming second in the 1995 presidential elections. The party also had disaffected Radicals.

Table 5A.2.   Democratically Elected Presidents

	Alignment	Term
Juan Perón	PJ	1946–1951
		1951–1955
Arturo Frondizi	UCR	1958–1962
Arturo Illia	UCR	1963–1966
Héctor Cámpora	PJ	1973–1973
Juan Perón	PJ	1973–1974
Isabel Perón	PJ	1974–1976
Raul Alfonsín	UCR	1983–1989
Carlos Menem	PJ	1989–1995
		1995–1999
Fernando de la Rúa	UCR/Alliance	1999–2001
Adolfo Rodríguez Saá	PJ	2001–2001
Eduardo Duhalde	PJ	2002–2003
Néstor Kirchner	PJ	2003–2007
Cristina Fernández de Kirchener	PJ	2007–2011
		2011–present

Note: Coup d'états led by the military in support of the traditional economic elites overthrew President Hipólito Irigoyen (UCR) in 1930, Juan Domingo Perón (PJ) in 1955, Arturo Frondizi (UCR) in 1962, Arturo Illia (UCR) in 1966, and Isabel Perón (PJ) in 1976.

NOTES

We thank the comments of Sebastián Mazzuca, the editors, and other participants in the Constructing Democratic Governance in Latin America conference organized by the Inter-American Dialogue in Washington, DC, on October 6–7, 2011.

1. In this chapter, democracy is understood as a form of government comprised of representatives elected in fair and competitive elections.

2. Rules to select the national executive included indirect election through an electoral college in 1983 and 1989; the use of popular vote with runoff in 1995; reinterpreting nominating rules in 2003 to allow multiple candidates from a same party; and using simultaneous, open, and compulsory primaries in the 2011 election. These changes were the result of a constitutional reform proposed by President Carlos Menem in 1994; an informal reinterpretation of the electoral code by President Eduardo Duhalde in 2003; and a change in the national electoral code through a political reform proposed by President Cristina Fernández de Kirchner voted by Congress in 2010.

3. Coup d'états led by the military in support of the traditional economic elites overthrew President Hipólito Irigoyen (UCR) in 1930, Juan Domingo Perón (PJ) in 1955, Arturo Frondizi (UCR) in 1962, Arturo Illia (UCR) in 1966, and Isabel Perón (PJ) in 1976.

4. Mora y Araujo (1980a, 1980b), Smith (1980), and Llorente (1980a) discuss the electoral support for Peronism in the 1946 election, when Perón was first elected

president, showing the support of urban workers in the most developed provinces and a more multiclass alliance with the poor in the less developed provinces. They also show how the increasing gains of this second component during his administration and until he was reelected in 1973.

5. The studies mentioned in the previous footnote compare the electoral coalitions of both parties. David Rock (1975) discusses the origins and evolution of the UCR.

6. This regime business cycle, with exchange rate appreciation and a decline in real salaries after every coup d'état, was masterfully described by Guillermo O'Donnell (1978) in "Estado y Alianzas en Argentina, 1956–1976."

7. Failures include a military defeat in the Malvinas war with the UK (April 2 through June 14, 1982), a decline in Argentina's international standing due to the systematic and brutal violation of human rights, severe economic mismanagement leading to the debt crisis, the nationalization of private debts benefiting big corporations and government allies, etc.

8. Thousands of Argentine citizens were "disappeared" by the military regime between 1976 and 1983. Details of the systematic torture and assassination of political opponents disappeared by the regime were detailed in the CONADEP report, as well as details about the detention camps used by the three forces of the military.

9. The "first historical movement" described the rise of the UCR to power under the presidency of Irigoyen and the "second historical movement" described the rise of Peronism in 1946. Dreams of a "third historical movement," however, would be crushed by the economic problems unfolded as a consequence of the debt crisis of 1982.

10. Prior to the Constitutional reform of 1994, the legislative bodies of each Province would select two senators. Those senators would generally be members of the majority party in the province.

11. A few holdouts have unsuccessfully sued the Argentine government and are still waiting for their payday.

12. In the conflict with the Clarín conglomerate, the government also supported human rights' groups accusations that the adopted children of Clarín's owner had been kidnapped by the military during the dictatorship—a common practice with the children of disappeared parents—and given to her. DNA tests found no evidence for this accusation but the event was polarizing in the relationship between the government and the media.

13. In 2007, she had not been the most voted presidential candidate in Córdoba, the City of Buenos Aires, Neuquen, and San Luis.

14. This section relies heavily on Murillo (2011).

15. Although Menem issued 103 decrees between 1989 and 1991, when the Argentine economy was in a tailspin, he issued more monthly decrees in his second administration than in the second half of his first administration. See www.adclegislativo.org.ar/listadodecreto.php, accessed November 14, 2011.

16. Not all radical reforms were adopted by decree, however. For instance, the privatization of the national oil-producing company under President Menem was approved by Congress, as was the subsequent renationalization of the same company by President Fernández de Kirchner.

17. The autonomy of the Central Bank was also resisted under Duhalde and Néstor Kirchner. Finance Minister Roberto Lavagna clashed with Central Bank presidents Mario Blejer, Aldo Pignanelli, Alfonso Prat-Gay, and Martin Redrado in both administrations.

18. In 2002, Finance Minister Lavagna had questioned the statistics on poverty and forced the resignation of the national statistics chief.

19. The two UCR presidencies were led by Raul R. Alfonsín (1983–1989) and Fernando de la Rúa (1999–2001). Five Peronist presidencies were led by Carlos Menem (1989–1995 and 1995–1999), Néstor Kirchner (2003–2007), and Cristina Fernández de Kirchner (2007–2009 and 2011–2015).

REFERENCES

Boas, Taylor C. 2013. "Mass Media and Politics in Latin America." In *Constructing Democratic Governance in Latin America*, edited by Jorge I. Domínguez and Michael Shifter. 4th ed. Baltimore: Johns Hopkins University Press.

Calvo, Ernesto, and Marcelo Escolar. 2005. *La nueva politica de partidos en la Argentina: Crisis politica, realineamientos partidarios y reforma electoral.* Buenos Aires: Prometeo, Pent.

Calvo, Ernesto, and María Victoria Murillo. 2005. "The New Iron Law of Argentine Politics? Partisanship, Clientelism and Governability in Contemporary Argentina." In *Argentine Democracy: The Politics of Institutional Weakness*, edited by Steven Levitsky and María Victoria Murillo. College Park: Pennsylvania State University Press.

Catterberg, Eduardo. R. 1991. *Argentina Confronts Politics: Political Culture and Public Opinion in the Argentine Transition to Democracy.* Boulder, CO: Lynne Rienner.

CENDA. 2010. *La anatomia del nuevo patron de crecimiento y la encrucijada actual: La economia argentina en el periodo 2002–2010.* Buenos Aires.

Etchemendy, Sebastian. 2011. "La 'Doble Alianza' Gobierno-Sindicatos en el kirchnerismo (2003–2011)." *Origenes, Evidencias y Perspectivas.* Buenos Aires: Universidad Torcuato Di Tella.

Etchemendy, Sebastian, and Ruth B. Collier. 2007. "Down But Not Out: Union Resurgence and Segmented Neocorporatism in Argentina (2003–2007)." *Politics & Society* 35 (3): 363–401.

Etchemendy, Sebastian, and Candelaria Garay. 2010. "Between Moderation and Defiance: Argentina's Left Populism in Comparative Perspective (2003–2009)." *Latin America's Left Turn: Causes and Implications*, edited by Steven Levitsky and Kenneth M. Roberts. Baltimore: Johns Hopkins University Press.

Ferreira Rubio, Delia, and Matteo Goretti. 1996. "Cuando el presidente gobierna solo: Menem y los decretos de necesidad y urgencia hasta la reforma constitucional (1989–1994)." *Desarrollo Economico* 141.

Gargarella, Roberto. 2011. *Notas sobre Kirchnerismo y justicia: La politica en tiempos de los Kirchner*, edited by A. Malamud and M. De Luca. Buenos Aires: EUDEBA.

Gibson, Edward. 1996. *Class and Conservative Parties: Argentina in Comparative Perspective.* Baltimore: Johns Hopkins University Press.

Gibson, Edward, and Ernesto F. Calvo. 2000. "Federalism and Low-Maintenance Constituencies: Territorial Dimensios of Economic Reform in Argentina." *Studies in Comparative International Development* 35 (5): 32–55.

Huntington, Samuel P. 1993. *The Third Wave of Democratization*. Norman: Unversity of Oklahoma Press.

Iaryczower, Matias, Pablo Spiller, et al. 2006. "Judicial Lobbying: The Politics of Labor Law Constitutional Interpretation." *American Political Science Review* 100 (1): 85–97.

INDEC 2011. Encuesta Permanente de Hogares (Permanent Survey of Households). Buenos Aires.

Jones, Mark P., Wonjae Hwang, and Juan Pablo Micozzi. 2009. "Government and Opposition in the Argentine Congress, 1989–2007: Understanding Inter-Party Dynamics through Roll Call Vote Analysis." *Journal of Politics in Latin America* 1 (1): 67–96.

Kanenguiser, Martin. 2011. *El fin de la ilusion: Argentina 2001–2011: Crisis, reconstrucción y declive*. Buenos Aires.

Leiras, Marcelo, Agustina Giraudi, et al. 2011. *Who Wants an Independent Court? Political Competition and Supreme Court Instability in the Argentine Provinces (1984–2008)*. Buenos Aires: Universidad de San Andres.

Levitsky, Steven. 2003. *Transforming Labor-based Parties in Latin America: Argentine Peronism in Comparative Perspective*. New York: Cambridge University Press.

Levitsky, Steven, and María Victoria Murillo. 2005. *Argentine Democracy: The Politics of Institutional Weakness*. University Park, PA: Pennsylvania State University Press.

Llorente, Ignacio. 1980a. "Alianzas politicas en el surgimiento del peronismo: El caso de la provincia de Buenos Aires." In *El voto peronista: Ensayos de sociologia electoral argentina*, edited by M. Mora y Araujo and I. Llorente. Buenos Aires: Editorial Sudamericana.

———. 1980b. "La composicion social del movimiento peronista hacia 1954." In *El voto Peronista: Ensayos de sociologia electoral argentina*, edited by M. Mora y Araujo and I. Llorente. Buenos Aires: Editorial Sudamericana.

Lupu, Noam. 2011. "Party Brands in Crisis: Partisanship, Brand Dilusion and the Breakdown of Political Parties in Latin America." *Politics*, Princeton University.

Mazzuca, Sebastián. 2013. Natural Resource Boom and Institutional Curses in the New Political Economy of South America. In *Constructing Democratic Governance in Latin America*, edited by Jorge I. Domínguez and Michael Shifter. 4th ed. Baltimore: Johns Hopkins University Press.

Mora y Araujo, Manuel. 1980a. "Introduccion: La sociologia electoral y la comprension del peronismo." In *El voto peronista: Ensayos de sociologia electoral argentina*, edited by M. Mora y Araujo and I. Llorente. Buenos Aires: Editorial Sudamericana.

———. 1980b. "Las bases estructurales del peronismo." In *El voto peronista: Ensayos de sociologia electoral argentina*, edited by M. Mora y Araujo and I. Llorente. Buenos Aires: Editorial Sudamericana.

Murillo, María Victoria. 2001. *Labor Competition and Partisan Coalitions in Latin America: Trade Unions and Market Reforms*. New York: Cambridge University Press.

———. 2009. *Political Competition, Partisanship, and Policy-Making in Latin American Public Utilities*. New York: Cambridge University Press.

———. 2011. "La fortaleza institucional Argentina en 2003–2011." *La política en tiempos de los Kirchner*, edited by A. Malamud and M. De Luca. Buenos Aires: Eudeba.

O'Donnell, Guillermo. 1978. "Estado y alianzas en la Argentina, 1956–1976." *Desarrollo Económico* 16 (64): 523–54.

———. 1994. "Delegative Democracy." *Journal of Democracy* 5 (1): 55–69.

O'Donnell, Guillermo, Phillippe C. Schmitter, and Laurence Whitehead. 1986. *Transitions from Authoritarian Rule: Comparative Perspectives*. Baltimore: Johns Hopkins University Press.

Poliarquía. 2011. "Presidential Approval Series, August 2006–July 2011." Buenos Aires.

Portantiero, J. C. 2002. "Los desafíos de la democracia." *Todavia* 1 (2): 1–3.

Rock, David. 1975. *Politics in Argentina, 1890–1930: The Rise and Fall of Radicalism*. Cambridge: Cambridge University Press.

Scartascini, Carlos, Ernesto Stain, and Mariano Tommasi. 2010. *How Democracy Works: Political Institutions, Actors, and Arenas in Latin American Policymaking*. Washington, DC: Inter-American Development Bank and DRCLAS, Harvard University.

Smith, Peter. 1980. "Las elecciones de 1946 y las inferencias ecologicas." In *El voto peronista: Ensayos de sociologia electoral argentina*, edited by M. Mora y Araujo and I. Llorente. Buenos Aires: Editorial Sudamericana.

Spiller, Pablo T., and Mariano Tommasi. 2007. *The Institutional Foundations of Public Policy in Argentina*. New York: Cambridge University Press.

Stokes, Susan C. 2001. *Mandates and Democracy: Neoliberalism by Surprise in Latin America*. New York: Cambridge University Press.

Torre, Juan Carlos. 2003. "Los huérfanos de la política de partidos sobre los alcances y la naturaleza de la crisis de representación partidaria." *Desarrollo Economico* 42 (168): 647–65.

CHAPTER SIX

Bolivia

Keeping the Coalition Together

George Gray Molina

B olivia is widely regarded as the *other* new Left story in Latin America: two landslide elections in 2005 and 2009, the presence of social and indigenous movements, and the figure of former coca growers' leader Evo Morales are all deemed unique in a regional and historical context. Academics contrast the Bolivian *proceso de cambio* (change process) favorably with respect to the Venezuelan, Nicaraguan, and Ecuadorian experiences (Touraine 2005; Castañeda 2006; Dunkerley 2007). Since Morales's reelection in December 2009, however, political mishaps have weighed against the Movimiento al Socialismo (MAS; Movement toward Socialism), including an attempt to raise hydrocarbon prices in December 2010 and police violence against an indigenous march in September 2011. During the most recent clash, sociologist Boaventura de Sousa Santos remarked that "Evo's government is no longer of the left, [but] a field of struggle," in a quote that resounded beyond academic circles (Página Siete 2011). Political infighting and confrontations with indigenous movements have weakened a broad-based political coalition that yielded a strong electoral majority for five years.

Despite this, the MAS political project has not unraveled. It is bolstered by a strong economy, a weak opposition, and a majority coalition that continues to include campesino unions, social movements, the urban poor, and fractions of the middle class. Many analysts have observed that the MAS is a loosely organized movement rather than an institutionalized political party (Harten 2011; Centellas 2011). I argue this feature has come to define the *proceso de cambio* beyond the refoundational agenda itself. This chapter addresses the tensions of building a broad-based political coalition—without becoming a party—in Bolivia. In contrast to *democracia pactada* (democracy by pact), where political elites bargained among themselves to sustain a political party system, the MAS coalition institutionalized direct bargaining between the state and civil society. This has both strengthened and weakened the prospects for keeping a broad popular coalition together. On the one hand, it raises the stakes for supporting the MAS, as it guarantees unmediated social and political inclusion. On the other hand, it also requires that social and indigenous movements surrender a degree of their political autonomy to uphold a grand coalition—as observed recently with the Territorio Indígena y Parque Nacional Isiboro-Secure (TIPNIS; Isiboro Sécure National Park and Indigenous Territory) affair. This is one of the key tensions faced by social and political actors since the National Revolution: how to construct a broad-based popular coalition together without becoming co-opted by the state it in the process.

The first part of the chapter describes the new political coalition that emerged with Morales's two landslide elections, and how the expanded political coalition created new challenges for democratic governance from within; the second part analyzes what issues were on and off the political agenda, as well as how that has affected the Movimiento al Socialismo (MAS; Movement toward Socialism) coalition. The final section describes future challenges for Bolivian democracy, as the refoundational aspects of Evo Morales's second term in office wane.

A New Balance of Power

From 2005 to 2009: MAS Inroads into Opposition Territory

The December 2005 elections delivered a blow to a twenty-year period that consolidated a pattern of political bargaining between established political parties— the Movimiento Nacionalista Revolucionario (MNR; Nationalist Revolutionary Movement), Acción Democratic Nacionalista (ADN; Nationalist Democratic Action), and the Movimiento de la Izquierda Revolucionaria (MIR; Leftist Revolutionary Movement). Table 6.1 shows voting for key parties in the presidential elections since 1985. These three parties accounted for over 60 percent of votes in the twenty-year period, and translated their electoral power into governing coalitions in parliament. Two features were essential to *democracia pactada*. First is what Eduardo Gamarra has termed "hybrid presidentialism," a form of presidentialism that combines a key role for Congress in the selection of the president, and

Table 6.1.   Votes Won in National Elections, 1985–2009 (in percentages)

	1985	1989	1993	1997	2002	2005	2009
MNR	26.4	23.0	*33.8*	18.2	22.5	6.5	
AP (ADN/ MIR)			20.3				
ADN	*28.6*	22.7		22.3	3.4		
MIR	8.9	19.6		16.8	16.3		
CONDEPA		11.0	13.6	17.2			
UCS			13.1	16.1	5.5		
MBL			5.1	3.1			
IU (ASP)	0.7	7.2	0.9	3.7			
PS-1	2.2	2.8			0.7		
NFR					20.9	0.7	
MAS					20.9	*53.7*	*64.2*
MIP					6.1	2.2	
MRTKL			2.2				
LyJ					2.7		
PODEMOS						28.6	
UN						7.8	5.6
CN							26.5
AS							2.3
Valid Votes	1,728,363	1,573,790	1,731,309	2,177,171	2,778,808	2,185,960	4,582,786

Sources: Gamarra and Malloy 1995; Yaksic and Tapia 1997; Dunkerley 2000; Assies and Salman 2005; Tribunal Supremo 2012

Note: Results for the party that won the election is in italics. ADN = Acción Democrática Nacionalista, Acuerdo Patriótico, AS = Alianza Social, ASP = Asamblea por la Soberanía de los Pueblos, CN = Concertación Nacional, CONDEPA = Conciencia de Patria, IU = Izquierda Unida, LyJ = Libertad y Justicia, MAS = Movimiento al Socialismo, MBL = Movimiento Bolivia Libre, MIP = Movimiento Indigenista Pachacuti, MIR = Movimiento de Izquierda Revolucionaria, MNR = Movimiento Nacionalista Revolucionario, MRTKL = Movimiento Revolucionario Túpac Katari de Liberación, NFR = Nueva Fuerza Republicana, PS-1 = Partido Socialista-Uno, UCS = Unidad Cívica Solidaridad.

also in crafting a governing parliamentary coalition. The executive needed parliament to rule, and parliament needed this power to consolidate a stable political party system. The mutual need cemented five government coalitions and averted a number of government crises along the way. The political space gained by the executive/legislative pacts were also lost in the quality of representation and overall weakness of the legislative branch. Second, the political system relied on patronage and clientelism to include the demands of popular organizations and, to some extent, to keep the popular vote within the system. The systemic reach was tested twice with neopopulist candidacies from Conciencia de Patria (CONDEPA; Fatherland Consciousness) and Unidad Cívica Solidaridad (UCS; Civic Unity of Solidarity) (Archondo 1991; Mayorga 2002; Assies and

Salman 2005). The MAS broke a pattern of systemic bargaining and expansion of the system. The Morales candidacy occurred at a point when indigenous or more radical demands for political participation became antisystemic. The period between 2002 and 2005 is a case study in the unraveling of a systemic political party regime.

The 2005 elections brought with them not only a new president, but also a new set of political actors and practices. The MAS won 53.7 percent of the vote, with 72 deputies and 12 senators out of a total of 157, and mostly prevailed in the Andean departments of the country. The outlines of a broad coalition were there: Morales won a vast majority of the rural vote and nearly half of the urban vote, which concentrates most potential voters. The rural coalition stood on the social strength of a group of indigenous and campesino organizations that provided a core organization: Confederación Sindical Única de Trabajadores (CSUTCB; Unified Syndical Confederation of Rural Workers), Colonizadores, Confederación de Pueblos Indígenas de Bolivia (CIDOB; Confederation of Indigenous Peoples of Bolivia), Consejo Nacional de Ayllus y Markas del Qullasusyu (CONAMAQ; National Council of Ayllus and Markas of Qullasuyu), and the Confederación Sindical Unica de Trabajadores Campesinos-Bartolina Sisa (CSUTCB-Bartolina Sisa; Unified Syndical Confederation of Rural Workers-Bartolina Sisa). Despite the concentration of the vote in Andean and rural areas, the MAS secured enough votes to elect a president without a congressional negotiation, which had been a hallmark of the past. The electoral margin proved strong enough to push through a law calling for a constituent assembly, which deliberated from 2007 to 2009.

In hindsight, the most significant political event during Morales's first term was the aftermath of the violence that erupted in Pando in October 2008. After that event, during which armed groups confronted *campesinos* in the outskirts of Cobija, the regional opposition that had led public opposition to Evo Morales collapsed. With the civic committees out of mainstream electoral competition, the "acuerdo de octubre" (October Agreement of 2008) paved the way to the approval of the new constitution and a new landslide victory for the MAS.

In the December 2009 elections, the MAS made significant inroads on what was considered "opposition territory," winning 64 percent of the vote, eighty-eight deputies and twenty-six senators out of a total of 166, but also majorities in seven of nine departments including the departments of Santa Cruz and Tarija. The regional sweep shows an embattled opposition cornered in certain pockets of lowland Bolivia. To the extent that the MAS vote thrived on the popular sectors and highland immigrants living in the lowlands, it defused a dangerous regional rift that had been threatening political stability along geographic lines.

Two issues define Morales's second term in office. First, it started with a clear mandate to implement the ambitious refoundational reforms included in the new constitution. These included changes to the judiciary power, electoral law, legislative assembly, and also in the quality of departmental, regional, municipal, and indigenous autonomies. The *campesino*, indigenous, and rural coalition that had led to the MAS's first victory, expanded to include numerous urban constituencies, including neighborhood councils, universities, informal sector associations, and middle class professional groups. Legislative activism was made easier by a two-thirds majority in the plurinational assembly. Second, the composition of the cabinet and key assembly leaders suggested a move away from the direct participation of indigenous and social movements and the rise of middle class and MAS party sympathizers. While the shift did not make waves at the time, it would eventually become a focus of debate within MAS circles (Almaraz 2012). The new MAS cadres would be perceived as being increasingly loyal to the president and vice president and less to the social organizations that delivered two electoral victories.

Post-2010: *The Problems of an Expanded Coalition*

A year after the 2009 elections, the political coalition ran into some trouble. Two policy decisions put a dent on the political agenda and affected the pace of reform itself. The first was an unsuccessful attempt to raise the price of hydrocarbons in December 2010. The measure, which liberalized prices for diesel and gasoline, amounted to a 73 percent increase in prices for gasoline and an 82 percent increase on diesel. After three days, a massive mobilization led by the Central Obrera Boliviana (Bolivian Workers' Central) and other popular organizations brought the country to a halt and called for the resignation of key economic authorities, including Vice President Garcia Linera himself. On New Year's Eve, Evo Morales repealed the decree and admitted that he had heard and seen the people's rage: "it's time to govern obeying the people" (Jornada 2011). Two effects of the *gasolinazo* lingered on.

The first effect was a critical indictment of economic policymaking and the nationalization of hydrocarbons. Five years after nationalization, the country still imported most of its diesel and jet fuel oil in 2010 and subsidized the internal market by as much as $500 million a year, at the peak of international oil prices—with a part of the subsidy leaving the country in smuggled canisters of liquefied gas—in a context of domestic shortages. The fiscal pressures that led to the decision to liberalize prices were as much an admission that a consolidated fiscal surplus actually hid an indebted treasury, and that Yacimientos Petrolíferos Fiscales Bolivianos (YPFB; National Oil Fields of Bolivia), which changed chief executives every year for five years, were perceived as being a political drag rather than a dynamo of broad-based economic growth.

The second effect was more profound, as it impacted over the narrative behind the *proceso de cambio* in Bolivia. The *gasolinazo* reminded people of past austerity measures approved during the holiday seasons, supposedly masterminded by the IMF and implemented by neoliberal policymakers throughout the 1980s and 1990s. Even the repeal sounded neoliberal. Both Morales and Garcia Linera made the case that gas subsidies were hurting the fiscal balance sheets of the Ministry of the Economy and Finances and that liberalization was "required to stop the drain on the economy." The *gasolinazo* showed that there was a wounding gap between policy messages and policy action. Evo Morales's popularity plummeted to a 32 percent approval rate, as the average citizen could neither understand nor share the technocratic rationale behind such an unpopular policy. The *gasolinazo* also initiated a second wave of ruptures within the MAS coalition. A group of former government officials wrote a six-page manifesto lamenting the derailment of the *proceso de cambio,* and received a 136-page reply by Vice President Garcia Linera. The effects escalated with the TIPNIS crisis.

In July 2011, the twenty-four indigenous communities of the Territorio Indígena y Parque Nacional Isiboro-Secure (TIPNIS) rejected a proposal to build a 174 km highway through their national park, linking the Chapare-Cochabamba with Trinidad-Beni. Tensions escalated as the Administradora Boliviana de Caminos (ABC; Bolivian Administrator of Roads) initiated preparatory clearing of forests on the highway inside the TIPNIS park. The communities of the TIPNIS decided on August 15 to initiate a march to the city of La Paz to protest the highway and denounce the lack of consultation over public works in their indigenous territory as described in the new constitution. President Morales at first ridiculed the march as being led by neoliberal environmental NGOs, later decried USAID and US Embassy involvement in the march, and eventually linked former president Sánchez de Lozada as someone behind the CIDOB's legal counsel vis-à-vis the OAS Inter-American Human Rights Commission.

As the march proceeded, numerous attempts at dialogue failed and highlighted the strength of an emerging coalition of indigenous peoples and urban middle classes. Indigenous peoples, under the new constitution, held consultation rights for any development initiatives in their territory. This message resounded with the urban middle classes and with other popular organizations, including CONA-MAQ and the Central Obrera Boliviana (COB; Bolivian Workers' Central). As the march reached the border between Beni and La Paz, a counter-blockade was set up outside the town of Yucumo by MAS sympathetic coca-leaf growers. Police forces were sent in to "make sure the march did not reach Yucumo," after a group of indigenous women forced Minister Choquehuanca to march with them toward the Yucumo blockade. The violence that erupted on September 25 led to the violent repression of *marchistas* and to the arrest and release of indigenous leaders.

A cabinet crisis ensued over the following days, with the resignation of the minister of defense objecting to police violence against *marchistas*. Later that day, Vice Minister of Government Marcos Farfán resigned to defend his actions as field leader of the Yucumo police operations. The next day, Minister of Government Sacha Llorenti also resigned to provide breathing space for President Morales in the context of a growing crisis. On September 29, the president put the highway project on hold until a two-department referendum could determine the issue. Massive street protests followed the presidential address, as blame was deflected with one government official after the other. The police violence is currently under investigation by three different commissions: the United Nations, Defensoria del Pueblo (the Bolivian Ombudsman), and the Union de Naciones Suramericana (UNASUR; Union of South American Nations).

The net effect of the TIPNIS conflict was a third wave of political splintering inside the MAS coalition. MAS indigenous deputies threatened to abandon the party and take with them the two-thirds majority votes required for a filibuster-proof majority in the assembly. Many urban MAS voters were also disenchanted and joined opposition forces in the null/abstention vote for the judicial election in October 2011. A weakened MAS led to a rise in social protest against the government around the country.

On the Agenda: Strengthening the State

Nationalization and Expanded Social Transfers

In Evo's first term, two key measures provided the backbone for electoral success: nationalization of hydrocarbons and expanded social transfers. The nationalization of Bolivian natural gas was achieved under two different administrations, with a law approved during the Mesa administration in July 2005 (Law 3058) and a decree passed by the Morales administration in May 2006 (Decree 28701).

Neither legal instrument nationalizes via expropriation or changes in property rights. Both measures increased the government's take by an order of magnitude: Law 3058 increased government participation from 18 to 50 percent of production value while Decree 28701 increased this figure up to 82 percent and included a renegotiation of contracts with close to a dozen multinational companies. Taken together, however, the two measures represented a swing away from the past.

The nationalization process made two important changes. The first was the new structure of the government's take. Government participation in hydrocarbons has four sources: the first is an 18 percent royalty over the value of production; the second is a 32 percent Direct Hydrocarbons Tax; the third is a payment to YPFB of recoverable costs, negotiated on a contract-by-contract basis; and the fourth is the distribution of the remainder as shared utilities between YPFB and the operator, based on a formula that accounts for new and depreciated capital investments, the price of natural gas, and volumes of production (Del Granado et al. 2010). Under the new contracts, the government's take fluctuates between 67 percent of gross production value (at US$1 dollar per million BTUs) and 75 percent of gross production value (if prices reach US$4.5 dollars per million BTUs) (Medinacelli 2007). Under the new contractual terms, hydrocarbons operators pay a little more than the 50 percent negotiated in Law 3058 and a little less than the 82 percent included in Decree 28701.

The increase in government revenues and new contracts have had at least two positive and three negative impacts. The first positive effect is that, due to extraordinary increases in prices and better bilateral negotiation with Argentina and Brazil, Bolivian GDP topped US$19 billion in 2010, a US$9 billion increase since 2005. The second positive effect is a significant increase in government revenues accruing from the hydrocarbons sector, reaching US$1.6 billion in 2010, about twice as much as Bolivia received in total foreign aid (donations plus credit). On the downside, the price effect of exports weighed heavily over the production effect in explaining additional export revenues. In 2006, average prices were 5.4 times greater than prices eight years earlier and three times greater than three years earlier. Second, the gas sector in Bolivia has become increasingly uncertain with respect to new investments in exploration and higher export volumes. This has been evident in negotiations with Brazil and Argentina, with Bolivia unable to fulfill existing contracts. Third, to the extent that the global gas market is expanding, Bolivia needs to look beyond the regional market, including the Pacific basin, to improve its leverage position over regional competitors and regional demand.

Additional revenues from the hydrocarbons sector financed expanded social transfer programs to school-age children (Juancito Pinto), pregnant and lactating women (Juana Azurduy de Padilla), and the elderly (Renta Dignidad), and account for over US$240 million, or approximately 1.8 percent of Bolivian GDP in 2010 (Garcia Linera 2011). The transfers reach close to 2,000,000 children and approximately 600,000 men and women over the age of 65. While the Juancito Pinto is modeled on the Bono Escuela program of the city of El Alto and similar programs in Brazil (Bolsa Família) and Mexico (Progresa), the Renta Dignidad is an expansion of the Bonosol payment implemented with the capitalization of public companies in the 1990s. The difference from the Bonosol is in how the transfer is funded: for nine years, funding for the payment came from utilities from capitalized companies and internal debt, while it is now paid with hydrocarbons taxes and royalty payments to the regions.

The Renta Dignidad is an annual payment to 600,000 Bolivians over the age of 65 who have no retirement income and an additional 130,000 Bolivians who do receive a retirement payment. The amount paid to those without retirement income is Bs$2,400 (about US$320), and the amount paid to salaried retirees is Bs$1,800 (about US$240). In 2010, the total annual cost of the Renta Dignidad was about US$240 million.

The Juancito Pinto payment was designed to increase school attendance and reduce desertion, and it has been in place since November 2006. In 2010, over 1.8 million children enrolled in public schools from first to sixth grade, in alternative and technical education schools, and in special education programs. The program expanded to two million children in grades first to eight by the end of 2010. Each child receives an annual Bs$200 payment (about US$26), subject to an annual evaluation confirming that the child is attending school. In 2010, the annual cost of the Juancito Pinto payment was expected to be about US$51.9 million. An additional grant, named after the republican hero Juana Azurduy de Padilla, reached 208,000 women and 341,000 children under the age of one. The total amount for this mostly rural program is $US13.4 million.

A recent simulation by Nora Lustig et al. (2011) compares the fiscal impact of the Bolivian transfer with similar programs in the region—Brazil, Argentina, Mexico, and Peru (Lustig et al. 2011). While Bolivia spends a relatively high proportion of its GDP in social transfers, and more of its goes to the poorest quintile than to the richest quintile of the population (making it progressive in absolute terms), the Bolivian program is still one of the least effective in reducing poverty in the region. This is mostly because of the universal characteristics of spending in Bolivia (a large amount of recipients spanning upper and lower deciles) and because most social transfers accrue to retired age population, rather than to children and mothers. A more targeted approach might accelerate social achievement in the poorest quintiles of the population with consequent impact on poverty and inequality reduction over the long run.

Behind the Agenda: Bargaining with Society

Weak State and Institutional Pluralism

The historical record suggests a "weak state / strong society" balance, despite state-building efforts in the mid-1950s and the mid-1990s. The nature of this relationship, however, has not been sufficiently discussed—with a tendency to focus on what was "missing" from democratic state building, rather than on what is driving the specificity of state and societal development in Bolivia.

I have argued elsewhere that the historical form taken by a "weak state / strong society" trajectory in Bolivia helps to explain a number of features that puzzle social and political analysts and policymakers today (Gray Molina 2005, 2008). Among them, the absence of large-scale violence in a society marked by pronounced ethnic cleavages, social inequality, and regional imbalances. The modus vivendi adopted by the Bolivian state includes various forms of institutional pluralism that accommodate social pressures from below and a society that takes on many features of de facto statehood from above in such important matters as the administration of justice, natural resource management, and political self-rule. The state is neither as weak as many political analysts suggest, nor is society as strong as many would like; the Bolivian modus vivendi has been based on shifting alliances of power between elites and social actors throughout the twentieth century.

And while the state/societal modus vivendi has kept the peace for over a century, recent events suggest that this form of governance is ill-equipped to manage the tasks of an increasingly urban, cosmopolitan, intercultural, and global society and economy. The Bolivian challenge, in the future, is not as simple as strengthening the state—either in the progressive strong-state mold or in the liberal rule-of-law sense. The most difficult challenge, it would seem, is for Bolivian social and state actors to construct a renewed modus vivendi able to tackle a set of important and intractable problems: pressure over natural resources, increased social services for new urban populations, and intercultural politics in the public sphere, among others.

Institutional pluralism is not exempt from problems. The proliferation of autonomous institutional rules tends to fragment the national public sphere—places where the joint construction of legitimacy, authority, and sovereignty are required to deal with national questions. There are many cases of judicial or natural resource disputes between communities, peoples, or groups that could not be addressed because each challenged the legitimacy of the rule of law as applied to their specific circumstance. For many group issues, community customary law has sufficed; for disputes between groups and communities, however, the cost of institutional pluralism can be high. Factional disputes over the nature and scope of the rule of law are often the rule, rather than the exception, at the national level.

A related question on institutional pluralism is whether it is withering or whether it is a structural feature of the state. The historical view is that the continuous process of negotiation over the legal and bureaucratic extension of the Bolivian state has resulted in a chronic process of accommodation, both for political institutions and for political practice. The state should not, in this view, be seen as "unfinished" or "noninstitutionalized," but rather, as a type of state that has institutionalized differently. Rather than conforming to a pure type of political regime—liberal, socialist, or communitarian—the Bolivian state is so hybrid that takes on a national-popular ideological umbrella. Hence, monolithic descriptions of the Bolivian state—the neoliberal, populist, or colonial state—tend to miss the point and misrepresent the nature of state-society relations.

While institutional pluralism is the predominant feature of political accommodation in the twentieth century, a less commented feature is that civil society organizations such as NGOs, churches, neighborhood councils, international donors, unions, and indigenous groups, among others, take on quasi-state-like authority. These include the self-regulation of land and natural resources, self-legislation concerning civil disputes, keeping the peace, and enforcing customary law. These discontinuities, places where bureaucratic or legal state presence is tenuous, are places where authority, legitimacy, and sovereignty are continuously contested.

For some, this is evidence of a failed or weakened state that should be filled with liberal democratic institutions. For others, it is evidence of indigenous and popular self-rule, self-government, and self-legislation. I argue that state discontinuities are evidence of neither. If we recognize that the discontinuous construction of state authority is a feature of state-society relations, we are more likely to see state discontinuities as evidence of a peculiar balance of power between state and society, rather than as a credit or debit with respect to state weakness or social strength.

A more important question to ask is whether state discontinuities are ruled by particularism or by some sense of public rule. Particularism includes a number of forms of patrimonial politics, clientelism, and *caudillismo* (political authoritarianism). It is a form of politics that privatizes or hoards power in the hands of few. Public rule can be defined as a form of politics that is open, public, and binding, even among adversaries or rivals. It includes the rule-of-law as traditionally discussed in the political science literature, but it may also include forms of customary or local law that do not inhibit open and public deliberations over political power. The public or private nature of discontinuities is something that is open to empirical verification. It is observable in the way local leaders are appointed and how they exercise local, regional, and national power.

Off the Agenda: Institutionalizing Achievements

Missing from the National-Popular-Indigenous Nexus: Material Impact

Pablo Stefanoni, writing on MAS politics, described recent political realignments as the struggle between a national indigenous movement that loosely united middle class and rural voters under a progressive umbrella and *pachamamistas*, indigenists, stemming from both a romantic indigenous narrative and an uncompromising antiglobalization position (Stefanoni 2011). The TIPNIS crisis splintered both the national-indigenous coalition by dividing urban middle class voters and also the *pachamamista* faction by pitting lowland indigenous organizations against other indigenous organizations (Colonizadores and MAS party organizations). Beyond the short-run confrontation, what seemed to be missing were incentives for a progressive policy coalition to stick together.

The national-popular-indigenous nexus continues to provide a broad political and electoral umbrella for the MAS, but is less and less a catalyst for social and political change. The current coalition faces two longstanding problems. The first is related to how successful electoral coalitions translate into successful policy coalitions. This was also a challenge during the 1990s wave of policy reform (Graham et al. 1999). Institutional reforms promise future benefits but tend to incur short-run costs that conspire against cumulative policy success from one administration to the next or within a single administration. The usual practice, which redistributes benefits to a political clientele on the basis of political patronage, is reaching its limit in a context of squeezed finances and over-extended central government bureaucracies.

The second challenge is how to strengthen institutions that channel political energy into cumulative social and policy achievements. As much as the state is being refounded in a political sense, it is also being dismantled in a policy sense. Although the public payroll has increased from 7 percent of GDP in 2006 to 10 percent in 2010, the effectiveness of social service delivery and economic support for broad-based growth has not increased (International Monetary Fund 2011).

The key issue is the lack of progress in social and economic affairs—not having material impact over poverty and inequality levels. The latest figures suggest a mixed picture. Economic growth rates, measured on a per capita basis, have been exceptional in the past half-decade. Per capita income increased from $1,147 in 2005 to an estimated $1,900 in 2010. According to official statistics, the poverty rate has dropped 11 percentage points, from 60.9 percent in 2005 to 49.9 percent in 2010. Despite the drop of about 2 percentage points per year, the absolute number of poor has only decreased by about 90,000 per year, with 5.1 million still under the poverty line. The greatest reduction in poverty has occurred in rural areas, particularly at the extreme poverty line. Recent studies have concluded that much of the redistributive impact comes from both a decline in the wage premium between skilled and unskilled workers, and to a lesser extent, from the impact of social transfers, which tend to be fiscally progressive, but not large enough to lift poor households up to the poverty line (Lustig et al. 2011).

The mismatch between high rates increases of per capita income and very moderate improvements in poverty reduction suggests that economic activity still reflects a commodity-driven economy, with little productivity improvements of the low-hanging fruit variety (labor movement from low-sector productivity agriculture to high-productivity manufacturing) and even less of the of the value-added improvements in productivity (through export upgrading from commodities to knowledge intensive or low-carbon sectors) (Gray Molina 2011). A narrow economic base, concentrated in natural gas and mining in the formal sectors and services and contraband/illicit activities in the informal sector continues to define Bolivia's pattern of economic development.

International Relations, between Loyalty and Exit

A turn to international relations has been increasingly important for domestic politics. At the beginning of the Morales administration, "pragmatic" and "ideological" strands of foreign policy competed: where pragmatism was the defining feature of bilateral talks with Brazil and Argentina on regional issues, and with Chile on the 13-point agenda, and ideological politics defined the embattled position with respect to the United States, Alianza Bolivariana para los Pueblos de Nuestra América (ALBA; Bolivarian Alliance for the Americas), and Climate Change talks. After the 2009 elections, the ideological strand became more visible and overtook most of the foreign policy agenda. Talks with Chile broke down in March 2011 and have since floundered with the threat of Bolivia taking its case to The Hague to recover access to the Pacific coast.

The move inward will have a sizeable effect over certain issues on the policy agenda: regional integration with Brazil, international trade and development, and climate change/environmental policies. The Brazilian relationship has grown increasingly important as other links to the region have receded. Three issues are key: the first has to do with antinarcotics and security policies. Following the expulsion of the DEA in 2009, Brazil has increased its presence in joint training activities with the Bolivian police and has shown interest in addressing narcotics interdiction in transit from Bolivia. Brazil has also shown concern over the recent fiscal amnesty on used cars, which included hundreds of stolen vehicles from the frontier region. Finally, the TIPNIS crisis has created tension, with the Brazilian construction company OAS, financed, in part by Banco Nacional de Desenvolvimento (BNDES; the Brazilian National Development Bank) infrastructure facility. Brazilian diplomats have been forced to make explicit communiques on Bolivian ownership of the highway project, and deference to national procedures on environmental and indigenous consultations.

Trade and development issues have been on the Bolivian back burner for years. Trade negotiations are deemed less important, given the importance of natural gas trade in the Southern Cone and minerals trade with Asia. To the extent that the export basket has been reconcentrated—close to 75 percent of exports are currently traditional hydrocarbons and minerals exports—the move for trade diversification has stalled and receded. The recent drop in commodity prices for soybeans, oil, and some minerals, is forcing diversification back on the agenda. To the extent that domestic economic indicators are still promising, Bolivian foreign policy is unlikely to change with respect to trade, investment, and development. New pressures would likely arise if a global recession sets in, affecting key prices.

Finally, the climate change agenda, although relatively minor in development and investment terms, is where Evo Morales has made the biggest splash since the Cancun Climate Change talks, in which Bolivia was the sole protest vote on a global agreement. The environmental agenda has been a test case for Bolivian foreign policy since the TIPNIS crisis erupted (Solon 2011). The gap between words and deeds has seen a backlash from the global environmental community that once supported the Bolivian position at the peoples' Climate Change Summit in Tiquipaya and later, at Cancun. If Evo Morales once commanded moral leadership on indigenous and environmental issues worldwide, that support is being presently eroded by the TIPNIS affair.

Conclusions

This chapter discusses one of the tensions behind Evo Morales's second term in office. In a political system that is still in flux, the most important issue for democratic governance continues to be the endurance of the broad-based popular coalition that brought Morales to power. While other issues linger in the background— the implementation of a new constitution, the scope of regional autonomies, and the independence of the judiciary power, among others—the future of the *proceso de cambio* hinges on whether urban, *campesino*, and indigenous organizations continue to support the MAS coalition. Despite electoral success and a broad electorate, the MAS has not become a political party itself (Zuazo 2009; Cortez Hurtado 2011). This predicament is not unique to this period in Bolivian history. It was a critical issue for the MNR (National Revolutionary Movement) in the late 1950s and early 1960s, and eventually led to its fracture and demise (Whitehead 2008). Also relevant, is that the current pattern of political bargaining between strong social movements and a relatively weak state did not follow from the new constitution and electoral law, but preceded it. Despite deliberate attempts to create a state that is responsive to social movements in its institutional design, the current challenge faced by the MAS runs deeper, to the question of how a political coalition can deliver lasting institutions at all.

Three challenges will affect Bolivian democratic governance in the future. The first has to do with the difficulty of translating successful electoral coalitions into successful policy and institutional coalitions. Much of the recent political unraveling of the MAS has been self-inflicted and ignited by controversial policy measures. The *gasolinazo* and the TIPNIS affair have tested the frailty of a political system that is prone to spill out onto the streets at the slightest provocation. Although Evo Morales has held the coalition in the past, he is facing growing skepticism about the *way* democratic politics develops in Bolivia (Oporto 2011). Political agreements are too frequently reached after a great deal of social and political conflict. In addition, agreements, even when reached, seem to push substantive unresolved issues into the distant future—effectively postponing solutions to poverty and inequality, environmental sustainability, devolved subnational government, and many other issues. Few cumulative policy successes have been possible in this environment, as each government has had an incentive to unravel fragile agreements and pursue a lone policy path.

The ambition of the new constitution, approved in 2009, multiplied governance challenges by opening numerous policy fronts: coalitions for and against the approval of indigenous autonomy statutes, controlling food prices, a fiscal amnesty for used cars, an indigenous slate in the judicial elections, a law on municipal and departmental borders, among many others. In addition to the policy-induced infighting, the MAS also faced its first electoral upset in the judicial elections of October 16, 2011. If in the past, the MAS has united around Evo Morales, this has become more and more unlikely as his second term faces challenges from within.

The second challenge has been institutions that have been weakened after a drawn-out constitutional reform process. Given the refoundational mandate of the constituent assembly, the incentives of the political game have been to continuously reinvent the rules of the game. This might begin to explain why a weak state-strong society balance of power has led to the proliferation of institutional solutions *outside* of the mainstream institutional framework. This "institutional pluralism"—institutional power-sharing mechanisms, dual powers, social control mechanisms, corporatist negotiations, patronage politics that coexist with the formal institutions of representative government—has been both an asset and a weakness for democratic governance. Institutional pluralism, although messy, has been effective at including excluded groups, at diffusing political power and, at times, keeping the peace in moments of violence and conflict. In the absence of a representative democratic system that works effectively, this patched-up system has provided a minimum democratic floor. However, it also weakens incentives to change gross inequality in land holdings, in income, and in access to social services, and promotes meritocratic mobility. It locks in past privilege and provides little momentum for cumulative policy successes of the type that will make a dent in living standards and equity.

Morales faces the challenge of institutional pluralism with each new policy initiative. The recent TIPNIS crisis was exacerbated by the lack of accountability in the public chain of command. The multiple layers of envoys, negotiators that move outside of official institutional channels, are dense and defined by the relative power of political stakeholders. With the TIPNIS episode, compromised political actors were able to sidestep responsibility and place blame on others; the open-ended process allowed the president himself to blame the media for dramatizing an antigovernment story.

The third challenge has to do with how domestic and international politics play off each other. Since 2006, foreign relations were mostly managed with both a "pragmatic" and "ideological" wing: pragmatic with the UNASUR members, with Chile until the breakup in March 2011, and with Brazil and Argentina during gas and integration negotiations. The ideological streak was most evident with the Climate Change Summit and with the expulsion of the US ambassador in 2008. The recent weakening of Venezuelan foreign policy and the domestic problems brewing at home have opened a gap between what is said and what is done in international relations.

Although Bolivia has championed a radical environmentalist position at global meetings—rejecting the concept of green economies, reduced deforestation mechanisms, carbon markets, and other market-based policy instruments—it has shown a clearly developmentalist position at home. This has been most evident during the TIPNIS conflict, but also for less public decisions on biodiversity, transgenic crops, funding for natural parks, allowing entry of polluting automobiles, and looking the other way on local and regional legislation that condones lax environmental standards in the domestic economy. These gaps affect Evo Morales's political credibility abroad, which has recently started to draw international attention (El Pais 2011).

If political infighting is on the agenda in Bolivia, what can be expected in the future? Two things seem certain. First, despite lulls in popularity and credibility, it is unlikely that the MAS will lose its power base any time before the national elections of 2014. Core electoral support is still strong, and Evo Morales has proven resilient in past political skirmishes. The MAS upset at the judicial elections will likely galvanize a new round of party building. However, the opposition is still fragmented, with growing support for Juan del Granado, Samuel Doria Medina, and Ruben Costas from different opposition constituents. The greatest political threats emerge from within the MAS itself, which is embattled and looking for a way to salvage the *proceso de cambio* in the near future.

Second, the learning curve is steep for institutional change in Bolivia. The many social and economic challenges that keep poverty and inequality high confirm that not much has changed in the labor market, with a commodity-driven growth boom with few links to broad-based growth, which also threaten environmental sustainability in the medium term. The institutions needed for a "different type of development" are not so different from the institutions needed for "development": they are likely to be transparent, effective, and allow for cumulative policy successes that may take twenty or thirty years—education policy, environmental policy, economic diversification, judicial reform, and sustainable urban planning are all in this category. The key difference in this historical period is in the process: the MAS legitimizes its actions in the process of governing, rather than waiting for policy outcomes to mature. This probably means that institution building will continue to be on the agenda for the foreseeable future. The question is whether this will build upon refoundational change, or whether less foundational change is brewing for the next decade. In any event, democratic governance will be at the center of Bolivia's quest to get beyond politics-as-usual and spur long-lasting social and economic progress.

NOTES

This essay is based on a paper presented at an Inter-American Dialogue workshop in Washington DC, October 6–7, 2011.

REFERENCES

Almaraz, Alejandro. 2012. *La mascarada del poder.* Cochabamba: Textos Rebeldes.

Archondo, Rafael. 1991. *Compadres al microfono: La resurrección metropolitana del ayllu.* La Paz: HISBOL.

Assies, Willem, and Ton Salman. 2005. "Ethnicity and Politics in Bolivia." *Ethnopolitics* 3:269–97.

Castañeda, Jorge. 2006. "Latin America's Left Turn." *Foreign Affairs* (August/September).

Centellas, Miguel. 2011. "Beyond Caudillos: The Need to Create a Strong Multiparty System." *Revista,* David Rockefeller Center for Latin American Studies. Cambridge: Harvard University.

Cortez Hurtado, Roger, ed. 2011. *Claves de la transición del poder, cuadernos de futuro.* La Paz: PNUD.

Del Granado, Hugo, Leila Mokrani, Mauricio Medinacelli, and Jorge Gumucio. 2010. *Generación, distribución y uso del excedente de hidrocarburos en Bolivia.* La Paz: PIEB.

Dunkerley, James. 2007. "Evo Morales, the 'Two Bolivias' and the Third Bolivian Revolution." *Journal of Latin American Studies* 39:133–66.

Gamarra, Eduardo, and James Malloy. 1995. "The Patrimonial Dynamics of Party Politics in Bolivia." In *Building Democratic Institutions: Party Systems in Latin America,* edited by Scott Mainwaring and T. R. Scully, 399–433. Stanford: Stanford University Press.

Garcia Linera, Alvaro. 2011. *El oenegismo: Enfermedad infantil del derechismo.* La Paz: Vicepresidencia del Estado Plurinacional de Bolivia.

Graham, Carol, Merilee Grindle, Eduardo Lora, and Jessica Seddon. 1999. *Improving the Odds: Political Strategies for Institutional Reform in Latin America.* Washington, DC: IDB.

Gray Molina, George. 2005. "Harmony of Inequalities: Ethnic Politics in Bolivia, 1900–2000." Oxford CRISE Working Paper. Oxford: CRISE.

———. 2008. "The Strength of Weak Ties: State/Society Relations in Bolivia." In *Unresolved Tensions: Bolivia Past and Present*, edited by John Crabtree and Laurence Whitehead. Pittsburgh: University of Pittsburgh Press.

———. 2011. "Crecimiento económico adaptativo." Paper presented at the Academia Boliviana de Ciencias Económicas. La Paz: ABCE.

Harten, Sven 2011. *The Rise of Evo Morales and the MAS*. London: Zed Books.

International Monetary Fund. 2011. "Article IV Consultations for Bolivia." Washington, DC: IMF.

Jornada. 2011. "Ante presiones para que renuncie Evo abrogó el 'gasolinazo.'" www.jornadanet.com/n.php?a=57666-1.

Lustig, Nora, et al. 2011. "Fiscal Policy and Income Redistribution in Latin America: Challenging the Conventional Wisdom." CAF Working Paper. Caracas: Corporacion Andina de Fomento.

Mayorga, Fernando. 2002. *Neopopulismo y democracia*. Cochabamba: Centro de Estudios Superiores Universitarios, Universidad Mayor de San Simón.

Medinacelli, Mauricio. 2007. *La Nacionalización del Nuevo Milenio: Cuando el Precio fue un Aliado*. La Paz: Fundemos.

Oporto, Henry. 2011. "Fin del Evismo." Fundación Pazos Canqui. La Paz: FPC.

Pagina Siete. 2011. "El gobierno de Evo ya no es de izquierda, es un campo de lucha." Interview with Boaventura de Sousa Santos, September 17. www.paginasiete.bo /2011-09-18/Nacional/Destacados/06-07nal-001-0918.aspx.

El Pais. 2011. "Las bases indígenas abandonan a Morales." September 27. http://internacional.elpais.com/internacional/2011/09/26/actualidad/1317050867_595306 .html.

Pearce, Adrian, ed. *Evo Morales and the Movimiento al Socialismo in Bolivia: The First Term in Context, 2005–2009*. London: Institute for the Study of the Americas.

Solon, Pablo. 2011. "Letter by Pablo Solon on the TIPNIS Highway Controversy." http:// climate-connections.org/2011/09/29/letter-from-pablo-solon-on-the-tipnis-highway -controversy/.

Stefanoni, Pablo. 2011. *¿Qué hacer con los indios? Y otros traumas irresueltos de la colonialidad*. La Paz: Plural.

Touraine, Alain. 2005. "Entre Bachelet y Morales: Existe una izquierda en America Latina?" *Nueva Sociedad*.

Tribunal Supremo Electoral-Organo Electoral Plurinacional. 2012. www.oep.org.bo/.

Whitehead, Laurence. 2008. "Bolivia's Latest Refoundation." In *Unresolved Tensions: Bolivia Past and Present*, edited by John Crabtree and Laurence Whitehead. Pittsburgh: University of Pittsburgh Press.

Yaksic, Fabian, and Luis Tapia. 1997. Bolivia: Modernizaciones empobrecedoras, desde su fundacion a la desrevolucion. La Paz: Muela del Diablo/SOS Faim.

Zuazo, Moira. 2009. *Como nació el MAS? La ruralización de la política*. La Paz: ILDIS.

CHAPTER SEVEN

Brazil

Democracy in the PT Era

David Samuels

On January 1, 2011, Luiz Inácio "Lula" da Silva left office with an 83 percent approval rating—the highest in Brazilian history—and passed the presidential sash to his successor, Brazil's first female president, Dilma Rousseff (Datafolha 2010). Lula's election and two administrations were historically significant for Brazil in several ways. Lula differed from all previous Brazilian presidents, and his party, the Partido dos Trabalhadores (PT; Workers' Party), differs substantially from Brazil's other parties: they are both "outsiders," in that they do not pertain to the traditional Brazilian economic, political, or social elites. The ascension to power of a poor and uneducated migrant metalworker who became a nationally prominent union leader and who helped found the PT carries substantial symbolic weight, signifying a deepening of democratic governance in Brazil.

As for the PT, it is the first important Brazilian party to be formed autonomously from the influence of the state or political and economic elites. The party grew out of a confluence of union, Catholic church, and social-movement activism in the 1970s and early 1980s, and matured into an organization that catalyzed, mobilized, and channeled a diverse network of individuals working to deepen the participatory contours of Brazilian democracy and to reorient government policy toward the interests of the poor and middle class. As it grew, the PT's organizational strength, programmatic coherence, and administrative innovation at the local and state levels transformed it into the anchor of the opposition and helped it amass a large following of partisan identifiers in the

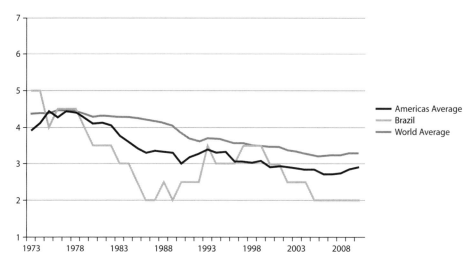

Figure 7.1. Freedom House Scores (1= "Free," 7= "Not Free")

electorate. These characteristics differentiate it from every other Brazilian party. And although it has moderated its political platform since 2002, the PT remains a distinct force in Brazilian politics—both within the halls of power as well as at the grassroots level (Samuels 2004, 2006; Amaral 2010; Hunter 2010; Ribeiro 2010).

The critical question for any evaluation of democratic governance in contemporary Brazil is, *"What difference has ten years of PT rule made for Brazilian democracy?"* To put the discussion of this question in context, consider both objective and subjective assessments of Brazilian democracy. Freedom House classifies the quality of Brazilian democracy today as not just above the world average, but better than average for Latin America (fig. 7.1).

Subjective data—an analysis of the evolution of popular support for democracy— also points toward an optimistic interpretation. Up through 2007, Brazil was a noted laggard in terms of the popular legitimacy of democracy in Latin America, a fact that concerned observers (Weyland 2005; Power 2010). However, satisfaction with democracy has increased since 2007 and now *exceeds* the regional average (fig. 7.2). Brazilian democracy is clearly enjoying a period of unprecedented vitality and durability. Yet room for improvement remains. At the level of the obvious, Freedom House's best score is a "1"—a ranking Brazil has never achieved. Why not? Brazil has come a long way, yet several factors impede further progress.

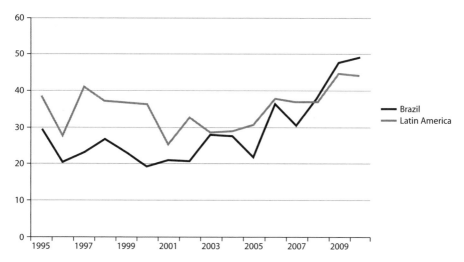

Figure 7.2. Satisfaction with Democracy (% Responding "Very" or "Well" Satisfied)

What difference has PT rule made for Brazilian democracy? Although the PT has always governed in coalition with several parties, including some that also participated in former President Fernando Henrique Cardoso's cabinets, the key difference between Lula's administration and Cardoso's is that Lula's successes and shortcomings reflect *partisan* goals. That is, the most important political dynamic occurring in Brazil today is the PT's effort to remake the country in its own image. Thus, the best way to assess the relative success of this effort is to compare the Lula government's actions against the PT's founding principles, articulated as the *modo petista de governar* or "PT way of governing."

Although the party never used these specific terms, the *modo petista de governar* can be described as an effort to transform Brazilian democracy by (1) strengthening links between state and society, (2) reducing socioeconomic inequalities, and (3) improving the rule of law. The first element focuses on problems of representation and accountability deriving from Brazil's party system and its formal institutional structure; the second deals with the tension between formal democratic equality and informal inequalities of opportunity based on race, class, or gender; and the third, focuses on the web of "illiberal" practices such as corruption, crime, police brutality, and lack of access to justice for average Brazilians.

Before 2003, Brazil had never experienced the combination of a popular leader backed by a highly organized and programmatic political party. The *modo petista de governar* represents a critical element in the PT's self-image and public presentation as "different" (Magalhães, Barreto, and Trevas 1999), and Lula's victory raised the hopes of those who expected his government to redirect government priorities and change the relationship between state and society. Any evaluation of Brazilian democracy must not only focus on policies enacted and those that were left on the table, but on how well government performance measured up to the PT's own vision.

Lula's 2002 campaign sent out conflicting signals about whether his government would put PT principles into practice. On the one hand, Lula sought to placate the market, choosing a prominent conservative businessman as his running mate and releasing a statement of principles that emphasized his acceptance of the rules of the economic game. Lula knew that to win he had to portray himself as someone who would not undo Cardoso's hard-won gains. Yet after winning, to what extent did Lula's government live up to the PT's cherished ideals? The clearest successes have come in terms of the first two "pillars" of the *modo petista de governar*—transforming state-society relations and addressing socioeconomic inequalities, while the clearest failures have come in terms of strengthening the rule of law.

State-Society Relations

The first pillar of the *modo petista de governar* focuses on state-society relations. In its published materials, the PT tends to focus on expanding participatory practices, but I interpret this more broadly, because efforts to deepen democracy can take many forms. The PT has long fought to broaden and strengthen the conception of citizenship, creating new channels of representation as well as expanded participatory opportunities. Three aspects of this pillar merit attention: (1) whether new forms of representation have emerged in Brazil's party system, (2) whether the Lula administration has created new channels of participation for civil society activists, and (3) whether state relations with organized labor have evolved in ways the PT has long advocated.

The Party System: "The PT versus the Rest"

In any democracy, the party system connects citizens to elites. Since Lula took office, have linkages between voters and elected officials been strengthened or weakened? Although the PT has moderated, it remains a distinct actor in Brazil's party system both in terms of its penetration in society and its programmatic positions. This suggests that unlike other Brazilian parties, the PT has strengthened its role as an agent of collective representation and accountability, enhancing democratic responsiveness.

Just after redemocratization, scholars settled on the view that Brazil's parties were weak and its party system "inchoate" (Mainwaring 1999). This interpretation gained traction because it resonated with longstanding notions about Brazilian culture, and because historic state-led labor incorporation efforts and the existing political institutions impeded the emergence of strong parties and a coherent party system. Other scholars challenged this notion, taking the view that party weakness is exaggerated and that the party system is consolidated rather than incoherent (e.g., Figueiredo and Limongi 1999; Hagopian et al. 2009; Limongi and Cortez 2010).

Numerically, the inchoate nature of the party system has increased. Although two-party competition has largely characterized presidential elections since 1994, presidential elections do not reflect party strength. Patterns of competition in legislative elections offer a clearer view; at their peak in 1998 the PT and Partido da Social Democracia Brasileira (PSDB; Brazilian Social Democracy Party) together only obtained about 30 percent of the seats in the lower chamber of Brazil's legislature (table 7.1). In 2010, 22 parties won at least one seat in the chamber; election results have consistently generated high (even increasing) levels of party-system fragmentation (table 7.2).

Table 7.1.   Seat Distribution in the Brazilian Chamber of Deputies, 1990–2010

Parties	1990		1994		1998		2002		2006		2010	
	Seats	%	Seats	%	Seats	%	Seats	%	Seats	%	Seats	%
PT (leftist)	35	7.0	49	9.6	58	11.3	91	17.7	83	16.2	88	17.1
PSDB (centrist)	38	7.6	63	12.3	99	19.3	71	13.8	65	12.7	53	10.3
PP (rightist)	42	8.3	51	9.9	60	11.7	49	9.6	42	8.2	41	7.9
PMDB (centrist)	108	21.5	107	20.9	83	16.2	74	14.4	89	17.3	79	15.3
PDT (leftist)	46	9.1	34	6.6	25	4.9	21	4.1	24	4.7	28	5.4
PTB (centrist)	38	7.6	31	6.0	31	6.0	26	5.1	22	4.3	21	4.0
PFL/DEM (rightist)	83	16.5	89	17.3	105	20.5	84	16.4	65	12.7	43	8.3
Other	113	22.6	89	17.3	52	10.2	97	19.0	123	24.0	160	31.7

Table 7.2.   Effective Number of Legislative Parties

1983	1987	1991	1995	1999	2003	2007	2011
2.39	2.83	8.67	8.17	7.13	8.50	9.3	10.4

The question is, "So what?" Since redemocratization, presidents have needed near-consensus to pass any contentious policy proposal (Ames 2001; Power 2010). This may generate incentives for clientelism and "wheeling and dealing," but it has not obviously harmed governance (Armijo, Faucher, and Dembinska 2006; Arantes and Couto 2009). Reformers continue to target Brazil's political institutions—particularly its electoral system—but the arguments in favor no longer focus on regime stability but on representation and accountability (e.g., Amorim Neto et al. 2011). That is, without a reasonable degree of ideological or programmatic differentiation, democratic responsiveness suffers—or so the argument goes.

Can Brazilian voters tell the major parties from each other? At the elite level, according to legislators' responses to a battery of questions over twenty years, the answer to this question is no, with one exception: legislators from the PT stand apart from those from other parties (Lucas and Samuels 2010), while the rest of the party system has grown relatively *more* incoherent (Power and Zucco 2009). Today, PT legislators stand on the center-left, while members of the PSDB, Partido do Movimento Democrático Brasileiro (PMDB; Brazilian Democratic Movement Party), and Democratas (DEM; Democrats) are all indistinguishable from each other on the center-right. At the elite level, the Brazilian party system remains largely inchoate; the only consistent distinction that matters is between the "PT and the Rest."

A similar dynamic characterizes the party system at the mass level. In comparative perspective, aggregate partisan identification is about average in Brazil—about 40 to 45 percent of voters affirm a party identity. However, only three parties—the PT, the PSDB, and the PMDB—have claimed more than 3 percent of voter preferences consistently since 1989. Figure 7.3 provides the share of Brazilians who identify with these parties, along with the total proportion of voters who identify with a party.

The PMDB has steadily lost identifiers over time, and the PSDB has never attracted a large number of partisan identifiers. This means that about 60 percent of Brazilians who declare a partisan attachment today are *petistas*—individuals who declare a partisan attachment with the PT. The proportion of Brazilians who identify as *petista* grew from about 5 percent in 1989 to 25 percent twenty years later. Even if Brazil were viewed as a *best* case in comparative perspective for the

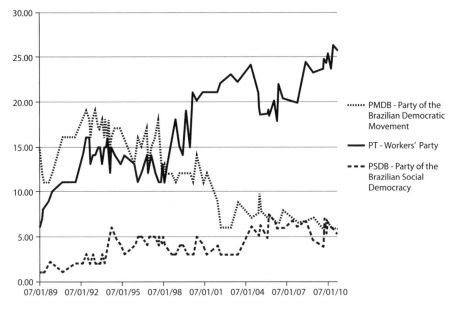

Figure 7.3. Evolution of Party Preferences in Brazil (%), 1989–2010

incubation of mass partisanship in society (which it is not), a single party growing from virtually nil in the 1980s to 25 percent of the population in one generation is an astonishing achievement. In short, developments at the mass level echo
those at the elite level: partisanship is evolving into "the PT versus the Rest"
(Samuels 2006). No other party possesses a collective, programmatic image that
resonates with a sizeable chunk of the electorate.

Representation and accountability in mass democracy presuppose that parties act as collective agents of the electorate. Yet since redemocratization, only
the PT has sought to cultivate a collective partisan reputation. Some degree of
party-system fragmentation would not necessarily weaken democratic representation or accountability, but a system as incoherent as Brazil's dilutes voters' ability to attribute responsibility for political outcomes in legislative elections. Over
the last twenty-five years only PT politicians have successfully appealed to voters
based on their personal qualifications as well as the party's policy positions.

The Evolving Role of Civil Society Organizations

To what extent did the Lula administration create new channels for civil society
to influence government priorities? Early on, civil society organizations (CSOs)

expressed frustration that Lula's government was ignoring this longstanding PT goal (Hochstetler 2006). Many had hoped Lula's election would give the PT the opportunity to scale up successful practices implemented at municipal or state levels, such as participatory budgeting. The perceived failure to put ideals into practice disappointed many, and several analyses concluded that civil society was marginalized during Lula's government (Goldfrank 2011; Hunter 2011).

This conclusion was premature. The Lula government opened various new opportunities for Brazilians to participate in shaping public policies. For space reasons I focus only on Brazil's "National Conferences" (NCs). NCs bring together CSO and government representatives to deliberate about and discuss policy issues. Topics of recent National Conferences include indigenous peoples' health, disability rights, LGBT (lesbian, gay, bisexual, and transgender) issues, sustainable development, human rights, and Afro-Brazilian rights. After a conference is called, thousands of local meetings are held across the country, involving hundreds of thousands of people. These meetings select delegates to state-level conferences, which repeat the deliberative process and then select delegates to the national conference, which aggregates all the lower-level deliberations.

Eighty conferences were held between 1989 and 2009, but were held most frequently under Lula (table 7.3). More pertinently, NCs held under Cardoso covered only seven policy areas, while under Lula their scope expanded dramatically, opening the doors for a far more diverse and heterogeneous set of activists to participate in deliberations about policy recommendations to be delivered to cabinet ministers and members of the legislative branch (see especially Pogrebinschi 2010; Pogrebinschi and Santos 2010).

Do the National Conferences embody the first pillar of the PT's *modo de governar*? Some are skeptical: Souza (2011, 81) suggests that Lula used the NCs instrumentally to intensify pressure on Congress to pass predetermined policy

Table 7.3.   National Conferences by President

Presidency	No. of Conferences	No. of Topics Covered
Fernando Collor (1989–1992)	2	2
Itamar Franco (1992–1994)	6	6
FHC (1995–2002)	17	7
Lula (2003–2010)	55	32
Total	**80**	**33**

Source: Pogrebinschi (2010).

proposals. Likewise, Hochstetler and Friedman (2008, 21–22) argue that CSOs did not influence the Lula administration's agenda, but rather that the PT and the administration dominated the social-policy agenda, subsuming CSOs' role nearly completely.

Avritzer (2010) and Pogrebinschi (2010) disagree, implying that NCs are not merely government efforts to claim popular legitimacy for policies it wants to pass. Both note that CSOs help formulate NC agendas, and that NCs' policy recommendations commonly result in executive decrees and new legislation. Specifically, Pogrebinschi (2010, 11) argues that NCs impact policy under the following conditions:

1. The conference covers an issue where no comprehensive policy framework exists, for example, youth culture, food security, or minority rights;
2. The conference topic is of relatively low political salience for the general population but high salience for an organized and active group; and
3. The conference outcome entails relatively low electoral stakes for the government.

These conditions frequently hold on many social-policy issues of interest to civil society, suggesting that participatory practices can have substantial influence. And apart from the question of influencing concrete outcomes, it is important to highlight the symbolic importance for Brazilian democracy of expanded and participatory mechanisms. It is certainly difficult to dismiss the importance of the fact that an estimated five *million* people participated in National Conferences between 2003 and 2010 (Pogrebinschi 2010, 9). Even if NCs are dominated by long-term activists, and even if not every NC recommendation makes it into law, the fact is that no previous government ever even *listened* to such a wide array of civil society representatives, much less offered them a seat at the policymaking table.

Under Lula, an ever-broader range of citizens gained the opportunity to voice their concerns and demands on issues dear to their hearts, and to participate in a deliberative process. Mechanisms such as the NCs expand the notion of "democratic governance" by drawing our attention away from elections and by highlighting new opportunities for average citizens to participate in the creation of public policy. And while it is true that expanded opportunities to participate may depend on having a friendly political party in power, Avritzer suggests that the rise of the PT has had a cumulative effect on Brazil's political opportunity structure, which is now far more open to grassroots influence than at any point in its history. Civil-society activism creates spaces for gradual political change, because thousands of local-level activists have become community leaders over the years—and many entered politics through the PT or other leftist parties. These new cadres are less clientelistic, have different policy priorities, and believe participatory processes are important for democratic governance.

Participatory mechanisms such as NCs clearly embody the *modo petista de governar*. If they did not, they would not have drawn the disdain of José Serra, the PSDB candidate for president, who argued on the 2010 campaign trail that the National Conferences "do not represent society, but rather a single political party" (Aguiar 2010). One of Lula's close aides lashed out in response, stating that Serra advocated an elitist conception of democracy that gave average Brazilians no right to influence government decisions, only to vote politicians up or down (Dulci 2010).

To what extent has the Lula government created new opportunities for civil society to influence policy priorities? On the one hand, the Lula government did wall off economic policy and the budget from participatory practices. Moreover, the PT still prioritizes the electoral process of representative democracy—that is, it showed no desire to radically transform Brazil's democratic institutions, as in Hugo Chávez's Venezuela, for example. Yet on the other hand, participatory practices put in place during the Lula administration have opened up new spaces for a more diverse set of voices to be heard. Perhaps the most important and lasting impact these participatory practices will have is symbolic—by opening the policy process up to a more diverse set of societal voices, these practices help strengthen the PT's image as the "party of participation"—precisely what the PT has long claimed.

Changing Union-State Linkages

In terms of the PT's ability to transform state-society relations, the last question to ask is whether relations between the state and organized labor have evolved in ways the PT long advocated. Lula was one of many labor leaders who helped found the PT, and the metalworkers union he led formed part of the Central Única dos Trabalhadores (CUT; Unified Worker's Central), an independent union federation which advocated reform of the country's model of labor relations, particularly its Consolidação das Leis do Trabalho (CLT; Consolidated Labor Law), promulgated under dictator Getúlio Vargas in 1943. The CLT model placed organized labor in a subordinate position relative to the state and made it weakly representative on the shop floor and ineffective in collective bargaining.

The exhaustion of the state-led model of development in the 1970s gave the CUT two targets to attack: that model *and* the political power of the state. Yet upon winning the presidency, Lula, the PT, and the CUT abandoned the goal of "new unionism" to reform Brazil's antiquated labor laws. When this tactic became clear, leftist critics accused Lula and CUT leaders of betraying their core principles for the easy benefits of *sindicalismo chapa branca*, the phrase used to describe the "you scratch my back, I'll scratch your back" relationship between government and "official" union leaders (Oliveira 2003).

This reversal did not merely reveal pragmatism's victory over ideology. Since the early 1990s many new unionist leaders had come to reconsider their antistatist positions and to defend the labor relations status quo. Both economic and political factors—economic crisis and neoliberal policies—account for this shift (A. Cardoso 2011). In the 1980s and early 1990s, economic crisis and structural changes in Brazil's economy generated rising unemployment and declining wages, weakening organized labor. Presidents Collor and Cardoso also privatized numerous state-owned industries and enacted labor-market reforms, further undermining unions (Cardoso 2008).

In this context, the PT and the CUT abandoned the principles of "new unionism" and focused on capturing power. Opposition to privatization and neoliberalism became key elements of the PT's electoral platform. Other parties accused the PT of wanting to revive Vargas-era state-led development policies, yet because economic stagnation and neoliberal policies were weakening the PT's union base, the party had good reason to reposition itself as patriotic defender of the Brazilian state. And in such a context it made less sense to advocate reform of the CLT, which would only weaken the state further.

The new approach to labor relations had two key implications: the PT and the CUT would strengthen the Brazilian state's involvement in the economy, and would maintain the historically close relationship between the state and organized labor. Thus, although Lula brought the leaders of the "new unionism" into the halls of power, the structure of labor relations in Brazil remains largely unchanged. Nevertheless, despite abandoning the reformist project of the new unionism, the inescapable fact is that under the PT, the workers won: they *are* the government. Consider the counterfactual: if José Serra had beaten Lula in 2002, and some other PSDB candidate had beaten Dilma in 2010, the government might have passed policies to weaken unions. PT victories brought about precisely what critics on the right have long feared: the CUT has entrenched itself in government so deeply that it may never be dislodged. Overall, organized labor today is in a much stronger position than at the end of Cardoso's terms.

Summary

To what extent did the PT and Lula follow through on longstanding promises to transform state-society relations? While Lula was reaping political rewards from his personal charisma and successful policies, the PT continued the grunt work of constructing political identity at the mass level. This is likely to remain the party's greatest legacy, because long after Lula is gone from the scene, *petismo* will remain a powerful resource the party can draw upon.

This effort to connect the party—and not just the party's leader—to average Brazilians is a key development in Brazil's party system, and which in terms of the distinctiveness of the parties from each other can now be characterized as "the PT versus the Rest." No other party has invested in creating a programmatic partisan image. Because of this, voters do not recognize any other large party as distinct—a fact that may present a future challenge for Brazilian democracy.

As for organized civil society, the Lula government did fulfill pledges to open up new participatory spaces. Many CSOs benefited from government largesse, and numerous civil society leaders gained spots on government advisory councils or jobs in social-service bureaucracies. More importantly, CSOs enjoyed expanded opportunities to influence public policies. Even if many of those policies gained relatively little academic or media attention, civil society influence may have considerable long-term symbolic importance, feeding back and helping to consolidate the PT's image in society as the "party of participation."

Finally, although organized labor under Lula enjoyed a period of vitality and although "new unionist" leaders gained unprecedented access and control over key government bureaucracies, a changing economic and political context in recent years has gradually pushed PT and the CUT leaders to abandon longstanding positions. Instead, accommodation with both capital and the usefulness of controlling the state to advance the party's and labor leaders' political projects became the order of the day.

The Second Pillar: An "Inversion of Priorities"?

To what extent did the Lula administration invert government priorities to favor historically excluded groups? On both the Left and the Right, critics whined that Lula was merely lucky, rather than good—that he reaped political rewards from a favorable international economic climate only because of policies Cardoso had implemented. Others complained that Lula was a Cardoso clone with a popular touch, given his administration's emphasis on fiscal austerity and its friendliness to big business. Such economic policy pragmatism did forestall accusations that Lula was a Hugo Chávez-style economic populist, yet they also implied that Lula would fail to address the PT's goal of greater social spending. Leftist critics perceived a disjuncture between the PT's promises and Lula's policies. To what extent is such criticism warranted?

Promotion of Economic Equality

Critical fire directed at the Lula administration diminished as the decade wore on—and such criticism that remained failed to resonate with average Brazilians, as Brazil's poor and middle classes were enjoying improved living standards. Millions of Brazilians benefited from economic growth: under Cardoso the average annual inflation rate was 14.9 percent, while under Lula it fell to 6.7 percent. Likewise, average annual real per capita GDP growth under Cardoso was 0.8 percent, while under Lula it was 2.4 percent.

Stable prices and a growing economy provided concrete gains for the poorest. Economic inequality has long been notoriously high in Brazil. After hardly budging at all under FHC, inequality declined under Lula to levels not seen since before the 1980s. Inequality declined not because the rich were getting poorer (in fact, they were getting richer too, just not as fast as everyone else), but because the poorest and middle class saw dramatic real income gains. This resulted in a reduction in poverty: although the percentage of the population living on US$1.25/day (the "absolute poverty" level) remained relatively steady under Cardoso, it declined significantly under Lula. Yet the poorest were not the only ones who gained: as has been the case in China and elsewhere, stability and growth helped millions consolidate their status as members of the middle class, driving expanded production and consumption of durable goods (Neri 2008).

The employment picture also improved dramatically under Lula, particularly benefiting poorer Brazilians. Reversing a trend from the Collor and Cardoso years, the last decade saw rising labor market formality: for every informal sector job created during that decade, three were created in the formal sector (Berg 2010). In short, economic gains for average Brazilians were not only palpable but were far greater under Lula than under Cardoso. Average Brazilians could see in their refrigerators and bank accounts that Lula's government was fulfilling its campaign promises to focus not just on stability but on growth that benefited all.

Lula also enjoyed drawing attention to the impact of the Bolsa Família program, which provides subsidies to families earning less than R$100 per month. This program expanded considerably under Lula, and by the end of 2010 it covered nearly everyone eligible—almost 12 million families or about a quarter of Brazil's population. Observers attribute a significant portion of Brazil's decline in inequality to the spread of conditional cash transfers (Paes de Barros et al. 2006).

Other government policies contributed to income gains by the poor and middle classes. For example, although Cardoso increased the minimum wage 24 percent in real terms during his two terms, Lula increased it 57 percent over the same number of years (DIESSE 2011). This improved the purchasing power of Brazil's poorest and improved the living standards of all Brazilians who receive a public pension or government benefit, all of which are indexed to the minimum wage.

Lula's government prioritized maintaining economic stability and growth, and improving the lot of Brazil's poorest through social assistance programs. Still, there were no large increases in public social welfare spending. Thus, while there was no "inversion" of spending priorities, far more Brazilians experienced welfare gains under Lula than under Cardoso. This is the "inversion" that Lula will be remembered for, particularly when compared against the Cardoso administration: the combination of economic stability, social assistance for the very poorest, and income gains for the working poor and middle classes.

Advances in Gender and Racial Equality

The question of "inverting priorities" should not focus exclusively on economic inequality. For example, the PT had long pledged to work with CSOs to strengthen women's participation and representation (Macaulay 2006). Although the percentage of women in the legislature—8.6 percent in 2011, up from 6.6 percent in 1997—still lags far behind both regional and world averages (International Parliamentary Union 2011), Lula named more women to his cabinet than any of his predecessors (Amorim Neto 2007). Fulfilling a campaign promise to women's movements, on his first day in office he also created a Special Secretariat of Women's Policies (with status of minister), something Cardoso had refused to do. Finally, the symbolic importance of Dilma's election as Brazil's first female president merits mention. Such developments certainly help cement the PT's image as the party that expands opportunities for all Brazilians.

Changes in terms of race relations also left an impact, both concretely and symbolically. The Lula government expanded affirmative action programs at public universities for Afro-Brazilians that were initiated under Cardoso. Moreover, under Lula, for the first time representatives of Brazil's Movimento Negro became truly engaged in the formulation of public policies and held key positions (Lima 2010). Such involvement was not mere window-dressing: in 2003 Lula created a

Special Secretariat of Policies to Promote Racial Equality, which was tasked with integrating practices of racial equality into all federal government policies (Lima 2010, 83). Lula also named four Afro-Brazilians to his cabinet, and appointed the first black Supreme Court justice since the return of democracy. Finally, Lula signed a law requiring public primary and secondary schools to include lessons about Brazil's history of slavery and race relations.

Summary

Did the Lula government follow through on the PT promise to "invert" socioeconomic priorities? Lula managed—like no previous president—to provide the mythical "free lunch"—inequality decreased and social spending increased, all without threatening the interests of the rich. Lula understood that the Brazilian state could be more generous to the poor—and that such generosity would generate massive political payoffs. The results of the 2006 and 2010 elections—and Lula's sky-high approval rating on leaving office—support the notion that most Brazilians believe Lula's government *did* invert government priorities (Zucco 2008).

Policies such as the expansion of Bolsa Família, promotion of formal-sector employment, and expansion of financial services to the poor go well beyond the achievement of economic stability because they expand and deepen the idea of democratic citizenship for all of Brazil's citizens. And while the success of Lula's government certainly favored the PT, these policies all increase individuals' contact with the state—largely without clientelistic or partisan intermediation—changing people's perceptions about what their government can and should be doing for them.

It is true that some of Lula's successes can be traced to Cardoso's policies, but Lula and the PT will get the credit. This is not simply because most of the gains occurred on Lula's watch, but because such gains do not fit with the PSDB's image. However, they do fit with the *modo petista de governar*. Consider the symbolic importance of Lula's eight years in office, which served to convince Brazil's poor that one of their own could not only lead the country but could do so effectively. *This* is an inversion—not a concrete one, but of popular perceptions of who has the capacity to participate in shaping Brazil's political future.

Consider as well the symbolic importance of many of Lula's less-well-known policies. For example, compared to economic stability, corruption, or Bolsa Família, the government's actions on racial and gender equality flew under the radar. Yet by elevating those policy areas to the same level as the Ministries of Foreign Affairs, Defense or Finance, by bringing representatives of socioeconomically disadvantaged groups into government, and by actively promoting policies of "social inclusion" Lula clearly sought to fulfill the PT's positions—and to differentiate his government from Cardoso's. The long-term consequences of efforts to "invert priorities" are both concrete and symbolic. Millions of Brazilians escaped poverty or even entered the middle class. Yet government bureaucrats under Lula were not just technocrats who single-mindedly focused on efficiently delivering policy. They cast their efforts to transform Brazilian society as part of a larger effort to use public policy to construct new forms of democratic citizenship. Concretely and abstractly, in terms of addressing socioeconomic inequalities the Lula administration sought and often succeeded in putting the *modo petista de governar* into practice, improving democratic governance by reducing the gap between the informal socioeconomic inequalities that pervade Brazilian society and the formal equality implied by universal suffrage.

The Third Pillar—The Rule of Law and "Ethical and Transparent Governance"

Prior to Lula's first term, most observers of Brazilian politics—and most *petistas*—believed that corruption pervaded every party *except* the PT. Lula and his party built their reputations not only by calling for broader participation and a reorientation of government priorities, but also by railing against corruption, political impunity, transparency in government, and other challenges to democratic accountability. Given this third pillar of the *modo petista de governar*, one might have expected significant attention to such issues. However, in contrast to its efforts to at least partially follow through on the promises implied in the first and second pillars, government performance on these issues disappointed.

Good economic performance, institutional stability, and competitive elections have improved Brazil's democratic performance. However, Freedom House has never given Brazil the top score because of concerns about issues surrounding the rule of law: the pervasiveness of corruption and impunity among government officials, and the way that such disregard for the law broadly manifests itself throughout Brazilian society through crime and violence in the streets, ineffective and brutal police forces, and an inaccessible legal system.

In contrast to other indicators of democratic governance, Brazil's performance on these issues has shown little improvement since redemocratization: Transparency International's Corruption Perceptions Index has hardly budged since the Cardoso years (www.transparency.org, August 27, 2011), and criminal violence has remained persistently high since redemocratization, in contrast to small improvements across the rest of the region (www.politicalterrorscale.org, August 27, 2011).

Corruption corrodes popular legitimacy of democracy because it short-circuits the notion of democratic equality, and weakens the possibility of holding government officials to accounts—from the street cop up to the president. Why did the Lula administration and the PT fail to follow through on the third pillar of the *modo petista de governar*? Fighting corruption was clearly never one of Lula's priorities, but the reason is not because he sought out kickbacks or even because he tolerated influence-peddling scams as "business as usual" on his watch. What is distinctive about corruption under Lula is precisely what was also distinctive about his administration's efforts to fulfill the promises implied by the first and second pillars of the *modo petista de governar*: at the core, the dynamic of corruption was driven by a *partisan* logic.

The connection between corruption and party politics lies with the dynamics of coalition presidentialism. At a superficial level, coalition dynamics under Lula might suggest that the PT had to capitulate to the incentives of Brazilian coalition presidentialism, because cabinet coalitions did not differ in terms of their raw "size" under Lula and Cardoso (Klein 2011). However, Lula made clear efforts to protect the PT from the power-sharing incentives that drive coalition presidentialism in Brazil (Abranches 1988). Brazilian presidents can choose between a unilateral governance strategy (represented by Fernando Collor) and a cooperative approach in which the president distributes the spoils of office and influence over policy equally among his or her party and the other parties in the cabinet (exemplified by President Cardoso).

Lula's approach to governing was neither as unilateral as Collor's nor as cooperative as Cardoso's. Upon taking office Lula confronted a complicated balancing act: how to build a legislative majority without alienating his base. After the 2002 elections, the parties in Lula's electoral coalition—including the PT—controlled only 25 percent of the seats in the Chamber of Deputies. To get anything done he would have to reach out—even to parties that had supported FHC. However, Lula confronted resistance from the PT to ceding power to the party's rivals. Thus, he sought to distribute as few ministries to nonleftist parties as possible.

Lula's first coalition failed to provide a legislative majority. To win legislative support he relied on *governismo*—politicians' pragmatic desire to obtain the clientelistic benefits of being in the government, rather than remaining in the opposition—by enticing individual deputies to abandon the party that helped them win election and switch into one of the parties in his cabinet. For a while this tactic worked, and during his first term the government passed several important reforms. However, this strategy ultimately proved fragile. Problems erupted when leftist supporters balked at a proposed social security reform that was so contentious that one of the leftist parties in Lula's cabinet withdrew from the government, and the PT expelled several members who had refused to support the president's position.

As his leftist support wavered, Lula sought additional support on his right by bringing the PMDB, which controlled about 15 percent of the seats, into his cabinet. This should have bolstered his support, but it didn't. The reason is that Lula continued to face pressure from the PT to not share the spoils of office. The PT controlled only 29 percent of the coalition's legislative seats but held 60 percent of the cabinet ministries. In contrast, the PMDB, PL, and PTB together held almost 50 percent of the legislative seats, but were awarded only 12 percent of the portfolios (Amorim Neto 2007). Lula's tactics angered both his leftist and his conservative allies, and his legislative support wavered.

The massive corruption scandals that came to light in 2005 are intimately connected to Lula's governing tactics (Pereira, Power, and Raile 2011). High-ranking members of the Lula government were accused of greasing the wheels of government through payola, by exchanging monthly cash payments (the *mensalão*) for legislators' support on particular votes. These accusations implied that Lula had constructed his first cabinet coalition not through perfectly legal pork barreling but through corruption. Yet the *mensalão* proved to be just the tip of the iceberg: media and congressional investigators soon discovered that to pay the *mensalão*, PT officials had constructed a massive off-the-books campaign finance scheme.

PT leaders admitted that the broad outlines of the accusations were true, and Brazil's prosecutor general stated that a criminal organization *within the PT* had taken root in Lula's administration immediately following the 2002 elections (Lopes 2006; Rangel 2006). Yet despite the prosecutor's statements, Lula downplayed the scandals' significance and resisted admitting that his close confidants had done wrong. At the height of the scandal, he lamely claimed that, "the PT only did what other Brazilian parties have done all along" (*O Globo*, July 18, 2005).

The scandals ultimately forced out several high administration and party officials, including Lula's chief of staff, the finance minister, and the president of the PT. They also caused Lula's approval ratings to temporarily plummet, and damaged the reputation as the party of clean government that the PT had built over two decades. In 1997, the PT conducted a national survey on party images, and found that only 4 percent of Brazilians believed the party to be the most corrupt—

the smallest percentage of any party mentioned. In 2006, after the *mensalão* scandal, the PT repeated the survey only to find that 27 percent of Brazilians now believed it was the most corrupt, 20 percent more than the next party mentioned (Fundação Perseu Abramo 2006, 55).

What explains the pervasive corruption at the top levels of the Lula government? First, instead of relying on legal political currencies such as pork-barreling and political appointments, the Lula government resorted to the illegal tactic of using *actual* currency to purchase legislative support. The *mensalão* reflects a choice about how to address the demands of coalition presidentialism: Lula's critical problem was not that other parties refused to enter his government, but the PT's unwillingness to *let* them participate as equals. The *mensalão* illustrates how Lula and the PT sought to sidestep the incentives of coalition presidentialism and dominate the executive branch.

Second, corruption was fruit of the PT's longstanding problematic relationship with campaign finance. PT candidates traditionally raised relatively less money than candidates from other nonleftist parties, largely because the party possessed few links to wealthy patrons (Samuels 2001; Samuels 2004). The PT compensated for its poverty by relying on coattail effects from Lula's popularity and, more importantly, on the strength of its organization and its party label (Samuels 2006). Yet as Lula and the PT moderated and adopted a more pragmatic approach, its leaders came to rely less on the party's traditional mobilizational techniques and increasingly on tactics similar to other parties. However, as it sought to expand its appeal, the PT consistently failed to obtain the funds it needed to compete successfully.

Given the party's persistent lack of sufficient *legal* sources of campaign finance, Lula's ascension to power opened innumerable doors to temptation. After all, Lula needed money to win reelection, and the PT needed money to continue to grow. Yet desperation for money does not explain why elements within the PT engineered a centrally organized, illegal scheme. After all, holding the reins of power tends opens the spigots of *legal* campaign finance. Here again we see a partisan logic: both legal and illegal campaign finance practices in Brazil are typically highly decentralized and individualized. The Lula administration's scandals are novel in Brazilian politics, because for the first time in Brazilian history a highly organized political party sought to leverage its control over the national government to raise funds on its own behalf, and to influence or even control the flow of money to its candidates—and to discriminate against its rivals. PT leaders did not engage in illegal activities simply to enrich themselves personally (although this certainly cannot be discounted); they did so as part of a quest for long-term power on behalf of their party and its candidates.

Power corrupts, to be sure. Yet if the scandals were really the fruit of power corrupting just a few individual bad apples, they would not have spoiled the PT's collective reputation. The scandals at the heart of Lula's administration hinted at deeper problems within the PT. The party has since sought to "clean house," but the success of such efforts remains incomplete. Accusations of corruption dogged Dilma's advisors on her campaign trail, and scandals erupted almost immediately after her inauguration. In politics it does not matter whether Caesar's wife *is* chaste; the PT no longer *appears* pure. The symbolic importance of Lula's accepting corruption as "business as usual" in Brazil spoke volumes, because it implied a deeply rooted hypocrisy at the party's highest levels about the PT's programmatic goals—that all the party's efforts to "expand democratic citizenship" through participation and to "invert priorities" was a bunch of hot air, because when push came to shove in terms of power politics, the ends always justified the means. And in this sense the PT is no different from any other party—indeed, one might say that because it is a highly organized and powerful bureaucratic institution, it now holds a tremendous advantage over its rivals in the field of Brazilian politics.

In short, the Lula administration can clearly be characterized by tensions between the PT's goal of winning power and its desire to transform Brazilian society. A key contextual factor to keep in mind is that only a small slice of Brazilian voters consistently regards corruption negatively—relatively well-off and educated voters—that is, a tiny minority. The masses tend to tolerate practices that wink at corruption such as the *jeitinho* and *rouba mas faz* (Almeida 2007; Souza and Lamounier 2010). Such attitudes are intimately tied to the low expectations that Brazilians have about the government's willingness or ability to attack corruption, organized crime, and police brutality.

Despite a growth of attention to issues of corruption and the rule of law by Brazilian academics, bloggers, mass media, and CSOs, without elite consensus on attacking corruption, it is unlikely that existing anticorruption institutions and mechanisms—many of which are innovative and which produce salutary effects (Power and Taylor 2011)—will substantially improve democratic accountability and citizens' faith in the efficacy of Brazilian democracy. No Brazilian president has made fighting corruption a centerpiece of his or her administration. The main challenges to democratic governance in Brazil—particularly in terms of accountability and citizens' perceptions of the legitimacy of government—will continue to be found in this area.

The PT stood for the principle that corruption in public life was unacceptable. Yet Lula's statements and failure to take more dramatic action indicated that he had accepted corruption as a normal part of politics—and that he was unwilling or unable to do anything about it. The broader problem for Brazilian democracy is that passivity in the face of corruption opens the door for unequal political influence—giving the lie to the notion that Brazil's formal institutions are functioning as well as one could expect. Corruption undermines the notion that the policy process reflects—even indirectly—voters' expressed demands, and undermines the PT's claim to have expanded the ideas and practice of democratic citizenship in Brazil.

Conclusion

Since its formation the PT has presented itself as an agent of grassroots political change, claiming that only it could transform state-society relations in Brazil. The party advertised its core principles as the *modo petista de governar*—a programmatic commitment to bringing greater popular participation, socioeconomic equality, honesty, responsiveness, and accountability to Brazilian politics. Lula's choices—and thus his legacy—were certainly shaped by the Cardoso administration's accomplishments, as well as by what Cardoso left on the table. Lula also had the good luck to benefit from a positive global economic environment. Yet the Lula administration is novel in a particularly important way in historical perspective, in combining a personally popular president with a highly institutionalized, programmatic political party with deep roots in society. For this reason, discussion of the Lula administration's legacy for Brazilian democracy must focus on the complicated question of the degree to which his administration's choices transformed Brazil *in the PT's image.*

Lula's victory forced the PT to confront several dilemmas, most importantly of balancing the PT's programmatic commitments with the pragmatic concerns of governance. This represents a new twist on the old concern about the alleged difficulty of combining presidentialism with multipartism. Lula had the most success in implementing the first two pillars of the *modo petista de governar*, strengthening the links between state and society and reducing socioeconomic inequalities. The PT had long sought to expand the idea of democratic citizenship by opening up new channels for popular participation for setting government priorities, and under Lula organized civil society did gain greater and more diverse opportunities to participate in the policy process, and organized labor gained unprecedented access to power. This does not mean that Lula's accomplishments fit the utopian goals of this first pillar to the letter. Scholars should explore *how much* influence civil society gained and evaluate the relative costs and benefits of orga-nized labor's abandonment of its autonomist project. Still, even if the glass is only half full, the administration's efforts also fit with the PT's self-image. The sym-bolic importance of expanding participatory opportunities have also helped the PT consolidate its image in society, distancing it from other parties in terms of the extent and depth of mass partisan identification.

The administration's successes on the second pillar—an inversion of socioeco-nomic priorities—are substantively greater, and also carry symbolic weight for the future of Brazilian democracy. Lula gets most of the credit for growing the economy, reducing socioeconomic discrimination, and bringing millions into the middle class not just because most of the actual gains occurred on his watch but also because such changes fit with the PT's declared goals of providing eco-nomic opportunity to a greater diversity of Brazilians. The accomplishments may not represent a complete inversion of priorities, but no president could have met *all* the needs of Brazil's poor majority. In any case, such success bolsters the Lula administration's symbolic legacy, and bodes well for the PT's future. In important ways, the PT strengthened its reputation as the party that collectively represents the interests of average Brazilians.

Unfortunately, the scandals that plagued the Lula administration may have sac-rificed many of the claims the PT made to have deepened Brazilian democracy. Lula faced a difficult task: finding a balance between maintaining the program-matic commitments and long-term goals of his own party and having to share power, due to the requirements of coalition presidentialism. The pragmatic pull to the center cost him the support of a good part of his leftist base, even as the ap-parent turn to clientelistic "politics as usual" ironically masked the PT's refusal to fully fairly share the spoils of office. To get around the constraints of coalition presidentialism, members of the PT's high command engaged in a massive, illegal campaign-finance scheme.

The Lula administration is likely to be remembered not just for relying on tradi-tional and perfectly legal forms of generating political support—exchanging con-trol over cabinet ministries and lower-level bureaucratic positions, for example—but also for rationalizing patently illegal practices as the normal way of conducting political business. The symbolic costs of failing to live up to the commitments of the third pillar of the *modo petista de governar* are high, as the adoption of illegal campaign finance techniques and their coordination from within nerve center of Brazil's strongest national party spells trouble for the prospect that Brazil can make headway on issues related to the rule of law. The PT long advertised itself as different—as rejecting the consensus that corruption was an acceptable way of conducting politics. However, the Lula administration scandals indicate that many in the party have now accepted these practices.

What does the growth of the PT hold for the future of Brazilian democracy? In terms of party competition, the emerging dynamic of the "PT versus the Rest" is striking. The PT continues to grow, spreading its organizational tentacles across the nation, and gaining adherents in regions where it had none just a few years ago (Samuels and Zucco 2011). The PSDB has led the opposition to the PT, but former President Cardoso admitted that his party has failed to develop its own vision for Brazil's future, and had failed to plant its values in voters' minds (F. Cardoso 2011). Even the PSDB's platform acknowledges the weakness of its relationship to civil society (PSDB 2007, 22).

There are two reasons why the PSDB has failed to articulate a distinct alternative vision for Brazil. First, unlike the PT, it is an elite party by birth and by nature. Its success is almost entirely due to having capable political leaders be in the right place at the right time: the almost-accidental presidency of Fernando Henrique Cardoso occurred only six years after the party formed. Its weakness is the same as all elite parties: a lack of a popular touch and an inability to capitalize on holding power to lay down roots in society.

Second, the PSDB has been outflanked by the political moderation of Lula and the PT. In the late 1980s the PSDB filled a space that had opened on the center-left, as the PMDB shifted rightward and the PT remained further to the left. Yet to this day the PSDB has failed to react to the PT's moderation, and it holds the position of standard-bearer of the opposition to the PT only because of even greater strategic ineptitude (or lack of desire) on the part of the parties to its right. The PSDB has failed to develop a recognizable programmatic profile, even seeming ashamed of some of its greatest policy successes, such as privatization. An opposition party can win campaigns based on the depoliticization of politics—individual leaders' technocratic competence—only when the incumbent screws up. Without establishing how it differs from the PT and building a connection with voters, the PSDB is left rooting for a crisis to burst the PT's bubble.

As for his legacy in the pantheon of Brazilian presidents, Lula is not an antiinstitutional populist in Chávez's mold. Quite the opposite, he may have sought autonomy from his party, but accusations that he undermined the PT and Brazil's institutional structure are not credible. There will be *petismo* long after Lula has faded from the scene. Lula also does not represent a reincarnation of Getúlio

Vargas—and the difference between the two helps us better comprehend Lula's and the PT's historical significance. For all his efforts to portray himself as "father of the poor," Vargas was a son of a segment of Brazil's traditional landholding elite. He did not embody the new urban working classes that emerged at the time, but rather sought to use the state to control and manipulate those groups.

In contrast, Lula and the PT represent a significant new development for Brazil in terms of the circulation of elites that is a necessary element of even a minimalist definition of democracy, and embody the aspirations and interests of the middle classes that have emerged over the last thirty years. Lula and the PT are the first true nonelites to rise to power and form a *new* elite from organized civil society— something that happened nearly a century ago in Western Europe, for example, with the election of the first socialist governments in Germany (1918), the UK (1924), or France (1936). Lula's election represents an unprecedented diversification of the political game in Brazil—an expansion of real democratic inclusiveness. The PT fought to accomplish this goal—and in many ways it has succeeded, even if only partially. The symbolic and long-term importance of this fact has been overlooked.

REFERENCES

Abranches, Sérgio H. Hudson de. 1988. "Presidencialismo de coalizão: O dilema institucional brasileiro." *Dados* 31:5–38.

Aguiar, Eduardo. 2010. "Serra acusa governo de cercear imprensa." Accessed August 11, 2011. www.jornaldelondrina.com.br/brasil/conteudo.phtml?id=1037800.

Almeida, Alberto Carlos. 2007. *A Cabeça do Brasileiro.* Rio de Janeiro: Editora Record.

Amaral, Oswaldo. 2010. "As transformações na organização interna do Partido dos Trabalhadores entre 1995 e 2009." PhD diss., UNICAMP.

Ames, Barry. 2001. *The Deadlock of Democracy in Brazil.* Ann Arbor: University of Michigan Press.

Amorim Neto, Octavio. 2007. "Algumas conseqüências políticas de Lula: Novos padrões de recrutamento ministerial, controle de agenda e produção legislativa." In *Instituições representativas no Brasil: Balanço e reformas,* edited by Jairo Nicolau and Timothy J. Power, 55–73. Belo Horizonte: Editora UFMG.

Amorim Neto, Octavio, et al. 2011. "Redesenhando o mapa eleitoral do Brasil: uma proposta de reforma política incremental." *Opinião Pública* 17 (1): 45–75.

Arantes, Rogério B., and Cláudio G. Couto. 2009. "Uma constituição incomun." In *A constituição de 1988: Passado e futuro,* edited by Maria Alice Rezende de Carvalho et al., 17–51. São Paulo: Editora Hucitec/ANPOCS.

Armijo, Leslie, Philippe Faucher, and Magdalena Dembinska. 2006. "Compared to What? Assessing Brazil's Political Institutions." *Comparative Political Studies* 39 (6): 759–86.

Avritzer, Leonardo. 2010. "Living under a Democracy: Participation and Its Impacts on the Living Conditions of the Poor." *Latin American Research Review* 45 (Special Issue): 166–85.

Berg, Janine. 2010. "Laws or Luck? Understanding Rising Formality in Brazil in the 2000s." Brasilia: International Labour Office.

Cardoso, Adalberto. 2008. "Los sindicatos: representación de intereses y acción política del capital y trabajo en Brasil." *Veredas* (UAM—Xochimilco) 16:63–83.

———. 2011. "'Tomorrow You Will Be the Government': Workers' Movement from Unions to Power in Brazil." IESP-UERJ. Unpublished.

Cardoso, Fernando Henrique. 2011. "O Papel da Oposição." Accessed August 27, 2011. http://oglobo.globo.com/pais/noblat/posts/2011/04/12/o-papel-da-oposicao-374379 .asp.

Datafolha. 2010. "Acima das expectativas, Lula encerra mandato com melhor avaliação da história." Pesquisa de opinião pública—December 20, 2010. Accessed August 13, 2011. http://datafolha.folha.uol.com.br/po/ver_po.php?session=1122.

DIESSE. 2011. "Tabelas e gráficos do Salário Mínimo Real—03/2011." www.dieese.org .br/esp/salmin.xml.

Dulci, Luiz. 2010. "Nota à imprensa: Resposta do ministro Luiz Dulci às declarações de José Serra." Accessed August 11, 2011. www.secretariageral.gov.br/noticias/ultimas_ noticias/2010/08/20-08-2010-nota-a-imprensa-resposta-do-ministro-luiz-dulci-as -declaracoes-de-jose-serra.

Figueiredo, Argelina, and Fernando Limongi. 1999. *Executivo e legislativo na nova ordem constitutional*. Rio de Janeiro: Editora FGV.

Fundação Perseu Abramo. 2006. "Pesquisa de opinião pública." www.fpa.org.br.

Goldfrank, Benjamin. 2011. "The Left and Participatory Governance: Brazil, Uruguay, and Venezuela." In *The Resurgence of the Latin American Left*, edited by Steven Levitsky and Kenneth M. Roberts, 162–83. Baltimore: Johns Hopkins University Press.

Hagopian, Frances, et al. 2009. "From Patronage to Program: The Emergence of Party-Oriented Legislators in Brazil." *Comparative Political Studies* 42 (3): 360–91.

Hagopian, Frances, and Scott P. Mainwaring, eds. 2005. *The Third Wave of Democratization in Latin America: Advances and Setbacks*. New York: Cambridge University Press.

Hochstetler, Kathryn. 2006. "Organized Civil Society in Lula's Brazil." Unpublished Paper presented at the Latin American Studies Association 2006 Conference, San Juan, Puerto Rico, March 15–18, 2006.

Hochstetler, Kathryn, and Elisabeth Friedman. 2008. "Can Civil Society Organizations Solve the Crisis of Partisan Representation in Latin America?" *Latin American Politics and Society* 50 (2): 1–32.

Hunter, Wendy. 2010. *The Transformation of the Workers' Party in Brazil, 1989–2009*. New York: Cambridge University Press.

———. 2011. "The PT in Power." In *The Resurgence of the Latin American Left*, edited by Steven Levitsky and Kenneth M. Roberts, 306–24. Baltimore: Johns Hopkins University Press.

Hunter, Wendy, and Timothy Power. 2005. "Lula's Brazil at Midterm." *Journal of Democracy* 16 (3): 127–40.

International Parliamentary Union. 2010. "Women in National Parliaments." Accessed August 10, 2011. www.ipu.org/wmn-e/classif.htm.

Klein, Christian. 2011. "Ministério da Dilma segue cartilha de Lula." *Valor*, March 10, 6.

Lima, Márcia. 2010. "Desigualdades raciais e políticas públicas: Ações afirmativas no governo Lula." *Novos Estudos CEBRAP* 87:77–95.

Limongi, Fernando, and Rafael Cortez. 2010. "As eleições de 2010 e o quadro partidário." *Novos Estudos CEBRAP* 88:21–37.

Lopes, Eugênia. 2006. "MPF denuncia 40 pessoas por envolvimento no mensalão." *O Estado de São Paulo*, April 11. Accessed July 31, 2006. www.estadao.com.br/ultimas /nacional/noticias/2006/abr/11/319.htm.

Lucas, Kevin, and David Samuels. 2010. "The Ideological 'Coherence' of the Brazilian Party System, 1990–2009." *Journal of Politics in Latin America* 2 (3): 39–69.

Macaulay, Fiona. 2006. "Sexual Politics, Party Politics: The PT Government's Policies on Gender Equity and Equality." Working Paper CBS-46-03, Centre for Brazilian Studies, University of Oxford.

Magalhães, Inês, Luiz Barreto, and Vicente Trevas, eds. 1999. *Governo e cidadania: Balanço e reflexões sobre o modo petista de governar*. São Paulo: Editora Fundação Perseu Abramo.

Mainwaring, Scott. 1999. *Rethinking Party Systems in the Third Wave of Democratization: The Case of Brazil*. Stanford: Stanford University Press.

Neri, Marcelo, et al. 2008. *A Nova Classe Média*. Rio de Janeiro: Fundação Getúlio Vargas.

O Globo. July 18, 2005. Quote from an episode of "Fantástico."

Oliveira, Francisco de. 2003. *Crítica à razão dualista/O ornitorrinco*. São Paulo: Boitempo.

Paes de Barros, Ricardo, et al. 2006. "Uma análise das principais causas da queda recente na desigualdade de renda Brasileira." Texto para Discussão no. 1203. Rio de Janeiro: Instituto de Pesquisa Econômica Aplicada.

Pereira, Carlos, Timothy Power, and Eric Raile. 2011. "Presidentialism, Coalitions, and Accountability." In *Corruption and Democracy in Brazil*, edited by Timothy Power and Matthew Taylor, 31–55. Notre Dame: University of Notre Dame Press.

Pogrebinschi, Thamy. 2010. "Moving away from Liberal Democracy: Participation, Representation, and Political Experimentalism in Brazil." Unpublished paper presented at the Ash Center Democracy Seminar, Harvard Kennedy School, September 8, 2010.

Pogrebinschi, Thamy, and Fabiano Santos. 2010. "Entre representação e participação: As conferências nacionais e o experimentalismo democrático brasileiro." Unpublished research report, IESP/UERJ.

Power, Timothy. 2010. "Brazilian Democracy as a Late Bloomer: Reevaluating the Regime in the Cardoso-Lula Era." *Latin American Research Review* 45 (Special Issue): 218–47.

Power, Timothy, and Matthew Taylor, eds. 2011. *Corruption and Democracy in Brazil*. Notre Dame: University of Notre Dame Press.

Power, Timothy, and Cesar Zucco Jr. 2009. "Estimating Ideology of Brazilian Legislative Parties, 1990–2005: A Research Communication." *Latin American Research Review* 44 (1): 218–46.

PSDB. 2007. "Programa do PSDB." Accessed August 26, 2011. www2.psdb.org.br/wp -content/uploads/2010/04/Programa_PSDB_2007.pdf, p. 22.

Rangel, Rodrigo. 2006. "Entrevista do procurador-geral da República, Antonio Fernando de Souza, à Revista Istoé." Accessed July 31, 2006. www2.pgr.mpf.gov.br/Institucional/procurador-geral/folder.2006-03-08.2946566637/entrevista_istoe_-23-04-06.pdf.

Ribeiro, Pedro Floriano. 2010. *Dos sindicatos ao governo: A organização nacional do PT de 1980 a 2005*. São Carlos: EdUFSCar.

Samuels, David. 2001. "Does Money Matter? Campaign Finance in Newly Democratic Countries: Theory and Evidence from Brazil." *Comparative Politics* 34:23–42.

———. 2004. "From Socialism to Social Democracy? The Evolution of the Workers' Party in Brazil." *Comparative Political Studies* 37 (9): 999–1024.

———. 2006. "Sources of Mass Partisanship in Brazil." *Latin American Politics and Society* 48 (2): 1–27.

Samuels, David, and Cesar Zucco. 2010. "The Roots of Petismo, 1989–2010." Unpublished paper presented at the annual meeting of the American Political Science Association, Washington, DC.

Souza, Amaury de. 2011. "The Politics of Personality in Brazil." *Journal of Democracy* 22 (2): 75–88.

Souza, Amaury de, and Bolivar Lamounier. 2010. *A classe média brasileira*. Rio de Janeiro: Editora Campus / Elsevier.

Weyland, Kurt. 2005. "The Growing Sustainability of Brazil's Low-Quality Democracy." In *Wave of Democratization in Latin America: Advances and Setbacks*, edited by Frances Hagopian and Scott Mainwaring, 90–120. Cambridge: Cambridge University Press.

Zucco, Cesar Jr. 2008. "The President's 'New' Constituency: Lula and the Pragmatic Vote in Brazil's 2006 Presidential Election." *Journal of Latin American Studies* 40:29–49.

CHAPTER EIGHT

Chile

Beyond Transitional Models of Politics

Peter M. Siavelis

The 6.9 magnitude quake shook the Chilean National Congress in Valparaíso as the presidential sash was passed to Sebastián Piñera of the right-wing Coalition for Change. The aftershock from the devastating February 25, 2010, earthquake prompted jokes of divine retribution for having elected a government of the Right for the first time in fifty-two years. The leader of the outgoing center-left Concertación coalition, Michelle Bachelet, was leaving power with an approval rating of over 70 percent. How is it that such a successful government could be forced to pass the reins to the opposition? Why was it that the Concertación coalition, almost universally considered one of the most successful coalitions in Latin America, was defeated? How could the Right, sectors of which were unwavering defenders of the Augusto Pinochet dictatorship not long ago, assume power where authoritarianism had left such deep political and social scars? Why have dramatic student and labor protests so thoroughly shaken the country that is often hailed as the economic and political model for Latin America?

Answers to these questions abound. Most center around either the increasing ineffectiveness of the Concertación governments or allegations of the coalition's growing corruption and arrogance of power (Fernández 2010). However, few have considered how the models of politics forged during the transition itself continue to deeply affect Chilean politics and have helped lead to these outcomes. Fewer still have explored how the answers to these questions have deeper meanings for how Chilean democracy has functioned over the last twenty years and what it might look like in the future.

This chapter will do so, proceeding in three sections. In the first, it argues that each of Chile's coalitions forged a particular model of politics that bears a profound imprint of the democratic transition. In the case of the Concertación, this model provided two decades of successful government and set down the basis for what became Chile's "model" democratic transition. Nonetheless, ultimately this deeply entrenched model came to undermine the Concertación's ability to continue to govern and to win elections, effectively making the coalition a victim of its own success. In the case of the Coalition for Change (from here on called the Alianza, as it has been known for the majority of time since the return to democracy), the transitional model of politics it adopted prevented it from being a viable option for governing for many years, and only when it successfully abandoned this model could it assume power. However, despite this transformation, since assuming government, the Right has been unable to overcome the image that it shares many of the problems that plague the Concertación, largely, and ironically, because it has accepted elements of the very governance model employed by the Concertación.

The second section of the chapter analyzes advances during the first twenty years of Chilean democracy, as well as remaining challenges, arguing that both can be tied to the governing models developed during the transition. In particular, successes in areas that are most evident (economic management, civil-military relations, and constitutional reform) have grown from the Concertación's elitist governance model, aimed at consensus building. At the same time, the major challenge and shortcomings in Chilean democracy (an emerging *partidocracia*—or party-dominated democracy—lack of accountability, and lackluster, limited reform) have also grown out of this model—a model with which the Right is also increasingly identified.

Finally, the chapter explores the implications of these findings for understanding the past and future of Chilean democracy, arguing that an excessive focus on governability during the transition exacted a cost on other dimensions of democracy and particularly representation and accountability. The establishment of new mechanisms of representation and accountability that will allow Chileans to demand and receive the kind of policy reforms they want is the major challenge for the future.

The Democratic Transition and the Genesis of the Twin Transitional Models of Politics

The Concertación coalition grew from a disparate collection of seventeen parties, initially formed to defeat Pinochet in the 1988 plebiscite on his continued rule. It eventually whittled down to five major parties, managing to overcome divisions to forge the longest lasting coalition in Chilean history, and one of the longest in South America. Four Concertación presidents followed: Christian Democrats Patricio Aylwin (1990–1994) and Eduardo Frei (1994–2000) and Socialist Presidents Ricardo Lagos (2000–2006) and Michelle Bachelet (2006–2010). Beginning in 1989 the Concertación won every presidential and legislative election until bested by the Alianza with the victory of Renovación Nacional's (RN; National Renewal) Sebastián Piñera in 2010. The Concertación also managed to win every subsequent legislative election at least with respect to the popular vote (it dropped below the Alianza in the number of seats in the 2009 election), and sometimes by margins as large as 18 percent (table 8.1).

When one reads accounts of the spectacular success of the Concertación in managing the economy and devising a successful model for politics, there is often a note of triumphant inevitability. However, to understand the models of politics that grew from the transition it is important to realize that the transition itself was extraordinarily constrained, politically and institutionally. The reestablishment and maintenance of democracy was not a foregone conclusion.

In political terms, though Concertación governments skillfully managed civil-military conflict, for many years there was enormous uncertainty given continu-

Table 8.1.   Valid Votes and Seats Received by the Concertación and the Alianza in Chamber of Deputies Elections, 1989–2009 (in percentages)

Year	1989		1993		1997		2001		2005		2009	
Coalition	V	S	V	S	V	S	V	S	V	S	V	S
Concertación	51.5	57.5	55.3	58.3	50.5	57.5	47.9	51.7	51.8	54.2	44.4	47.5
Alianza	34.2	40	36.7	41.7	36.3	38.4	44.3	47.5	38.7	45	43.5	48.3
Others	14.3	2.5	7.9	0	13.3	4.2	7.8	0.8	9.5	0.8	12.2	4.2
Concertación's Margin	17.3	17.5	18.6	16.6	14.2	19.1	3.6	4.2	13.1	9.2	0.9	−0.8

Note: V = votes, S = seats.

ing veto power of the military (Weeks 2003). While in many countries former dictators fled the country in disgrace, Pinochet simply moved across the Alameda (Santiago's main avenue) to the Armed Forces building, literally in view of the presidential palace. In response to what he perceived as political threats to his family and the military, Pinochet put troops on full alert in December 1990 and May 1993 (Loveman 2001, 313). Scotland Yard's October 1998 arrest of General Pinochet during a visit to London was the final chapter in civil-military conflict. He was arrested in response to an extradition request by renegade Spanish judge Baltasar Garzón on the grounds of human rights violations. Pinochet's arrest initiated a 17-month period during which some of the most important changes in Chilean politics took place, providing the basis for the reestablishment of a normalized pattern of civil-military relations (Roht-Arrizaz 2005).

These three crucial events are emblematic of an extraordinarily uncertain transition. During the initial phases of the transition the establishment and maintenance of democracy was very much in doubt, and the military retained de facto veto authority—functionally, and even constitutionally. Indeed, former president Aylwin noted that Pinochet "always thought we were going to fail and that the country was going to call him back to replace me."[1] Angell notes that during this time, "there seemed to be two parallel systems of power in Chile, one democratic" and "another a carryover from the authoritarian past posing a veiled threat to the civilian authorities—in Pinochet's words, a sleeping lion" (Angell 2007, 147).

Institutional variables also complicated the democratic transition and left an imprint on the Concertación's transitional political model. Chilean elites inherited an institutional structure they did not design and that was extraordinarily difficult to reform (Siavelis 2000; Barros 2002). In contrast to most political systems where elites craft institutions to serve their own interests, Chile's democratic institutions were imposed in the form of Pinochet's 1980 constitution. Though ultimately reformed in 2005, the constitution held sway for most of the transitional period. It provided effective veto power for the armed forces, established a strong and military-dominated National Security Council, limited the presidents' power of appointment and dismissal of military officers, and provided for a number of appointed senators (who for most of the transitional period were appointed by the military or other forces sympathetic to the Right). This further heightened the sense of insecurity and uncertainty and made governing more complex, delicate, and difficult.

What is more, the military imposed an electoral system with two member districts, doing away with Chile's traditional multimember district PR (proportional representation) system. This electoral system, in a context where five parties existed within the Concertación, obliged them to engage in a complex game of deal making and power sharing in order to divide electoral slates. Only through coalition making could the constellation of parties within the Concertación assure representation for each (Siavelis 2002).

Finally, there were also partisan limits to the Concertación's manoeuvring room. At the beginning of the transition, several hard Right sectors were firmly in the camp of Pinochet and were expecting Concertación governments to fail. In addition, the leaders of right-wing parties, even more moderate ones, made clear that they would accept no changes to Pinochet's institutional framework or constitution (Valenzuela 1995). The highly disciplined parties of the Right prevented any constitutional reforms early on, stating that any reform attempts would be considered threats against Chile's constitutional order.

The dilemmas of the Alianza were different. However, just as on the center-left, the politics of the democratic transition left a deep imprint on the Right. Only when it abandoned this political model would it achieve decisive electoral victories.

First, it was very difficult for the Right to distance itself from the dictatorship. At the beginning of the transition, key sectors of the Right actively supported Pinochet and defended him and his legacy. Given the importance of maintaining the Alianza, it was difficult for more moderate sectors to differentiate themselves from the more extreme (Garretón 2000; Angell 2007). This was particularly difficult for members of Renovación Nacional (RN; National Renovation), which sought to expand its appeal to the ideological center while also maintaining its core Right constituency. The Concertación was consistently able to draw legitimacy and popularity from its foundational moment as opposition to the Pinochet dictatorship, exacting a cost on the electoral fortunes of the Right.

Second, the Right was for years unable to articulate a policy program distinct from that of the Concertación. On the one hand, the Right's stance was largely defensive, with few innovative ideas beyond protecting Pinochet's economic and constitutional legacy. On the other hand, the Concertación itself had largely co-opted the Right's economic policies, tinkering with only a few of them, and then taking credit for Chile's dramatic economic success (Guardia 2010). This left little policy space in which the Right could move.

Third, the Right faced difficulties in maintaining unity, often because of an inability to agree on single presidential candidates in two of the four presidential races that it lost, detracting from the perceived coherence of the Right as an option (Altman 2008, 249). In both the 1993 and the 2005 elections, two significant candidates of the Right participated, projecting an image of disunity and disorganization.

Finally, early in the transition the Right, and primarily the Unión Democrática Independiente (UDI; Independent Democratic Union), had a dogged commitment to not allow constitutional reform because it was seen as one of the most important legacies of Pinochet's transformation of Chile. Nonetheless, this commitment to what was clearly an antidemocratic document only reinforced the idea that the Right had a legitimacy deficit (Pollack 1999, 149).

Thus the democratic transition left a deep imprint on both coalitions. On the Left this was a largely positive one in terms of electoral politics and governing, while on the Right this model damaged the sector electorally until it was left behind. However, with the passage of time and changing contexts, each coalition faced distinct challenges with respect to the constraints imposed by the political models that grew from the transition.

The Transitional Model in Action: The Concertación

At the outset of democracy, the Concertación faced an uncertain transition, a potentially destabilizing military, and a constraining constitution. Furthermore, the interaction of a multiparty system and the institutional structure inherited from the dictatorship provided an imperative to engage in deal making to guarantee the transition. It was universally recognized that the best way to underwrite the transition and ensure success was to strike agreements among parties to assure policy coherence, governing stability, and ultimately, the maintenance of democracy (Boeninger 1989). The transitional model it devised included mechanisms and policymaking norms designed to successfully achieve these goals.

El Cuoteo

The Concertación coalition was based on an elaborate form of party power sharing known as the "*cuoteo.*" The details of this bargain included careful division of ministerial portfolios among its constituent parties. Vice ministers were generally chosen from a different party (and usually of a different ideological sector) than the minister. What is more, throughout the ministries, and particularly in the "political" ministries, each postauthoritarian administration sought to provide representation for the complete constellation of the Concertación's parties in upper level staffs.

The *cuoteo* was one of the keys to success of the Concertación and the democratic transition. This form of portfolio distribution and job sharing reinforced trust by insuring widespread party input into governmental decision making. The dispersion of cabinet authority prevented the verticalization of particular ministries into patronage-dispensing institutions for a single party (Rehren 1992). Without this representation and voice, parties would have had little incentive to remain loyal to the coalition; it would have likely fallen apart, and Chile would not have achieved the textbook democratic transition that it has today.

Nonetheless, while at first viewed positively by the public as a consensus-generating mechanism, the *cuoteo* increasingly became viewed derisively by the Chilean public. It created the perception that ministerial positions were not awarded based on the talents or experience of the minister, but rather on the exigencies of party politics. Chileans increasingly view the *cuoteo* as a form of *politiquería* (crass politicking) and as a way to insure political positions for politicians, some of who have been unsuccessful in winning elections. Perhaps more seriously, from the level of the cabinet (and especially the recent cabinets of President Bachelet) down to the level of public administration, the *cuoteo* has been blamed for government incompetence, given the lack of preparation of officials appointed for partisan reasons. In November 2008, politicians on the Right called for elimination of the *cuoteo* in the Ministry of Health because of a series of errors and irregularities in the nation's hospitals (Renovación Nacional 2008).

Thus, though the *cuoteo* emerged as a successful informal tool to manage coalition building and maintenance during a democratic transition, it became an impediment to the establishment of more representative patterns of political recruitment in Chile, with important consequences for the ability of citizens to hold their leaders accountable. Nonetheless, the exigencies of coalition management and maintenance prevented the Concertación from abandoning it.

Elite Domination of Political Recruitment and Candidate Selection

Elites have consistently dominated candidate recruitment and selection for a variety of institutional and political reasons. The legislative election system imposed by the outgoing Pinochet government, known as the binomial system, establishes two-seat districts for elections to Congress, for which each coalition can present two candidates. The details of the electoral system have been analyzed in depth elsewhere and need not be recounted here (Rabkin 1996; Scully and Valenzuela 1997; Siavelis 2002; Navia 2005). However, in terms of representation, its most significant feature is that the highest polling coalition in a district can only win both seats if it more than doubles the vote total of the second-place list; otherwise, each list wins one seat. So within the context of Chile's postauthoritarian pattern of two-coalition competition, a coalition must poll 66 percent of the vote to win both seats, but can usually win one seat with only 33 percent. Because both major alliances almost invariably poll between 33 percent and 66 percent in each district, the outcome of elections is a foregone conclusion: except in a few cases one member of the Concertación and one member of the Alianza are likely to win in each district.

In addition, because the binomial system only provides two candidate slots to each coalition, and the Concertación is composed of five major parties, the number of candidacies that each party in each coalition receives is subject to arduous negotiations before the elections. The complexity of this negotiation process and the political horse-trading involved leave candidate selection completely in the hands of party elites and works at cross purposes with any efforts to democratize the selection process (Siavelis 2002; Navia 2008). The complexity of this negotiating environment in a multilevel game, where considerations of coalition maintenance also come into play, necessitates purposeful party elite intervention if parties are to achieve their goals.

Despite repeatedly stated intentions to democratize the process, Concertación presidential candidates also have been effectively chosen by elites. In 1989, Patricio Aylwin was chosen purely by elites. In 1993, only party militants and adherents participated in a primary process, but both candidates, Eduardo Frei and Ricardo Lagos, were put forward by the elites of their respective parties. Accordingly, in 1999 given that a PDC candidate had been named the standard bearer for two elections in a row, it was widely accepted that it was Socialists Lagos' "turn." He was confirmed in a primary that was a foregone conclusion. In 2005, a primary in the Concertación was planned, but Soledad Alvear dropped out before it took place because she was so far behind in the polls, and it is widely acknowledged that Bachelet's success grew out of the fact that Lagos had tagged her as his successor (Altman 2008). The selection process in 2009 involved a single regional primary between candidates chosen by the elites of their respective parties in the Maule and O'Higgins regions between former President Eduardo Frei and José Antonio Gómez from the Partido Radical Socialdemocrata (PRSD; Social Democrat Radical Party). Frei won with 65 percent versus 35 percent for Gómez. Had the percentage difference between both candidates been less than 20 percent, the selection process would have continued with additional primaries in other regions, but it did not. The process of popular inclusion or real popular influence in determining the outcome was minimal in any of the presidential primaries.

The legislative electoral system created strong incentives for coalition formation, and the selection of candidates by way of negotiations assured political voice for all members of the coalition in Congress. Indeed, without elite selection it is likely that the coalition would have fallen apart given that important party actors would have been excluded with a more open process. On the presidential level, elite selection assured the designation of moderate candidates acceptable to all actors in the coalition and provided for alternation of its two ideological sectors. However, elite domination of political recruitment and candidate selection exacted a cost in terms of the representative capacity of the political system, reinforcing the notion that politics was a game played only by the powerful.

Extrainstitutional Policymaking

The post-transitional policymaking model also involved a series of deals between party and executive branch elites within the Concertación and between the Concertación and potential veto players on the Right outside of Congress. In terms of the Concertación's relationships with veto players on the Right, the bargain included a tacit agreement that the president should negotiate with powerful economic actors and leaders on the Right to arrive at consensus solutions for the most controversial legislation before it was presented to Congress. This model, dubbed *democracia de los acuerdos* (democracy by agreement), was used to reform the tax code, expand social welfare and anticorruption legislation, and in the comprehensive constitutional reforms of 2005. These major policy deals involved little popular or congressional involvement (see Silva 1992; Boylan 1996; Fernández 2010).

Once again, this policymaking pattern was crucial to success of the democratic transition. Given the number of parties involved in the coalition it was necessary to facilitate agreement among parties. In addition, the fragility of the transition during much of the early years of democracy coupled with the controversial nature of many political issues and the existence of veto players made direct negotiation with those players a smart strategy. However, over the years this politics of elite accommodation has created a perception among the public that citizen preferences matter little and that politics is a negotiated rather than representative game. Finally, in negotiating directly with social actors outside of the Congress, presidents have consistently ignored the country's principal representative institution and created the perception (even among legislators) that the president bypasses Congress (Siavelis 2000).

Moderate (but Frustratingly Piecemeal) Reformism

Even more than its political model, Chile's economic model has been lauded around the world, with high rates of growth and impressive achievements in eliminating poverty. Still, the question of the underlying roots of economic success and where to place the credit or blame are still divisive in Chile. For his supporters, Pinochet's neoliberal economic policies transformed Chile into the free-market dynamo that it is today, and Concertación governments have managed the success without altering the Pinochet model. Many of Pinochet's critics, however, acknowledge that he set the country on the economic course it is on today, but are more critical of the reform process and its outcome. They contend that Concertación governments have improved the imperfect model that they inherited from Pinochet, but the fundamentals of the model remain intact (Silva 1995). In addition, they argue, despite impressive macroeconomic indicators, Chile is one of the most unequal countries in the world, and the Pinochet government's comprehensive privatization of the health, education, and social security systems has created an effectively two-tiered system where those with access to privatized social goods enjoy much higher standards of quality and access (Ffrench-Davis 2002).

Political actors across the spectrum agree that part of the unwritten deal underwriting the transition was that the neoliberal economic model inherited from Pinochet would remain untouched in its essentials (Silva 1992). Early democratic leaders recognized that the economy was the Achilles' heel of the transition. Had a substantial change in economic course taken place, the integrity of the democratic transition would have been compromised. The commitment of presidents to leave the economic model untouched calmed powerful economic elites, whose reaction to a potential change in policy could have been destabilizing. International investors were assured of economic stability and a dependable investment panorama. Finally, the process of veto player consultation on the economy facilitated later more widespread agreement on other issues with groups whose sympathies lay with the Right.

The Right: The Transitional Model Transformed

During the height of Concertación governments, it appeared that the Right was doomed to perpetual exile from government. At the midpoint of the Concertación's twenty years of government, Garretón noted that the Right might become a "permanent minority," without a shift in its fundamental political orientations (2000, 72). Gradually the dynamic of each of the dimensions of the Right's political model outlined above began to change—partly as result of public opinion regarding the exhaustion of the Concertación and the search for a new political alternative, but also because of a few key variables and turning points that shaped the platforms and image of the Right. These include: a transformed relationship with the military and the acceptance of the desirability and durability of democracy, transformations in the electoral strategies of parties, the acceptance of deep constitutional reforms in 2005, and attempts to develop a "new" Right. The transformation in the political model of the Right inherited from the democratic transition has been a crucial advance in the development of democracy in Chile. Nonetheless, the Right remains plagued with problems as it is increasingly perceived to differ little from the Concertación.

A Transformed Relationship with the Military and the Acceptance of Democracy

Early in the democratic transition many on the Right were convinced that Concertación governments would fail. These sectors maintained their commitments to the authoritarian regime as a way to hedge their bets against an eventual return to military rule. Garretón goes further to contend that the Chilean right had an "atavistic" link to the military regime, doggedly portraying itself as the political, institutional, and economic inheritor of the military's successful project (2000, 66). However, as it became clear that not only were Concertación governments going to succeed but were likely to remain in power for some time, the Right gradually realized it would need to work with the Concertación or it would be seen as a simple impediment to the establishment of full democracy (Pollack 1999).

In addition, during Chile's protracted transition, civilian governments have had to deal with several direct military challenges to their authority. In each of these cases, democratic authorities faced down threats yet resisted antagonizing the military. Eventually, as the public lost patience with the political machinations of the military, it became politically inopportune for the parties of the Right to continue to support the military, and both of its parties came to support civilian subordination of the armed forces (Weeks 2003).

Following Augusto Pinochet's arrest in London, the majority of parties across the spectrum and (even within the Concertación) agreed that the arrest represented an affront to civilian sovereignty. In addition, in 2001 a roundtable on human rights required that the armed forces provide more information on the detained and disappeared, and the Lagos administration pushed for a new commission on human rights abuses (Fuentes Forthcoming, 19). This forced the Right to acknowledge the extent of abuses and to distance itself from them and, in turn, the military. This corresponded with a simultaneous effort by the military itself to reform and become an institution more in tune with the norms of militaries in established democracies. Finally, in 2004, following the discovery of an excess of $30 million of cash that Pinochet had stashed in Riggs Bank in Washington, DC (belying Pinochet's assertion that he was unlike other Latin American dictators who simply sought to enrich themselves), the parties of the Right largely abandoned outright support for him, transforming their relationship with the military to appeal to a wider electorate.

Transformed Electoral Strategies

While Chile's right-wing parties have been historically more institutionalized than other rightist parties in Latin America, Garretón notes that while on the center and Left, civil society organizations tended to be dominated by Chile's parties in pre-Pinochet Chile, the opposite is true for the Right (2000, 55). In fact, powerful economic groups tended to be the most important social bases of the Right, and party organizations were simply their expression. The story of the transformation of Chile's Right is partly told in a transformation of this dynamic. That is not to say that powerful socioeconomic groups do not continue to dominate Chilean politics. However, the UDI in particular has made a real effort to broaden its electoral bases from the wealthiest and most conservative sectors of Chilean society, experiencing dramatic growth in support from the poorest sectors of Chilean society (Luna 2010, 338).

Unlike RN, the UDI reached out to organize among Chile's poor with campaigns and party centers in Chile's *poblaciones* (shanty towns) as early as the mid-1980s. The UDI brought an anti-Marxist and antiparty message to this socioeconomic sector, stressing the importance of order, stability, and work. It also exploited the position of its local level activists within the Pinochet government to distribute patronage and cultivate support, promoting knowledge of how the poor could take advantage of state resources and particularly the Programa de Empleo Mínimo (PEM; Minimum Employment Program) and the Programa de Ocupación para Jefes de Hogar (POJH; Occupational Program for Heads of Households) (Klein 2004). In advocating these programs, the UDI simultaneously attempted to promote its image as a technocratic, problem-solving party rather than a "political" or "ideological" party.

Organizational factors were also at play. The UDI is a cohesive, disciplined, and centralized party that set out from its strong electoral base in the capital to conquer new electoral districts throughout the country with the passage of every election (Joignant and Navia 2003). The Renovación Nacional (RN; National Renewal), however, is a rather loose, heterogeneous, and decentralized party, lacking the kind of explicit conquering strategy characteristic of the UDI. In terms of candidate selection and placement, the UDI has used a consistent strategy to pick up new seats. Unlike RN, the UDI has a centralized candidate selection process. The party's electoral commission works to identify the districts where the UDI has the best chance of winning, and, even in nonelection years, seeks to identify potential candidates and where they should run (Navia 2008). In contrast, the RN's candidate selection process has hurt it. Because the party is really something of a "loose association of leaders, party elites are more than willing to give up other districts to the UDI if they can be guaranteed that they will not face strong competition from UDI candidates in their own districts" (Navia 2008, 111). RN also lacks the kind of concerted strategy of candidate cultivation given its more independent orientation.

Acceptance of Constitutional Reform

The 1980 constitution was one of the legacies of the Pinochet government most fiercely defended by the parties of the Right, and particularly the UDI. The constitution established a number of provisions that provided effective veto power for the Right. This veto power was tied largely to the ability of Pinochet and his supporters to name high-level political authorities before leaving power (Siavelis 2000). The most egregiously authoritarian aspects of the constitution were reformed during the Lagos administration in September 2005 with the support of the Right. The reforms eliminated the positions of appointed senators and senators for life, reduced the powers of the National Security Council, returned to the president the authority to remove the commanders-in-chief of the armed forces, and reduced the presidential term from six to four years. These reforms prompted president Lagos to declare that the Chilean democratic transition was finally complete. Some have traced the Right's abandonment of its unyielding defense of Pinochet's constitution to a "forward looking" strategy (Fuentes Forthcoming). However, it is undeniable that the Right's acceptance of reform also grew from the reality that increasingly the power of appointment of these authorities fell to

Concertación governments with the passage of time and that it had increasingly come to work to the center-left's advantage. However, the Right's abandonment of its absolutist commitment to not reform the constitution improved its image by burnishing its democratic credentials.

The Building of a New Right

Certain leaders on the Right, and particularly Sebastián Piñera, have also been central in restoring its electoral viability by remaking it in the eyes of the public. One of the main objectives of Piñera's 2009–2010 campaign was to build what he termed a "new Right." In his campaign he advocated a *nueva derecha con una mayoría social* (a new right with a social majority) both inserting an implicit criticism of the existing Right and suggesting that the new Right would be attractive to many more Chileans. To do this, Piñera's based his campaign on two themes and markedly moved certain key policy positions of the Right towards the center. The first was a negative one aimed at the Concertación. Piñera had to be cautious. Bachelet left power with the highest rating of any modern president. So rather than attacking personalities or policies, Piñera focused his campaign on the idea that the Concertación had failed, was out of gas, and had not fulfilled its campaign promises. The attack focused on the growing sense that the Concertación had spent too many years in power and had become "corrupt" and exhausted (*agotado*). He criticized the politics of the *cuoteo*, capitalizing on a growing public perception that power was distributed based on political connections rather than talent. In terms of the positive elements, he argued that Chile needed a new form of government based on efficiency and expertise and not on political connections. In this sense, he drew on the technocratic appeals of the old Right. However, there was also something new here. It was not just a new model of government that Chile needed, but a "second transition." Rather than lauding the military regime at all, Piñera's plan for government referred to a first "old transition" that "we" completed (note the use of "we" as an effort to distance himself from the old Right) and that "we" needed to initiate a "second transition: the new, the young, belonging to the future and transforming Chile into a developed country without poverty" (Piñera 2009, 8).

In addition, Piñera tacked toward the center during the campaign to pick up centrist voters and build a new vision of the Right, particularly with respect to social issues. Because this was a three-way race, with dissident candidate Marco Enríquez-Ominami competing on the Left, Eduardo Frei, the Concertación candidate had the most difficult position, squeezed into a shrinking center—losing votes to the Right and attempting to attract voters from the Left. This left competition for centrist voters wide open for Piñera. He played up his family's Christian Democratic roots and the fact that he had voted against Pinochet in the 1988 plebiscite. Perhaps most important, with respect to economic policy, Piñera simply stole the Concertación's thunder, advocating many of its policy positions. Piñera's main economic policies were clearly acceptable to the broadest ideological spectrum in Chile with a pledge to create a million jobs, eliminate poverty, and to make Chile a developed country. The two major alliances waged similar campaigns in the 2009–2010 elections, with the dissident leftist candidate being the only one to propose deep changes to the post-transitional models of politics accepted by both major alliances.

The three campaigns differed on key issues (table 8.2). Though variations in policy positions were slight (especially between the Concertación and Alianza candidates), they reflected the historical orientations of the three major ideological sectors. Nonetheless, many of Frei's policy positions were farther to the Left than has been the norm for most Christian Democratic candidates. With respect to economic policies, both Frei and Ominami supported a state option within the AFP retirement system, while Piñera, in line with his more market-oriented stance, campaigned on keeping the system as it is. In addition, there were some differences with respect to tax policy that one would expect, and differing views on the status of the state-owned CODELCO copper company.

Only Enríquez-Ominami advocated a complete transformation of the Pinochet public education system, while Frei advocated dramatic increases in spending and Piñera proposed limited reforms around the edges. Something similar can be said about higher education and social welfare. Enríquez-Ominami proposed a dramatic change to how higher education is financed, and Frei advocated an increase of state spending on healthcare, without transforming the fundamental outlines of the model inherited from Pinochet. Piñera's proposals were more modest all around, recognizing a role for the state, but one that was relatively constrained.

Piñera also took liberal stances on social issues. While stopping short of a full endorsement of gay marriage, in a controversial campaign ad, Piñera called upon Chileans to respect homosexual couples. Both he and Frei supported civil unions, while Enríquez-Ominami was the only candidate to support gay marriage. Breaking with the Catholic Church, Piñera also came out in favor of legalization of the morning-after contraceptive pill, as did the other candidates. The only deep policy difference in the social area related to legalizing abortion, with Piñera against, Enríquez-Ominami in favor, and Frei advocating for the legality of therapeutic

Table 8.2. Policy Positions of Major Candidates in 2009–2010 Chilean Presidential Election

Issue Area	Marco Enríquez-Ominami (IND)	Edudardo Frei (Concertación)	Sebastián Piñera (Coalition for Change—Alianza)
Economic Policies			
Retirement System	Include a state option for retirement within the AFP system.	Include a state option for retirement within the AFP system.	Maintain the system as is.
Employment	Establishment of unemployment insurance and a national employment agency.	State subsidies for job creation	Establish a million new jobs. Employment and training subsidies.
Taxes	Tax reform. Reduce gas taxes, increase corporate taxes.	Increase corporate income tax.	Decrease IVA and gas taxes.
Status of CODELCO	Limited privatization	Leave state owned.	Privatize 50%.
Education and Health			
Educational Reform	End municipal administration, reestablish state control.	Dramatically increase spending to 5%–6% of GNP in 10 years.	Increase student subsidies, provide incentives for quality teachers.
Higher Education System Financing	Directly and fully finance students from lowest 2 economic quintiles.	Preferential admission for underepresented groups	Increase scholarships for low income students and for necessary professions.
Health Care	Construct new hospitals, train more specialists.	Build 10 new hospitals, 76 new medical offices, eliminate AUGE waiting lists.	Build new hospitals, establish centers of excellence.
Social Policy			
Abortion	Supports legalized abortion	Favors legislation on therapeutic abortion	Against legalization
Day after Pill	Supports	Supports	Supports
Homosexual Unions	Legal marriage	Civil Unions	Civil Unions
Political and Constitution			
Constitutional Reform	Adopt a new constitution.	Adopt a new constitution.	Maintain constitution as is.
Binominal Election System	Eliminate.	Eliminate.	Perfect through other reforms (primaries, etc.).
Campaign Finance	Public financing campaigns	Reform of spending law	Reform of spending law and a new law regulating political parties

Sources: www.votainteligente.com, Zuñiga (2010), Olivares (2010).

abortion. Indeed, Frei's stance on these issues, despite being a Christian Democrat, is a remarkable testament to his desire to draw support from his left flank.

The candidates differed most with respect to constitutional and political reform, an area that public opinion polls show the Chilean public cares least about. With respect to constitutional reform, Piñera stuck to the Right's long-time position that the constitution does not need reform, while Frei favored wholesale reform, and Enríquez-Ominami favored the adoption of a semipresidential system. In terms of the binomial legislative electoral system, Piñera maintained the Right's long-held position that it should be maintained and "perfected."

Successes, Challenges, and Fault Lines of Chilean Democracy

The many successes of Concertación governments are well accounted for and need not be extensively reviewed here (for a complete summary and references to literature, see the 3rd edition of this volume). In short, however, the economy was extraordinarily well managed, with average growth rates of 4.74 percent between 1995 and 2005 (reaching as high as 10.8 percent in 1995) and 3.73 percent between 2005 and 2010 (despite the worldwide economic downturn). Indeed, as world economic growth again sputtered in 2011, Chile's per capita growth averaged 5.2 percent for 2010 and was on target for a growth rate of over 6.5 percent for 2011. Real per capita gross income adjusted for PPP almost doubled between 1995 and 2009, from $7,160 to $13,420. While unemployment has ticked up from its low of 6.1 percent in 1997, between 1995 and 2005 it averaged 8.1 percent, and despite the world downturn, it averaged 8.0 percent between 2005 and 2010. Indeed, unemployment was projected to fall from 9 percent in 2010 to 7.7 percent for 2011 (Banco Central de Chile 2011; Instituto Nacional de Estadísticas 2011). Significant reforms have been undertaken to the tax code, the labor code, the social welfare system, and health and to Santiago's transport system; however, the fundamental structural elements of the Pinochet model have not really been transformed in these areas.

As this chapter and other analysts have noted, civil-military relations transformed from a situation where the military as an institution posed a real threat to the maintenance and stability of democracy to one where the military is firmly ensconced in the barracks. This is a remarkable transformation for a military that was, a relatively short time ago, responsible for vicious human rights abuses and a wavering commitment to democracy.

The country's deeply authoritarian constitution has been transformed. The 1980 constitution established myriad authoritarian provisions that placed it outside the norms for constitutions in a democratic society. The Lagos government worked with the opposition to consensually pass a series of deep constitutional reforms in 2005 that place the constitution fully within the norms of those of established constitutional democracies.

Finally, the coalition ceded power to a deeply reformed Right, that while once reactionary is now a viable governing option. It did so peacefully and without the emergence of the type of populist leftists that have emerged in many countries in the region.

For all of these reasons, it is undeniable that the country is among the most successful in Latin America, and Chile is repeatedly referred to in the press and academic work as a model of successful democratization and balanced development. Nonetheless, the streets have been full of angry protestors for months, and levels of dissatisfaction with government and the opposition are at an all-time high. While some point to Piñera's 27 percent level of support in the polls as a harbinger of the Concertación's bright electoral future, this overlooks the fact that the latter has a level of support of 17 percent (Centro de Estudios Públicos 2011).

More seriously there are problems with systemic support for democracy. There is widespread disillusionment with democracy in Chile, reflecting a wider crisis of representation in the country. Only 15 percent of Chileans think democracy functions well or very well, and after two decades of democracy, only 45 percent think in all cases democracy is the best regime, with the number who believe so decreasing. Indeed, the total percentage of Chileans who think that in some circumstances an authoritarian regime is acceptable (18 percent) or that it really does not matter whether a regime is authoritarian or democratic (29 percent) outnumber the 45 percent who think that democracy is always preferable (Centro de Estudios Públicos 2008). While some might contend this is a trend across Latin America, on several key indicators of mass public opinion, other countries rank higher, and some of Chile's indicators are disturbing. Thirty-six percent of Chileans report being satisfied or very satisfied with democracy, placing Chile in the eighth position among eighteen countries included in the 2007 Latinobarómetro survey. Uruguay and Costa Rica, often grouped with Chile as "poster children" for democracy, reported much higher rates of satisfaction with democracy at 66 percent and 47 percent respectively (Corporación Latinobarómetro 2007). More worrying for the future, while 95 percent of Chileans over 55 are registered to vote, only 22 percent of 18 to 24 year olds are (Centro de Estudios Públicos 2008). Voter participation is quite low. There are 12 million eligible voters in Chile, yet 5 million of them did not vote in the 2009–2010 presidential election. Of these 5 million, 3.8

million did not register, and roughly 1.2 million stayed home even though voting is obligatory if one is registered (Fernández 2010, 292).

What explains the apparent contradiction of success with high levels of dissatisfaction? In essence, despite the success of the transition, there are some by-products of the increasingly converging transitional models of politics shared by both coalitions, which help explain both the widespread citizen dissatisfaction in Chile, and that at the same time constitute the major challenges and fault lines of democratic governance for the future.

Emerging Partidocracia

Strong and well-institutionalized parties are central actors in quality democracies (Mainwaring and Scully, 1995). Indeed, strong parties were crucial to the success of the Chilean transition, because only strong parties with the capacity to discipline members could negotiate and enforce the agreements that sustained the democratic transition. However, increasingly, the domination of the Chilean political system by parties with low levels of popular adhesion is bordering on the development of a *partidocracia*. This argument may come as a surprise to those who have followed the coverage of the progressive erosion in support for parties among the Chilean population, both in the press and in academic literature (Rodríguez 2006; Luna 2008).

However, while *popular* support has eroded for parties, at the elite level the party system seems remarkably like that of the preauthoritarian period, and numerous studies attest to the extent of continuity. Given the continued centrality of parties one might be tempted, therefore, to argue that parties still form the "backbone" of Chilean politics, as Garretón once argued with respect to parties in the preauthoritarian era (Garretón 1987, 64). However, while they remain the "backbone" for structuring elite politics, the nature of society-party relations is very different from the preauthoritarian period.

When surveys began immediately following the return of democracy in 1990, 62.5 percent of the Chilean public attested to identifying with a political party. By 1992, the number of Chileans self-identifying with political parties increased to 87 percent. From there, this percentage has registered gradual declines to the point that in 2008, only 43 percent of Chileans said they identified with a particular political party, and none of the parties registered a level of adherence above 10 percent.[2]

Nonetheless, at the elite level, parties—and in particular party elites—remain the most important political actors in Chile. First, parties are recognized as one of the central policymaking actors. Party elites in concert with the president by-pass Congress to work out legislative deals with major social actors and veto players before they are presented to Congress for approval. Members of parliament also recognize the centrality of party leaders to legislation. Chile was the only country of fifteen included in a recent study where *party leaders* were ranked as most important, ahead of voters and party militants in terms of whose opinions deputies take into account when making decisions (Marenghi and Montero 2008).

Second, party elites are remarkably powerful actors within their own parties. Elites exercise almost complete control over the legislative candidate selection process, and in the few cases where primaries are undertaken, party elites have overridden the decisions of popular contests to satisfy deals related to coalition maintenance (Siavelis 2002; Navia 2008). With respect to internal party democracy, legislators perceive it as quite low, albeit growing, when measured in terms of the power and influence of party militants. During the first three legislative periods of the democratic government, 16 percent of deputies termed levels of party democracy as "high" or "very high" during the first (1994–1998), 31 percent during the second (1998–2002), and 44.4 percent during the third (2002–2006). Overall, among the fifteen countries included in the PELA (Parliamentary Elites of Latin America) study, Chile ranked third from the bottom in terms of perceived internal party democracy, only behind Argentina and the Dominican Republic (Rodríguez 2008).

Finally, as detailed throughout this chapter, parties and considerations of party identification are central in determining which posts people receive, where parliamentary candidates run, and how the spoils of Chile's coalition government are distributed. In this sense, and as Luna (2008) has argued, there remains a highly institutionalized and stable party system at the level of elites, but it has weak ties to the population.

In writing on pre-Chávez Venezuela, a country previously touted as a "model" and an island of stability in Latin America, Coppedge contended that "The institutions that make Venezuela a stable polity also tarnish the quality of its democracy" (1994, 2). Coppedge noted that Venezuela's highly institutionalized parties had come to completely dominate the political system in the form of a "partyarchy" or *partidocracia*. In a similar way, the institutions and political dynamic which made Chile's transition to democracy a success have also tarnished the quality of democracy, and many of these are tied to a developing *partidocracia*.

This is not to say that powerful parties are bad for democracy. In their study of Uruguay, Buquet and Chasquetti refer to the *partidocracia de consenso* (party dominated consensus), noting the extraordinary strength of Uruguayan parties (2004). However, the crucial difference is that Uruguayan parties demonstrate many of the same prerogatives as Chilean parties, but unlike Chile, they enjoy high levels of cohesive support among the mass public. Therefore, while parties in Chile are strong and influential at the elite level, they lack the deep roots in society that characterized parties in the past and which has been recognized as central to effective party representation (see Rodríguez 2006; Luna 2008).

The electoral system obligates parties to stand together if they have any chance of winning, and purposeful action in building coalitions is at the core of continuing to win. Without strong party elites who structure and enforce agreements, it would have been difficult to forge the types of collaborative efforts that have been central to maintaining the Concertación. However, hopefully for Chile and unlike Venezuela, the extent of party domination *over* civil society institutions and groups is much less. Therefore an antidote to this *partidocracia*, in the form of electoral reform, can stave off the development of one that is as entrenched and damaging as the one that gave rise to Hugo Chávez in Venezuela. However, such a reform has consistently fallen victim to debates over how a new electoral system should look.

Lack of Accountability

The dynamic interaction of coalition politics and the electoral system also limits accountability. The legislative election system with few exceptions provides each coalition an effective assurance of one of the two seats in each electoral district, creating what has been often termed a permanent *"empate político"* (a permanent tie). One could argue that voters could reassert control by ousting incumbents nominated by party elites. However, the binomial system also makes it almost impossible to defeat incumbents. Barring incompetence or extreme indiscipline, Chilean parties consider incumbents to have a right of renomination (Siavelis 2002). The election system in the context of two coalitions strongly limits the ability to unseat an incumbent. Rarely will one list contain two candidates from the same party, providing incumbents the luxury of not facing intraparty competition at least in the electoral arena. More importantly, if a voter seeks to unseat an incumbent there are two potential strategies. The voter can either completely abandon his or her ideological convictions and vote for an opposition list, or cast a likely more ideologically sincere vote for the list partner of the incumbent. However, because votes are pooled in determining seat distributions, a vote for one candidate on a list is in many respects a vote for both. Therefore, by voting for an incumbent's list partner, a voter may actually be contributing support to the very incumbent the voter aims to defeat (Navia 2005). Further, as Navia goes on to note, because of the thresholds of the system, a candidate who loses support in a district could conceivably go from a level of 60 percent support to 35 percent without losing the congressional seat. Accountability is central to democracy. The current coalitional configuration combined with the properties of the binominal system does not provide voters the opportunity to hold their representatives accountable.

Public opinion survey data suggest that citizens perceive and object to this elite dominance, lack of turnover, and the elite lock on power. When asked whether members of Congress are concerned about the problems of average people, only 14 percent of the population answered in the affirmative. When asked to name the two principal defects of political parties, the top three responses were "they are not transparent" (36 percent), "they are always the same . . . "there is no turnover" (33 percent), and "they pass out government positions among themselves" (31 percent) (CEP 2007).

Lackluster and Limited Reform (and Nagging Inequality)

The conduct of politics that grew out of the transition has also profoundly influenced the content of policy outcomes. The restrictions placed on elites as a result of the veto power of the military and the Right limited the scope of potential reforms. Elites have consistently avoided destabilizing change and have been loath to address deep public dissatisfaction by engaging in any fundamental reform of the economic system inherited from Pinochet.

Nonetheless, the unwillingness of democratic governments to enter into a discussion of the economic model beyond some minor piecemeal reforms like the Acceso Universal con Garantías Explícitas plan (AUGE; Universal Access with Explicit Guarantees), a limited reform of the healthcare system undertaken by President Ricardo Lagos to address the most egregious inequalities, left the Concertación open to charges that nothing has changed with democracy. Despite success in fighting poverty, levels of inequality in Chile are among the highest in the world, and weaknesses in lines of citizen representation underscored throughout this chapter leave citizens with few avenues to affect the political economy of the country. Once again, high-level negotiations rather than popular or legislative consultation have been the norm in making economic policy.

With such clear signals of trouble with the inherited economic model, why have governments not acted more aggressively to more fundamentally transform its key aspects? Once again, the economic policymaking process since the return of democracy has been based on two sets of tacit agreements that are underwritten by the interaction of political party context and the election system.

The first is a tacit agreement between the Concertación and the Alianza. The Concertación has agreed to preserve the economic and social security structures set up by the Pinochet dictatorship. Although the Concertación governments have significantly increased fiscal expenditure on social policies, for example, they have not in any way touched the privatized structures of healthcare and pensions, or attempted any form of redistribution that would even out the highly unequal structure of income distribution or educational opportunities. They have kept the state out of economic activities as much as possible, precluding the discussion or implementation of any kind of development strategy. What is more, even today the Concertación must avoid charges of irresponsible economic policymaking or populism, and an unwillingness to engage in fundamental economic transformations is deeply entrenched in a habitually risk-averse group of political elites.

The second agreement is within the Concertación. As repeatedly noted, the parliamentary election system obliges the Concertación to run as a coalition, which requires at least limited policy consensus. Engaging in fundamental structural economic reforms risks fracturing the Concertación among its various ideological flanks, a disastrous outcome for either the center or the Left, given the dynamics of a parliamentary electoral system that will exclude at least one ideological sector in the context of a three-bloc competition.

The unwillingness or inability of governments to address severe inequality and devise more inclusive patterns of economic policymaking have contributed to the wider pattern of dissatisfaction analyzed here. Recent student protests and labor unrest are indications of public disgust with inequality and the lack of fundamental economic reform. The significance of these protests is deeper, however, and more complex on a number of levels.

While in the international press the protests have been portrayed as about the educational system per se and lack of reform of Pinochet era educational laws and institutions, they really grow from much deeper frustrations. Indeed, many of the protesters are middle class students, and the demands they make could potentially widen inequalities between the middle class and poor. However, what is at the root of the protests is a sense of fairness. The protesters object to the policies pursued by elites, who have ensured that the fruits of Chile's economic success continue to be funneled to the top, within a system rigged to underwrite the continuing power of economic elites. Protestors argue that the private educational system with its elite schools is central to how the system is rigged to perpetuate this inequality. The over forty protests in Chile during 2011, in this sense, like political protests erupting around the world (and now in other Latin American capitals), are about justice and fairness. This is why the protestors have widened their demands from basic educational reforms to also include demands for inclusion, equality of opportunity, reform of the political system, and deeper labor and tax reforms.

In addition, the explosion of protests can also be tied to Piñera's victory. The Concertación held fairly tight oversight of the internal components of the coalition, including social movements, to prevent them from embarrassing transitional governments. However, with a president of the Right, these groups have been liberated from such restraints, while the Right and President Piñera underestimated the extent of pent-up frustration.

Some elites within the Concertación understand these problems and the origins of the fault lines set out here. Socialist Carlos Ominami went as far as to say that while the Concertación did oversee a successful transition, it did not oversee the successful transformation of Chile. He went on to argue that in many respects the Concertación "situated itself within a logic of administration rather than a logic of transformation" (Ominami 2010, 49).

Conclusion

Democracy is multidimensional, involving tradeoffs between its various elements. One dimension is *representation*, or the channeling of public will into policy through elected representatives. According to this idea, the policy preferences of elected officials ideally should reflect those of the electorate. There is reason to believe that a model of "mandate representation" (where congruence exists between the policy preferences of the population and politicians) is more likely to facilitate the positive functioning of democracy (Kitschelt 1999).

In addition, democracy entails *accountability*. Citizens should be able to participate in periodic elections to award or punish (i.e., reelect or remove) the elected for the quality and nature of the representation provided. In short, "Governments are 'accountable' if citizens can discern representative from unrepresentative governments and can sanction them appropriately, retaining in office those incumbents who perform well and ousting from office those who do not" (Manin et al. 1999, 10).

Finally, democracy entails *governability* or the "ability of governments to make policy decisively" (Coppedge 2001, 8), which is "mostly a top-down phenomena," that entails "governing effectively" (Mainwaring and Scully 2010, 2), and is certainly tied to generalized stability and adherence to the rules of the game.

Earlier editions of this volume, though underscoring the potential fault lines of democracy, consistently pointed to Chile as a model economy and democratic transition in comparison to other countries in the region. These assertions are made mostly based on the impressive stability and *governability* that have characterized Chile since the return of democracy, with little reference to representation or accountability.

This is the case because in Chile the two transitional models of politics have consistently privileged governability over representation and accountability. The success of the Concertación coalition (and, in turn, the democratic transition) was based on a complex power-sharing arrangement; but it is one that increasingly brings charges of elite domination and politics by quota, with little citizen participation. The sharing of electoral spoils through negotiated assignment of legislative candidacies guaranteed peace between Chile's parties, but could only be undertaken through elite selection of candidates and precluded significant citizen input. With respect to the policymaking process, party elites in concert with the president bypass Congress to work out legislative deals with major social actors and veto players before they are presented to Congress. This was certainly a stabilizing phenomenon, but one that sidelined Congress and the public and resulted in a pattern of piecemeal reform that fell short of public demands for deeper transformations to country's socioeconomic structure. Finally, the electoral system and the system of nominations consistently sidelined citizens and prevented the effective exercise of accountability.

While the Right has undergone the deep transformations necessary to govern, it never seriously questioned or departed from the basic consensus between it and the Concertación. Where the Concertación has lacked audacity, the Right has lacked imagination and commitment to fundamentally reshape the political model and commitments it now shares with the Concertación. Indeed, the Right has been perceived as so complicit in this way of doing politics that it has been difficult for the Piñera government to distinguish itself from Concertación governments.

Chile's citizens demand a new model that performs better on *all* measures of democracy and not just governability and stability. This is not to suggest that this growing dissatisfaction will bring the military from the barracks, but rather that Chile is not immune from the widespread dissatisfaction with the quality of the functioning of democracy that plagues much of Latin America, despite being held up as a "model" democracy in the region.

While it is perhaps an exaggeration to suggest that Chile could fall victim to the type of populist leaders that have come to power or aspired to power in the region, there are some troubling realities that underscore the potential for a rockier future for democracy. First, recent protests and the level of dissatisfaction being expressed by citizens in public opinion polls are emerging within the context of a relatively successful and healthy economy, based in large part on a commodity boom. If the world economic slowdown reaches Chile, it is likely that even more vocal demands for change would rock the system.

Second, it will be very difficult to put the party system genie back in the bottle. That is to say that levels of dissatisfaction and disgust with political parties have reached such a level that it is difficult to imagine what actions elites could take to restore parties to their traditionally accepted roles as the main interlocutors between the governed and those who govern.

Third, while public opinion surveys give the Piñera government low marks, the Concertación polls are even worse, that is to say, voters hold neither the government nor the opposition in high regard, creating a ripe environment for a transformational figure from outside the traditional party system.

However, perhaps most worrying, the chapter on Chile in the third edition of this volume underscored that the "success" of Chile (i.e., governability and stability) was based on the construction of a new social pact between social sectors regarding the fundamental outlines of Chile's socioeconomic structure. That consensus now appears to have broken down, with potentially negative consequences for the future performance of Chilean democracy.

Parties traditionally were the most important interlocutors of politics in Chile, and historically no successful democracy has conducted the business of representation any other way. However, it appears that parties have lost such legitimacy in the eyes of the public that it is difficult to imagine that they could reassume the historical role they played. Electoral reform would certainly help, as would completely abandoning the entrenched model of politics that proved so central to a successful democratic transition and so damaging to the consolidation of a more complete democracy in all of its dimensions. Perhaps a real second transition is in order, one that will bring new faces and new models of politics to Chile, and one that moves beyond those of Chile's historic, but completed, transition.

NOTES

1. Interview, August 20, 2008.
2. Data collected and aggregated by author from a series of surveys from the Centro de Estudios Públicos. See www.cepchile.cl/dms/lang_1/home.html.

REFERENCES

Altman, David. 2008. "Political Recruitment and Candidate Selection in Chile, 1990–2006: The Executive Branch." *Pathways to Power: Political Recruitment and Candidate Selection in Latin America*, edited by P. M. Siavelis and S. Morgenstern, 241–71. University Park, PA: Pennsylvania State University Press.

Angell, Alan. 2007. *Democracy After Pinochet*. London: University of London Institute for the Study of the Americas.

Banco Central de Chile. 2011. "Indicadores Macroeconómicos."

Barros, Robert. 2002. *Constitutionalism and Dictatorship: Pinochet, the Junta, and the 1980 Constitution*. New York: Cambridge University Press.

Boeninger, Edgardo. 1989. "Gestión de gobierno y proceso de decisiones púbicas." SEGPRES. Santiago: Unpublished memorandum.

Boylan, Delia. 1996. "Taxation and Transition: The Politics of the 1990 Chilean Tax Reform." *Latin American Research Review* 31 (1): 7–31.

Buquet, Daniel, and Daniel Chasquetti. 2004. "La Democracia en Uruguay: Una partidocracia de consenso." *Política y Gobierno* 42 (Fall): 221–47.

Centro de Estudios Públicos. 2007. "Documento de trabajo: Estudio nacional de opinión pública." Santiago: Centro de Estudios Públicos.

———. 2008. "Estudio nacional sobre partidos políticos y sistema electoral, Marzo–Abril 2008." Santiago: Centro de Estudios Publicos.

———. 2011. "Estudio nacional de opinión pública, junio–julio 2011." Santiago: Centro de Estudios Publicos.

Coppedge, Michael. 1994. *Strong Parties and Lame Ducks: Presidential Partyarchy and Factionalism in Venezuela*. Stanford: Stanford University Press.

———. 2001. "Party Systems, Governability, and the Quality of Democracy in Latin America." Paper presented at the conference, Representation and Democratic Politics in Latin America, University of San Andrés, Buenos Aires.

Corporación Latinobarómetro. 2007. Informe, Latinobarómetro.

Fernández, María de los Ángeles. 2010. "La derrota electoral de la Concertación y del progresismo en Chile: Ideas para un debate." *Chile en la Concertación: 1990–2010*, edited by Y. Quirogo and J. Ensignia, 285–99. Santiago: Friedrich Ebert Stiftung.

Ffrench-Davis, Ricardo. 2002. *Economic Reforms in Chile: From Dictatorship to Democracy*. Ann Arbor: University of Michigan Press.

Fuentes, Claudio. Forthcoming. "The Long Process of Democratizing Chile." In *Concertación Governments in Chile 1990–2010: Politics, Economics and Social Policy under the Rainbow*, edited by P. Siavelis and K. Sehnbruch. Boulder CO: Lynne Rienner.

Garretón, Manuel Antonio. 1987. *Reconstruir la política: Transición y consolidación democrática en Chile*. Santiago: Editorial Andante.

————. 2000. "Atavism and Ambiguity in the Chilean Right." *Conservative Parties, the Right, and Democracy in Latin America*, edited by K. J. Middlebrook, 53–109. Baltimore: Johns Hopkins University Press.

Guardia, Alexis. 2010. "Relación entre economía y política: La experiencia chilena." *Chile en la Concertación: 1990–2010*, edited by Y. Quirogo and J. Ensignia, 79–122. Santiago: Friedrich Ebert Stiftung.

Instituto Nacional de Estadísticas. 2011. "Tasa de desocupacion." Santiago: Instituto de Nacional de Estadistísticas.

Joignant, Alfredo, and Patricio Navia. 2003. "De la política de los individuos a los hombres del partido: Socialización, competencia política y penetración electoral de la UDI (1989–2001)." *Estudios Públicos* 89 (Summer): 129–71.

Kitschelt, Herbert. 1999. *Post-Communist Party Systems: Competition, Representation, and Inter-Party Cooperation*. New York: Cambridge University Press.

Klein, Marcus. 2004. "The Unión Demócrata Independiente and the Poor (1983–1992): The Survival of Clientelistic Traditions in Chilean Politics." *Jahrbuch fur Geschichte Lateinamerikas* 41:301–24.

Loveman, Brian. 2001. *Chile: The Legacy of Hispanic Capitalism*. New York: Oxford University Press.

Luna, Juan Pablo. 2008. "Partidos políticos y sociedad en Chile: Trayectoria histórica y mutaciones recientes." *Reforma de los partidos políticos en Chile*, edited by A. Fontaine, 75–126. Santiago: CIEPLAN.

————. 2010. "Segmented Party-Voter Linkages in Latin America: The Case of the UDI." *Journal of Latin American Studies* 42:325–56.

Mainwaring, Scott, and Timothy Scully. 2010. "Democratic Governance in Latin America." *Democratic Governance in Latin America*, edited by S. Mainwaring and T. R. Scully, 367–97. Palo Alto: Stanford University Press.

Marenghi, Patricia, and Mercedes García Montero. 2008. "The Conundrum of Representation." In *Politicians and Politics in Latin America*, edited by M. Alcántara Sáez, 29–64. Boulder, CO: Lynne Reinner.

Navia, Patricio. 2005. "La transformación de votos en escaños: Leyes electorales en Chile, 1833–2004." *Política y Gobierno* 12 (2): 233–76.

————. 2008. "Legislative Candidate Selection in Chile." In *Pathways to Power: Political Recruitment and Candidate Selection in Latin America*, edited by P. Siavelis and S. Morgenstern, 92–118. University Park, PA: Pennsylvania State University Press.

Ominami, Carlos. 2010. "Chile: Una transición paradojal: Notas para un examen crítico." In *Chile en la Concertación: 1990–2010*, edited by Y. Quirogo and J. Ensignia, 21–62. Santiago: Friedrich Ebert Stiftung.

Piñera, Sebastián. 2009. "Programa de gobierno para el cambio, el futuro, y la esperanza: Chile 2010–2014." Santiago: Coalición por el cambio.

Pollack, Marcelo. 1999. *The New Right in Chile 1973–1997*. New York: St. Martin's.

Przeworski, Adam, Susan C. Stokes, and Bernard Manin. 1999. "Introduction." In *Democracy, Accountability and Representation*, edited by A. Przeworski, S. C. Stokes, and B. Manin, 1–26. New York: Cambridge University Press.

Rabkin, Rhoda. 1996. "Redemocratization, Electoral Engineering, and Party Strategies in Chile, 1989–1995." *Comparative Political Studies* 29 (3): 335–56.

Rehren, Alfredo. 1992. "Organizing the Presidency for the Consolidation of Democracy in the Southern Cone." Unpublished paper presented at the Latin American Studies Association, Los Angeles.

Renovación Nacional. 2008. "Parlamentarios piden terminar con el cuoteo en el MINSAL," Renovación Nacional website, November 3, 2008. http://rn.cl/2008/11/03/parlamentarios-piden-terminar-con-el-cuoteo-en-el-minsal/.

Rodríguez, Leticia. 2006. "El sistema de partidos chileno: ¿Hacia una desestructuración ideológica?" In *Chile: Política y modernización democrática*, edited by M. Alcántara Sáez and L. Rodríguez, 73–110. Barcelona: Edicions Bellaterra.

Roht-Arrizaz, Naomi. 2005. *The Pinochet Effect: Transitional Justice in the Age of Human Rights*. Philadelphia: University of Pennsylvania Press.

Scully, Timothy, and Samuel Valenzuela. 1997. "Electoral Choices and the Party System in Chile: Continuities and Changes at the Recovery of Democracy." *Comparative Politics* 29 (4): 511–27.

Siavelis, Peter. 2000. *The President and Congress in Post-Authoritarian Chile: Institutional Constraints to Democratic Consolidation*. University Park, PA: Pennsylvania State University Press.

———. 2002. "The Hidden Logic of Candidate Selection for Chilean Parliamentary Elections." *Comparative Politics* 34 (4): 419–38.

Silva, Eduardo. 1992. "Capitalist Regime Loyalties and Redemocratization in Chile." *Journal of Interamerican Studies and World Affairs* 34 (4): 77–117.

———. 1995. "The Political Economy of Chile's Regime Transformation: From Radical to 'Pragmatic' Neo-liberal Policies." In *The Struggle for Democracy in Chile*, edited by P. W. Drake and I. Jaksic, 98–127. Lincoln: University of Nebraska Press.

Valenzuela, Samuel. 1995. "Orígenes y transformaciones del sistema de partidos en Chile." *Estudios Públicos* 58 (Fall): 5–80.

Weeks, Gregory. 2003. *The Military and Politics in Postauthoritarian Chile*. Tuscaloosa: University of Alabama Press.

CHAPTER NINE

Colombia

Democratic Governance amidst an Armed Conflict

Eduardo Posada-Carbó

P oor Colombia," a columnist in the Spanish daily *El País* observed with pity in 2000: "a country of cursed richness, *la amapola opiácea*. A country with talent, beauty, citizenship, is destroyed." Indeed a decade ago, the notion of Colombia as a "failed state" had been widely accepted among important academic and policymaking circles. As Julia Sweig noted in 2002 in the publication *Foreign Affairs*, "Between drugs, paramilitaries, guerrillas, and a collapsing state, Colombia's condition is steadily worsening." Sweig echoed critics who argued "the whole idea of Colombia as a functioning nation was a fiction." She came to favor a radical approach to the country's problems: "Unless Colombia was reinvented and new institutions were created from scratch, the nation risked collapse" (Tagle 2000; Sweig 2002). Not surprisingly, when the Fund for Peace together with *Foreign Policy* published their first Failed State Index in 2005, Colombia ranked fourteenth among the twenty most vulnerable countries in the world, next to Haiti, Afghanistan, Rwanda, and North Korea (The Fund for Peace and the Carnegie Endowment for International Peace 2005).[1]

Colombia did not collapse. To acknowledge this fact does not mean to deny the severe crisis that the country underwent, fueling such diagnoses of despair. However, by the end of 2010, it was clear that Colombia was on a different path, one far from that of doom and failure so widely predicted. Reports in the international press reflected a drastic change in perceptions: "Colombia stands as a beacon of hope for South America," read a headline from the *Daily Telegraph* in 2008 (Hannan 2008).[2] In 2011, the "Failed State Index" had moved Colombia to forty-fourth on the list, still in the "danger" zone, but nowhere near the top failing candidates, as had been the case just a few years earlier (Foreign Policy and the Fund for Peace 2011). Colombian leaders, who naively adopted the "failed state" rhetoric, now boasted about their achievements: "This failed state that we had eleven years ago is today a vibrant democracy," President Juan Manuel Santos told President Barack Obama when they met in 2011.

An assessment of the state of democratic governance in Colombia, the aim of this chapter, has to start by providing an explanation for the country's transformation from "collapse" to success over the last decade. Thus, the first section will offer an account of such developments, with a special focus on the Álvaro Uribe Vélez administration (2002–2010). This will be followed by looking at some of the major advances and setbacks in democratic governance under Juan Manuel Santos, the new president since August 7, 2010. A third and concluding section will briefly discuss the prospects and challenges faced by Colombia in the task of constructing democratic governance.

While it is possible to measure the level of achievements in democratic governance (Mainwaring, Scully, and Vargas 2010, 11–51), the analysis that follows is more qualitative than quantitative. My major concern is not to provide a balance sheet of successes and failures, but rather to examine the conditions— the challenging conditions in this case—under which Colombia has been pursuing the dualistic goal of democratic governance: "governing democratically, but also governing more effectively" (Mainwaring and Scully 2010, 2). The concept of governance may invite us to move beyond state institutions and focus more on civil society. Colombia has indeed embraced such agenda of governance since 1991. Contrary to what some theoreticians tell us about the "crisis of faith in the state" (Bevir 2010)—the apparent inspiration behind the ideas of new governance—what the Colombian experience shows is the need to rely on the central state to guarantee the basic conditions for free social interaction and coexistence. The assumption underpinning this chapter is that there cannot be governance without traditional government, thus my emphasis on state institutions and state policies. By no means does this imply abandoning civil society altogether. Indeed, the conditions for democratic governance in Colombia have improved during the last decade, partly thanks to significant policy innovations determined to some extent by important shifts in the climate of public opinion (Weir 1992).[3]

Coming Out of the Abyss

A familiar story that should not detain us here is that by 2000, Colombia had been suffering a prolonged and profound crisis (Cepeda Ulloa 2003; Pizarro Leongómez 2004). However, it is important to appreciate the gigantic dimensions of the problems, how Herculean these were (and still are), in order to have a yardstick to assess the level of progress made in the last decade. It is also important to emphasize that the country has been trying to solve such colossal problems within the natural constraints of a liberal democratic regime.[4] This section highlights the magnitude of the crisis by the end of the twentieth century and offers both an account and an explanation of the main achievements, limits, and failures of Colombian democratic governance during the last decade.

The Colombian crisis has often been described as one of multiple angles, simultaneously affected by guerrillas, paramilitaries, and narcotraffickers, among many other factors. Nevertheless, what has characterized the country's crisis since the 1970s is the endurance of guerrilla warfare that has seriously threatened social and political stability—the prolonged "internal armed conflict." Money from illegal drugs fuelled the conflict by undermining the rule of law, diminishing the capacity of state forces to combat organized crime, and by strengthening the finances of guerrilla organizations. During the Barco (1986–1990) and Gaviria (1990–1994) administrations, the Colombian government was able to demobilize and integrate a handful of guerrilla movements into the political system—most notably the M19. However, the oldest guerrillas persevered in their rebellious activities, above all the Fuerzas Armadas Revolucionarias de Colombia (FARC; Revolutionary Armed Forces of Colombia) and also the Ejército de Liberación Nacional (ELN; National Liberation Army).

These organizations not only endured throughout the 1990s, but they grew stronger.[5] Their survival and growth tends to obscure the significant achievements that the country accomplished during the 1990s. Two achievements merit particular attention. First, a successful peace process allowed the integration of former armed rebels into politics. This was accompanied by the adoption of a new constitution in 1991 through an assembly where former members of guerrilla movements had important representation, and indeed significantly contributed to the shaping of the new charter.[6] Second, the Colombian authorities were able to prevail over the major drug cartels that had posed a serious threat to the state and society. Pablo Escobar, the feared head of the Medellín Cartel, was gunned down by police forces, and the Rodríguez Orejuela brothers, leaders of the Cali Cartel, were captured and extradited to the United States. Such successes in themselves suggest the need to question the stereotype of the Colombian "failed state."[7] Faced with a multifront conflict, the state proved to have the capacity both to dismantle strong criminal organizations and to negotiate with guerrilla groups.

Yet, while the Colombian state managed to succeed in some areas, it was certainly failing in others. Above all, it had failed to guarantee security to its citizens, its most basic duty. The number of homicides since 1980 is staggering. In 1991, the homicide rate peaked at 79.3 per 100,000 inhabitants—at the time, perhaps the highest homicide rate in the world. It decelerated afterward, but then spiked again to an upward trend after 1998: almost 29,000 homicides were committed in 2002 (Departamento Nacional de Planeación, Colombia 2005; Colombia, Ministerio de Defensa 2010). Similarly, the number of kidnappings also skyrocketed through the 1990s, reaching a peak in 2000 when some 3,700 people were kidnapped (Moor and Zumpolle 2002). Partly in reaction to increasing levels of general insecurity, paramilitary groups started forming, sometimes with the collaboration of members of the state forces, leading to the creation of the Autodefensas Unidas de Colombia (AUC; United Self-Defenses of Colombia) in 1997, which was responsible for a series of massacres and political assassinations that shocked the country. In 1998, General Jorge E. Mora, then commander of the armed forces, told Andrés Pastrana as he took power: "Mr. President, [our] democracy is at risk, this war [with the FARC] is lost." Violence forced people to migrate from their homes. Estimates of the *desplazados* (displaced people) vary, but by 2004 the official register of *desplazados* was over 1.5 million (Departamento Nacional de Planeación, Colombia 2005). The state was also failing by the mere physical absence of its forces and agents in significant sections of its territory. In 2002, over 150 municipalities out of 1,100 had no police presence, the result of the FARC's strategy to bomb police stations. Threatened by criminal groups, almost 400 *alcaldes* (city mayors) had moved their offices outside their own towns. The Pastrana administration established a 42,000 square km demilitarized zone to hold peace talks with the FARC in 1998, an apparent example of the lack of control over its territory, which fed the fears of a "failing state" (Pastrana 2005).

The above picture, based on selective data, is incomplete; however, it does offer an idea of the dismal circumstances that surrounded the country a decade ago. It is against this picture that the developments of the last decade ought to be assessed. By the end of 2010, a story of utter failure had been turned into one of limited success. The homicide rate was down to 34 per 100,000 inhabitants, the lowest in the last twenty-eight years (El Tiempo 2010a). The successes against kidnapping were far more striking: the numbers of kidnappings drastically decreased from 2,883 in 2002 to 283 in 2010. The government was also able to rescue some of the hostages, including former presidential candidate Ingrid Betancourt, who became an international symbol of the victims of this horrendous crime after being held in captivity for more than six years by the FARC. Paramilitary groups were dismantled and thousands of their members demobilized, while a significant number of their leaders were extradited to the United States, where they faced narcotrafficking charges. The power of the FARC was curtailed, both militarily and politically, with severe blows against its hierarchical structure. All municipalities regained police presence. *Alcaldes* were able to dispatch from their own towns. While the conflict is far from over, Colombians have been coming to terms with the tragic past of the most recent decades: a group of *Memoria Histórica*, led by the historian Gonzalo Sánchez, has published a series of reports with details of some of the most notable violent episodes, including the paramilitary's massacre at La Rochela and the FARC's bombing of Bojayá. Some socioeconomic indicators add further elements to the success story. The economy grew at an annual average rate of 4.8 percent between 2002 and 2009. During the same period, total investment in the country grew 50 percent, much higher than the average in Latin America (20 percent) (Gaviria 2010). The coverage of primary, secondary, and higher education significantly expanded—with higher growth rates in the public sector (Ministerio de Educación Nacional, Colombia 2010). Coverage of the health care service has also expanded. All in all, Colombians regained confidence about their own country and their own future.

Of course, this story of success must be qualified. During the last decade, Colombia advanced less in fighting poverty and inequality than the average rate of progress in Latin America. Similarly, unemployment rates in Colombia were the highest in the region, while the informal employment sector grew. Above all, none of the problems related to the internal conflict and organized crime around narcotrafficking have been fully solved. Despite the advances, problems of high homicides, forced displacement, and abuses of human rights remain severe. Indeed, some people argue the story is "largely untrue" (Wilkinson 2011), particularly among those fierce critics of the Uribe administration, haunted by accusations of the president's support of paramilitary activities. Some of the facts, however, are indisputable—like the "dramatic drop" in homicides and the diminishing power of the FARC, acknowledged by his critics (Wilkinson 2011). The range of interpretations, however, remains open to question.

How do we explain Colombian developments in the last decade? Both supporters and critics of Uribe tend to center their attention mostly on his leadership. It is undeniable that Uribe played a fundamental role, but exclusive focus on presidential leadership cannot provide a full, satisfactory explanation. There are at least two other variables that merit serious consideration: the strengthening of state institutions and the design and implementation of new policies, in turn conditioned by a changing climate of public opinion.[8] While Uribe might have influenced both, these variables were at work before Uribe came to power.

Leadership does matter in politics, and Uribe proved to be an outstanding and committed leader.[9] He served for two consecutive four-year terms with his successful reelection in 2006—the longest presidency in Colombian history. Throughout his tenure, he held extraordinarily high popularity rates. Well-known for his style of "micromanagement," Uribe's leadership in conducting the country's affairs was present in many areas, including matters of local government, which Uribe dealt with in weekly *consejos comunales* (open town hall meetings) in municipality after municipality, where he personally chaired the meetings. Above all, and where the "leadership" variable matters most, Uribe was an effective leader in facing the guerrilla threat. He seems to have provided "supreme command," the sort of civilian leadership that Elliot A. Cohen considered crucial in wartime, where "political leaders immerse themselves in the conduct of their wars no less than in their great projects of their legislation" (Cohen 2002, 206). Uribe pursued with tenacity his "democratic security" policy, closely overseeing its implementation (Ministerio de Defensa, Colombia 2003). Curtailing the power of the FARC was no mean achievement, and the important advances on this front had wide implications for the improvement of democratic governance in Colombia.

Uribe's leadership in itself, however, did not necessarily foster either governance or democracy in all respects. Reforming the constitution in 2005 to favor the reelection of the incumbent was already questionable during his first term. The second attempt, although blocked by the decision of the Constitutional Court in 2010, was a truly detrimental affair. It may be that the two consecutive terms provided the necessary framework for the success of some policies, like the strategy to combat the FARC. But there are reasons to believe that his reelection and his second attempt at reforming the constitution to stand for a third term had a negative impact on democratic governance.[10] Efforts to guarantee those reforms diverted the attention of high officials including cabinet ministers and the presidential office, from the business of governing, while it led to grave scandals. Progress in some areas may have slowed down as a result, particularly during his second term. The decline in the number of homicides is a relevant example: they drastically declined during the first years of Uribe, but progress to combat homicides seems to have stagnated between 2005 and 2010 (Granada, Restrepo, and Vargas 2009).

Uribe's leadership did not operate in an institutional or historical vacuum. Indeed, his actions took place against a background of an ongoing process of reform, which resulted in the overall strengthening of the state. Consider the reforms of the police (Llorente 1999; Vásquez 2009)[11] and the justice system, including the establishment of the Fiscalía following the adoption of the 1991 constitution, which helped to explain the successes against the Medellín and Cali cartels. The armed forces also underwent significant changes. Plan Colombia, in particular, launched under the Pastrana administration with US collaboration in 1999, was a major contribution to the modernization and professionalization of the army. As James D. Henderson notes, it "was formulated at a crucial moment in a 'silent revolution' in military reorganization that had been going on in Colombia for almost a decade." Thus, Uribe "had the immense advantage of coming into office with a much-improved military" (Henderson 2011).[12] The state reforms were not just confined to its security apparatus. They were wide-ranging, both in scope and aim, as they intended not just to strengthen the state, but also to relegitimize its democratic credentials (Posada-Carbó 1996). The division of power—a distinct, long-standing constitutional tradition in Colombia—was reinforced, which enhanced the possibilities of horizontal accountability. Perhaps no other institution better captured this reformist trajectory than the establishment of the Constitutional Court (CC) in 1991. Although the Supreme Court of Justice had exercised the role of an independent constitutional tribunal of last resort since 1886, the new Constitutional Court was given more powers to protect citizens' rights. Since its inception, the CC has proved to be an active and independent court (Cepeda 2004, 537–700; Cepeda 2005a). Its 2010 ruling against the proposal for a referendum that would have allowed Uribe to run for a third consecutive term reconfirmed Colombian democratic traditions while becoming a historical landmark of liberal constitutionalism in Latin America (Posada-Carbó 2011).[13]

The achievements of the last decade were partly the result of a strengthened state in which various agencies often acted independently from (and even sometimes against) the wishes of the executive branch. For example, it was a Supreme Court decision that gave the final shape to the *Ley de Justicia y Paz* (Law of Justice and Peace), a key legal instrument in the dismantling of the paramilitaries during the Uribe administration. In economic matters, the government did not have a free hand, as its policymaking was limited by the decisions of the Central

Bank, an autonomous institution since 1991. The local government of the capital city, Bogotá (which now concentrates around 25 percent of the country's population), substantially improved throughout the 1990s, led by a succession of elected *alcaldes* who governed independently from, and often in opposition to, the presidents. Some of the achievements in Bogotá, with national implications, are just impressive: between 1993 and 2002, the homicide rate in the Colombian capital was drastically curtailed from 80 to 27.3 per 100,000 (Sánchez, Espinosa, and Rivas 2007).

A strong state in itself is no guarantee of effectiveness. Thus, any examination of the achievements in the struggle against the guerrillas and crime in general also ought to underscore the significant changes in state policies during the last decade. Traditionally, individual specific policies in tackling the armed conflict and violence have hardly been considered as possible variables with explanatory power of their own. The long survival of guerrilla warfare and high levels of violence in Colombia have instead been explained in structural terms, the alleged result of historic, socioeconomic, or political factors, be they grievances tied to social problems in rural areas, the exclusionary nature of the political system, or the lack of legitimacy of the Colombian state. Since at least the late 1970s, state policies to tackle the armed conflict and violence were informed by such traditional structuralist views, which favored negotiation over confrontation with guerrilla groups. The relative success of Uribe's "democratic security" program suggests bringing state policies to the center of the discussion (Restrepo and Spagat 2005). Of course, Uribe's leadership should be credited for the final design and implementation of what became the flagship of his government. But the conception of Uribe's security policy, and its successes, cannot be isolated from developments that took place during previous administrations. Its adoption was partly the result of important changes in the climate of opinion. Again, Uribe's leadership, both as candidate and president, helps to explain the wide popular support that backed his security program. Nonetheless, the public acceptance of the new policy did not take place overnight, nor was it a sudden innovation. Rather, it reflected a long-term process of intellectual transformation, during which old assumptions about the roots of the conflict and the causes of crime and violence had been systematically challenged. Throughout the 1980s and 1990s, the dominant views on the subject tended to favor policies of negotiation and dialogue with the guerrillas. Even the expression "security" was often absent from the public debate (Deas 1999, 11–20). The prevailing diagnosis, Montenegro and Posada concluded in 2001, had a negative influence on the public policies toward the problems of violence: the guerrillas, not the government, were the agenda-setters at the negotiating table; state officials did not believe in their own legitimacy to enforce the law; the capacity of the army and the police to respond to the threat of illegal armed groups was weakened; and, a general atmosphere of self-defeatism paralyzed collective action (Montenegro and Posada 2001, 45–47). During the 1990s, a new wave of studies encouraged drastic reconsiderations (Deas and Daza 1995; Rubio 1999). By 2002, "a shift in the basic policy paradigms guiding the search"[14] for a solution to the armed conflict, and to the more general problems of violence, had already taken place.

In sum, during the last decade, the conditions for democratic governance improved substantially in Colombia. This was due, above all, to general improvements in security, which in turn encouraged a stronger economic performance while motivating confidence about the prospects of a country that had been perceived as a failed state just a few years earlier. Some of this success is justly attributed to the leadership of former President Uribe. Without denying the significant role of his agency, this section has emphasized other variables in trying to understand Colombian developments: the strengthening of state institutions and the adoption of new policies, conditioned by shifts in public opinion. Furthermore, the prolonged presence of Uribe in the presidency affected democratic governance. It was precisely the strength of institutions that put an end to the populist temptations of a third term for Uribe, thus allowing for the alternation of power in 2010.

Democratic Governance under Santos

Juan Manuel Santos was elected to the Colombian presidency in June 2010 on a platform of continuity. He pledged, in particular, to persist on the security efforts of his predecessor, he himself having being in charge of the defense portfolio during the second Uribe administration (Santos 2009). Santos, however, was not handpicked by Uribe; given the choice, the latter would have selected his former minister of agriculture, Andrés Felipe Arias. Neither was Uribe constitutionally allowed to campaign in favor of any candidate.[15] After an overwhelming majority in the second round, and with the largest number of votes for a presidential candidate in Colombian history, Santos reached power with a clear and strong mandate from the electorate (Posada-Carbó 2011). By looking at the first sixteen months of Santos in power, this section will show that conditions for democratic governance in Colombia continued to improve, although the challenges to overcome are still immense. While the narrative focuses on Santos, it builds on the argument outlined above: a stronger state and the continuities of the security policy are the major explanations behind Colombian advances. These have continued to take place notwithstanding changes of leadership.

Santos was elected with the backing of a wide coalition, which included the two main parties that had supported Uribe 'Partido de la U' (PU; the Social Party of National Unity) and the Partido Conservador (PC; Conservative Party), support from Cambio Radical (CR; Radical Change) whose leader distanced himself from Uribe during his second administration, and the Partido Liberal (PL; Liberal Party), one of the main parties hitherto in the opposition. Once elected, Santos widened his coalition further by incorporating the Partido Verde (PV; Green Party), a relatively new party that had gained five seats in the Senate and three in the Chamber during the congressional elections in March 2010. Thus, the only party currently in the opposition is the Polo Democrático Alternativo (PDA; Alternative Democratic Pole).

In contrast to what happened in other Latin American countries when facing crises, the Colombian party system has not collapsed (Leongómez 2006). But it has been undergoing a process of transformation, to some extent determined by a series of electoral reforms specifically aimed at breaking the dominance of the so-called "traditional two-party system," formed by the Liberal and Conservative parties (Better 2003).[16] Such process was characterized, firstly, by increasing party fragmentation followed by party regrouping. Some of the measures adopted by the new constitution of 1991—including a single national constituency to elect senators—had stimulated fractionalization to an extreme, while it encouraged the formation of small "parties" and "electoral micro-enterprises," as labeled by Eduardo Pizarro Leongómez (2006). By 2003, over forty parties and movements had representation in Congress. In addition, the Liberal and Conservative parties were often displaced from the control of local government in the major cities, shortly after the introduction of elections of city mayors in 1986. Over the last two decades, for example, the *alcaldía* of Bogotá has been in the hands of either "Independents" or of the leftist PDA. Gustavo Petro, a former member of the M19 and a PDA dissident, was elected in the October 2011 elections. In 2003, Congress passed a new electoral reform that, as Shugart, Moreno, and Fajardo have shown, had an immediate effect in the "dramatic . . . reduction of the number of different party labels contesting elections and winning seats" in the 2006 elections (2007, 257), an outcome reiterated in the subsequent elections of 2010. The final result of this process of transformation is uncertain. What has so far emerged is a multiparty system, with possibly five or six major protagonists: the two traditional parties, PL and PC, the PU (formed around the leadership of Uribe), the Cambio Radical (CR: Radical Change), a splinter party from the PL, the PDA (a coalition of leftist movements), and perhaps the PV (table 9.1).[17]

Any possible obstacle that this emerging multiparty system might have posed to governance under a presidential regime was overcome by Santos through the formation of the strong coalition that controls over 90 percent of seats in Congress. Partly as a result of such a strong coalition, Santos was able to push ahead an ambitious agenda in Congress during his first year in office. Among other measures, the package included legislation to enhance the fiscal capacity of the central state, reforms to the criminal code, an anticorruption statute, and the reestablishment of an independent Ministry of Justice, which had been merged with

Table 9.1. Main Parties Represented in the Colombian Congress (no. of seats)

Parties	2006	2010
Senate		
U Party	20	28
Conservative Party	18	22
Liberal Party	18	17
Radical Change	15	8
PDA	10	8
Green Party	0	5
Others	21[a]	14[b]
House of Representatives		
U Party	29	47
Conservative Party	29	37
Liberal Party	37	35
Radical Change	19	16
PDA	8	4
Green Party	0	3
Others	39[c]	22[d]

Sources: Instituto de Ciencia Política, "Los retos del nuevo Congreso," Bogotá, August 2010, www.icpcolombia.org/archivos /conceptos/los_retos_del_nuevo_congreso.pdf.
    [a] Includes six parties and representatives from the two special constituencies for indigenous peoples.
    [b] Includes two parties and representatives from the two special constituencies for indigenous peoples.
    [c] Includes fourteen parties, some of them regionally based.
    [d] Includes seven parties and representatives from five special constituencies.

the Ministry of Interior under Uribe. It also included the *Ley de Víctimas y Restitución de Tierras* (Law of Victims and Land Restitution), a legal framework to compensate the victims of the armed conflict and restitute land to the dispossessed peoples displaced by the conflict. This was highlighted as one of the most important pieces of legislation passed by Congress under Santos, though its approval met serious resistance and indeed opposition from landowners, Uribistas, and former President Uribe himself. In the end, the government prevailed, and the bill was signed in a symbolic ceremony attended by the Secretary General of the United Nations. A critical review of the first legislature under Santos considered that "the general balance is positive" (Barrera 2011, 21). As its author, Victor Barrera, observed, such efficiency in executive-legislative relations cannot be explained solely by the existence of a majoritarian coalition. Barrera outlined other contributing factors: Santos's personal commitment to the legislative agenda; the role of some key ministers together with the leaders in Congress; and the establishment of a Mesa de Unidad Nacional, an informal board where the government and leaders of the parties in the coalition try to reach a common position regarding the legislative agenda (Barrera 2011, 22–23).

It is his approach toward consensual politics that has mostly characterized the Santos administration. In this regard, he resembles his great-uncle, former President Eduardo Santos (1938–1942), a man of compromise whose personality during his times was identified with the centrist character of the Colombian nation. Just as the first Santos represented then a break with the confrontational style of Alfonso López Pumarejo (1934–1938), so the second Santos—moderate and conciliatory—now stands in sharp contrast to his predecessor. Throughout Uribe's eight years of tenure, for example, there was never a formal meeting between the president and the leaders of the opposition party, PDA. In contrast, shortly after his victory, Santos met with Gustavo Petro, the defeated PDA candidate. Later on as president, Santos and members of his government have held official meetings with the leaders of the PDA to discuss the need of further guarantees for the opposition (Semana 2011d). Surprisingly, where his conciliatory approach has been perhaps most seriously tested has been in his reaction to the recurrent attacks he has received from former President Uribe. Time and again in his responses to Uribe's criticism, Santos has reiterated his intentions to make compromise a principle of his government. He has applied this principle in both domestic and foreign affairs. Domestically, in addition to reestablishing a dialogue with the opposition, he has tried to mend fences with the judiciary, a sector in constant friction with Uribe. Internationally, he restored diplomatic relations with

Colombian neighbors Venezuela and Ecuador, "dangerously tense" by the time he came to office (Ramírez 2011, 56). On both fronts, a new language now dominates the presidential discourse. As *El Tiempo* observed, Santos has encouraged a "new political climate" by putting an end to "the verbal public confrontation" which had become a "paradigm" during the previous administration (El Tiempo 2010b).

Santos's political style and general progress has gone over well with the public. Confidence in the economy continues to be strong. GDP grew 7.7 percent during the third trimester of 2011. Unemployment was down to 9 percent from 11.2 percent the previous year. Optimism among industrialists prevails. Fiscal conditions overall seem promising (Andi 2011; BBVA Research 2012). Santos's foreign diplomacy gets the highest rates of approval in the polls. His popularity rates were perhaps at their peak in late September 2010 when an army raid killed the FARC's military chief, Mono Jojoy (Victor Julio Suárez). By the end of his first year, with an 85 percent popularity rate, he had managed to keep similarly high rates of approval to those of his predecessor (Semana 2011f). According to a Gallup poll conducted in June 2011, 76 percent of those surveyed approved of the way Santos was conducting his presidency. The approval was strongest in areas such as the handling of foreign relations, rural problems, and narcotrafficking; it was still relatively high in the management of the economy, the environment, and in dealing with corruption and guerrillas. However, in some critical areas, the Gallup poll showed high rates of disapproval, such as health, cost of living, and unemployment. Notable among the areas where the president received the lowest rates of approval was "security" (Gallup Colombia 2011). A different poll, conducted by Ipson-Napoleón Franco, did give Santos positive approval rates in "security," although in decline from 80 to 59 percent between November 2010 and July 2011 (Semana 2011a). Both pollsters provided a similar picture: the overwhelming majority of Colombians supported Santos's presidency.

"It does not cease to be a paradox," the influential magazine *Semana* observed, "that the main failure Colombians see in the current government is in security" (Semana 2011b). That Colombians remain highly concerned with security despite the advances of the previous decade is not surprising, given the severity and dimensions of the problem. Yet the picture continues to be positive, one of overall improvements, despite some apparently mixed results and criticisms. While homicide rates have gone down just over 10 percent since December 2010, kidnappings and mass killings have gone up slightly. Security conditions have improved in some cities, but urban insecurity has increasingly attracted the attention of the public debate (El Tiempo 2011a). The FARC continues to represent a destabilizing force, whose threatening capabilities should not be underestimated. A July 2011 report in *The Economist* summarized the reasons behind Colombian security concerns: signs that the FARC may be "bouncing back" through a different strategy; the "rise in activity by former paramilitary groups, recycled as criminal bands"; and the lowering of the morale in the army as a result of unfavorably rulings by Colombia's courts (The Economist 2011). Additionally, the fears of deteriorating security conditions have been fuelled by open criticisms from hardline Uribistas and former President Uribe himself. Under Santos, however, the armed forces have continued to hit the guerrillas hard, including the killing of FARC's military commander Mono Jojoy. More importantly, on November 4, 2011, Alfonso Cano, the FARC's chief, was killed in what can be considered the most significant army operation against the leadership of the FARC's since its foundation.[18]

The formal opposition to the Santos government was originally confined to the PDA, a party that has a minority representation in Congress and is suffering from fragmentation. Its limited representation in Congress, however, does not reflect the level of the party's presence in the public debate. Although the party lost this post in the 2011 elections, the new *alcalde* Gustavo Petro is a PDA dissident who will play a central role in either reshaping the party or reconfiguring the Left with an eye on the 2014 elections. The party also influences the unions, and its voice in the media, at home and abroad, is significant. Even if the formal opposition is limited, this does not mean that Santos has governed free of criticism. His most surprising and indeed strongest critic has been former President Uribe and some of the closest allies of his administration.

"*Uribismo* won the elections, but lost the government," Luis Carlos Restrepo, High Commissioner for Peace under Uribe, observed (El Espectador 2011b). Uribe and his most loyal followers have taken issue with Santos in at least four major areas. First, in their establishment of relations with Venezuela and Ecuador, a move that the former president despised as a "*diplomacia cosmética y de apariencia*," "*meliflua y babosa*" (a cosmetic diplomacy of mere appearances) (Semana 2011c). Second, in policies and measures related to the armed conflict. The sole inclusion of the term "armed conflict" in the *Ley de Víctimas* was a source of open dispute between the government and Uribe, who unsuccessfully rejected the use of the expression (Semana 2011e). Any suggestion of a dialogue with the FARC has been met with the strong opposition of the Uribistas. Third, Uribe has also criticized the anticorruption campaign launched by the Santos administration. While the actions of the judiciary against members of the previous administration are independent from the executive, Uribe has accused the government of making a "*show publicitario*" out of its anticorruption campaign (El Tiempo 2011). Finally, Uribe has strongly opposed Santos's initiative to reopen negotiations with the FARC, formally announced in August 2012. By May 2012, Uribe's attacks against Santos had already increased to the point that *Semana's* cover portrayed the former president as "the leader of the opposition" (Semana 2011h). For almost two years, Santos has been generally prudent in his responses to Uribe. He did say once that when he retires from office, Colombians will see him "lecturing as ex-President instead of troubling the incumbent presidents." But, Santos has also reiterated that he admires and respects his predecessor, that he is continuing some of the previous key policies, and that "my goal is not to fight with Uribe . . . because it is not convenient either to President Uribe, or the government, or the country" (El Espectador 2011a; Semana 2011g). But by mid-2012 the relationship between the two leaders had soured. Uribe will continue to be an important factor in Colombian politics; nonetheless, it is Santos who has had the upper hand since August 2010.

Democratic governance has thus continued to improve under Santos. His renewed leadership gave the country a new sense of direction based on the successes of his predecessor, but also marked a fresh departure toward consensual politics. That conditions have continued to improve under a new government may serve to underline the argument that political leadership matters, but other variables are perhaps more important in explaining Colombian achievements.

Conclusion: Challenges and Prospects

Conditions for democratic governance in Colombia have improved during the last decade. Above all, such improvements were due to substantial progress in the security front, particularly in the fight against the FARC and in the dismantling of the paramilitaries. A better security environment encouraged self-confidence among Colombians about the future of the country. The economy has benefitted from higher levels of investment, both domestic and international. While political leadership accounts for an important part of Colombian achievements, this chapter has stressed the significance of other factors: the strengthening of state institutions and effective policies conditioned, in turn, by shifts in the climate of opinion.

Despite the advances, the challenges that the country faces are of extraordinary dimensions. Colombia's poverty and inequality levels are among the worst in the region (The Economist 2011b, 101). Homicide and kidnapping rates, together with the number of *desplazados* (displaced) constitute a truly humanitarian catastrophe. Guerrillas and other criminal organizations continue to pose serious security threats. Indeed, unless further substantial progress is made in tackling security problems, the prospect of an unstable and violent future still looms large on the horizon.

Two immediate challenges need special attention. The first relates to the increasing polarization within the political elites (Bermeo 2003). In an interview published in *El Espectador* on September 10, 2011, Fabio Echeverri Correa, former president of the Asociación Nacional de Industriales (ANDI; National Association of Industrialists), expressed his concerns about the rift between Santos and Uribe. After blaming those who were instigating the distance between the two leaders, Echeverri noted that what worried him most was the possible "catastrophic effects" of such rift, which could lead to similar conflicts to those suffered by Colombians in the 1940s and 1950s. The prospect of yet another cycle of violence in a country haunted by its violent history should not be taken lightly. It was urgent, Echeverri suggested, that the two leaders meet to settle their differences (El Espectador 2011c). The differences between Santos and Uribe may be manageable. They do not seem to constitute yet the sort of polarization that threatens regime stability and social order. The political antagonism that has taken sectarian turns is that between *Uribistas*—with the former president at the front—and their radical opponents, mostly the Polo Democrático, but also in the Liberal Party. Such antagonism is not simply caused by ideological polarization; it is mainly driven by mutual criminal accusations, which severely undermine trust in the democratic process and in the judiciary. The other urgent meeting that has been long delayed is that between Uribe and his older political antagonists.

Such polarization impinges on the second challenge: the perseverance of the armed conflict. In his inaugural speech, President Santos stated that the door to peace negotiations was open, although under certain conditions: above all that the guerrillas renounce violence and free the kidnapped. "We will not be deceived again," he said on Christmas Eve in 2011, reiterating that his government is ready to engage in dialogue, but only if the FARC demonstrates their willingness to embark upon a serious peace process (Santos 2011b). Indeed, following the strike against Cano, the FARC's leader, there was a growing perception among opinion makers that the Colombian armed conflict was reaching a turning point. The improved combat capacity of the army, the "efficacy of the state" Alejandro Vargas wrote in *El Colombiano*, may persuade the FARC to come to terms with a negotiated settlement (El Colombiano 2011).[19]

Any prospect of bringing the armed conflict to an end in the near future, however, may be doomed without "peace" among the political elites. Further polarization within the political system will continue to fuel hopes of survival among the guerrillas: that all they need is to persevere and wait for future deteriorations of security conditions. Polarization among the political elites thus sends the wrong signals to the guerrillas, while potentially becoming the source of further violence. There is no doubt that the search for peace continues to be the first priority for Colombia. It is naïve to think that a country, any country, can develop an agenda of democratic governance amid an armed conflict with no end in sight.

NOTES

1. For an academic approach, see Mason 2001. For an early article that raised skepticism about such diagnoses, see McLean 2002.

2. The change in perceptions had apparently taken place earlier in the United States; see Shifter 2005.

3. Although Weir is more interested in explaining the limits and boundaries of policy innovation, her approach is useful in appreciating how changes in ideas influence the processes of policymaking.

4. Scholars working on Colombia have reflected very little on this. For an interesting and relevant analysis, see Restrepo 2005. An easy response to the dilemmas posed by Restrepo has been to deny the existence of democracy in Colombia.

5. For an account of the recent history of the FARC, see Pécaut 2008. On how diminished and almost insignificant the threat of the ELN was in the 1970s, see Broderick 2000.

6. The constituent assembly was cochaired by representatives of the Liberal and Conservative parties together with a former member of the M19, representing their newly formed political movement, AD-M19.

7. I have questioned elsewhere the simplistic notion of the Colombian "failed state." See my articles for the Fundación Ideas para la Paz in www.ideaspaz.org, in "Publicaciones/Serie Comentarios." See also my short essays Posada 2003 and Posada 2004. For a collection of essays that examine the sources of the country's strength at a time when predictions of failure flourished, see Cepeda Ulloa 2004.

8. A stronger state, as Hillel Soifer and Matthias von Hau note, is identified with the "institutional capability to exercise control and implement policy choices within the territory it claims to govern." See Soifer and von Hau 2008.

9. For an account of key aspects of Uribe's first term by a close adviser, who praises his leadership qualities, see Bermúdez 2012. Regarding leadership, Fukuyama refers to the literature that distinguishes "institutional" from "interpersonal" leaders, the former linked to the "promotion and protection of values," while the latter to the "efficiency of the enterprise." See Fukuyama 2004.

10. For an alternative view on this, see Cepeda Ulloa 2008.

11. In the immediate past, one of the most intense periods of reform of this institution took place between 1993 and 1997, including the expansion of the police force and

the increasing enrollment of women. However, the important measure of centralizing the police dates back to the origins of the Frente Nacional (1958–1974). The Mexican police, by contrast, remain a highly decentralized organization, "divided up into over 2,000 separate state and local forces"; see Shannon O'Neil's chapter in this volume.

12. Predating the publication of Plan Colombia, the army's successful response to the FARC's attack of Mitú in November 1998 is considered as an important turning point in reversing the series of setbacks suffered by state forces; idem, p. 6. In his memoirs as Uribe's Minister of Defense, Juan Manuel Santos acknowledged Pastrana's contribution to the transformation of the military (see Santos 2009). It should be noted that, while very significant, US aid has been relatively marginal to the overall effort at strengthening the state in Colombia, particularly if approaching the subject from the long-term historical perspective suggested here. Regarding Plan Colombia alone, as former President Gaviria has observed, "nine out of every ten dollars have come from the Colombian state"; see Gaviria 2011, xi. This is not the case of Afghanistan, examined by Fukuyama, where "state building [. . .] had to begin from the ground up, with resources and guidance provided entirely from the outside." Furthermore, it could be argued that the US policies towards Colombia during the Samper administration weakened the state's capacity to combat the guerrillas. Consider here the general comment by Fukuyama on how the international community has often been "complicit in the *destruction* of institutional capacity in many developing countries"; Fukuyama 2004, 39, 101.

13. For a longer historical perspective of Colombian liberal-democratic traditions, see also Posada-Carbó 2006.

14. I have borrowed this expression from Hall 1992.

15. Note here the contrast with the United States or with Brazil, where the then President Lula accompanied the candidate Dilma Rousseff at electoral rallies.

16. A revision of the "traditional two-party system" in Colombia is long overdue. See, for example, the composition of the House of Representatives during the National Front (1958–1970), as described in Taylor 2009, 50–51. Giovanni Sartori was probably right when he questioned the bipartisan label for Colombia: "If that is a two-partism, then I do not know what two-partism is"; see Sartori 1994, 180–81. I have discussed this in Posada-Carbó 2006a and 2006b.

17. There are speculations about the eventual merge of the PL and CR—the latter consisting mainly of dissident Liberals. The PDA is suffering from serious divisions, after Gustavo Petro, its former presidential candidate, formed a dissident group from the party to fight successfully for the *alcaldía* of Bogotá. Similarly, the PV has also suffered divisions.

18. Manuel Marulanda, better known as "Tirofijo," who had been the leader of the FARC since its creation over forty-two years ago, died of natural causes in 2008. By contrast, Cano, his successor, was killed in an army operation after just three years in command. President Santos claimed that the operation against Cano had been the most important historical strike of the state against the FARC (Santos 2011a).

19. At the time of revising this chapter, representatives of the government and the FARC were preparing their first formal encounter in Havana, after a meeting in Oslo, where the new round of peace talks were officially launched.

REFERENCES

Asociación Nacional de Industriales (ANDI; National Association of Industries), Centro de Estudios Económicos (Centre for Economic Studies). 2011. "Encuesta de opinión industrial conjunta" (July 1–31): 1–11.

Barrera, Víctor. 2011. "Legislar para la prosperidad." *Ciendías* 73 (August–November): 21. www.cinep.org.co.

BBVA Research. 2012. "El futuro es ahora." *Análisis Económico* (September). www .bbvaresearch.com/KETD/fbin/mult/110914_NotaForoBBVA_tcm346-268740.pdf?ts =10112012.

Bermeo, Nancy. 2003. *Ordinary People in Extraordinary Times: The Citizenry and the Breakdown of Democracy*. Princeton: Princeton University Press.

Bermúdez, Jaime. 2010. *La audacia del poder*. Bogotá: Planeta.

Better, Arturo Sarabia. 2003. *Reformas políticas en Colombia: Del plebiscito de 1957 al referendo del 2003*. Bogotá: Norma.

Bevir, Mark. 2010. *Democratic Governance* (Princeton: Princeton University Press), 1–3, 252–55.

Broderick, Walter J. 2000. *El guerrillero invisible*. Bogotá: Intermedio.

Cepeda, Manuel. 2004. "La defensa judicial de la constitución: una tradición centenaria e ininterrumpida." In *Fortalezas de Colombia*, edited by Cepeda Ulloa, 537–700. Bogotá: Ariel.

———. 2005a. Chapter in *Colombia: The Politics of Reforming the State*, edited by Eduardo Posada-Carbó. Institute of Latin American Studies Series.

———. 2005b. "The Judicialization of Politics in Colombia: The Old and the New." In *The Judicialization of Politics in Latin America*, edited by Rachel Sieder, Line Schjolden, and Alan Angell, 67–104. New York: Palgrave Macmillan.

Cepeda Ulloa, Fernando. 2003. "Colombia: The Governability Crisis." In *Constructing Democratic Governance in Latin America*, edited by Jorge I. Domínguez and Michael Shifter, 193–219. 2nd ed. Baltimore: Johns Hopkins University Press.

———. 2008. "Colombia: Democratic Security and Political Reform." In *Constructing Democratic Governance in Latin America*, edited by Jorge I. Domínguez and Michael Shifter, 209–41. 3rd ed. Baltimore: Johns Hopkins University Press.

Cohen, Elliot, A. 2002. *Supreme Command: Soldiers, Statesmen, and Leadership in Wartime*. New York: Free Press.

Colombia, Ministerio de Defensa. 2010. "Comportamiento homicidio común." March 3. www.mindefensa.gov.co.

El Colombiano. 2011. "Impactos de la muerte de 'Cano,'" *El Colombiano*. November 9.

Deas, Malcom. 1999. "Introduction." In *Reconocer la guerra para construir la paz*, edited by Malcolm Deas and María Victoria Llorente, 11–20. Bogotá: Norma.

Deas, Malcolm, and Fernando Gaitán Daza. 1995. *Dos ensayos especulativos sobre la violencia en Colombia*. Bogotá: Tercer Mundo.

Departamento Nacional de Planeación, Colombia. 2005. *Visión Colombia*.

———. 2009. *Visión Colombia II centenario: Propuesta para discusión*. Bogotá: Planeta.

The Economist. 2011a. "The FARC Is Not Finished Yet." *The Economist*, July 7.

———. 2011b. "Income Inequality." *The Economist*. April 23–29, p. 101.

El Espectador. 2011a. *www.elespectador.com*. April 15.

————. 2011b. "Crece distancia entre Uribe y Santos." *www.elespectador.com*. April 15.

————. 2011c. "Los oportunistas incitan la pelea entre Santos y Uribe." *www.elespectador*
.com. September 10.

Foreign Policy and the Fund for Peace. 2011. "The Failed States Index." *Foreign Policy*.
September 10. www.foreignpolicy.com/failedstates.

Fukuyama, Francis. 2004. *State Building, Governance, and World Order in the 21st Cen-*
tury. Ithaca: Cornell University Press.

The Fund for Peace and the Carnegie Endowment for International Peace. 2005. "The
Failed States Index Rankings." *Foreign Policy* (July/August). www.foreignpolicy.com
/articles/2005/07/01/the_failed_states_index_2005

Gallup Colombia. 2011. "Gallup Poll: Bimestral." June 2011. www.elpais.com.co/elpais
/archivos/encuesta-gallup-junio-2011.pdf.

Gaviria, Alejandro. 2010. "Corte de cuentas." *El Espectador*. August 1.

Gaviria, César. 2011. "Prólogo." In *Políticas antidrogas en Colombia: Éxitos, fracasos y*
extravíos, edited by Alejandro Gaviria and Daniel Mejía. Bogotá: Universidad de los
Andes.

Granada, Soledad, Jorge A. Restrepo, and Andrés R. Vargas. 2009. "El agotamiento de la
política de seguridad: Evolución y transformaciones recientes en el conflicto armado
Colombiano." In *Guerra y violencias en Colombia: Herramientas e interpretaciones*, edited by Jorge A. Restrepo and David Aponte, 27–124. Bogotá: Universidad Javeriana.

Hall, Peter, A. 1992. "The Movement from Keynesianism to Monetarism: Institutional
Analysis and British Economic Policy in the 1970s." In *Structuring Politics*, edited by
Steven Steinmo, Kathleen Thelen, and Frank Longstreth, 90–113. Cambridge: Cam-
bridge University Press.

Hannan, Daniel. 2008. "Colombia Stands as a Beacon of Hope for South America."
Daily Telegraph, March 5.

Henderson, James D. 2011. "Plan Colombia's Place in the Democratic Security Program
of Alvaro Uribe Vélez." *The Latin Americanist* (March): 3–15. http://onlinelibrary.wi
ley.com/doi/10.1111/j.1557-203X.2011.01103.x/pdf.

Instituto de Ciencia Política. 2010. "Los retos del nuevo Congreso." Bogotá. www.icp
colombia.org/archivos/conceptos/los_retos_del_nuevo_congreso.pdf.

Leongómez, Eduardo Pizarro. 2006. "Giants with Feet of Clay: Political Parties in Colombia." In *The Crisis of Political Representation in the Andes*, edited by Scott Mainwaring, Ana María Bejarano, and Eduardo Pizarro Leongómez, 78–99. Stanford:
Stanford University Press.

Llorente, María Victoria. 1999. "Perfil de la policía colombiana." In *Reconocer la guerra*
para construir la paz, edited by Malcolm Deas and María Victoria Llorente, 391–473.
Bogotá: Norma.

Mainwaring, Scott, and Timothy Scully, "Introduction." In *Democratic Governance in*
Latin America, edited by Scott Mainwaring and Timothy Scully, 1–8. Stanford:
Stanford University Press.

Mainwaring, Scott, Timothy Scully, and Jorge Vargas. 2010. "Measuring Success in
Democratic Governance." *Democratic Governance in Latin America*, edited by Scott
Mainwaring and Timothy Scully, 11–51. Stanford: Stanford University Press.

Mason, Ann C. 2001. "Colombia State Failure: The Global Context of Eroding Domestic Authority." Unpublished paper presented at the conference on Failed States, Florence, Italy, April.

McLean, Phillip. 2002. "Colombia; Failed, Failing, or Just Weak?" *Washington Quarterly* (Summer): 123–34.

Ministerio de Defensa, Colombia. 2003. *Política de Defensa y Seguridad Democrática.* Bogotá: Ministerio de Defensa.

Ministerio de Educación Nacional, Colombia. 2010. *Revolución educativa: Acciones y lecciones, 2002–2010.* Bogotá: Ministerio de Educación Nacional.

Montenegro, Armando, and Carlos Esteban Posada. 2001. *La violencia en Colombia.* Bogotá: Libros de Cambio.

Moor, M., and L. Zumpolle. 2002. *La industria del secuestro en Colombia: ¿Un negocio que nos concierne?* La Haya: Pax Christi Holanda.

Pastrana, Andrés, with Camilo Gómez. 2005. *La palabra bajo fuego.* Bogotá: Planeta.

Pécaut, Daniel. 2008. *Las FARC: ¿Una guerrilla sin fin o sin fines?* Bogotá: Norma.

Pizarro Leongómez, Eduardo. 2004. *Una democracia asediada. Balance y perspectivas del conflicto armado en Colombia.* Bogotá: Norma.

Posada-Carbó, Eduardo. 1996. *Colombia. The Politics of Reforming the State.* London: Macmillan/ILAS.

———. 2003. "Colombian Institutions: On the Paradox of Weakness." *ReVista: Harvard Review of Latin America* (Spring): 14–17.

———. 2004. "Colombia's Resilient Democracy." *Current History* (February): 68–73.

———. 2006a. *La nación soñada: Violencia, liberalismo y democracia en Colombia.* Bogotá: Norma.

———. 2006b "Colombia Hews to the Path of Change," *Journal of Democracy* (October).

———. 2011. "Colombian After Uribe." *Journal of Democracy* 22 (1): 137–51.

Ramírez, Socorro. 2011. "Los milagros de la diplomacia." *Ciendías* 73 (August–November): 56. www.cinep.org.co.

Restrepo, Jorge A., and Michael Spagat. 2005. "Colombia's Tipping Point?" *Survival* 47 (2): 131–52.

Restrepo, Luis Alberto. 2005. "Los arduos dilemas de la democracia en Colombia." In *Nuestra guerra sin nombre: Transformaciones del conflicto en Colombia,* edited by Francisco Gutiérrez Sanín et al., 315–46. Bogotá: Norma.

Rubio, Mauricio. 1999. *Crimen e impunidad en Colombia.* Bogotá: Tercer Mundo.

Sánchez, Fabio, Silvia Espinosa, and Angela Rivas. 2007. "¿Garrote o zanahoria? Factores asociados a la disminución de la violencia homicida y el crimen en Bogotá, 1993–2002." In *Las cuentas de la violencia,* edited by Fabio Sánchez, 301–56 Bogotá: Norma.

Santos, Juan Manuel. 2009. *Jaque al terror: Los anos horriblesd de las FARC.* Bogotá: Planeta.

———. 2011a. "Alocución del presidente Juan Manuel Santos tras la caída de 'Alfonso Cano,' Popayán." November 5. www.presidencia.gov.co.

———. 2011b. "Seguir perseverando, le pidió el Presidente Santos a la Fuerza Pública, desde la base de Tolemaida." December 23. wsp.presidencia.gov.co/Prensa/2011/Diciembre/Paginas/20111223_04.aspx.

Sartori, Giovanni. 1994. *Comparative Constitutional Engineering: An Inquiry into Structures, Incentives and Outcomes.* London: Macmillan.

Semana. 2011a. "Un año de luna de miel." Semana.com. August 1.

———. 2011b. "Un año sorpresa." Semana.com. August 1.

———. 2011c. "La descarnada mirada de Uribe al gobierno de Santos." Semana.com. August 3.

———. 2011d. "Gobierno y oposición reactivaron diálogo institucional." Semana.com. March 25.

———. 2011e. "Las tres tesis de Uribe derrotadas en la Ley de Víctimas." Semana.com. May 12.

———. 2011f. "Santos cumple primer año en el poder con el 85% de imagen positiva." Semana.com. August 5.

———. 2011g. Semana.com. August 4.

———. 2011h. "Alvaro Uribe, el jefe de la oposición. Semana.com. May 27.

Shifter, Michael. 2005. "Colombia ya no es un país colapsado: Así piensan en E.U." *El Colombiano* (Medellín), May 13.

Shugart, Matthew, Erika Moreno, and Luis E. Fajardo. 2007. "Deepening Democracy by Renovating Political Practices: The Struggle for Political Reform." In *Peace, Democracy, and Human Rights in Colombia*, edited by Christopher Welna and Gustavo Gallón, 202–66. Notre Dame: Notre Dame University Press.

Soifer, Hillel, and Matthias von Hau. 2008. "Unpacking the Strength of the State: The Utility of State Infrastructural Power." *Studies in International Comparative Development* 43 (3–4): 219–30.

Sweig, Julia E. 2002. "What Kind of War for Colombia?" *Foreign Affairs* (September /October): 124–25.

Tagle, Eduardo Haro. 2000. "Colombia." *El País* (Madrid). September 1.

Taylor, Steven L. 2009. *Voting Amid Violence. Electoral Democracy in Colombia.* Boston: Northeastern University Press.

El Tiempo. 2010a. "Disminución histórica de la tasa de homicidios en Colombia." eltiempo.com. January 22. www.eltiempo.com/justicia/ARTICULO-WEB-NEW_NOTA_INTERIOR-8794653.html.

———. 2010b. "Juan Manuel Santos: Un presidente que ha sorprendido." eltiempo.com. November 13.

———. 2011a. "Cuadrando la seguridad urbana." eltiempo.com. September 13.

———. 2011b. "Tensión con Álvaro Uribe durante el primer año de gobierno de Santos." eltiempo.com. August 6.

Vásquez, Juan Ruiz. 2009. "Colombian Police Policy: Police and Urban Policy, 1991–2006." PhD diss., University of Oxford.

Weir, Margaret. 1992. "Ideas and the Politics of Bounded Innovation." In *Structuring Politics: Historical Institutionalism in Comparative Perspective*, edited by Steven Steinmo, Kathleen Thelen, and Frank Longstreth, 188–261. Cambridge: Cambridge University Press.

Wilkinson, Daniel. 2011. "Death and Drugs in Colombia." *The New York Review of Books* 23 (June).

CHAPTER TEN

Mexico

Democratic Advances and Limitations

Shannon O'Neil

M exicans should take some considerable pride in their democracy. In just two short decades, Mexico has moved from what Peruvian novelist and Nobel laureate Mario Vargas Llosa described as a "perfect dictatorship" to a vibrant, if at times messy, democratic system. Since the official transition in 2000, when the opposition Partido Acción Nacional (PAN; National Action Party) candidate won the presidency, the nation has held thousands of elections at the cumulative federal, state, and local levels, most of which are considered free and fair. Mexico boasts three strong political parties (as well as a handful of smaller ones), autonomous electoral and transparency-oriented government institutions, a competitive and independent press, and an emerging civil society.

Yet while its electoral achievements are substantial, all is not well in Mexico's democracy. Citizen support for the democratic system remains relatively weak, ahead of only Peru, Guatemala, and El Salvador in Latin America.[1] Surveys show that political participation and civic involvement has changed little in the last decade (Paras García, Lopez Olmedo, and Vargas Lopez 2010). Other studies suggest that participation rates by Mexico's poor—a large minority of the overall population—have actually declined with democratization (Holzner 2010). These findings are troubling for those who view widespread and inclusive involvement as vital to democracy's consolidation.

Mexico struggles with deep-rooted vested interests, authoritarian legacies, and a still limited set of tools to ensure open, accountable, and responsive government. But perhaps the weakest link in Mexican democracy today is the third branch of government, the judiciary. Here, the most difficult fights are still ahead, as the struggle to reform the court system, and law enforcement generally, is only beginning. Establishing the rule of law will prove the true test of Mexico's future democratic governance.

This chapter begins by evaluating the democratic gains of the last decade. It then turns to the continuing limitations to democratic consolidation, focusing particularly on the functioning of Mexico's law enforcement and court systems. The chapter concludes with a discussion of the challenges ahead for consolidating Mexico's still nascent democracy.

Mexico's Democratic Advances

While election watchers among the chattering classes today (often rightly) decry the undue influence of backroom politics, money, and the media in political campaigns, these concerns pale in comparison to those of the not too distant past, when the ballot box itself was in question. For decades the Partido Revolucionario Institucional (PRI; Revolutionary Institutional Party) orchestrated elections to legitimize its control. Many voted sincerely—reflecting the trickled-down benefits of years of strong economic growth and the mobilizing force of the party's corporatist organization of social and economic interests. But the PRI's heavier hand was always present. Party stalwarts ensured that the PRI won nearly every single election for decades. They started with proverbial carrots: a mix of public goods (roads, bridges, or new municipal facilities) and private handouts (ranging from a sandwich to paint for houses willing to emblazon the PRI logo on their newly whitewashed walls to washing machines or even to promises of government jobs and contracts). These specialists perfected more fraudulent and coercive methods—stuffing ballot boxes, rigging voter rolls, violating the secrecy of the voting booth, and threatening opposition candidates and voters alike.

These once common practices are now largely relics of the past, hard won through years of striking personal courage and, less prosaically, institution building. One of the most important in promoting and later safeguarding Mexico's young democracy is the Instituto Federal Electoral (IFE; Federal Electoral Institute). Created in 1990 primarily as window dressing for electoral reforms, President Salinas pursued to shore up the PRI's domestic and international electoral legitimacy, and further legislative changes in 1993 and 1994 expanded its jurisdiction and freedom. A 1996 electoral reform finally freed the IFE from the powerful Interior Ministry, as well as from any one political party, by empowering citizen councillors and reducing political party representatives to nonvoting observers, and gave it sweeping powers to manage the electoral process, monitor campaign finances, and police political parties (Estévez, Magar, and Rosas 2008, 260). The reform also expanded the jurisdiction of the Tribunal Electoral del Poder Judicial de la Federación (TEPJF; Federal Electoral Tribunal) to handle challenges relating to elections throughout the land, and removed it from the executive branch's control (placing it instead under the jurisdiction of the Supreme Court).

Initially weak, dependent, and underfunded, the two institutions would slowly evolve into vital, autonomous, and quite powerful defenders of Mexico's electoral democracy. The IFE used its voice to ensure fairer and freer elections, actions that in no small measure helped ensure the 1997 midterm opposition gains and 2000 opposition presidential win. The TEPJF, too, showed its mettle in the newly democratic period, annulling a controversial 2000 Tabasco governor's race, and disbanding the PRI-stacked local election monitoring council in the Yucatán in 2001. These highly regarded institutions emerged a bit battered from the controversial 2006 election (during which losing presidential candidate Andrés Manuel López Obrador refused to accept a razor thin loss), and the ensuing 2007 electoral reform, which increased partisanship within IFE's ranks by allowing the reelection of its president and by establishing an internal review board more responsive to Congress (Serra 2009). Many observers worry that in the long run these changes will undermine IFE's autonomy and objectiveness. Nevertheless, now twenty-plus years on, it is still one of the strongest and most respected institutions in the nation.

In 2002, Mexico created another vital institutional tool for improving democratic governance: the Instituto Federal de Acceso a la Información (IFAI; Federal Institute for Access to Public Information). Charged with facilitating and implementing the new Federal Transparency Law, the agency has taken many important and innovative steps to help open up the black box of Mexico's governance. It proactively requires bureaucracies and agencies to post basic information such as budgets, staffs, salaries, and contracts, and interprets the public's right to other information held by the government quite broadly (Michener 2010). Since its creation, nearly 700,000 requests have been made and granted (Instituto Federal de Acceso a la Información y Protección de Datos 2011).

Political parties, secretive bureaucracies, and individual actors have pushed back, at times successfully, on these watchdog institutions. Nevertheless, they remain powerful tools for illuminating the mechanics of elections and governance more broadly.

As important as these institutions are for democracy, Mexico's political parties are also important. Though social movements, interest groups, and even the media play important roles in communicating popular demands to the state, only political parties can provide the direct and consistent access to governance structures necessary to maintain a healthy democracy. As scholars have noted, parties are particularly vital for representation in Latin America, where alternative forms of interest intermediation are often less influential and poorly organized (Mainwaring and Scully 1995). Public opinion supports this notion, as the vast majority of Mexicans feel political parties are vital for democracy.[2]

Unlike many of its Latin American neighbors, Mexico can boast a quite stable and disciplined three-party dominant system. While for years the electoral cleavage centered on a PRI/anti-PRI dichotomy, within the more competitive electoral arena, voter identification with one of the three main parties has remained strong (though the number of independent voters has grown), and increasingly identified along a left-right ideological spectrum, suggesting more programmatic (versus clientelistic) ties (McCann 2009).

This is not to say that Mexico's political parties have always or even consistently acted in the public good. Indeed, there are important and downright shameful cases of each party flouting the basic rules of the game—for instance working to disqualify an attractive presidential candidate, to politicize the IFE, or to undermine electoral rules and regulations. But even while there has not been wholehearted acceptance of the democratic rules of the game by every politician, on a relative scale Mexico's democratic rules are robust and characteristically enforced; most of these attempts to subvert democracy failed.

There are also indications that Mexico's established parties and politicians have at least begun to learn the art of compromise. Behind the partisan grandstanding and vitriol, alliances between parties are now commonplace, with politicians working together to pass legislation. Though many Mexicans bemoan legislative gridlock, statistics question that assumption. Since democratization, more bills have passed through the divided Congress than under Presidents Zedillo and Salinas combined.[3] These include the annual budget, approved every year since the opposition assumed the presidency (far better than the US Congress's track record in this regard). The Congress worked closely with President Vicente Fox's government to push forward Mexican foreign policy interests, ratifying 176 of the 195 treaties submitted for review from 2000 to 2005. Only once did the Congress rule against the president's recommendation during this period (Domínguez and Fernández de Castro 2001, 172). Under President Calderón, the Congress approved laws privatizing the public pension system, transforming the court system, expanding access to health insurance, amending the tax system, and changing the rules regarding the structure of the state-owned oil company and the avenues for private investment, among others.

Still, many things have been left undone. The structural and labor reforms that experts and policymakers alike agree are urgently needed still languish in Congress. A more fundamental tax reform has also fallen by the wayside, leaving Mexico still at the bottom of the barrel among Organisation for Economic Co-operation and Development (OECD) countries and even its Latin American neighbors in terms of tax revenue as a percent of GDP. In fact, Mexico's government seems unable to pass or enforce any laws or regulations that would threaten the monopolies and oligopolies that dominate so many sectors of the country's economy. Political reforms too seem a nonstarter, despite a broad national and international academic and technical policy consensus on the benefits of change, leaving the political concentration of power intact.

Fundamental changes in executive-legislative relations have, of course, occurred. The legislative agenda is no longer driven by the executive branch; political parties in the Congress have now assumed that mantle. When introducing initiatives the president rarely gets all he wants: the last three *sexenios* signature programs—including fiscal, energy, electoral, and judicial reforms—have often failed or been watered down dramatically. But for all the frustrations, slow moving and incremental legislative reform is a hallmark of a working democracy (as political processes in the United States or the United Kingdom also show).

At the state and local level, Mexico's political parties at times have joined together in an effort to gain office. An illustrative case is the 2010 gubernatorial elections in the state of Oaxaca. One of Mexico's poorest states, it had remained a bastion of the worst of the PRI's cronyism and heavy hand. In 2004, the election of Governor Ulises Ruiz Ortiz was mired in controversy that included allegations of vote rigging and even murder. During his time in office, he used the state apparatus to harass independent news outlets, indigenous groups, and civil society organizations, and unleashed its lethal force on renegade teacher union protests in the state's capital. Yet six years later, the head of the Partido de la Revolución Democrática (PRD; Party of the Democratic Revolution)-PAN alliance, Gabino Cué Monteagudo, toppled the PRI's candidate, as did his legislative slate. In a massive turnout, ordinary voters ended some eighty years of PRI domination, opening up at least the possibility of a different future for the poverty-stricken state. Strategic cooperation and compromise between the parties was essential to this victory.

While perhaps the most vivid example, Oaxaca was not an isolated case. A similar dynamic occurred that year in the state of Puebla, which too fell for the first time from PRI control. Whether through electoral coalitions or on their own, in each election cycle more and more states and municipalities have changed political hands. In 1988, the PRI held a virtual representation monopoly, with just thirty-nine of Mexico's nearly 2,500 municipalities (and no states) in opposition hands. By 2000, nearly half of Mexico's population had been or was governed by non-PRI elected officials; in 2010 this rose to nearly 90 percent (Lujambio 2000). This alternation in power has been important for the evolution of Mexico's party system, giving all parties actual governing experience, helping dismantle the PRI's old clientelist machines and ways of doing things, and enabling a greater possibility for programmatic policies and representation.

The rise and expansion of federally mandated universal assistance programs are also signs of this shift. *Oportunidades* (which expanded upon a previous initiative of the Zedillo administration) provides economic assistance to Mexico's poorest, now reaching a quarter of the population. It rewards families for keeping their kids healthy and in school, in an effort to break the cycle of poverty. *Seguro Popular*, started in 2002 under Fox, provides affordable health care to the half of Mexico's population effectively shut out of the social security based health system. Nearly ten years later, it claims near universal coverage, accessible to over 50 million Mexicans. These popular programs' budgets outpaced nearly every other sector of government expenditure, reflecting in part their electoral attractiveness for "retrospective voters," who base their votes on past government performance rather than direct personal benefits (e.g., vote buying).[4] But unlike economic assistance programs of the past (which were primarily clientelistic in nature), most analysts laud these programs for their rigorous selection process, effective targeting, and generally clean delivery of funds and services (Levy 2006; Frenk et al. 2006).

Democratic competition has visibly raised the costs of not responding to a broader set of voters than in the past. Political parties have learned—sometimes the hard way—the importance of nominating well-known and liked candidates rather than old school party hacks. The most vivid lesson occurred in the 2006 presidential race, when the PRI's Roberto Madrazo, a powerful behind-the-scenes party leader, trailed far behind the PAN and PRD candidates, finishing an embarrassing third in the contest. This contrasts to the nomination process and outcomes of more recent state level elections. In the lead up to the 2009 gubernatorial election in Nuevo Leon, PRI leaders resolved their differences based on public name recognition and citizen support. The clear winner of internal polls, Rodrigo Medina de la Cruz went on to win the seat.[5] In 2011, the outgoing governor of the State of Mexico, Enrique Peña Nieto, chose the popular Eruviel Ávila as the PRI's candidate, who went on to decidedly win the post by a margin of 40 percent (Grillo and Mascareñas 2011). Though many knew that Peña Nieto preferred his cousin and close aide Alfredo del Mazo Maza, he astutely chose voter over personal preferences (shattering the possibility of a PAN-PRD alliance in the process, which further strengthened the PRI's electoral prospects) (Dávila and Salinas 2007; García Rosario 2011; Barrera 2011). In fact, much of the PRI's heralded electoral "comeback" has to do with the party's internalization of the democratic rules of the game. PRI leaders recognized that, though not perfectly or directly, voters' preferences increasingly matter, and adjusted their strategies accordingly.

These positive changes within the government, its bureaucracies, and its political parties have been matched by changes outside the state's official reach. Mexico's now free and competitive press routinely exposes corruption, investigates scandals, and questions the official line. While some complain about the coverage's bloody tinge, the so-called fourth estate has utterly transformed in the last three decades from its days as a virtual extension of the PRI's communication team (Lawson 2002; Lawson and Hughes 2005).

Citizens too have had moments of power and influence, due to an expanding, if still somewhat weak, civil society. For years mobilization occurred primarily within the corporatist PRI structure, which created or co-opted social organizations such as labor unions, peasant groups, business associations, and other popular movements. Independent organizations began their uphill trek in opposition to this regime, the first prominent few focusing primarily on election monitoring and human rights. Dedicated but disparate activists came together in the early 1990s through Alianza Cívica, an umbrella association of some 300 organizations to monitor the polls, do voter quick counts, and denounce electoral shenanigans. Gaining domestic and international recognition and support, Alianza Cívica helped push open the political system, making outright fraud increasingly difficult to hide.

After democratization, many militants turned their energy and efforts to improving the new system. A group of journalists, editors, and civil society leaders successfully forced the hand of the newly minted Fox government to pass the 2002 Freedom of Information Act. The 2008 judicial reform, too, resulted from ongoing efforts by civil society groups to right the wrongs of a broken justice system. These activists first pressured state governments, successfully reforming local level courts in Nuevo Leon, Chihuahua, and Oaxaca. In 2007, with judicial reform back on the table as part of Calderón's larger security agenda, they fought for and ensured that the final reforms incorporated a much more comprehensive overhaul of the justice system and greater protections for individual rights. Unlike in the past, those outside government are increasingly able and willing to supervise, denounce, and at times punish poor governance.

The Limits on Democratic Governance

These notable instances of progress do not excuse the often glacial speed of change, nor hide Mexico's many remaining democratic weaknesses. While the political arena is now much more competitive, the challenge remains how to make the political parties—and the system in general—more representative, responsive, and accountable. Political parties have more often than not overlooked or even actively stymied citizen participation.

Part of the problem lies with Mexico's rigid term limits, which give elected officials few direct incentives to fulfill their campaign promises. A sacred mantra of the Mexican Revolution, the constitution forbids reelection from the president of the nation down to the local mayor. Designed to limit the consolidation of power by strongmen, this institutional choice has instead made politicians only tenuously interested in and accountable to voters. Since no politician will remain in his or her post, career advancement depends not on good service to one's constituents but rather on the favor of party leaders. The lack of electoral consequences combined with weak oversight can bring out the worst in human nature—sloth, greed, and a lust for power. But even for the more civic-minded elected officials, these rigid term limits leave them little time to make a mark. For instance, local mayors have three-year terms. After spending the first year learning the ropes, they have only the second to try and make changes, because by the third they are looking forward to their next position—somewhere else. Citizens have no direct way to punish them for poor job performance, or to reward them for a job well done. As a result of the rules, politicians are indebted to party leaders (who nominate them for future posts) rather than voters. Though enhancing governability by strengthening parties, these rules limit accountability to the average citizen.

To be fair, democracy has changed these calculations, providing at least indirect accounting. Dissatisfied voters have on several occasions punished the governing party, even if they could not punish the individual. For example, in 2009 the PRI's candidate lost his sizable lead and later the Sonora gubernatorial race after a tragic fire in a local daycare revealed systematic public mismanagement and potential graft under the existing PRI administration that ultimately took the lives of forty-nine toddlers. That same year voters, dissatisfied with the status quo, threw the PAN out of the governor's office in San Luis Potosí. But these are still indirect checks at best.

Finally, democracy has not ended, nor even perhaps diminished, corruption within the system. Once largely the purview of Mexico's politicized bureaucracy, the decentralization of power through federalism and divided government expanded the opportunities for corruption to elected and appointed officials across branches and levels of government.[6] Regulatory schemes and conflict of interest codes lag behind, encouraging (or at least not dissuading) these dynamics. Transgressors, even when discovered, often go unpunished, as autonomous investigative bodies such as the Auditoría Superior de la Federación (ASF; Superior Auditory Agency) are underfunded, understaffed, and lack independent sanctioning power (Morris 2009).

Outside of government, many rightly worry that the duopoly controlling the all important television market has nefarious effects on politics and political representation. The most telling event occurred during the lead-up to the 2006 presidential election, when Congress (its members more worried about bad publicity than doing the right thing by their constituents) passed the Federal Television and Radio Law. Dubbed the Televisa law, it protected Televisa and TVAzteca against new competition by automatically renewing their licenses, giving them preferential access to new bandwidth, and limiting the president's or regulator's ability to foster new competition (Becernil 2007; Malkin 2007). The Supreme Court later struck the law down as unconstitutional.

Many too see the successful cases of citizen involvement and influence in passing the transparency law and judicial reform as notable exceptions rather than trends. Civil society on the whole remains quite shallow and weak. Mexico has anywhere from ten to thirty times fewer civil society organizations per capita than Latin American countries at similar levels of development, such as Chile, Argentina, and Brazil.[7] Part of the discrepancy may arise because of the lack of social capital needed for the growth of civic associations, as in the World Values Survey it scores low on measures of tolerance and interpersonal trust compared to advanced democracies (Moreno and Méndez 2002). But it also likely reflects the legacy of corporatist cooptation by the PRI, which for decades discouraged independent activism and organization. It also stems from legal limits on donations that dissuade domestic companies and individuals from supporting nonprofits, and the other vagaries of tax law that, for instance, make it harder for nonprofits to attract talented individuals with competitive salaries. Whatever the balance and combination of factors, the more limited number of organizations, in turn, lessens their ability to counter the weight of vested economic and other interests within the political process, or to successfully promote greater transparency and accountability within the system.

These democratic weaknesses are particularly prevalent at the local level. While renowned for decades for its imperial presidency, de jure Mexico's top elected official is surprisingly weak, limited by the bicameral and federal nature of the system, as well as relatively weak agenda-setting powers. Historically, the bulk of the president's de facto powers stemmed from his position as party head, and depended on his party's control over both houses of Congress (Weldon 1997, 225). With democratization, the executive's domination of the legislature ended, and federalism became a reality. Where once appointed and dismissed at will by PRI presidents, governors are increasingly powerful. Many see them now as de facto veto players within the system, blocking or changing political and fiscal reforms for their benefit. This has brought the fight for democratic governance to the state and municipal level, where in many places it is much less advanced.

Local institutions too are uneven and generally much weaker than at the federal level. State-run IFE offices are less competent and organized than their federal counterpart, and in recent years have become increasingly vulnerable to corruption and general mismanagement.[8] The limited reach of the IFAI at the local level also shows up in evaluations; a recent study found only 30 percent of Mexico City public agencies in compliance with the baseline openness mandated by the law and regulated by the capital's agency.[9]

Overall Mexico's democratic transition has been a positive one, even if slower and less comprehensive than many had hoped. The remaining challenges show that while clean elections are necessary, they are far from sufficient. Mexico now needs to move beyond the focus on elections to develop more robust checks and balances and increase the accountability of politicians and public officials to voters and citizens.

In many ways the successes of Mexico's electoral democracy, and of the workings of the executive and legislative branches, highlight the greatest challenge facing its democracy today. Where democratic governance repeatedly fails Mexico's citizens is within the third branch of government, the judiciary (and law enforcement more generally). Escalating violence and the woefully slow and inadequate governmental responses directly affect citizens' daily lives and, more fundamentally, threaten the integrity of Mexico's democracy.

The Rising Security Threat

Ask most Mexicans today and their number one worry is security, which now surpasses economic concerns in poll after poll (Calderón 2011). Open any newspaper or turn on the television, and the news coming out of Mexico more likely than not features ever more grisly forms of torture and murder. The government estimates that more than 60,000 people have been killed in drug related violence since 2006, rivaling the better-known war zones of Iraq and Afghanistan. Violence, of course, in Mexico is nothing new, and the recent spike comes after a twenty-year-long decline (Escalante Gonzalbo 2009). It is also highly concentrated (though expanding)—relegated to approximately 10 percent of all municipalities—with nearly one-fifth of all drug-related killings occurring in just one border town, Ciudad Juárez (Shirk and Rios 2011). Statistically, with twenty-two homicides per 100,000, the violence is no higher than and in some cases much lower than that in many other Latin American nations, including Brazil, Colombia, and Venezuela. Whatever the appropriate comparisons, the rapid escalation and gruesome public nature of the violence have dramatically affected the country.

Mexico's increasing insecurity reflects many factors. Some are external, namely the evolution of the hemispheric drug trade. Thirty years ago, Colombian organizations dominated not just the production of cocaine but its wholesale distribution networks throughout much of the United States, the world's largest market. Mexican cartels played a smaller role within this larger production and distribution chain. But enforcement actions by the United States and the Colombian governments, combined with market forces and Mexico's comparative geographic advantage, changed this dynamic. Today, it is the Mexican cartels that dominate the business, working with local and international producers to supply, transport, and distribute some 90 percent of cocaine, as well as the vast majority of imported marijuana, heroin, and methamphetamine in the United States. Four decades and billions of dollars destined for the "war on drugs" succeeded in moving the epicenter of the Western Hemisphere drug trade 2,000 miles north to Mexico.

These international shifts overlapped with Mexico's slow democratization process. Political opening throughout the 1990s interrupted the long-standing collusion between some members of the ruling PRI political party and favored drug traffickers. In return for a cut of the profits (and few high profile killings), PRI officials implicitly guaranteed limited interference by law enforcement and potential competitors, using public force to ensure local trade route monopolies (commonly referred to as *plazas*). The PRI's eroding political control undermined these deals, and opened up the illicit sector to new actors and entrepreneurs. Indeed, violence picked up in states where the PAN first broke the PRI's monopoly on power. In Baja California and Chihuahua, for example, homicide rates increased by one-third and two-thirds respectively following the election of the first opposition governors.[10] The 2000 elections put an end to the final vestiges of old collusion, setting the stage, in conjunction with other factors discussed below, for the escalation of violence in recent years.

Increasing resources and domestic competition spurred Mexico's criminal organizations to become both more organized and militarized. Sophisticated accounting and money-laundering outfits developed to process, clean, and disperse billions of dirty dollars. Complicated logistical operations and supply chains developed to produce and transport their wares from the fields and labs to their final markets in a timely manner. To protect this trade, Mexican drug cartels militarized their operations. The most notorious case involves the Zetas, whose leaders defected from the Mexican army's special operations units, first to the Gulf Cartel and then later to form their own independent criminal organization.[11]

Even as Mexican cartels dominated the drug trade north, they diversified their business models, supplying the domestic retail drug market and branching into kidnapping, human smuggling, extortion, and contraband. These new and growing businesses escalated the violence.

Calderón directly confronted the drug cartels. He significantly expanded the role of the military in the fight, sending some 50,000 troops into states such as Michoacán, Chihuahua, and Tamaulipas to take organized crime head on. He also vastly expanded the breadth and depth of the security relationship with the United States through the Merida Initiative, a multiyear security assistance program that provides hundreds of millions of dollars and closer bilateral operational and intelligence cooperation. These strategic choices and policies led to record numbers of interdictions, arrests, and extraditions, interrupting business as usual and leading to greater fragmentation within these illegal markets. Higher stakes, enhanced competition, increasing firepower, and growing market uncertainty have all led to heightened violence, as disputes and "mergers and acquisitions" are settled through blood on the streets.

Mexico's Achilles' Heel

Facing this increasingly professional and armed threat has been a weak, outdated, and still largely undemocratic judicial sector. Under the PRI, the police and courts were just one more part of the party machine, more instruments of social control than protection or justice. For those with the party, infractions—minor or major— could often be forgiven. But for regime opponents, law enforcement and the legal system were useful instruments of harassment and intimidation (Magaloni 2006; Uildriks 2010).

This long-standing politicization of the courts and police left them weak in the face of increasingly sophisticated crime organizations. In fact, some argue "not only do they [the judiciary] allow crime to go unpunished because of their incompetence . . . but in some instances they have actually been 'captured' by criminals" (Magaloni and Zepeda 2004; Morris 2009, 41).

The dysfunction within Mexico's law enforcement institutions went farther, to the very structure and operation of the bureaucracies themselves. In return for potential mortal danger, police officers are paid a pittance—on average just over $600 a month—far short of the $850 officials estimate are required to just meet basic necessities (García Luna 2007; Secretariado Ejecutivo del Sistema Nacional de Seguridad Pública 2011). They often have to pay for the basic tools of the job—a gun, bullets, even gasoline for their patrol cars—themselves. An honest cop has to deal with a corrupt hierarchy, where higher ups often expect and demand payoffs to climb the career ladder and even to avoid punishment. Stories of superiors punishing straight arrows by giving them graveyard shifts, docking their pay arbitrarily, even locking them in stationhouse rooms for hours are too prevalent to be easily dismissed. The perverse pseudo-franchise scheme weeds out the optimistic, idealistic, and able. The remaining corps are often less capable, less effective, and less motivated.[12] Their jobs are made all the harder by wide distrust between the police and local communities.[13] Though levels of professionalism vary between governmental levels (federal, state, and local), and from location to location, overall it is fair to say that "Mexico's finest" has a hard time enticing the most talented and able into its ranks.

The courts are perhaps even worse. An estimated 80 percent of crimes are never even reported (Ch and Rivera 2011). Only one in five is fully investigated, and fewer are prosecuted (Zepeda Lecuona 2007, 141–43). Studies show that out of every one hundred crimes committed, just one or two convictions occur.[14] And of the few actually convicted, the majority are guilty of theft, caught in the act of stealing (Rivera 2011), rather than the more serious crimes of kidnapping, extortion, or murder.[15]

Once an investigation begins, the chances of acquittal are slim, regardless of the evidence. Defense attorneys have few tools to help their clients, as they are unable to cross-examine witnesses or challenge the prosecutor's evidence. Judges often skip court proceedings, preferring to read the transcripts rather than meet the parties in person.[16] And they often refuse to consider the evidence in front of them, as so poignantly depicted in the now highest grossing and Emmy award winning Mexican documentary *Presunto Culpable*, the story of José Antonio (Toño) Zúñiga's quest to overturn an unjust murder conviction.[17] His harrowing tale shows that even when convictions occur, they can result in grave miscarriages of justice.

The rising violence exposed this weak rule of law, decades in the making and relatively untouched by democracy's advances. As competitive elections in Mexico transformed the executive and legislative branches, Mexico's judicial sector remained largely unchanged. This in part reflects the nature of the third branch of government. By democratic design courts are not—and should not—be affected by the logic of elections. This insulation has its benefits, including limiting the politicization of justice. But it also means that electoral democracy in and of itself will not make the changes necessary to move beyond the old decrepit system. If anything, democracy makes it all the harder, as needed reforms languish under divided government.

The criminals are years, perhaps decades, ahead in terms of professionalizing themselves with weapons, systems, and efficient and effective logistical practices. For Mexico's democratic governments, the challenge is nothing less than fundamentally transforming a broken system years in the making while simultaneously fending off a sustained assault by Mexico's criminals.

Judicial Sector Reform Efforts

The previous democratizing and democratic governments tried to address these problems. Starting with President Zedillo and then with both Fox and Calderón, each president tried to revamp law enforcement agencies, and in particular federal police forces (those within their direct control). Amid public worries over crime and outrage over perceived police corruption and inefficiency, Zedillo proposed a new Sistema Nacional de Seguridad Pública (SNSP; National System of Public Security). The initiative increased transfers to states for public safety measures, expanded the role of the military in counternarcotics efforts, and created the Policía Federal Preventiva (PFP; Federal Preventive Police), a force comprised of police and intelligence officers from multiple federal security agencies (Macías and Castillo 2002; Sabet 2010). It also purged more than 15 percent of the notoriously corrupt Policía Judicial Federal (PJF; Federal Judicial Police), filling the empty posts with military officials (Sabet 2010).

Riding the democratic wave into office, Fox, too, focused on centralizing and professionalizing the public security system. He first replaced the Federal Judicial Police with a new Federal Investigative Agency (AFI), modeled on the US Federal Bureau of Investigation (FBI). He then eliminated the Interior Ministry's supervisory functions over the police, creating a separate Ministry of Public Security.

Calderón continued to transform Mexico's security institutions, starting with a new Federal Police force under the command of the autonomous Secretaría de Seguridad Pública (SSP; Secretary of Public Security). The biggest investment here has been on the human side, mandating new ways of recruiting, vetting, and training the corps. Added to this is a strong technology component called Plataforma México, a comprehensive national crime database to aid intelligence and investigatory work (as well as better monitor and vet law enforcement staff) (García Luna 2011).

Through these various efforts, Mexico has made some progress, improving the national police corp. The number of federal police officers has risen from nearly 6,500 when Calderón took office to over 35,000. More than 7,000—or roughly 20 percent—are college educated, practically unheard of under previous national forces. Pay is better, vetting procedures more strenuous, and training both more comprehensive and ongoing. Using information gleaned from the new systems (and through cooperation and intelligence sharing with the United States), the federal police and military have made numerous high level takedowns of cartel leaders. In fact, as of October 2012, twenty-four of the thirty-seven "most wanted" were either dead or behind bars (Luhnow 2011).

Yet the limits to these reforms are still woefully apparent. Though legally required, crime report submissions to the national database are uneven and sobering. Sources show that many municipalities and states file less than one report a month. Plataforma México—no matter how sophisticated the technology—is only as good as its inputs. Recruitment too has been a problem, particularly the search for the more skilled and educated, to the point of leaving positions unfilled. Institutionally, these new forces have not been immune from corruption—the Calderón administration fired more than 10 percent of the federal forces and levied criminal charges against 465 of them following a 2010 screening test that exposed multiple instances of malfeasance and, in some cases, personal ties to criminal organizations (Ellingwood 2010). There has been much less advancement in terms of creating active internal affairs boards, instituting merit-based promotion standards, and improving crime statistics reporting, all necessary building blocks to create a truly professional police force.

Even if one assumes the federal police are moving in the right direction, they represent just 10 percent of Mexico's law enforcement officers. The majority of Mexico's roughly 400,000 police officers are divided up into over 2,000 separate state and local forces, where professionalism, accountability, and even basic capacity are uneven at best, largely dependent on the will and resources of state and local governments. While Calderón has pushed to centralize these myriad forces into thirty-two state and federal district level corps, governors and local representatives so far have stymied these initiatives.[18]

Judicial reform, too, has been attempted across multiple administrations. In one of his first acts as president, Ernesto Zedillo "re-founded" Mexico's Supreme Court. The 1994 reforms cut the number of justices from twenty-six to eleven, replaced their life terms with fifteen-year tenures, established more stringent nonpolitical experience-based standards for appointment, and gave the Senate a greater say over nominations (Finkel 2005). They granted the Supreme Court a greater role in governance, expanding the grounds for judicial review. Since these changes, the highest court in the land has gained independence and gravitas, becoming a real check on and balance to executive and legislative power, and providing a judicial alternative to the more traditional (and less democratic) conflict resolution through backroom political negotiations.

During his tenure, Fox tried to push through more sweeping changes to the judicial system. His 2004 judicial reform would have introduced oral trials, strengthened due process, and made criminal procedures more transparent had it passed.[19] While this more encompassing effort failed, his administration did succeed in reforming the juvenile justice system, establishing a separate system for those under eighteen years of age for the first time in Mexican history.

Calderón's legislative efforts were more successful, culminating in 2008 in a wide-ranging package of constitutional and legislative reforms. The final compromise melded the executive branch's desire to strengthen crime-fighting tools with Congress's and civil society groups' interests in better guaranteeing individual rights. The new legal framework, when enacted, will fundamentally transform Mexico's judicial system. Elaborating on Fox's efforts, it introduces oral trials, strengthens the presumption of innocence and due process, and improves access to an adequate defense. It also introduces alternative arbitration mechanisms and plea-bargaining to limit case backlogs and help prosecutors prioritize their time and resources more strategically. And it strengthens investigatory and prosecutorial tools against organized crime, including easing restrictions on wiretapping and enabling prosecutors to detain potential organized crime suspects for up to eighty days, effectively suspending habeas corpus for especially serious crimes (Carbonell 2008).

If fully implemented the reforms will transform Mexico's justice system in ways that should increase transparency and accountability, improving its functioning and outcomes. But the challenge to make this vision a reality before the 2016 deadline is enormous. At both the federal and state levels judges, lawyers, and court officials need to be retrained, courtrooms renovated or built from scratch, law school curricula revamped, forensic labs expanded, and evidentiary collection and analysis skills developed. While some progress is being made on these fronts, both the federal and state level governments still struggle in many cases to pass the basic implementing statues and regulations necessary to propel the process forward.

Some blame the holdup on the tragic death of the first person designated to shepherd the process (and the slow designation of his successor), others on delays in establishing and activating the eleven-member Coordinating Council (comprised of representatives from the three branches of government, several bureaucracies, as well as civil society and academia), to the recalcitrance of the Supreme Court, and to opposition to the content of the reforms by some experts, political party leaders, and segments of the voting public.[20] But whatever the reasons, the designated transition years have passed with only slow advances.

As important as these actions are the costs. So far no federal or state entity has publicly estimated the substantial costs of the transition, much less begun to budget for them. Yet the costs will undoubtedly be enormous. If the history of state-level reforms is any guide, it will require billions of dollars in the coming years. Lessons from the state level show that without proper funding, the reforms will likely fail—leaving true justice still in limbo.

Added to these costs are the resources needed to strengthen the Procuraduría General de la República (PGR; Attorney General's Office). The PGR currently fairs poorly when compared to other security institutions, with its total budget of Mex$12 billion (roughly US$900 million), just over a third that of the SSP (Sabet 2010, 14). This was not always the case: just a decade ago the Mexican government allocated slightly more funds to the justice branch than to its public security agency.

In recent years the PGR has been on the losing end of many bureaucratic battles, confusing its mandate and limiting its resources. Since the 2008 security reform the federal police has built up its own investigation units, ending the PGR's previous monopoly on criminal investigations (Sabet 2010). Yet how these newly minted federal police detectives do, should, and will work with Mexico's public prosecutors remains unclear. No systematic process yet exists even to hand off evidence to their PGR counterparts. Cooperation between these two judicial sector branches is vital if Mexico is to reduce violence and crime.

The cost of this dysfunction shows up in the ever-growing gap between the number of arrests and successful prosecutions. Drug trafficking arrests soared during Calderón's tenure to over 80,000 (Ellingwood 2011). Though the PGR doesn't release official conviction rates (in part because their systems are not yet automated), anecdotal evidence strongly suggests these rates have not increased, much less kept up with the blistering rise in apprehensions. Official data show that while overall criminal complaints rose over the last five years, the number of convictions has at best remained steady (Rivera 2011).

The failure of the PGR in even the highest profile cases highlights its shortcomings. For instance, in 2009, the arrest of thirty-five mayors, police chiefs, and other officials from the state of Michoacán on alleged drug trafficking ties made huge headlines, with officials opining that this showed the government's commitment to rooting out "cancerous" corruption, even within its own ranks.[21] Two years later, all had (more quietly) been released due to the lack of evidence for their purported crimes.

Mexico's Challenges Ahead

Most analysts argue that it takes at least a generation to transform police and justice systems, and to strengthen democratic institutions and mores more generally. A decade plus out from Mexico's official transition (and two plus from the first rumblings of democratization), there is serious work left to do.

To construct a democratic rule of law—a lynchpin for responsible and responsive governance—Mexico needs to improve the institutional performance of its judicial sector. This means deepening and consolidating the current federal police reform efforts and extending and expanding these efforts to encompass state and local law enforcement. It requires transforming the justice system by the 2016 deadline—making the new vision a reality. And it means investing in the PGR to ensure that justice can be served.

In addition to institutional performance, Mexico needs to increase accountability. This will require stronger internal affairs and watchdog organizations within the security apparatus, stronger and more independent courts, and broader political reforms, beginning with reelection. Though not a panacea for Mexico's ills, reelection—particularly at the local level—is an important step for bolstering representation and responsiveness. It should also benefit security. A main challenge to strengthening the rule of law, especially at the local level, is the lack of policy continuity. Time constrained, local officials have no incentive to take on long term, laborious reforms to police or court systems. Instead, short term public works—roads and bridges (often to nowhere)—dominate budgets and staffs. For those that invest in these more thankless tasks, initial steps are often thrown out by the next administration just a few years later, leaving citizen security hanging in the balance.

Only in rare cases, such as the northern city of Chihuahua, have local governments been able to overcome this problem, with positive results. While usually the upper- and even midlevel echelons of the security system are prime patronage slots, creating turnover with each new administration needing and wanting to reward allies, over the last nearly twenty years in Chihuahua, police chiefs have routinely outlasted their mayoral bosses. And since the mid-1990s, rather than start over with new policies (also the norm), each new head instead deepened the work of his predecessors. This has allowed them not only to obtain official standing with CALEA (the US-based Commission on Law Enforcement Accreditation), but to *maintain* it over many years—distinguishing them from other reformer-led municipalities. Ongoing basic efforts, rather than particularly innovative policy measures, have made a difference. The city's police force now boasts improved working conditions, longer initial and more ongoing job training, and better accountability mechanisms, becoming a much more professional (though still far from perfect) operation (Sabet 2009). Citizens recognize the transformation, rating their cops much more positively than in the past, and compared to residents in other places.

Yet this example is the exception that generally proves the rule. Almost no other city—much less state—has been able to replicate Chihuahua's success, in large part because the pull of patronage norms makes it very difficult to change the way things are done for very long, if at all. Reelection could change this dynamic, fostering the emergence of more Chihuahuas by rewarding good policies, good staff choices, and most importantly encouraging the continuity necessary for sustainable, systematic change.

Today many worry that Mexico's advances have stalled, leaving the nation with a procedural but not a substantive democracy. In addition to judicial sector and electoral reforms, many call for the creation of new watchdog organizations, the expansion of regulatory powers, the changing of campaign finance laws, and even the overhauling of the presidential system itself in order to strengthen Mexico's political system.

But to truly improve democratic governance, more attention must be paid to implementing legislative rules already on the books than writing new ones. While it is true that many of its current laws do not help the situation, Mexico's challenges today point out the limits of tinkering with institutional designs. Even with democratization, it remains a country known for the vast discrepancies between de jure laws and de facto power, with many well-written and balanced laws stymied by weak, nonexistent, or counterproductive implementation. Legislative, even constitutional reforms may surprisingly be the easiest part of the fight. The real work to improve Mexico's democratic governance must take place in the bureaucratic trenches, transforming the informal rules and institutions that shape how democracy actually works (Helmke and Levitsky 2006).

This has yet to start in earnest. So far, each president in the democratizing and democratic era, perhaps seeking to distinguish themselves from their predecessor, has preferred to "start over," disbanding problematic institutions, creating new bureaucracies and agencies, renaming and restructuring police forces, and changing reporting lines. While addressing some of the problems of the system, the frequent upheavals limit the deepening of institutions, and the efforts to take on the informal rules and norms block fundamental change. Instead, the positive steps of the previous administration are often lost by the next, as the focus on big legislative changes leaves little time, and little political capital, to penetrate these informal interactions, accepted practices, and working cultures within the state's bureaucracies. This is nowhere more apparent than in the judicial sector. Nearly twenty years since Zedillo's first reforms, Mexico still struggles to establish the basics for a democratic rule of law.

A final crucial question that remains for Mexico's government is if today's violence is undermining tomorrow's democracy. So far there are worrisome signs. At the local level there are numerous instances of criminal gangs silencing journalists, corrupting politicians, and killing anyone that stands in their way, destroying the freedoms necessary for democracy. The government's reaction, in particular sending out the military, has brought its own challenges to democratic governance, most notably the rise in alleged human rights abuses. A recent Human Rights Watch investigation found concrete evidence that from 2006 to 2010 law enforcement—including the army, navy, federal police as well as local and federal judicial investigative police—participated in 170 cases of torture, thirty-nine "forced disappearances," and twenty-four extrajudicial killings of civilians (Human Rights Watch 2011). As witnessed with the rise of *mano dura* (tough on crime) type policies region wide, many politicians and citizens alike assume that security and democracy are substitutes rather than complements.

But there is also the possibility that the current security crisis could bolster Mexico's democracy. To start, it has pushed Mexico to address its weak rule of law. It is hard to imagine that without the immediate threats, recent governments would have dedicated so much political capital and effort to making the necessary legislative changes. Second, the escalating security crisis may force Mexico's elites to engage and, as importantly, invest. As a percentage of GDP, Mexico's tax intake is one of the lowest in the hemisphere. Though oil revenues fill in in part for this citizen distance, the lack of funds does mean less for public goods, including security. Colombia's difficult struggle with its own security challenges illustrates a path Mexico too could follow: a democratic security tax. This asset tax on the wealthiest not only bolstered Colombia's law enforcement but also increased accountability, as it came with strong transparency and evaluation requirements attached (O'Neil 2011). One could imagine a similar path in Mexico.

The security challenge too could galvanize Mexico's civil society, increasing its depth and role in governance. The initial steps have already been taken. Think tanks, universities, and other nonprofit organizations have begun to conduct studies and surveys to better understand the root of the problems and inform potential policy solutions. Peace-oriented marches have brought out hundreds of thousands of citizens. Influential leaders such as Alejandro Martí and Javier Sicilia (both fathers whose sons were murdered) command center stage. But these efforts still remain somewhat marginal to the policy process, having yet to enter into a real and constructive dialogue with the political establishment. Democratization unwittingly helped fuel today's drug-related violence. The question now for Mexico is if it can use the current crisis to its advantage, ultimately ending up not just safer but more democratic.

NOTES

1. According to the 2010 Political Culture of Democracy in Mexico report, only 66 percent of Mexicans support democracy (Paras García, Lopez Olmedo, and Vargas Lopez 2010).

2. Seventy-one percent agree or strongly agree with the statement, "Without political parties there can be no democracy." See table 2.5 in Moreno 2010, 45.

3. To be fair, more have been proposed as well. Still, the passage rate over the last ten years is well above 50 percent (Casar 2010, 127–28).

4. A recent study shows that participation in Mexico's cash transfer programs, such as *Oportunidades*, increases voter support for the incumbent party (Diaz-Cayeros, Estévez, and Magaloni n.d., 240).

5. The candidate favored by PRI leaders on the national executive committee (as opposed to the Nuevo Leon's PRI governor at the time) was a union boss, who fared poorly in terms of voter recognition and preference.

6. E.g., as Congress has become more influential, it has also become more "bribable." See Morris 2009, 37.

7. One of the reasons for the disparity may be a lack of funding. Mexico's philanthropic giving hovers at around .04 percent, far below the rates for its peers in the region. See Layton 2008; Salomon and Wojciech Sokolowski 1999.

8. According to the 2011 Annual Report of IFE's internal review board, many local IFE departments could not account for a number of irregular charges, such as the unapproved purchase of suspiciously overvalued office space. See "Demandan consejeros" 2011; Caporal 2011.

9. "Justice in Mexico" 2011.

10. www.seguridadcondemocracia.org/atlas_2009/homicidios_por_entidad_federativa_y_regiones_1990-2007_16.pdf.

11. They later split from the Gulf cartel, becoming one of the most aggressive and violent criminal organizations in Mexico today.

12. Studies show that Mexican police suffer from low self-esteem, further crippling their ability to perform well under such pressures. See Azaola 2009.

13. A whopping 85 percent of Mexicans have little to no trust of the police. See Bailey and Chabat 2002, 14.

14. "Índice de incidencia" 2009.

15. For instance, public prosecutors are more than ten times more likely to open investigations into robberies than homicides.

16. "Global Corruption Report 2007: Corruption in Judicial Systems," 2007.

17. Roberto Hernández and Geoffrey Smith, "Presumed Guilty" (Cinépolis, 2011).

18. Supporters of the "mando único" reform rightly argue that with fewer forces it will be easier to mandate and enforce standards, conduct training, and professionalize Mexico's police. Many point to Colombia, suggesting that part of its success in overcoming the drug cartels rested in their national police force. Critics argue local community police are more likely to be accountable to local citizens, addressing their needs rather than higher up political agendas. They point to the United States, with its 18,000 individual police forces, which are seen as both reasonably effective and as a hallmark of democracy.

19. "Reforma integral" 2004.
20. There is opposition to the reforms on several (sometimes conflicting) grounds. Some think the reforms concede too much to the accused, and would prefer a system in which suspects enjoy fewer pre-trial rights. Others, however, believe the reforms do not do enough to respect basic human rights in criminal procedures, citing the *arraigo* provision as an unnecessary violation of international habeas corpus standards. See Zepeda Lecuona 2009, 4–5.
21. "Calderón Lanza Advertencia" 2009.

REFERENCES

Amparo Casar, Maria. 2010. "Executive-Legislative Relations: Continuity or Change?" In *Mexico's Democratic Challenges: Politics, Government, and Society*, edited by Andrew Selee and Jacqueline Peschard, 117–34. Stanford: Stanford University Press.

Azaola, Elena. 2009. "The Weaknesses of Public Security Forces in Mexico City." In *Police and Public Security in Mexico*, edited by David Shirk and Robert Donnelly, 125–47. San Diego: University Readers.

Bailey, John, and Jorge Chabat. 2002. *Transnational Crime and Public Security: Challenges to Mexico and the United States*. La Jolla: Center for US-Mexican Studies.

Barrera, Victor. 2011. "Ante el temor de perder su candidatura Peña Nieto elige a Eruviel." *Cuadrante Informativo*. March 28. Accessed August 10. http://cuadranteinformativo .com/index.php?option=com_content&view=article&id=3175:ante-el-temor-de -perder-su-candidatura-pena-nieto-elige-a-eruviel&catid=118:desde-nuestras-plu mas&Itemid=643.

Becernil, Andrea. 2007. "La *Ley Televisa*, una imposición previa a las elecciones de 2006, según Creel," *La Jornada*, May 5. Accessed August 8, 2011. www.jornada.unam .mx/2007/05/05/index.php?section=politica&article=005n1pol.

"Calderón: Evaluacíon 18 trimestres de gobierno." 2011. *Consulta Mitofsky* (May).

"Calderón Lanza Advertencia Contra Funcionarios Corruptos." 2009. *El Economista*, June 1. Accessed August 11, 2011. http://eleconomista.com.mx/notas-online/politica /2009/06/01/Calderón-lanza-advertencia-contra-funcionarios-corruptos.

Caporal, José Antonio. 2011. "Irregularidades en juntas locales y distritales del IFE." *Vértigo Politico*, May 16. Accessed August 11, 2011. www.vertigopolitico.com/es/ver tigo/noticia?id=n165090.

Carbonell, Miguel. 2008. "Sobre el Nuevo Artículo 16 Constitucional." *Biblioteca Jurídica Virtual del Instituto de Investigaciones Jurídicas de la UNAM*, 143–45. www.juridicas .unam.mx/publica/librev/rev/refjud/cont/15/cle/cle8.pdf.

Ch, Rafael, and Marien Rivera. 2011 "Numeros Rojos del Sistema Penal." CIDAC, 5.

"Claroscuros de una oportunidad histórica para transformar el sistema penal mexicano." 2009. *Análisis Plural* 3 (June): 4–5.

Dávila, Israel, and Javier Salinas. 2007. "Videgaray y Némer allanan el camino para postulación de Alfredo del Mazo," *La Jornada*, March 25. Accessed August 10, 2011. www.jornada.unam.mx/2011/03/25/estados/034n1est.

"Demandan consejeros del IFE sancionar a malos funcionarios electorales." 2011. *Yahoo! Noticias*, April 27. Accessed August 11, 2011. http://mx.noticias.yahoo.com/deman dan-consejeros-ife-sancionar-malos-funcionarios-electorales-044600534.html.

Diaz-Cayeros, Alberto, Federico Estévez, and Beatriz Magaloni. n.d. "Strategies of Vote-Buying: Democracy, Clientelism, and Poverty Relief in Mexico." Unpublished book manuscript.

Domínguez, Jorge I., and Rafael Fernández de Castro. 2009. *The United States and Mexico: Between Partnership and Conflict.* New York: Routledge.

Ellingwood, Ken. 2010. "Mexico Fires 3,200 Police Officers." *Los Angeles Times,* August 31. Accessed August 11, 2011. http://articles.latimes.com/2010/aug/31/world/la-fg-mexico-police-fired-20100831.

———. 2011. "Bravery May Not Be Enough to Bring Justice to Mexico." *Los Angeles Times,* July 2005. Accessed August 11, 2011. http://articles.latimes.com/print/2011/jul/05/world/la-fg-mexico-morales-20110705.

Escalante Gonzalbo, Fernando. 2009. "Homicidios 1990–2007." *Nexo,* January 9. Accessed August 11, 2011. www.nexos.com.mx/?P=leerarticulo&Article=776.

Estévez, Federico, Eric Magar, and Guillermo Rosas. 2008. "Partisanship in Nonpartisan Electoral Agencies and Democratic Compliance: Evidence from Mexico's Federal Electoral Institute." *Electoral Studies* 27 (2): 257–71.

Finkel, Jodi. 2005. "Judicial Reform as Insurance Policy: Mexico in the 1990s." *Latin American Politics and Society* 47 (1): 91–94.

Frenk, Julio, Eduardo González-Pier, Octavio Gómez-Dantés, Miguel A Lezana, and Felicia Marie Knaul. 2006. "Health System Reform in Mexico 1." *Lancet* 368 (October). www.thelancetglobalhealthnetwork.com/wp-ontent/uploads/2008/04/health_system_reform_in_mexico1.pdf.

García, Pablo Paras, Carlos Lopez Olmedo, and Dinorah Vargas Lopez. 2010. "Cultura politica de la democracia en Mexico, 2010: Consolidación democratica en las Americas en tiempos dificiles." *Latin American Public Opinion Project.* www.vanderbilt.edu/lapop/mexico/2010-culturapolitica.pdf.

García, Rosario. 2011. "El PRI rompe la línea de sucesión del llamado Grupo Atlacomulco en Edomex," *CNN México,* April 1. Accessed August 10, 2011. http://mexico.cnn.com/nacional/2011/04/01/el-pri-rompe-la-linea-de-sucesion-del-llamado-grupo-atlacomulco-en-edomex.

García Luna, Genaro. 2007. "Palabras del secretario de seguridad publica." Speech presented at The Reunion Nacional de Municipios, Seguridad Publica y Procuracion de Justicia. July.

———. 2011. *El nuevo modelo de seguridad para México.* México D.F.: Nostra Ediciones.

"Global Corruption Report 2007: Corruption in Judicial Systems." 226: Transparency International, 2007.

Grillo, Ioan, and Dolly Mascareñas. 2011. "Mexico's Old Ruling Party Scores a Youthful Resurrection." *Time,* August 7. Accessed August 10, 2011. www.time.com/time/world/article/0,8599,2081384,00.html.

Helmke, Gretchen, and Steven Levitsky, eds. 2006. *Informal Institutions and Democracy: Lessons from Latin America.* Baltimore: Johns Hopkins University Press.

Hernández, Roberto, and Geoffrey Smith. 2011. "Presunto Culpable." 87 minutes: Cinépolis.

Holzner, Claudio. 2010. *Poverty of Democracy: The Institutional Roots of Political Participation in Mexico.* Pittsburgh: University of Pittsburgh Press.

Human Rights Watch. 2011. "Neither Rights Nor Security Killings, Torture, and Disappearances in Mexico's 'War on Drugs.'" New York: Human Rights Watch.

"Índice de incidencia delictiva y violencia." 2009. *CIDAC* 1 (August). www.icesi.org.mx /publicaciones/PDF/Indice_violencia.pdf.

Instituto Federal de Acceso a la Información y Protección de Datos. 2011. "Solicitudes de información, tipo de respuestas emitidas y cuantos recursos son interpuestos." *Instituto Federal de Acceso a la Información y Protección de Datos.* www.ifai.org.mx /Estadisticas/#estadisticas.

"Justice in Mexico." 2011. *University of San Diego Trans-Border Institute* (July): 12. http:// justiceinmexico.files.wordpress.com/2011/02/2011-07-july-news-report1.pdf.

Lawson, Chappell H. 2002. *Building the Fourth Estate: Democratization and the Rise of A Free Press in Mexico.* Berkeley: University of California Press.

Lawson, Chappell H., and Sallie Hughes. 2005. "The Barriers to Media Opening in Latin America." *Political Communication* 22 (1): 9–25.

Layton, Michael. 2008. "Financiando la sociedad civil en México: Una aproximación a través de la II Encuesta Nacional Sobre Filantropía y Sociedad Civil, 2008." Seminar presented for the Proyecto Sobre Filantropía y Sociedad Civil, ITAM, Puebla. www.filantropia.itam.mx/docs/Finance.pdf.

Levy, Santiago. 2006. *Progress against Poverty: Sustaining Mexico's Progresa-Oportunidades Program.* Washington, DC: Brookings Institution Press.

Luhnow, David. 2011. "Mexico Police Arrest Chief of 'La Familia' Drug Cartel." *Wall Street Journal,* June 22. Accessed August 11, 2011. http://online.wsj.com/article/SB10 001424052702304887904576400291848238236.html.

Lujambio, Alonso. 2000. *El poder compartido: Un ensayo sobre la democratización Mexicana.* México, DF: Océano.

Macías, Vivianna, and Fernando Castillo. 2002. "Mexico's National Public Security System: Perspectives for the New Millennium." In *Transnational Crime and Public Security: Challenges to Mexico and the United States,* edited by John Bailey and Jorge Chabat, 53–70. La Jolla: Center for US-Mexican Studies.

Magaloni, Beatriz. 2006. "Weak and Powerful Courts under Autocracy: The Case of Mexico." Unpublished paper presented at the conference The Politics of Courts in Authoritarian Regimes, The University of Pennsylvania Law School, August 30–31.

Magaloni, Beatriz, and Guillermo Zepeda. 2004. "Democratization, Crime and Judicial Reform in Mexico." In *Dilemmas of Change in Mexican Politics,* edited by Kevin Middlebrooke, 168–97. London: Institute of Latin American Studies at the University of London.

Mainwaring, Scott, and Timothy Scully. 1995. *Building Democratic Institutions: Party Systems in Latin America.* Stanford: Stanford University Press.

Malkin, Elisabeth. 2007. "Mexican Court's Media Ruling Shows Support for Competition." *New York Times,* June 6. Accessed August 8, 2011. www.nytimes.com/2007/06 /06/business/worldbusiness/06mextv.html?scp=5&sq=televisa+law&st=nyt.

McCann, James. 2009. "Ideology in the 2006 Campaign." In *Consolidating Mexico's Democracy,* edited by Jorge Domínguez, Chapell Lawson, and Alejandro Moreno, 268–84. Baltimore: Johns Hopkins University Press.

Michener, Greg. 2010. "The Surrender of Secrecy: Explaining the Emergence of Strong Access to Information Laws in Latin America." PhD diss., University of Texas at Austin.

Moreno, Alejandro. 2010. "Citizens' Values and Beliefs toward Politics: Is Democracy Growing Attitudinal Roots?" In *Mexico's Democratic Challenges*, edited by Andrew Selee and Jacqueline Peschard, 29–49. Stanford: Stanford University Press.

Moreno, Alejandro, and Patricia Méndez. 2002. "Attitudes towards Democracy: Mexico in Comparative Perspective." *International Journal of Comparative Sociology* 43 (3–5): 350–67.

Morris, Stephen D. 2009. *Political Corruption in Mexico: The Impact of Democratization*. Boulder, CO: Lynne Rienner.

O'Neil, Shannon. 2011. "Mexico Can Win Drug War Colombia's Way." *Bloomberg*, June 17. Accessed January 19, 2012. www.bloomberg.com/news/2011-06-17/how-mexico -can-win-the-drug-war-colombia-s-way-shannon-o-neil.html.

Paras García, Pablo, Carlos Lopez Olmedo, and Dinorah Vargas Lopez. 2010. "Cultura Politica de la democracia en Mexico, 2010: Consolidación democratica en las Americas en tiempos dificiles." *Latin American Public Opinion Project*. www.vanderbilt.edu /lapop/mexico/2010-culturapolitica.pdf.

"Reforma integral al sistema de justicia, anuncia el Presidente Vicente Fox." 2004. Página de la Presidencia de la Republica, March 10. Accessed August 8, 2011. http://fox .presidencia.gob.mx/actividades/?contenido=7678.

Rivera, Marien. 2011. "The Fight Worth Fighting: Reforming the Mexican Criminal Justice System." *CIDAC* (March). www.cidac.org/esp/uploads/1/Reforma_penal-_la _guerra_util.pdf.

Sabet, Daniel. 2009. "Two Steps Forward: Lessons from Chihuahua." In *Police and Public Security in Mexico*, edited by David Shirk and Robert Donnelly, 247–69. San Diego: University Readers.

———. 2010. "Police Reform in Mexico: Advances and Persistent Obstacles." *Woodrow Wilson International Center for Scholars Mexico Institute* (May): 9.

Salomon, Lester M., S. Wojciech Sokolowski, and Associates. 1999. *Global Civil Society: Dimensions of the Nonprofit Sector*. Vol. 2. Baltimore: Johns Hopkins Comparative Nonprofit Sector Project.

Secretariado Ejecutivo del Sistema Nacional de Seguridad Pública. 2011. "Sueldos de policías estatales y municipales."

Serra, Gilles. 2009. "Una lectura crítica de la reforma electoral en México a raíz de la elección de 2006." *Política y Gobierno* 16 (2): 413–15.

Shirk, David, and Vidriana Rios. 2011. *Drug Violence in Mexico: Data and Analysis through 2010*. San Diego: Trans-Border Institute.

"Solicitudes de información, tipo de respuestas emitidas y cuantos recursos son interpuestos." 2011. *Instituto Federal de Acceso a la Información y Protección de Datos* 10. www.ifai.org.mx/Estadisticas/#estadisticas.

Tobar, Hector. 2008. "Judicial Overhaul in Mexico Okd." *Los Angeles Times*, March 7. Accessed August 8, 2011. http://articles.latimes.com/2008/mar/07/world/fg-mexjustice7.

Uildriks, Neils. 2010. *Mexico's Unrule of Law: Implementing Human Rights in Police and Judicial Reform under Democratization*. Lanham, MD: Lexington Books.

Weldon, Jeffrey. 1997. "The Political Sources of *Presidencialismo* in Mexico." In *Presidentialism in Latin America*, edited by Scott Mainwaring and Matthew Soberg Shugart, 225–58. New York: Cambridge University Press.

Zepeda Lecuona, Guillermo. 2007. "Criminal Investigation and the Subversion of the Principles of the Justice System in Mexico." In *Reforming the Administration of Justice in Mexico*, edited by Wayne A. Cornelius and David Shirk, 133–52. South Bend: University of Notre Dame Press.

———. 2009. "La reforma constitucional en materia penal de junio de 2008: Claroscuros de una oportunidad histórica para transformar el sistema penal mexicano." *Análisis Plural* 3 (June): 1–9.

CHAPTER ELEVEN

Peru

The Challenges of a Democracy without Parties

Steven Levitsky

For many observers, post-Fujimori Peru was a success story. The economy boomed in the 2000s, and unlike neighboring Bolivia, Ecuador, and Venezuela, democratic institutions remained intact. Nevertheless, Peruvians remained deeply dissatisfied with their government and democratic institutions. Public discontent was made manifest in the 2011 presidential election. Despite 9 percent economic growth, two candidates from outside the democratic establishment—Ollanta Humala, a populist former military officer, and Keiko Fujimori, the daughter of imprisoned ex-authoritarian leader Alberto Fujimori—qualified for the runoff. Humala, an outsider who had once modeled himself on Hugo Chávez, won the runoff, bringing Peru to the brink of political crisis.

This chapter examines the evolution of Peruvian democracy since 2000. It argues that despite a sustained economic boom, the institutional foundations of democracy in Peru remain weak. As an analysis of the post-Fujimori regime makes clear, weak state and party institutions create severe challenges for democratic governance even in the best of economic times.

Economic Boom, Political Bust? Democratic Governance under Toledo and García

In many ways, the 2000s were a successful decade for Peru. The economy boomed under Presidents Alejandro Toledo (2001–2006) and Alan García (2006–2011). Due to a combination of sound macroeconomic policies and soaring commodities prices, GDP grew 5.7 percent a year between 2001 and 2010, nearly double the regional average (Economic Commission of Latin America 2010b, 94). Incomes soared, and the official poverty rate fell from more than 50 percent in the early 2000s to just over 30 percent.

The performance of democracy was mixed, however. On the one hand, democratic institutions remained intact. Unlike most of its Andean neighbors, Peru did not experience a constitutional crisis or a slide into competitive authoritarianism. Yet democracy did not work well. Despite overseeing a remarkable economic recovery, Alejandro Toledo's presidency was crisis-ridden. A political novice without a real party, Toledo's government was plagued by infighting, unforced errors, and petty scandals (Degregori 2008). In 2004 and 2005, Toledo's approval rating fell into single digits, triggering calls for his resignation or impeachment. Governability problems were exacerbated by rising social conflict. The number of protests nearly quadrupled (Garay and Tanaka 2009, 60–61), and several conflicts descended into praetorian violence, including the 2002 antiprivatization uprising in Arequipa (the *Arequipazo*); the 2004 mob lynching of the mayor of Ilave; and the January 2005 armed uprising in Andahuaylas, led by Ollanta Humala's brother, Antauro, in which four police officers were killed.

Finally, beyond its macroeconomic success, the Toledo government did little to address structural problems such as poverty, inequality, and state weakness. Having inherited a crisis-ridden economy, Toledo focused on attracting investment and restoring growth. The government launched a conditional cash transfer program, *Juntos*, in 2005, but it remained a pilot project—benefiting fewer than 100,000 families—when Toledo left office. Toledo was thus unable to ensure that the benefits of Peru's incipient economic boom were broadly distributed, particularly in the interior. As a result, the specter of populism persisted.

In the 2006 presidential race, Peruvians nearly elected Ollanta Humala, a populist outsider with a dubious commitment to liberal democracy. As a young army commander in the early 1990s, Humala had been accused of human rights violations, and in 2005, he supported (but later repudiated) his brother's rebellion in Andahuaylas. Backed by Hugo Chávez, Humala adopted a radical antisystem discourse in 2006, attacking the Toledo government as a "dictatorship" dominated by "traditional politicians" and pledging to establish a new constitutional order.[1] He also rejected market-oriented policies and called for the nationalization of strategic industries and natural resources.

Yet Humala lost the 2006 election. Ex-president Alan García, who had presided over a hyperinflationary collapse during his first presidency (1985–1990), made a stunning comeback. A master politician, García ably positioned himself in the political center (Vergara 2007). His promise of "responsible change" placed him to the left of conservative candidate Lourdes Flores but to the right of Humala, whose polarizing discourse alienated many voters, particularly in Lima and along the coast (Vergara 2007). Although Humala won a first round plurality, García narrowly beat Flores to qualify for the runoff. Whereas Humala maintained his polarizing, antisystem appeal in the second round, García positioned himself as the antipopulist candidate, appealing to coastal voters who had supported Flores (Cameron 2011). Humala won broad support in the interior, but amid an incipient economic boom, the bulk of the coastal electorate opposed a radical break with the status quo (Cameron 2011). Backed by the Lima establishment, García won the runoff with 53 percent of the vote.

Alan García inherited favorable conditions for democratic governance. Due to soaring commodity prices, Peruvian exports—particularly minerals such as gold and copper—were booming, generating high growth and unprecedented revenue. Unlike Toledo, García was an experienced politician with a real party, Alianza Popular Revolucionaria Americana (APRA; American Popular Revolutionary Alliance). Although APRA controlled only 36 of 130 seats in Congress, it quickly forged a working legislative majority. Moreover, having established himself as a bulwark against Humala, García enjoyed broad support among the economic elite and the media. Given these favorable circumstances, the García government might have embarked on a moderate reformist path similar to Left governments in Brazil, Chile, and Uruguay.

Yet García governed solidly on the Right (Cameron 2011). Not surprisingly, he maintained Toledo's orthodox macroeconomic policies and pro-US foreign policy. Although García had criticized Toledo's negotiation of a US-Peru free trade agreement during the campaign, he quickly pushed for its ratification and implementation once elected. García also aggressively promoted foreign investment, particularly in the mineral sector. Private investment in mining nearly quadrupled, transforming Peru into the leading recipient of mining investment in Latin America.[2]

More surprising was García's neglect of redistributive issues. Real wages remained stagnant (Economic Commission on Latin America 2010a, 77), and the minimum wage lagged far behind productivity increases. Social spending increased, but only modestly (Cameron 2011, 389). Although the government expanded the Juntos program nearly tripling its budget and quadrupling its coverage (Diaz Rueda 2009), coverage remained far lower than that of other conditional cash transfer programs in the region. Whereas Brazil's Bolsa Família and Mexico's Oportunidades covered more than 70 percent of the poor, and Colombia's Familias en Accion covered 39 percent of the poor, Juntos covered only 17 percent of the poor (Johannsen, Tejerina, and Glassman 2009). Finally, despite mining companies' record profits, the government did not raise taxes in the mineral sector. Indeed, so striking was García's neglect of redistribution that conservative politician Lourdes Flores—tagged as the "candidate of the rich" in the 2006 election—accused García of being a "president for the rich."[3]

García's aggressive promotion of foreign investment and neglect of social policy contributed to rising protest in the interior. According to the *Defensoría del Pueblo* (ombudsman), the number of social conflicts increased from 65 in mid-2008 to 250 in late 2010.[4] Most of these conflicts were local communities protesting environmental damage created by mining projects. The García government adopted a hard line against protesters, accusing them of subversive motivations and threatening to impose legal restrictions on NGO activities.[5] García had a particularly conflictive relationship with indigenous groups protesting the expansion of mining and other development projects. A principal demand of indigenous protesters was a Previous Consultation Law (required by the UN Declaration on the Rights of Indigenous People), which would mandate that governments consult communities before approving major development projects. Although Congress approved such a law, García vetoed it. García's hardline orientation had tragic consequences in 2009, when two executive decrees aimed at facilitating oil and gas exploration in the Amazon resulted in a large-scale protest in the province of Bagua. In June, following a two-month road blockade, the government ordered police to break up the protest, triggering a violent conflict in which twenty-five police and nine civilians were killed.

Why, given abundant resources and APRA's left-of-center tradition, did García opt to govern on the Right? It may be that García "over-learned" from the mistakes of the 1980s, when his heterodox and statist policies resulted in hyperinflation. An alternative explanation is constituency-based. As Cameron (2011, 376–77) argues, García won the presidency in 2006 with votes from Lima and the coast, and with the strong support of leading conservative business and media groups. Whereas these groups wielded considerable power, left-wing and popular sector organizations were weak and posed little threat. Arguably, then, a conservative government was the path of least resistance. This path may have been reinforced by state weakness. Due to Peru's ineffective state bureaucracy, past efforts to implement redistributive social policies in Peru—including García's in the 1980s—had been marred by ineffectiveness and corruption (Graham 1992; Soifer n.d.). Thus, a redistributive strategy would have either risked failure or required a significant investment in state capacity—something García had little interest in. These costs may have contributed to his decision to opt for a laissez faire approach to poverty alleviation.[6]

The results of the García presidency were thus mixed. On the one hand, macroeconomic performance was excellent. GDP growth—nearly 10 percent in 2007 and 2008—was the highest in South America, inflation remained low, and international reserves more than doubled (Economic Commission on Latin America 2010a, 67). The government's fiscal and monetary prudence facilitated a Keynesian response to the 2009 global financial crisis (Peru was one of the few South American countries to avoid recession). Despite this impressive macroeconomic performance, however, García was strikingly unpopular. His public approval rating rarely exceeded 35 percent, and it was considerably lower among the poor and in the interior.[7] Even more troubling were signs of deeper public dissatisfaction with the status quo. For example, the 2010 Latinobarómetro survey (2010, 40) found that only 28 percent of Peruvians were satisfied with their democracy— one of the lowest levels in Latin America.

In the third edition of *Constructing Democratic Governance in Latin America*, Carlos Iván Degregori (2008) characterized the Toledo presidency as a "missed opportunity." Yet the truly missed opportunity may have been the García presidency. Whereas Toledo was a political novice who inherited difficult economic conditions in 2001, García was an experienced politician, with a real political party, who presided over an unprecedented economic boom. With ample resources and relative political stability, García had an extraordinary opportunity to combat some of the structural problems that have long plagued Peruvian democracy, such as social inequality and state weakness. Yet he did not.

The 2011 Presidential Election: A Surprising Left Turn

Notwithstanding signs of public dissatisfaction, the 2011 presidential race was expected to be a status quo election. The economic boom had reinforced an emerging elite consensus around orthodox free market policies, and most of the leading presidential candidates—including ex-President Toledo, Lima mayor Luis Castañeda, and Toledo's former prime minister, Pedro Pablo Kuczynski (known as PPK)—were establishment figures that embraced the political and economic status quo. The two main nonestablishment candidates, Humala and Keiko Fujimori, were considered long shots. Humala retained support in the highlands, but a radical populist appeal was not expected to resonate broadly in a booming economy. Although Humala had moderated since 2006, he was despised by the Lima elite and enjoyed little middle class support. Keiko Fujimori was also a flawed candidate. Unlike the postauthoritarian Right in Chile (Siavelis 2013), Fujimorismo had not renovated or broken with its authoritarian past. Rather, it had spent the previous decade defending Fujimori. Keiko, who had served as her father's First Lady, called his government the "best in Peruvian history" and promised that if elected, her "hand would not tremble" in pardoning him.[8]

Prior to the campaign's final stretch, a Fujimori-Humala runoff—described by Nobel laureate Mario Vargas Llosa as a choice "between AIDS and terminal cancer"—was considered a low probability event. As is often the case in countries with weak parties, however, the race generated surprises. Both of the early front-runners, Castañeda and Toledo, faltered as the campaign shifted into high gear, allowing Humala and Fujimori to qualify for the runoff. Humala's Gana Perú (forty-seven seats) and Fujimori's Fuerza 2011 (thirty-seven seats) also finished first and second in the legislative vote, although neither captured a majority of the 130-member body (table 11.1).

Explaining the First Round Results

Why, given Peru's economic boom, did two politicians from outside the democratic establishment qualify for the 2011 presidential runoff? In part, the outcome was rooted in party weakness. Where party organizations and identities are weak,

Table 11.1.   Results of Peru's 2011 Elections (as percentage of valid vote)

Party/Coalition	Presidential Candidate	Presidential Vote Round 1	Presidential Vote Round 2	Legislative Seats Won
Gana Perú	Ollanta Humala	31.7	51.5	47
Fuerza 2011	Keiko Fujimori	23.6	48.5	37
Alianza Por el Gran Cambio	Pedro Pablo Kuczynski	18.5		12
Perú Posible	Alejandro Toledo	15.6		21
Solidaridad Nacional	Luis Castañeda Lossio	9.8		9
APRA	None			4
Others	Others	0.7		0

Source: National Office of Electoral Processes (ONPE).

as they are in Peru, electoral campaigns weigh heavily. Critical to the 2011 campaign was the fact that the coastal middle class electorate split among three candidates: Castañeda, Toledo, and PPK. PPK—a naturalized US citizen who combined an image as a capable market-oriented technocrat with an effective marketing campaign—capitalized on Castañeda and Toledo's mistakes. However, his success was confined mainly to Lima. Rather than consolidating the coastal middle class vote, PPK split it, and as a result, all three establishment candidates failed to qualify for the runoff.

Fujimori and Humala benefited from the fragmentation of the establishment candidates because they enjoyed solid minority support. Fujimorismo maintained a stable core electorate of roughly 20 percent, particularly among lower income voters, who credited Alberto Fujimori for ending hyperinflation and defeating the Sendero Luminoso (Shining Path) insurgency. Humala benefited from widespread discontent (and anti-Lima sentiment) in the interior. Although radical voters—those who sought a radical change in the economic model—constituted only about a third of the electorate, no other candidate campaigned on the Left, leaving the field open for Humala.

Yet campaign dynamics do not fully explain the first round results. Why, despite a booming economy, did a majority of Peruvians vote for two candidates from outside the democratic establishment? Despite their ideological differences, Humala and Fujimori were both outsiders with respect to the political establishment. As this chapter will show, public distrust of political elites and institutions remains widespread in Peru, particularly in the interior. Whereas Castañeda, Toledo, and PPK had strong ties to the Lima elite, Humala, who was despised by the Lima elite, and Fujimorismo, which had been ostracized by much of the elite for more than a decade, did not.

The Second Round: Why Humala Won

The conventional wisdom during the second round was that Fujimori would win. Because the coastal middle class voters who had backed Castañeda, Toledo, and PPK in the first round were major beneficiaries of export-led economic boom, it was expected that they would overwhelming opt for the free market-oriented Fujimori over the more statist Humala. Indeed, fear of a return to statism was a central issue among the Lima elite and in the mainstream media. Most major newspapers (including the influential *El Comercio*) and all major television networks engaged in biased coverage aimed at heightening public fear of Humala,[9] which tilted the playing field in Fujimori's favor.

Yet economic fear did not carry the day. Although the wealthy voted overwhelmingly for Fujimori, the urban middle class split. Fujimori won Lima and other coastal cities, but her margin of victory was insufficient to offset Humala's overwhelming majorities in the interior. Ultimately, much of the middle class vote was driven not by economic fear but by anti-Fujimorismo.

Anti-Fujimorismo trumped economic fear in part because Humala moderated more successfully than did Fujimori. Guided by advisors from Brazil's Workers' Party, Humala charted a course toward the center during the first round, abandoning his antisystem discourse, softening his constitutional reform proposals, and emphasizing "social inclusion" over nationalization and radical economic change. After the first round vote, Humala reconfigured his campaign, bringing in mainstream technocrats from the Toledo camp and drafting a new platform that positioned him solidly on the moderate Left. The new platform pledged to maintain orthodox fiscal and monetary policies and respect international trade agreements, while proposing a 20 percent minimum wage increase, a windfall profits tax on mining companies, expansion of the Juntos conditional cash transfer program, and a new pension for the elderly. Humala also held a public "Oath for Democracy," in which he swore to respect the constitution, checks and balances, and human rights and pledged to stay in office "not a minute beyond" his five-year term.[10]

Humala's moderation won him the support of liberal establishment figures such as Vargas Llosa and ex-President Toledo, as well as numerous intellectuals, journalists, human rights advocates, and other public figures that had opposed him in the past. These endorsements enhanced the credibility of Humala's shift to the center and softened his image among middle class voters. And crucially, they transformed the Humalista coalition from a leftist outsider campaign into a broad anti-Fujimorista front that included centrist, proestablishment figures.

By contrast, Keiko Fujimori failed to credibly break with her party's corrupt and authoritarian past. Years of struggle in defense of Fujimori had transformed Fujimorismo into an ideological social movement with a strong identity and subculture (Urrutia 2011), which hindered its capacity to pursue independent voters. Although Keiko attempted to distance herself from her father's authoritarian past, "swear[ing] to God" that she would not pardon him,[11] she was constrained by her party's commitment to the imprisoned ex-president. Efforts to soften Keiko's image were undermined by the presence of old guard Fujimoristas in the front lines of the campaign. For example, hardline legislator Martha Chávez, who was reelected in 2011, publicly threatened Supreme Court President Cesar San Martin, who had presided over Fujimori's conviction;[12] and Alejandro Aguinaga, who was

Fujimori's health minister when thousands of forced sterilizations were carried out on poor women, was a top campaign advisor.[13] Finally, efforts to distance Keiko from her father's government were belied by evidence that Alberto was active in the campaign from his prison cell.[14] Ultimately, then, Fujimorismo's moderation lacked credibility. Indeed, surveys showed that nearly two-thirds of Peruvians believed Fujimori would pardon her father if elected.[15]

In sum, despite intense efforts by much of the mainstream media to heighten public fear of Humala, anti-Fujimorismo trumped economic fear among many middle class voters. Humala's winning coalition thus combined a radical protest vote, concentrated in the interior, with a middle class anti-Fujimori vote, concentrated in Lima and along the coast. The radical vote helped Humala win a first round plurality, but it was the anti-Fujimorista vote that ultimately delivered him the presidency.

State Weakness and the Persistence of Populism

Why, amid a sustained economic boom, would Peruvians elect a political outsider with a radical past and dubious democratic credentials? Do Peruvians simply prefer heavy-handed *caudillos* (strongmen) to liberal democratic rights and institutions? Such a cultural explanation is not convincing. Although Peru clearly lacks the broad societal consensus around liberal democracy that exists in Costa Rica and Uruguay, Latinobarómetro and other cross-national surveys show that the level of public support for democracy in Peru does not differ significantly from that of Brazil, Chile, Colombia, or Mexico.[16]

Where Peru truly stands out is on the dimensions of satisfaction with, and confidence in, democratic institutions. According to the 2010 Latinobarómetro survey (2010, 40), only 28 percent of Peruvians were satisfied with their democracy, compared to 44 percent in Latin America as a whole (table 11.2). Confidence in political institutions in Peru is the lowest in Latin America (table 11.3). Peru ranks dead last in terms of public trust in Congress (14 percent), the judiciary (15 percent), and political parties (13 percent). And whereas a solid majority of Brazilians and Chileans say they trust their government, only 25 percent of Peruvians do (Latinobarómetro 2010, 73). What is striking about Peruvian public opinion, then, is not widespread authoritarianism but rather widespread discontent and distrust.

What explains the persistence of public discontent in a context of sustained growth and rising incomes? The most plausible explanation lies in state weakness. The Peruvian state is among the weakest in Latin America (Soifer n.d.). Peru's tax

Table 11.2.   Support for and Satisfaction with Democracy (in percentages)

	Support for Democracy	Satisfaction with Democracy	Gap between support and satisfaction
Brazil	54	49	5
Chile	63	56	7
Colombia	60	39	21
Ecuador	64	49	15
Mexico	49	27	22
Peru	61	28	33
Latin America	61	44	17

Source: Latinobarómetro 2010: 39.

Table 11.3.   Specific Latinobarómetro Respondents Who Say They Trust Institutions (2010) (in percentages)

	Congress	Judiciary	Political Parties	Government
Brazil	44	51	24	55
Chile	41	38	23	58
Colombia	33	34	23	45
Peru	14*	15*	13*	25**
Latin America	34	32	23	45

Source: Latinobarómetro 2010: 73.
    * Lowest in Latin America
    ** Second Lowest in Latin America

capacity has also historically been among the lowest in the region (Soifer n.d.), and the state's limited regulatory capacity has long manifested itself in a sprawling urban informal sector in housing, commerce, and transportation (De Soto 1989). According to an IDB-sponsored report published in 2006, Peru's "bureaucratic functional capacity" ranked near the bottom in Latin America, below Bolivia, Guatemala, and Nicaragua, and it ranked last in terms of de facto judicial independence (Stein et al. 2006, 69, 88).

State weakness is especially pronounced in the interior (Soifer n.d.). Peru's postcolonial elite limited state-building efforts to Lima and the coast, leaving rural governance in the hands of local landowners (Soifer n.d.). Landowners remained the primary guarantor of rural social order into the twentieth century, and subsequent state-building efforts, such as that of the leftist military government led by General Juan Velasco (1968–1975), were largely unsuccessful (Soifer n.d.). Although Velasco's land reform destroyed the rural oligarchy, its failure to re-place the old social order with minimally effective state institutions created a vacuum of authority in many parts of the highlands (Starn 1999), which permit-ted the spread of coca production and the brutal Shining Path insurgency (Kay 1999; Burt 2004). In the 1980s, the guerrilla war and a severe economic crisis brought a "rapid disintegration of the state" (Mauceri 1997, 152). Tax collection plummeted, the justice system broke down in much of the country, and the secu-rity forces were "incapable of detaining [the Shining Path's] rapid expansion" (Mauceri 2004, 154). By decade's end, "increasing swaths of territory were no longer controlled by the government" (Burt 2004, 250–51).

The Fujimori government brought the state back from the brink of collapse, re-storing a minimum of tax capacity, extending the state's presence in the country-side, strengthening the armed forces, and defeating the Shining Path (Mauceri 1996, 1997; Wise 2003; Burt 2004). However, these initiatives did not result in an enduring or effective state presence in the interior. Much of the state's territorial extension was undertaken by the military, under a state of emergency that gave local army commanders vast authority. Consequently, the demilitarization that followed the 2000 transition brought a retreat of the state in much of the inte-rior. Moreover, many of the networks of state actors—including army, police, and judicial officials—that penetrated the interior in the 1990s were linked to the corruption ring operated by Fujimori's spymaster, Vladimiro Montesinos. These, too, were disrupted by democratization. Hence, state infrastructural power remains limited (Soifer n.d.). Throughout much of the interior, state authorities are "unable to enforce rules or regulations" (Mauceri 1997, 156), police and judicial authorities are often absent; schools, health clinics, and state bureaucracies are barely operative, and local officials are widely viewed as corrupt or ineffec-tive. Manifestations of state weakness in the 2000s include the persistence of large-scale coca production, the expansion of drug trafficking, the resurgence of armed groups, and frequent incidents of lawlessness, such as the 2004 lynching of the mayor of Ilave, Puno.

As Mainwaring (2006) has argued, state incapacity is a major source of public discontent. In the absence of minimally effective state agencies, even well-meaning governments routinely fail to deliver the (public) goods. Security, justice, educa-tion, other basic services go under-provided, resulting in widespread perceptions of government corruption, unfairness, ineffectiveness, and neglect. Where such perceptions persist, many voters conclude that "all parties are the same," that "all politicians are corrupt," or that no one in the political elite represents them. Such voters are more likely to support antisystem outsiders (Mainwaring 2006; Meléndez forthcoming).

The problems generated by state weakness are not necessarily ameliorated by economic growth. Rising incomes do not enhance public security, make state bureaucracies more effective, or improve the quality of public services. Indeed, the incomes of many Peruvians improved considerably in the 2000s, but in much of the interior, the quality of the state did not. As a Fujimorista congressional candidate from Arequipa put it:

> Do you want to know why people [in my district] voted for Humala? Because they step outside their homes and things are booming. People drive by in new cars. Huge shopping malls are popping up everywhere. But their lives are still miserable. Why? Well, the street isn't paved and their kids have lung problems because of the dust. Their kids get sick and miss school because there is no potable water or sewage. And the public school is barely operational anyway. Plus, there is no security, so they are afraid every time they leave their houses.[17]

State weakness was a major cause of democratic breakdown in 1968 (Lowenthal 1975) and 1992 (Mauceri 1995). It is also underlies the pattern of "serial populism" that characterizes contemporary Peruvian politics (Roberts 2007, 12). Even amid a growing economy, a state's persistent failure to protect citizens, uphold the law, and deliver basic services deepens public disaffection, erodes trust in government, and generates support for antiestablishment candidates who promise to "throw everyone out."

Democracy without Parties

Another challenge for Peru's democracy is the absence of political parties. The Peruvian party system collapsed in the late 1980s and early 1990s under the weight of a deep socioeconomic crisis and the mounting Shining Path insurgency (Cameron 1994; Tanaka 1998). The vote share of the countries' four dominant parties—APRA, the conservative Partido Popular Cristiano (PPC; Popular Christian Party), the centrist Acción Popular (AP; Popular Action), and the Marxist Izquierda Unida (IU; United Left)—fell from 97 percent in 1985 to just 6 percent in 1995. Party collapse permitted the election of a populist outsider, Alberto Fujimori, in 1990 (Cameron 1994). Fujimori created a personalistic vehicle, Change 90, to run for president but abandoned it after taking office. By the time he left power in 2000, he had created and abandoned three more parties: New Majority, Let's

Go Neighbor, and Peru 2000. Fujimori's success—he was overwhelmingly re-elected in 1995—convinced politicians that parties were no longer necessary for (and indeed, might be an obstacle to) winning public office. Thus, many emerg-ing politicians either abandoned established parties (e.g., Lima mayors Alberto Andrade and Luis Castañeda) or were newcomers, which, like Fujimori, created personalistic vehicles (e.g., Toledo). The pattern was repeated at the local level, as mayoral candidates abandoned parties for "independent movements" that were, in reality, personalistic vehicles (Planas 2000).

The 2000–2001 democratic transition generated hope for the rebirth of politi-cal parties. The strong performance of established party candidates Alan García (APRA) and Lourdes Flores (PPC) in the 2001 presidential election was viewed as evidence of a traditional party comeback (Kenney 2003a; Schmidt 2003). At the same time, various electoral reforms were undertaken to strengthen parties (Tuesta 2005; Vergara 2009). Thus, the Fujimori-era electoral system, in which all 120 legislators were elected from a single national district was replaced by one in which candidates were elected from twenty-five districts, thereby reducing the average district magnitude from 120 to five (Tanaka 2005, 105, 125). In addition, a minimum threshold of 5 percent for entry into Congress was introduced in order to weed out smaller parties. Finally, the 2003 Political Parties Law banned indepen-dent candidacies, granted national parties a monopoly over legislative represen-tation, and established a set of organizational requisites for national parties: to be legalized, new parties would require signatures from 135,000 supporters, as well as sixty-seven provincial branches—each with at least fifty activists—in two-thirds of the country's regions (Vergara 2009, 23).

Yet neither democratization nor institutional engineering halted the process of party decomposition. Indeed, the "rebirth" of established parties was illusory. Na-tional parties' survival after 2000 was largely an artifact of their legal monopoly over national candidacies. Because presidential and congressional candidates must run on party tickets, the "parties" headed by leading presidential candidates' necessarily achieve electoral success. Thus, the electoral revival of APRA and the PPC (via a coalition called National Unity, or UN) in 2001 and 2006 was driven almost entirely by the success of García and Flores.

Post-Fujimori Peru was thus a democracy without parties. Although parties per-sisted on paper, they were increasingly mere "name plates" (Planas 2000, 38). All significant parties to emerge after 1995 were personalistic vehicles. Toledo's Perú Posible (PP; Possible Peru), Andrade's Somos Perú (We are Peru), Castañeda's Soli-daridad Nacional (National Solidarity), and Humala's Partido Nacionalista Peruano (PNP; Nationalist Party) were created by, and exclusively for, their founders. They lacked organization, activists, or any internal life, and they were unlikely to survive their founder's departure from politics. Indeed, *all* of the major presidential candidates in 2011 either had no party (PPK) or led personalistic vehicles (Humala, Toledo, Castañeda, Fujimori).[18]

Party system collapse was also seen in the disintegration of parties' local linkages. National parties were increasingly displaced in local elections by provincial or regional "movements" (table 11.4). Whereas in the 2002 local elections, national parties captured more than 70 percent of the vote and most regional and provincial governments, by 2010 the national party vote had fallen to 34 percent, and provincial and regional parties captured more than two-thirds of local governments.[19]

By 2010, then, national parties had been largely displaced from local and regional politics. Yet emerging regional movements were as loosely organized, personalistic, and ephemeral as the parties they replaced (Tanaka and Guibert 2011; Zavaleta 2012), and as a result, local and regional politics grew increasingly fragmented and fluid. An average of twelve parties contested each regional election in 2010 (Seifert 2011, 27–28), and few of these parties endured beyond a single election or two. Manuel Seifert (2011) measured regional "party volatility" by dividing the number of new parties by the overall number of parties in each regional election. In 2006, the average level of party volatility was 62.5, meaning that most of the parties competing in that year's regional election were new (Seifert 2011, 23). In 2010, the figure increased to 68.3, meaning that on average, more than two-thirds of the parties in each region were new (Seifert 2011, 23).

Far from experiencing a rebirth in the 2000s, then, Peru's party system decomposed to a degree that was striking even by Latin American standards. Not only were established parties displaced by personalistic vehicles, but at the local

Table 11.4.   Regional and Provincial Governments Won by National Parties and Regional Movements, 2002–2010

	2002		2006		2010	
	Regions	Provinces	Regions	Provinces	Regions	Provinces
National parties	17	110	7	109	6	68
Regional/ provincial movements	8	84	18	86	19	126

Sources: Vera 2010, Coronel and Rodríguez 2011, Tanaka and Guibert 2011.

level, national parties of all types were displaced by short-lived, candidate-centered "movements." The following sections examine how democracy without parties works, as well as its consequences for democratic governance.

Amateurs, Free Agents, and *Transfugas*: How Democracy without Parties Works

Electoral politics in post-Fujimori Peru is organized almost exclusively around individual candidates. Notwithstanding parties' legal monopoly over national candidacies, their capacity to channel political careers has evaporated. From the perspective of individual candidates, national parties no longer provide the resources needed for election to public office. For one, in the absence of partisan identities, national party labels have little value; hence, local politicians "prefer their own label."[20] National parties also lack what Hale (2006) calls "administrative capital." Gutted of their local organizations, most parties have no activists, campaign infrastructure, or financial or patronage resources to offer local candidates. Consequently, as PPC leader Lourdes Flores put it, they are "completely unable to recruit good candidates. The good ones all want to go it alone."[21]

For those seeking major executive office, "going it alone" means creating a personalistic vehicle. Unable to rely on a national party for the resources needed to run a campaign, candidates for executive office turn to "party substitutes" (Zavaleta 2012; Hale 2006). For example, many businessmen mobilize the financial resources, employees, and infrastructure of their firms as a substitute for partisan organization.[22] An example is Cesar Acuña, who built Alianza para el Progreso (APP; Alliance for Progress) out of his consortium of private universities and a Trujillo-based charitable foundation. Acuña deployed his staff and students as activists, university administrators and faculty as candidates, and his foundation's resources for electoral clientelism (Meléndez 2011). This infrastructure helped Acuña become mayor of Trujillo and place his brother in the regional presidency of neighboring Lambayeque. Acuña used his wealth to sponsor APP candidates across the country, with the goal of running for president in 2016. Though an extreme case, Acuña was hardly alone. The number of "business-parties" increased markedly in the 2010 local and regional elections.[23]

Media outlets also serve as party substitutes, particularly in remote mountainous areas (Zavaleta 2012). In Puno, for example, outsider Hernán Fuentes used his radio station in Juliaca to capture the regional presidency in 2006 (Zavaleta 2010). Fuentes had no real party organization, but he gained fame by using his radio station to repeatedly denounce the incumbent regional president (Zavaleta 2010).

Likewise, television and radio journalist Carlos Cuaresma used his media presence to capture Cusco's regional presidency in 2002 (Muñoz 2010a).

Finally, candidates turn increasingly to local independent "operators" as a substitute for party organization (Zavaleta 2012). Operators are independent agents who orchestrate the campaign activities that are normally undertaken by local party organizations: they recruit candidates to fill out party tickets, build ties to local business or farmers' associations, buy off local media, and organize campaign activities (Zavaleta 2012). In other words, local candidates rent the administrative capital that in most democracies is supplied by parties.

Whereas candidates for major executive offices create personalistic vehicles and then base their electoral campaigns on party substitutes, lower-lever politicians operate as "free agents," renegotiating their partisan affiliation at each election. Although legislative candidates must by law be nominated by a party and local candidates frequently join big city mayoral or regional presidential slates in pursuit of coattails effects, these affiliations are generally short-term contracts that cover a single election cycle. To maximize their electoral prospects, candidates seek to join slates headed by a viable presidential (in the case of aspirants to Congress) or regional presidential (in the case of local mayoral aspirants) candidate. Because elections are highly volatile, politicians must renegotiate these partisan affiliations at each election.

This practice of strategic defection—known in Peru as *transfuguismo*—first gained notoriety in 2000, when Fujimori's spymaster, Vladimir Montesinos, forged a congressional majority by bribing eighteen opposition legislators (known as *tranfugas*, or "turncoats") to join the Fujimorista ranks. A leaked video of one of these bribes triggered the collapse of the regime, and the original *tranfugas* fell into disgrace. However, the practice of *transfuguismo* not only persisted but grew increasingly widespread during the 2000s. By 2011, it was not uncommon to find politicians who had been affiliated with six, seven, and even eight parties. The following are three examples.

Máximo San Román. A businessman from Cusco, San Román was elected vice president on Fujimori's Change 90 ticket in 1990. He broke with Fujimori after the 1992 coup, and in 1995, he was elected to Congress with Public Works, the party of Lima mayor—and presidential candidate—Ricardo Belmont. In 2000, San Román ran for president as candidate of the Unión por el Perú (UPP; Union for Peru). When new elections were held after Fujimori's fall, he joined Castañeda's National Solidarity ticket—as vice presidential candidate—until Castañeda dropped out of the race. In 2006, San Román ran as the vice presidential candidate of

National Restoration. Later that year, he ran unsuccessfully for Cusco's regional presidency with the Inka Pachakútec Regional Movement. He ran again for Cusco regional presidency in 2010, this time with his own National Alternative Party. In 2011, San Román joined PPK's presidential ticket, again as a vice presidential candidate. Thus, San Román participated in eight elections, with *eight different parties*, between 1990 and 2011.

Michel Azcueta. A longtime leftist, Azcueta served two terms as IU mayor of Villa El Salvador in the 1980s. After the IU's collapse, Azcueta joined Alberto Andrade's We Are Lima and was reelected. He was elected to Lima's city council with We Are Lima in 1998. In 2002, Azcueta sought to return as mayor of Villa El Salvador, but with Andrade in decline, he defected to Toledo's PP. He was defeated by his former deputy, Jaime Zea, who had followed him to We Are Lima in the 1990s but joined Unidad Nacional (UN; National Unity) in 2002. Azcueta ran unsuccessfully for mayor in 2006 with an "independent movement" called Peru Trust and again in 2010 with Alliance for Progress. Overall, then, Azcueta ran for mayor of Villa El Salvador with five different parties.

Tito Chocano. Chocano was first elected mayor of Tacna as a PPC member in 1986. He was subsequently reelected three times, each time with a different party. In 1989, he ran with the Union of Independents of Tacna; in 1993, he was the candidate of Fujimori's Change 90 / New Majority; and in 1995 he was reelected with his own vehicle, Strength and Development. In 2000, Chocano won election to Congress with We Are Peru. When new elections were held in 2001, however, Chocano abandoned the weakened Andrade and was reelected with UN. In 2010, he won Tacna's regional presidency with his seventh party: AP.

Although *transfuguismo* is viewed by most Peruvians as unprincipled, opportunistic, and even corrupt, it is critical to political survival in a democracy without parties. Due to a combination of extreme party volatility and strong coattails effects, aspirants to legislative or local executive office must continually secure positions on tickets headed by rising regional and national presidential candidates. Politicians who remain loyal to declining parties are almost certain to lose.

The generation of politicians that emerged in the 1990s and 2000s thus had no stable partisan ties. Rather, they were free agents who negotiated short-term contracts with parties prior to each election. In 2010, for example, thirty-one of Lima's forty-three district-level mayors had belonged to at least two parties, and nearly half had belonged to at least *three* parties. Likewise, a stunning 63 percent of congressional candidates in 2011 had no prior affiliation with the party that nominated them.[24]

Increasingly, then, the organizations competing for public office are temporary "coalitions of independents," linked together by short-term contracts that dissolve after each election (Zavaleta 2012). The one-shot nature of these alliances can be seen in the behavior of parties' legislative blocs in the aftermath of elections. During the 2001–2006 legislative period, the governing PP—perceived as nonviable because Toledo could not seek reelection—suffered thirteen defections.[25] Declining parties such as the Moralizing Independent Front lost nearly half their members to defection, and a few Unión por el Perú (UPP; Union for Peru) lost a majority of them. A similar dynamic occurred during the 2006–2011 legislative period. By 2008, more than two-dozen legislators had left their party (Loayza 2008, 7–8).

Consequences of Party Disintegration

Schattschneider (1942, 1) famously described democracy without parties as "unthinkable." More recently, Aldrich (1995, 3) called it "unworkable." Peruvian democracy provides a test of these claims. How does the absence of parties affect democratic governance? This section examines four implications of partylessness.

Hyper-Individualism and Problems of Political Coordination

The absence of parties limits politicians' time horizons and undermines coordination. Because institutionalized parties are collective and enduring organizations, they create incentives for more public-oriented and far-sighted behavior. Individual politicians may be self-interested, but they are constrained by their parties, which must serve the needs of politicians across the territory and those in future electoral cycles. Where parties are reduced to personalistic vehicles, these organizational incentives disappear. Personalistic vehicles are designed to pursue individual politicians' short-term objectives—usually their own immediate election. Where such organizations predominate, coordination becomes difficult: parties created for individual politicians to seek office in this election cycle are unlikely to coordinate around strategies focused on collective or future benefits. The consequences can be costly. In the late 1990s, when Fujimori was vulnerable to defeat in his illegal bid for a third term, the leading opposition candidates, particularly Andrade, Castañeda, and Toledo, failed to coordinate around a single candidacy, which debilitated anti-Fujimori forces (Levitsky and Cameron 2003). In the 2011 presidential election, Castañeda, Toledo, and PPK—all establishment candidates with similar platforms—failed to coordinate around a single candidacy and consequently split the center/center-right vote, allowing Humala and Fujimori to qualify for the runoff.

Amateur and "Semi-Professional" Politicians

Party disintegration has dramatically changed the nature of political careers. Because national party linkages to local and regional politics have disintegrated, politicians cannot rise up "through the ranks," from party activist to local and then national politician. With the partial exception of APRA, "the ranks" simply do not exist. At the same time, extreme electoral volatility makes it difficult— even with strategic defection—for politicians to secure reelection. Between 1995 and 2008, for example, Peru's legislative reelection rate was 20 percent, compared to 51 percent in Brazil, 52 percent in Argentina, and 63 percent in Chile (Tanaka and Barrenechea 2011). Likewise, only three of twenty-five regional presidents were reelected in 2006, and only seven were reelected in 2010 (Muñoz and García 2011, 13).

Extreme turnover almost invariably results in the rise of amateur politicians.[26] In the 2006–2011 and 2011–2016 legislative periods, for example, a stunning 82 percent of congresspeople were new. Of the legislators elected in 2011, 70 percent had no experience in elected office.[27] A similar pattern exists at the regional level. A study of the winners and runners up in the 2006 regional elections found that only twenty-eight of fifty had previously held elected office (Muñoz and García 2011, 11). Of the twenty-five regional presidents elected in 2010, fourteen had been in politics for less than a decade.

The 2000s thus saw the rise of the "semiprofessional" politician. Rather than working their way up the party ranks, most individuals who entered politics in the 2000s did so as a second career. Because aspiring politicians cannot rely on the label or administrative capital of national parties, they must make a name for themselves or accumulate resources *prior to* entering the political arena. Many of these new politicians were successful businesspeople (Muñoz and García 2011); others were media figures, religious leaders, famous athletes (four ex-members of Peru's national volleyball team won seats in Congress in 2011), and prominent leaders of other local institutions (e.g., university rectors, local police, or military commanders). Due to the uncertainty generated by low reelection rates, most new politicians remained active in other professions, allowing them to exit the political arena as quickly as they entered it.

The spread of amateur and semiprofessional politics may have important consequences for democratic governance. Outsiders who do not expect to sustain a political career have little incentive to invest in the development of political organizations and institutions. Moreover, they may have stronger incentives to engage in corruption—in effect, to "take the money and run" (see Muñoz 2010b).

Governability via Legislative Weakness

Weak parties have been widely linked to problems of governability in Latin America. Presidential systems with fragmented, inchoate party systems are said to be prone to executive-legislative conflict, institutional crises, and democratic breakdown (Mainwaring 1993; Mainwaring and Scully 1995). In post-Fujimori Peru, however, party weakness did not generate governability crises. Although divided government became a permanent fixture of Peruvian politics, party weakness enhanced the executive's capacity to co-opt individual legislators into an effective legislative majority.[28] Because most parties could not offer their legislators the prospect of reelection, legislators—most of whom had little or no prior history with the party—had little incentive to remain loyal. Governments could thus buy their support quite cheaply, via congressional perks, patronage jobs for friends or relatives, cash bribes, and blackmail (i.e., threats to investigate corrupt behavior).

Indeed, notwithstanding a decade of divided government, executive-legislative conflict was minimal in post-Fujimori Peru. Despite controlling barely a quarter of the legislature, Toledo had surprisingly few problems with Congress.[29] García was even more successful at legislative co-optation. Although APRA held only 36 of 130 seats in Congress, the García administration used a variety of perks to induce opposition legislators to vote with the government (Loayza 2008). For example, one group of legislators, known as "the Romans," abandoned the opposition after receiving trips to Italy.[30] Thus, despite its minority status, APRA controlled Congress throughout the 2006–2011 period, winning all leadership elections and losing few important votes.

Governability rooted in party weakness comes at the cost of democratic governance. The prevalence of amateur legislators undermines horizontal accountability. Indeed, Congress repeatedly failed to check executive abuse during the García presidency. It engaged in virtually no oversight of the executive, and opposition initiatives to investigate abuse or censure cabinet ministers repeatedly failed. For example, APRA blocked a legislative committee report on the 2008 "Petroaudios" corruption scandal that implicated top government and party officials, approving instead a report that effectively cleared those officials of wrongdoing.[31] And following the tragic June 2009 violence in Bagua, in which clashes between police and indigenous protestors resulted in the deaths of over thirty people, opposition-led votes of censure against Prime Minister Yehude Simon and Interior Minister Mercedes Cabanillas fell short.[32]

Amateur, single-term congresspeople are also less likely to invest in legislative capacity. Career legislators are critical to the development of a strong Congress. Not only do they possess the experience necessary to effectively oversee executive power, but because they have devoted their career to the Congress, their own power and prestige is closely linked to that of the Congress (Morgenstern and Manzetti 2003). In a Congress where 80 percent of legislators are novices and fewer than one in five are reelected, investment in institutional capacity is likely to be low.

Finally, a Congress dominated by amateurs may be especially prone to corruption. Amateur legislators with no prospect for reelection are often tempted to "get what they can" during their period in office. Indeed, post-2000 legislatures were plagued by personal corruption scandals. For example, the legitimacy of the 2006–2011 Congress was undermined by a series of public scandals involving individual legislators. The legislators involved in the most notorious scandals—nearly all whom were first termers—became household names, with monikers such as "electricity thief," "foot washer," "chicken eater," and "dog killer." Overall, a whopping 82 of 130 legislators were accused of corruption *at least once* between 2006 and 2009.[33]

Opening Politics (and Reinforcing Anti-Politics)

The breakdown of parties had a paradoxical effect on political representation. On the one hand, the narrow and predominantly white-skinned elite that dominated democratic politics prior to 1990 collapsed, opening up the political process to an unprecedented degree. Party collapse and fragmentation lowered the barriers to entry in the electoral arena, giving rise to a political elite that, while highly unstable, is far more socially representative than in the past. Politicians from diverse racial and socioeconomic backgrounds are now routinely elected to office. Alberto Fujimori (the son of working class Japanese immigrants) and Alejandro Toledo (who emerged from an impoverished and indigenous background) are but the most prominent examples of a pattern that has taken hold across the country.

Yet the collapse of the established party system and the emergence of a more open political elite has not reduced public hostility toward politicians. Indeed, it may have exacerbated it. According to the 2010 Latinobarómetro report, Peruvians' trust in parties and Congress was the lowest in Latin America, and the percentage of Peruvians who believe that politicians "govern for the public good" (16 percent) was the second lowest in the region (Latinobarómetro 2010, 73, 33).

Why do Peruvians distrust nonparty politicians as much as, if not more than, party politicians? Politicians everywhere are ambitious and power seeking. However, strong parties cloak politicians' individual ambitions behind a collective project. Politicians seek reelection, but as part of a collective project, and with a platform aimed at some longer-term public good. Without parties, politicians lack such cover: their ambition is naked, for all to see. Take *transfuguismo*. *Transfugas* jump from party to party in pursuit of the same goal as Swedish politicians: political survival. But whereas Swedish politicians advance their political careers within a single party, in Peru extreme party volatility creates distinct incentives: politicians who do not abandon declining parties will lose, putting their careers at risk. *Transfuguismo* is thus a strategy of political survival in a democracy without parties. The problem is that it is ugly. *Transfugas* appear nakedly opportunistic, without even a minimum of loyalty, principle, or interest in the public good. This perception may have reinforced Peruvians' hostility toward politicians.

Problems of Party Rebuilding (and the Paradox of Fujimorismo)

The question of how to rebuild parties has been a central—and unanswered—question in post-Fujimori Peru. The primary response of scholars and practitioners alike has been institutional. Electoral reforms such as smaller electoral districts, a 5 percent threshold for entry into Congress, a ban on independent candidacies, and organizational requisites for national parties were designed to reduce the overall number of parties and induce politicians to strengthen existing ones. Indeed, even as it became clear that these efforts at institutional engineering had failed (Vergara 2009), analysts continued to seek institutional remedies. Whereas some scholars focused on the enforcement of existing rules (Tanaka 2005, 109–23; Tuesta 2011), others proposed additional reforms, such as the introduction of a plurality electoral system (Sardón 2010).

Electoral reform is unlikely to resuscitate Peruvian parties. Strong parties are rarely, if ever, a product of institutional engineering. As both older and more recent research has shown, robust parties tend to be rooted in periods of intense political mobilization and conflict.[34] Polarization and conflict induce politicians to invest in political organization, mobilize activist bases, create bonds of loyalty and solidarity, and crystalize partisan identities and subcultures that often endure for generations.

Historically, most of Latin America's strongest parties emerged or were consolidated during periods of large-scale mobilization or conflict. The major parties in Colombia, Costa Rica, Uruguay, and El Salvador emerged out of civil war. The largest parties in Mexico, Bolivia, and Nicaragua were born of social revolution. Mass parties such as Argentine Peronism, Venezuela's Democratic Action, and Peru's APRA were born during periods of social mobilization and consolidated during periods of violent repression. Post-Fujimori Peru experienced relatively little polarization or social mobilization; consequently, conditions for party building were not favorable.[35]

Paradoxically, Fujimorismo may be a partial exception to this pattern. Although President Fujimori openly disparaged parties and never invested seriously in one of his own, his fall from power ushered in a period of political struggle for his supporters. Fujimorismo was ostracized after 2000, particularly during the 2000–2001 transition and the Toledo presidency. Pro-Fujimori politicians were confined to the margins of the political establishment, subjected to unfavorable media coverage, and at times insulted in public. Processes of transitional justice such as the Truth and Memory Commission excluded—and often vilified—Fujimoristas. Moreover, many Fujimorista officials were prosecuted for corruption or human rights violations,[36] and in 2002, three Fujimorista legislators, including former President of Congress Martha Chávez, were expelled from Congress. Finally, Fujimori himself was tried, convicted, and imprisoned in 2007. Although these trials were generally viewed—in Peru and abroad—as legally sound and legitimate, Fujimoristas viewed them as political persecution (Navarro 2011, 53–54; Urrutia 2011).

The "persecution" of the post-2000 period helped to remobilize Fujimorismo. Motivated by "indignation," "anger," and "hatred" (Urrutia 2011), Fujimorista activists transformed a "broken down" organization into a relatively vibrant social movement seeking Fujimori's return.[37] They organized meetings across the country in which Fujimori communicated directly with locals (in later years, via Skype); operated radio programs that transmitted Fujimori's messages, held events to celebrate key Fujimorista anniversaries, and mobilized protests against Fujimori's trial and imprisonment, the Truth and Memory Commission, and other transitional justice measures.[38]

Although Fujimorismo was hardly a mass party, it exhibited several party-building characteristics in the 2000s. First, it developed a strong identity and subculture (Navarro 2011; Urrutia 2011). Fujimorista identities were rooted in a set of shared referents, symbols, and language that crystalized during the post-2000 period. As ex-legislator Martha Moyano put it, the post-transition "persecution" was a "source of unity" that "helped to sustain us."[39] Likewise, Fujimorista Jorge Morelli observed that "there is no better glue for a political movement than a feeling of injustice. . . . We were like Christians in Rome."[40]

Fujimorismo also had a unifying ideology.[41] Though widely viewed as pragmatic and nonideological, Fujimoristas shared a national security ideology that emphasized the centrality of the state in ensuring order and public security. All Fujimoristas embrace the 1990s counterinsurgency, advocate a hardline against subversion, and deeply distrust human rights advocacy, which they view as soft on terrorism. During the 2000s, they denounced human rights trials, the Truth and Memory Commission, and other transitional justice measures as unjust—even treasonous—attacks on the armed forces. This national security ideology, which is rooted in the 1990s counterinsurgency,[42] is a major unifying force within the party.

Finally, Fujimorismo has a larger organizational base than is often believed, particularly in the low-income districts on the outskirts of Lima (Urrutia 2011). The main pillars of this organization are soup kitchens.[43] The Fujimori government invested heavily in building clientelist networks among soup kitchens, neighborhood daycare centers, squatters' movements, and other popular organizations. Because these organizations were largely ignored by Toledo and García, Fujimoristas had little difficulty rebuilding ties to them.[44] Due in large part to these linkages, Fujimorismo was easily the best-organized political force among the urban popular sectors in 2011 (Urrutia 2011).

In sum, the political conflict generated by the post-2000 transition reinforced a Fujimorista identity, ideology, and subculture among a modest-sized group of leaders and activists. These characteristics may facilitate Fujimorismo's institutionalization and survival beyond Fujimori himself.

Democratic Governance under Humala

Ollanta Humala's election in 2011 generated considerable fear among the Lima elite. Conservative commentators warned that Humala would install a leftist authoritarian regime like that of Hugo Chávez or Peruvian General Juan Velasco (1968–1975). *Peru21* editor Fritz Du Bois wrote that Peru would join an Andean "axis of evil" led by Chávez,[45] while *Correo* editor Aldo Mariategui claimed that a Humala government would be "worse than Chávez."[46] Indeed, many feared that Humala would, like Chávez (and Fujimori), use plebiscitary means to undermine liberal democratic institutions and impose a new—authoritarian—constitutional order.

Yet conditions in 2011 differed considerably from those in Chávez's Venezuela—or Fujimori's Peru. First, there was no crisis. Although many Peruvians were unhappy with the status quo, the kind of deep economic or political crisis that induces elites and masses to accept risky or radical change was absent (Weyland 2002). Indeed, surveys showed that most Peruvians opposed radical change. Unlike Chávez or Evo Morales, then, Humala did not win a mandate for radical change. Not only did he not wage an antisystem campaign in 2011, but his alliance with establishment figures such as Vargas Llosa and Toledo was essential to his second-round victory.

A radical or authoritarian turn would also generate opposition from a range of important actors, including a domestic private sector that was larger, wealthier, better organized, and more self-confident than at any time in the recent past; foreign investors, upon which the economy had grown highly dependent; the bulk of the national media, the Catholic Church, and Congress. Hence, a radical turn would risk generating broad public opposition, throwing a vibrant economy into crisis, and triggering an opposition countermobilization that could imperil Humala's presidency.

Finally, the regional context differed markedly from that of 2006. When Humala first ran for president, Chávez was at the peak of his power and influence. The Venezuelan economy was growing, oil revenue was peaking, and leftist victories in Bolivia and Ecuador generated regional momentum for the Chavista project. Five years later, the Venezuelan economy was in crisis and Chávez's prestige and regional influence were waning. At the same time, the political and economic success of the Lula government increased the regional attractiveness of the Brazilian model. This shift was manifested in the decision of new Left governments in El Salvador and Paraguay to eschew the Chavista path for a moderate one. In Peru as well, surveys showed an overwhelming preference for the Lula model.[47]

Given the potential cost of a radical turn and the attractiveness of the Brazilian model, a Venezuela-like scenario appears unlikely. A populist-authoritarian turn would run a substantial risk of failure—and perhaps a fall from power, as occurred to Lucio Gutiérrez in Ecuador (2005) and Manuel Zelaya in Honduras (2009).

Humala attempted to replicate the Lula model during his initial months in office, combining macroeconomic orthodoxy and redistributive social policies. He named an orthodox minister of the economy, retained García's Central Bank president, and declared a commitment to macroeconomic orthodoxy, foreign investment, and existing international agreements. At the same time, however, Humala announced a gradual 25 percent increase in the minimum wage, pushed through a Prior Consultation Law demanded by indigenous groups, expanded the Juntos conditional cash transfer program, and launched new programs to provide pensions for low-income retirees, college scholarships for low income students, and child care for working parents. To finance these programs, Humala negotiated a new windfall profits tax on mining companies that was expected to generate $1 billion a year in new revenue.[48]

Yet if Humala had little incentive to follow a Chávez-like path, he may have lacked the *capacity* to follow a Lula-like path. Three factors that were critical to the moderate Left's success in Brazil, Chile, and Uruguay were either weak or absent in Humala's Peru: a minimally effective state, a strong governing party, and experienced democratic leadership. With a notoriously weak state and a virtually nonexistent party, even the most skilled democratic leaders would face serious challenges in implementing socioeconomic reform in Peru. For Humala, who had never held elected office, the challenges were even steeper.

It was not long before such challenges emerged. In late 2011, a large-scale anti-mining protest in Cajamarca generated a cabinet crisis. Under pressure to establish the credibility of its new proinvestment orientation, the government declared that the disputed Conga mining project would go forward, imposed a state of emergency in Cajamarca, and briefly detained several protest leaders. The heavy-handed response generated opposition from leftists (and some liberals) in the government, dividing the cabinet. Humala responded by sacking left-of-center Prime Minister Salomón Lerner, his main leftist advisors, and several progressive cabinet members. Lerner was replaced by Oscar Valdés, a former military officer with no ties to the Left. The Conga crisis thus cost Humala his original team of advisers and destroyed his alliance with the Left. Moreover, the government's repressive response to anti-mining protests was viewed as an act of betrayal by many of Humala's original constituents, particularly in the interior. Under Valdés, the government abandoned its initial center-left profile for a more technocratic— and arguably center-right—orientation. It maintained a hardline stance toward anti-mining protest, and on two occasions (May 2012 in Espinar, Cusco, and July 2012 in Celendín, Cajamarca), protesters were killed in violent crackdowns. Humala's public support eroded, and in July, he shifted gears again, replacing Valdés with Justice Minister Juan Jiménez. The Jiménez cabinet adopted a more centrist profile, promising "dialogue" with protesters rather than repression. Having presided over three different cabinets and clumsy programmatic lurches from center-left to center-right and then back to the center, Humala finished his first year in the presidency with an approval rating of 40 percent. By mid-2012, he was more popular among the wealthy than among the poor. Humala's presidency seems unlikely to resemble that of either Chávez *or* Lula. Indeed, the more appropriate comparative references may be Fujimori and Toledo. Like Fujimori and Toledo, Humala was a politically inexperienced president without a real party. Like Fujimori, he underwent an abrupt and rather dramatic programmatic reorientation. And like Toledo, his initial months in office were marred by unforced errors and petty scandals.[49] Like both Fujimori and Toledo, Humala's first cabinet was highly heterogeneous (including neoliberal technocrats, ex-military officers, and leftists), which, in the absence of effective leadership, led to inconsistency and infighting. And in the absence of partisan linkages or effective state institutions to mediate social conflict, local protests became national-level crises.

A key question, of course, is whether the Humala government will ultimately threaten democratic institutions, like Fujimori, or respect them, like Toledo. Reasons for pessimism include Humala's illiberal background and near-total inexperience with democratic institutions, as well as the presence of ex-military officers in his inner circle. Indeed, the ascendance of ex-military advisors generated fear—now among the Left, rather than the Right—of a Fujimori-like authoritarian turn. Yet there are also reasons for optimism. For one, there is no crisis even remotely comparable to that which Fujimori inherited in 1990. Economic growth makes governing under democracy considerably easier. Second, given the weakness of parties in the legislature, a centrist Humala government should be able to co-opt a sufficient number of congresspeople to ensure a working legislative majority. Without a crisis or a recalcitrant Congress, incentives to assault democratic institutions should be weaker.

In some ways, these are the best of times for Peruvian democracy. The economy has boomed for nearly a decade, and the twelve-year-old democratic regime appears poised to become the longest-lived democracy in the country's history.[50] Yet public discontent with democratic institutions remains pervasive. This chapter has argued that persistent public discontent is rooted primarily in state weakness and party collapse. Unfortunately, political elites tend to invest seriously in state and party building only during periods of crisis or conflict.[51] Given the current boom, it is doubtful that contemporary Peruvian politicians have an incentive to make such investments. If they do not, Peru's democratic institutions will remain precarious, which does not bode well for their future when the good times (inevitably) end.

NOTES

The author thanks Eduardo Dargent, Jorge Domínguez, Carlos Meléndez, Paula Muñoz, Michael Shifter, Peter Siavelis, and Alberto Vergara for helpful comments on earlier drafts of this chapter.

1. *La Republica*, March 25, 2006. Also McClintock 2006.

2. Agencia Andina, May 13, 2010.

3. Quoted in Cameron 2011, 389.

4. Defensoria del Pueblo, *Reporte de Conflictos Sociales*, no. 64 (June 2009) and no. 89 (July 2011).

5. In 2007, García published a column in the newspaper *El Comercio* entitled "The Dog in the Manger," which compared protesters to the dog in Aesop's fable, whose snarling prevents hungry cattle from eating. The protesters, he argued, neither eat nor let others eat.

6. The author thanks Augusto Alvarez Rodrich for suggesting this point.

7. In April 2011, for example, García's approval rating among the wealthiest stratum of society was 66 percent, whereas his approval among the poorest sectors was only 18 percent. Ipsos-Apoyo, "Resumen de Encuestas de Opinión Pública" 11, no. 139 (April 2011).

8. El Comercio, June 9, 2008.

9. See Rivera 2011.

10. *La Republica*, May 15, 2011.

11. *Peru21*, April 25, 2011, and April 18, 2011.

12. *Diario16*, April 16, 2011.

13. *La Republica*, March 6, 2011.

14. *La Republica*, May 15, 2011, and May 18, 2011.

15. See *La Tercera*, May 24, 2011

16. According to the 2010 Latinobarómetro survey, for example, 61 percent of Peruvians agreed with the statement, "democracy is preferable to all other forms of government," which is equal to that of Chile and higher than those of Colombia (60 percent), Brazil (54 percent), and Mexico (45 percent).

17. Author's interview with Guido Lucioni, June 16, 2011.

18. With García off the ballot, APRA failed to even field a candidate.

19. Taken from Vera 2010; Coronel and Rodríguez 2011; Remy 2011; Tanaka and Guibert 2011.

20. Author's interview with PPC President Lourdes Flores, Lima, March 30, 2011.

21. Author's interview with PPC President Lourdes Flores, Lima, March 30, 2011. Also author's interviews with AP legislator Victor Andres García Belaunde (Lima, May 5, 2011) and PP leader Juan Sheput (Lima, May 5, 2011).

22. See Muñoz 2010a; Mendoza 2011; Zavaleta 2010, 2012.

23. See Ballón and Barreneachea 2010; Muñoz 2010a; Meléndez 2011; Muñoz and García 2011.

24. *Diario 16*, February 26, 2011, 8.

25. Taken from Degregori and Meléndez 2007, 136, and *La Republica*, May 27, 2005.

26. Where political parties are strong, low reelection rates do not necessarily inhibit political careers. In Mexico, for example, reelection is banned for all public offices.

However, politicians maintain their careers through institutionalized parties, which coordinate movement from one office to another.

27. Tanaka and Barrenechea (2011) and *Diario* 16, February 26, 2011, 8.

28. Similar patterns could be observed in Ecuador and Brazil during much of the 1980s and 1990s. See Mejía Acosta 2009.

29. Carlos Ferrero, who served as President of Congress and Prime Minister under Toledo, was so effective in co-opting legislative support that opposition leaders spoke of a "Pax Ferrerino." (Author's interview with ex-legislator Lourdes Flores, Lima, March 30, 2011).

30. Author's interviews with PP leader Juan Sheput (Lima, May 5, 2011) and ex-legislators Lourdes Flores (Lima, March 30, 2011), Guido Lombardi (Lima, May 4, 2011), and José Barba Caballero (Lima, May 4, 2011).

31. *Peru21*, January 16, 2009.

32. *Peru21*, June 30, 2009.

33. See *La Republica*, October 1, 2009.

34. See Lipset and Rokkan 1967; Huntington 1968; Hanson 2010; Slater 2010; and LeBas 2011.

35. By contrast, Bolivia and Venezuela *did* experience such polarization and conflict in the 2000s, which may give rise to more structured party systems. See Luna, Bidegain, and Reserve 2011.

36. Many of these figures were convicted and imprisoned, including Montesinos, ex-Prime Minister Victor Joy Way, ex-Interior Minister Juan Briones, and ex-Attorney General Blanca Nélida Colán. Others, such as ex-ministers Carlos Boloña, Cesar Saucedo, Absalón Vasquez, and Jaime Yoshiyama, legislator Martha Chávez, and Santiago Fujimori, received suspended sentences or were charged but not convicted.

37. Author's interview with Fujimorista leader Guido Lucioni (Lima, June 16, 2011). Also Navarro 2011.

38. Author's interviews with Jorge Morelli (Lima, June 18, 2011), Martha Moyano (May 6, 2011), Guido Lucioni (June 16, 2011), and Santiago Fujimori (Lima, March 24, 2011).

39. Author's interview, Lima, May 6, 2011. According to Fujimorista politician Guido Lucioni, "it is quite simple: more persecution, more Fujimorismo" (author's interview, Lima, June 18, 2011).

40. Author's interview (Lima, June 18, 2011).

41. On the importance of ideology for party cohesion, see Hanson 2010.

42. Author's interviews with Jorge Morelli (Lima, June 18, 2011) and Martha Moyano (May 6, 2011).

43. Author's interviews with Jorge Morelli (Lima, June 18, 2011), Martha Moyano (May 6, 2011), and Guido Lucioni (June 16, 2011).

44. Author's interviews with Martha Moyano (May 6, 2011), and Guido Lucioni (June 16, 2011). According to Moyano, Fujimorismo had ties to 2,000 of the roughly 3,000 soup kitchens in Lima in 2011.

45. *Peru21*, May 11, 2011.

46. Personal communication, May 31, 2011.

47. According to one postelection survey, 61 percent of Peruvians wanted Humala to be "more like Lula," whereas only 11 percent wanted him to be "more like Chávez" (*El Comercio*, June 19, 2011, p. A8).

48. *Gestión*, August 25, 2011.

49. Most notably, Vice President Omar Chehade—also a political amateur—was implicated in an influence-peddling scandal less than three months after taking office.

50. No Peruvian democracy has ever endured beyond twelve years.

51. See, for example, Slater 2010.

REFERENCES

Aldrich, John. 1995. *Why Parties? The Origin and Transformation of Political Parties in America*. Chicago: University of Chicago Press.

Ballón, Eduardo, and Rodrigo Barrenechea. 2010. "El Poder Regional: Mito y Realidad." *Poder 360* (December).

Barrenechea, Rodrigo. 2010. "Elecciones Regionales 2010: Liderazgos Políticos en Ciernes." *Argumentos* 4 (5).

———. 2011. "Que se Vayan Todos? Ya se Fueron!" *NoticiasSer.pe*. February 23.

Burt, Jo-Marie. 2004. "State Making against Democracy: The Case of Fujimori's Peru." In *Politics in the Andes: Identity, Conflict, Reform*, edited by Jo-Marie Burt and Philip Mauceri, 247–68. Pittsburgh: University of Pittsburgh Press.

Cameron, Maxwell A. 1994. *Democracy and Authoritarianism in Peru: Political Coalitions and Social Change*. New York: St. Martin's Press.

———. 2011. "Peru: The Left Turn that Wasn't." In *The Resurgence of the Latin American Left*, edited by Steven Levitsky and Kenneth M. Roberts. Baltimore: Johns Hopkins University Press.

Coronel, Omar, and María Ana Rodríguez. 2011. "Introducción: Continuidades y Cambios." In *El Nuevo Poder en las Regiones: Análisis de las Elecciones Regionales y Municipales 2010*, edited by María Ana Rodríguez and Omar Coronel, 3–7. Lima: Pontificia Universidad Católica del Perú.

Degregori, Carlos Iván. 2008. "Peru: A Missed Opportunity." In *Constructing Democratic Governance in Latin America*, edited by Jorge I. Domínguez and Michael Shifter, 264–84. 3rd ed. Baltimore: Johns Hopkins University Press.

Degregori, Carlos Iván, and Carlos Meléndez. 2007. *El naciemiento de los otorongos: El congreso de la república durante los gobiernos de Alberto Fujimori*. Lima: Instituto de Estudios Peruanos.

De Soto, Hernando. 1989. *The Other Path: The Invisible Revolution in the Third World*. New York: Harper and Row.

Diaz Rueda, Carlos. 2009. "CCT Programs in Peru." *Americas Quarterly* (Spring).

Economic Commission on Latin America. 2010a. "Economic Survey of Latin America and the Caribbean, 2009–2010: The Distributive Impact of Public Policies." New York: United Nations.

———. 2010b. "Preliminary Overview of the Economies of Latin America and the Caribbean." Briefing Paper. New York: United Nations.

Garay, Carolina, and Martín Tanaka. 2009. "Las protestas en el Perú entre 1995 y el 2006." In *Entre el crecimiento económico y la insatisfacción social: Las protestas sociales en el Perú actual*, edited by Romeo Grompone and Martín Tanaka, 59–123. Lima: Instituto del Estudios Peruanos.

Graham, Carol. 1992. *Peru's APRA: Parties, Politics, and the Elusive Quest for Democracy.* Boulder, CO: Lynne Rienner.

Hale, Henry. 2006. *Why Not Parties in Russia? Democracy, Federalism, and the State.* New York: Cambridge University Press.

Hanson, Stephen E. 2010. *Post-Imperial Democracies: Ideology and Party Formation in Third Republic France, Weimar Germany, and Post-Soviet Russia.* New York: Cambridge University Press.

Huntington, Samuel. 1968. *Political Order in Changing Societies.* New Haven: Yale University Press.

Johannsen, Julia, Luis Tejerina, and Amanda Glassman. 2009. "Conditional Cash Transfers in Latin America: Problems and Opportunities." Inter-American Development Bank Working Paper.

Kay, Bruce. 1999. "Violent Opportunities: The Rise and Fall of 'King Coca' and Shining Path." *Journal of Interamerican Studies and World Affairs* 41 (3): 97–123.

Kenney, Charles D. 2003a. "The Death and Re-Birth of a Party System: Peru 1978–2001." *Comparative Political Studies* 36 (10): 1210–39.

———. 2003b. *Fujimori's Coup and the Breakdown of Democracy in Latin America.* Notre Dame: University of Notre Dame Press.

Latinobarómetro. 2010. *Informe 2010.* Santiago: Corporación Latinobarómetro.

LeBas, Adrienne. 2011. *From Protest to Parties: Party-Building and Democratization in Africa.* New York: Oxford University Press.

Levitsky, Steven, and Maxwell Cameron. 2003. "Democracy without Parties? Political Parties and Regime Change in Fujimori's Peru." *Latin American Politics and Society* 45 (3): 1–33.

Lipset, Seymour Martin, and Stein Rokkan. 1967. *Party Systems and Voter Alignments: Cross-National Perspectives.* New York: Free Press.

Loayza, Jorge. 2008. "Decepción Nacional: El Reino de los Otorongos." *La Republica, Revista Domingo* (August 24): 6–8.

Lowenthal, Abraham F. 1975. "Peru's Ambiguous Revolution." In *The Peruvian Experiment*, edited by Abraham Lowenthal, 3–43. Princeton: Princeton University Press.

Luna, Juan Pablo, Germán Bidegain, and Roody Reserve. 2011. "Flourishing in the Desert? Socio-political Polarization and the Programmic Structuring of (Some) Andean Party Systems." Unpublished paper presented at the conference Polarization and Conflict in Latin America, ICIP, Barcelona, May 5–6.

Mainwaring, Scott. 1993. "Presidentialism, Multipartism, and Democracy: The Difficult Combination." *Comparative Political Studies* 26 (2): 198–228.

———. 2006. "The Crisis of Representation in the Andes." *Journal of Democracy* 17 (3): 13–27.

Mainwaring, Scott and Timothy R. Scully. 1995. "Introduction: Party Systems in Latin America." In *Building Democratic Institutions: Party Systems in Latin America*, edited by Scott Mainwaring and Timothy Scully, 1–34. Stanford: Stanford University Press.

Mauceri, Philip. 1995. "State Reform, Coalitions, and the Neoliberal *Autogolpe* in Peru." *Latin American Research Review* 30 (1): 7–37.

———. 1996. *State Under Siege: Development and Policy Making in Peru*. Boulder, CO: Westview Press.

———. 1997. "State Development and Counter-Insurgency in Peru." In *The Counter-Insurgent State: Guerrilla Warfare and State Building in the Twentieth Century*, edited by Paul B. Rich and Richard Stubbs, 152–74. London: Macmillan.

———. 2004. "State, Elites, and the Response to Insurgency: Some Preliminary Comparisons Between Colombia and Peru." In *Politics in the Andes: Identity, Conflict, Reform*, edited by Jo-Marie Burt and Philip Mauceri, 146–63. Pittsburgh: University of Pittsburgh Press.

McClintock, Cynthia. 2006. "An Unlikely Comeback in Peru." *Journal of Democracy* 17 (4): 95–109.

Mejía Acosta, Andres. 2009. *Informal Coalitions and Policymaking in Latin America: Ecuador in Comparative Perspective*. New York: Routledge.

Meléndez, Carlos. 2011. "Del chambar al 'Sancochado': El proyecto político de César Acuña." In *Anti-candidatos: Guía analítica para unas elecciones sin partidos*, edited by Carlos Meléndez. Lima: Mitin.

———. Forthcoming. "Perú: Las elecciones del 2011; Populistas e integrados; Las divisions políticas en un sistema 'partido.'" In *Elecciones y Política en América Latina*, edited by Manuel Alcántara Sáez and María Laura Tagina. Rosario: Homo Sapiens.

Mendoza, Raúl. 2011. "Partidos-empresa: La política como inversión." *La Republica Domingo*, March 30, 2011, 22–24.

Morgenstern, Scott, and Luigi Manzetti. 2003. "Legislative Oversight: Interests and Institutions in the United States and Argentina." In *Democratic Accountability in Latin America*, edited by Scott Mainwaring and Christopher Welna. New York: Oxford University Press.

Muñoz Chirinos, Paula. 2010a. "Consistencia política regional o frágiles alianzas electorales? El escenario cuzqueño actual." *Revista Argumentos* 4 (3). Online.

———. 2010b. "Political Organization as a Condition for 'Modern' Clientelism: The Case of Peru." Unpublished paper presented in the 29th International Congress of the Latin American Studies Association, October 6–9, Toronto.

Muñoz Chirinos, Paula, and Andrea García. 2011. "Balance de las elecciones regionales 2010: Tendencias, particularidades y perfil de los candidatos más exitosos." In *El Nuevo Poder en las Regiones: Análisis de las Elecciones Regionales y Municipales 2010*, edited by María Ana Rodríguez and Omar Coronel, 8–17. Lima: Pontificia Universidad Católica del Perú.

Navarro, Melissa. 2000. *La democracia volátil: Movimientos, partidos, líderes políticos y conductas electorales en el Perú contemporáneo*. Lima: Fundación Friedrich Ebert.

———. 2011. "La organización partidaria Fujimorista a 20 años de su origen." Undergraduate thesis, Department of Political Science, Pontifícia Universidad Católica del Perú.

Remy, María Isabel. 2010. "Elecciones regionales 2010 o el sueño de la candidatura propia." *Revista Argumentos* 4 (3). Online.

————. 2011. "Un balance final de las elecciones municipales y provinciales: En qué punto quedaron los partidos políticos?" *Revista Argumentos* 5 (1). Online.

Rivera, David. 2011. "Podrá el grupo comercio detener a Ollanta Humala?" *Poder* 27 (April).

Roberts, Kenneth M. 2007. "Latin America's Populist Revival." *SAIS Review* 27 (1): 3–15.

Sardón, José Luis. 2010. "Como optimizar el sistema electoral." PerúEconómico.com. October.

Schattschneider, E. E. 1942. *Party Government*. New York: Farrar and Rinehart.

Schmidt, Gregory D. 2003. "The 2001 Presidential and Congressional Elections in Peru." *Electoral Studies* 22:344–51.

Seifert, Manuel. 2011. "Colapso de partidos nacionales y auge de partidos regionales: Las elecciones regionales, 2002–2010." MA thesis, Pontificia Universidad Católica del Perú, Lima.

Siavelis, Peter M. 2013. "Chile: Beyond Transitional Models of Politics." In *Constructing Democratic Governance in Latin America*, edited by Jorge I. Domínguez and Michael Shifter. 4th ed. Baltimore: Johns Hopkins University Press.

Slater, Dan. 2010. *Ordering Power: Contentious Politics and Authoritarian Leviathans in Southeast Asia*. New York: Cambridge University Press.

Soifer, Hillel David. n.d. "The Origins and Persistence of State Power in Latin America." Unpublished book manuscript, Department of Political Science, Temple University.

Starn, Orin 1999. *Nightwatch: The Politics of Protest in the Andes*. Durham, NC: Duke University Press.

Stein, Ernesto, Mariano Tommasi, Koldo Echebarría, Eduardo Lora, and Mark Payne. 2006. *The Politics of Policies: Economic and Social Progress in Latin America, 2006 Report*. Cambridge, MA: Inter-American. Development Bank and David Rockefeller Center Latin American Studies / Harvard University Press.

Tanaka, Martín. 1998. *Los espejismos de la democracia: El colapso del sistema de partidos en el Perú*. Lima: Instituto de Estudios Peruanos.

————. 2005. *Democracia sin partidos: Perú, 2000–2005*. Lima: Instituto de Estudios Peruanos.

Tanaka, Martín, and Rodrigo Barrenechea. 2011. "Evaluando la oferta de los partidos: Cual es el perfil de los candidatos al próximo parlamento?" *Revista Argumentos* 5 (1). Online.

Tanaka, Martín, and Yamilé Guibert. 2011. "Entre la evaporación de los partidos y la debilidad de los movimientos regionales: Una mirada a las elecciones regionales y municipales desde las provincias, 2002-2006-2010." In *El nuevo poder en las regiones: Análisis de las elecciones regionales y municipales 2010*, edited by María Ana Rodríguez and Omar Coronel, 18–28. Lima: Pontificia Universidad Católica del Perú.

Tuesta, Fernando. 2005. *Representación política: Las reglas también cuentan*. Lima: Fundación Friedrich Ebert.

————. 2011. "Partidos frágiles y un congreso débil para los próximos 5 años." *La Republica*, April 23, 12–13.

Urrutia, Adriana. 2011. "Hacer campaña y reconstruir partido: Fuerza 2011 y su estrategia para (re)legitimar al Fujimorismo a través de su organización." *Revista Argumentos* 5 (2). Online.

Vera, Sofia. 2010. "Radiografía a la política en las regiones: Tendencias a partir de la evidencia de tres procesos electorales." *Revista Argumentos* 4 (5). Online.

Vergara, Alberto. 2007. *Ni amnésicos ni irracionales: Las elecciones peruanas de 2006 en perspectiva histórica*. Lima: Solar Central de Proyectos.

———. 2009. "El choque de los ideales: Reformas institucionales y partidos políticos en el Perú post-Fujimorato." Working paper, International Institute for Democracy and Electoral Assistance (IDEA). Lima.

Weyland, Kurt. 2002. *The Politics of Market Reform in Fragile Democracies*. New York: Cambridge University Press.

Wise, Carol. 2003. *Reinventing the State: Economic Strategy and Institutional Change in Peru*. Ann Arbor: University of Michigan Press.

Zavaleta, Mauricio. 2010. "Como se compite sin partidos? Política electoral en Cusco y Puno." *Revista Argumentos* 4 (5). Online.

———. 2012. "La competencia política post-Fujimori: Partidos regionales y coaliciones de independientes en los espacios subnacionales peruanos." Undergraduate thesis, Department of Political Science and Government, Pontifícia Universidad Católica del Perú.

CHAPTER TWELVE

Venezuela

Political Governance and Regime Change by Electoral Means

Ángel E. Álvarez

B y his death on March 5, 2013, President Hugo Chávez had ruled continuously for 14 years. The former president's coalition argues that four elections in support of Chávez represent a mandate to continue his socialist revolution, whereas the opposition claims that nearly half of the country opposes these policies. Elections under Chávez were peaceful, but extremely polarized, which is a serious impediment to democratic governance.

The late president and his changing political coalition have demonstrated remarkable resilience, not only winning the majority of the elections since 1998 but also enduring a military coup, two general strikes, and numerous street protests and riots. Boosted by his enduring popularity, President Chávez led a Bolivarian revolution that has shifted much of the economy into state-owned enterprises and centralized power in the hands of the president. Yet as the revolution advanced, the country fell in global comparative indicators, including democratization, transparency, freedom, and human rights. Still, the majority of Venezuelan voters believe they live in a democracy. While President Chávez demonstrated that he was capable of winning elections in a hostile environment, this chapter argues that democratic governance is much more than the staying power of an elected government.

The main challenges of democratic governance in Venezuela result from a three-level game of elite competition that prioritizes politics (namely, political competition) over policies. Each game—the regime game, the political coordination game, and the electoral game—revolves around elections as the arena in which politicians compete for regime change. High inflation rates, weak economic growth, extreme dependence on oil-rents, rising crime rates (particularly kidnapping and murder), and social unrest continue to challenge democracy in Venezuela. Yet the critical threat to democratic governance under Chávez stemmed from the contradiction between the goals of the revolution and the restoration of political and civil rights.

The Regime Game: Revolution and Democracy

The democratic credentials of Chávez's Bolivarian revolution are questionable. His government gradually imposed a radical transformation of state and property relations legitimized by electoral, "peaceful but armed" means ("Chávez insta a los cadets" 2010). Chávez stigmatized the opposition and labeled them traitors, while his followers alleged that only Chávez guaranteed peace and true democracy ("Cabello" 2012). The opposition has contested these claims, and has demanded the restoration of electoral political and civil liberties.[1]

According to international comparative indices of democratization, Chávez's regime set at a crossroads between democracy and dictatorship. Freedom House allocates a score from 1 to 7 for political rights and civil liberties, with 1 indicating the highest level of freedom; 7 corresponds to the lowest level. During the so-called "partyarchy" era (from 1973 to 1993), Venezuela scored on average 1 in political rights and 2 in civil liberties (Freedom House 2012). By 2011, it had declined to 5 on both indicators. The World Bank Worldwide Governance Indicators rank countries on a percentile rank, ranging from 0 (lowest) to 100 (highest). From 1998 to 2010, Venezuela's performance declined in five of the six dimensions of governance: in voice and accountability, Venezuela fell from 50.5 to 22.3 percentile rank; in political stability, it fell from 28.4 to 10.4; in government effectiveness the country fell from 20 to 14.8; in regulatory quality, from 40.7 to 4.3; in rule of law, from 21.5 to 1.4; and in terms of corruption, the country dropped from 16.1 to 7.2 (World Bank Group 2011). On each indicator, Venezuela compares poorly with the Latin American average, which averages a percentile rank of 53.8 for political stability and 61.5 for voice and accountability.

The Chávez government concentrated both political and economic power to undermine democratic processes. The president concentrated political power by centralizing oil revenue, reducing resources available to subnational elected authorities, packing the judiciary with progovernment judges, manipulating electoral rules to control the majority of seats in the legislature, and increasingly legislating by decree. The economic dimension of Chávez's revolution aimed to change the structure of property relations by nationalizing foreign companies and confiscating domestic private properties. The government progressively appropriated private property despite constitutional protection of economic rights. From 2005 to 2011 the central government confiscated 2,826 commercial and rural properties without payment and allowed the illegal appropriation of 529 private urban buildings and rural lands by nongovernment individuals and entities. Many of the private occupiers are essentially squatters, often characterized as "invaders" in Venezuelan media, who have been displaced from their own properties by natural disasters or difficult family situations (table 12.1). Ninety-five percent of the expropriated urban buildings and lands remain unpaid.

According to Latinobarómetro, 50 percent of Venezuelans are either "very satisfied" or "rather satisfied" with the way democracy works in the country, while the other half say they are "not very satisfied" or "not satisfied at all" (fig. 12.1). While Venezuela is not alone in being politically polarized—citizens of other democracies governed by left-wing parties such as Argentina, Ecuador, and Brazil are equally divided—disagreements over regime type are particularly heated in Venezuela.

Venezuelans have been divided on the democratic nature of Chávez's governance since 1999. On the day of Chávez's first inauguration, the president provoked a constitutional crisis by demanding a referendum on the election of a

Table 12.1.   Government Violations of Private Property in Venezuela, 2005–2011

Sector	Number of violations	Percentage
Appropriated by the government		
Industry and commerce	915	27.27
Rural lands	1911	56.96
Subtotal	**2826**	**84.23**
Appropriated by nongovernment		
Rural and urban properties	529	15.77
Total	**3355**	**100.00**

Source: Author's calculations based on unpublished data compiled and provided by Felipe Benites from the Observatorio de Derechos de Propiedad at the NGO Liderazgo y Vision (www.liderazgoyvision.org).

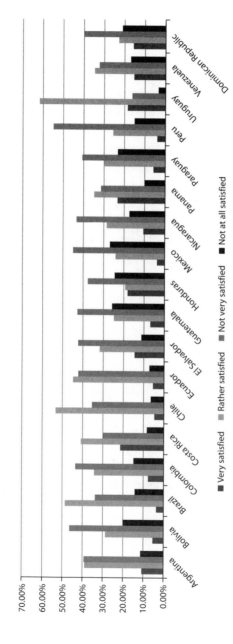

Figure 12.1. Satisfaction with Democracy According to Latinobarómetro, 2010

■ Very satisfied ■ Rather satisfied ■ Not very satisfied ■ Not at all satisfied

national constituent assembly. The 1961 constitution reserved such a power to the Congress, but the Supreme Court circumvented the provisions, exceeding its constitutional powers in the process (Brewer-Carías 1998). The Congress made weak attempts to avoid being shut down by the assembly but Chávez (with the support of the majority of the judiciary) easily won that round.

Due to the country's disproportional electoral system, in 1999, the Patriotic Pole—the pro-Chávez coalition formed by the Movimiento V República (MVR; Fifth Republic Movement), Movimiento al Socialismo (MAS; Movement toward Socialism), and Patria para Todos (PPT; Fatherland for All)—won 95 percent of seats in the assembly with just 62 percent of the vote, controlling 125 out of 131 seats. Chávez was reelected by a landslide in 2000. He won 59.8 percent of the vote, and his coalition controlled the majority in the new legislature although the turnout at 56 percent of registered voters was a record low.

The opposition parties' strategy at the time was misguided. Rather than support a traditional politician, they selected Lieutenant-Colonel Francisco Arias Cárdenas, second in charge during the February 4, 1992, coup attempt and personal friend of President Chávez. The alleged "divide-and-conquer" strategy failed, not only because Chávez won by a landslide margin but also because the ruling coalition remained unified, and Arias Cárdenas himself eventually reconciled with Chávez during the April 11, 2002, coup.

The regime game was played peacefully between 1998 and 2000, but from 2001 to 2003 bullets and stones progressively replaced ballots. Demonstrations began in 2001 as unions, business organizations, mass media, the Catholic Church, and education NGOs claimed that forty-nine decrees enacted by President Chávez unconstitutionally restricted property rights and civil liberties. In 2002, they were joined by several top managers of the government-owned oil company Petróleos de Venezuela (PDVSA; National Petroleum Corporation of Venezuela), who opposed the appointment of allegedly unqualified directors and criticized Chávez's oil policy, particularly Venezuelan subsidies to Cuba. In February 2002, the president fired seven managers during a nationwide mandatory radio and TV broadcast (one of his first long televised speeches, known as *cadenas*). The decision provoked a strong reaction from most PDVSA workers, who gained support from opposition politicians, mass media, military officials, and civil society leaders. Venezuelans (mostly from the middle and upper classes) crowded the streets of the major cities, demanding Chávez's resignation. The largest and more violent demonstration took place in Caracas on April 11, 2002, and led to a military revolt and the alleged resignation of Chávez.

Demonstrations against the coup, along with divisions among those who had staged it, saw Chávez return to power on April 13. The failed coup was followed by a three-month oil strike, more antigovernment riots (many of them violent: the so-called *guarimbas*), and the symbolic military takeover of Plaza Francia, a public square in the exclusive Altamira neighborhood of Caracas. The government reacted with pro-Chávez demonstrations and violent attacks against opposition demonstrations and independent journalists. The oil strike failed. Chávez finally fired about 20,000 out of 30,000 PDVSA workers and increased government control over the military.

In 2003, the opposition attempted to recall the president. The government implemented different strategies to delay the referendum. The Consejo Nacional Electoral (CNE; National Electoral Council), overtly controlled by Chávez's followers, disqualified about 75 percent of the signatures. The MRV leaders launched a campaign of political harassment in public workplaces by means of the infamous Tascón's List—a web-published list of about two million recall petition signers, obtained by the radical pro-Chávez legislator Luis Tascón from the CNE.[2] Several public servants included in the blacklist were fired, and voters were systematically intimidated. In 2004, the opposition tried again, collecting over 2.4 million signatures; this time the referendum was held on August 15, 2004.

Voter turnout was high at around 70 percent, and Chávez was reaffirmed with 59.1 percent of the vote. The opposition coalition—led by the Coordinadora Democrática, (CD; Democratic Coordinator)—claimed fraud ("CD Presentará" 2004), but they were unable to provide convincing proof or mobilize voters to defend their own results. This lost the opposition both credibility and electoral support. In the 2004 regional and local elections, opposition voters did not turn out in crucial regions, such as the Miranda state, where CD leader Enrique Mendoza was the incumbent candidate. Mendoza was defeated by Diosdado Cabello, a Chávez strongman. The opposition coalition, which suffered from severe coordination problems in many states and mayoralties, won a mere two states, Zulia and Nueva Esparta.

In another round of the regime game, in 2005, the opposition parties boycotted the legislative elections, alleging that the electoral roll was defective and the use of fingertip scanners for identity verification jeopardized secrecy of the ballot. They argued that the resulting legislature would lack legitimacy and would eventually lead to the collapse of the regime. The boycott succeeded, and the ruling coalition controlled the National Assembly until September 26, 2010.

In 2006, Chávez gained another term in office, with approximately 63 percent of the vote and a turnout of about 75 percent, which gave a boost to the revolution. That was the last opposition attempt to delegitimize Chávez's regimen by nonelectoral means. Since that year, the opposition has progressively abandoned confrontational strategies. Opposition leaders have come to understand that elections play a dual role in Venezuela: they legitimize the government's authoritarianism (which is its regime-game dimension) and create incentives for the ruling coalition to coordinate their efforts to maximize their chances of winning legislative seats and executive office (which is its electoral dimension).

Despite the intimidating practices used by the government and its "punishment and reward" strategies (Rodríguez 2008), opposition parties helped defeat a 2007 referendum that would have reformed sixty-nine constitutional articles, including the ban on consecutive reelection after two terms. This was the first electoral triumph for the opposition since Chávez came to power. Then, in 2008, the opposition coalition won important regional and local offices. They retained power in the two states they won in 2004 (Zulia and Nueva Esparta), and obtained a sound victory in three others (Miranda, Carabobo, and Táchira) as well as in Caracas Capital District, which was previously controlled by Chávez's Partido Socialista Unido de Venezuela (PSUV; Unified Socialist Party of Venezuela). The opposition also won some emblematic mayoral offices, including Petare—one of the largest, poorest, and most dangerous slums in Latin America, which had been under the administration of a pro-Chávez mayor since 2000.

In the 2010 legislative elections, the opposition won seven out of twenty-four states. The opposition won in the four most populated states (Zulia, Miranda, Caracas Capital District, and Carabobo), the seventh most inhabited one (Anzoátegui), and the largest cities with the highest concentration of urban poverty. It suggests that the electoral coalition behind each side of the Venezuelan polarized party system had changed. Today, the government is disproportionately stronger in rural, less economically diversified areas, whereas the Mesa de la Unidad Democrática (MUD; Democratic Unity Platform) coalition is disproportionately stronger in urban and more economically diversified areas.

The government disregarded the voters' mandate. The first and most emblematic distortion of the popular will was made evident when Venezuelans voted down the 2007 constitutional reform proposed by the president. Yet Chávez requested extraordinary power from the National Assembly to emit twenty-six decrees, which imposed many of the reforms rejected by popular vote. Indefinite reelection, the linchpin of the 2007 referendum, was put to voters again in 2009, and Chávez prevailed. There was one crucial difference between the two referendums: in 2007, only the president could be reelected, while the 2009 referendum provided that all offices were subject to reelection. Similarly, in 2008, after losing the election for the metropolitan mayor's office, the assembly created the Head of Government of the Capital District, an office appointed at will by the president. Most of the financial resources, buildings (including the mayor's working locations), and legal powers were transferred to the newly appointed authority. Finally, in the September 2010 legislative session, the main opposition coalition (MUD) won 49 percent of the vote to the ruling party's 48 percent. Despite gerrymandering and government-imposed reforms that allow members elected in overhang seats to keep their seats, Chávez's PSUV did not win the number of seats required to provide legislative powers to the president (60 percent). The opposition (MUD and PPT) won 52 percent of the popular vote and 41 percent of the legislative seats. To circumvent this relatively minimal check on his authority, Chávez requested, and was granted, decree powers until June 2012. These powers extended into the new legislature's term, and were considered unconstitutional by most Venezuelan legal experts. The Ley Habilitante (Enabling Act) clearly exceeded the constitutional powers of the National Assembly. In 2010, the government-controlled judiciary violated the parliamentary privilege (immunity from persecution), and denied three elected representatives the right to take the oath. The government also neglected to transfer resources to the states governed by opposition parties, despite constitutional mandate. This has been repeatedly denounced by governors Herique Capriles (Miranda), Herique Salas (Carabobo), César Pérez Vivas (Táchira), and Antonio Ledesma (metropolitan mayor). Although Venezuelan opposition parties have legal and effective opportunities to win office, their victories are often hampered by the electoral system and government practices. The 2012 presidential election was as unfair as the previous ones. The opposition organized by the MUD accepted the unfair conditions. They denounced the biases and failures of the CNE, but in the end they did not question Chávez's victory.

The Political Coordination Game

From 1998 to 2002, Chávez was supported by a heterogeneous coalition, with the Polo Patriótico (PP; Patriotic Pole), formed by the MVR, PPT, MAS, and Partido Comunista de Venezuela (PCV; Communist Party of Venezuela), winning the 1998 and 2000 national elections and referendums. Yet, the coalition heterogeneity created problems of coordination and discipline. In 2002, the MAS split into three factions; one of them, the most radical (PODEMOS) remained in the ruling coalition; a small faction (Vamos; Let's Go) attempted to create a form of "critical *Chavismo*"; while a third faction, which retained the original name of the party (MAS), moved toward the opposition field. At the same time, a few traditional social-democratic leaders who had played a critical role in the creation of the Chavista popular movement (namely, Luis Miquilena, Alejandro Armas, and Alberto Alvarenga) abandoned the ruling coalition, eliminating the moderate center-left wing of Chávez's movement. The pro-Chávez coalition became more ideologically homogenous as a result.

In 2007, the MVR was renamed Partido Socialista Unido de Venezuela (PSUV; United Socialist Party of Venezuela). Chávez ordered the fusion of the fourteen national parties and ten regional and local organizations into the PSUV. The largest satellites—Por la Democracia Social (PODEMOS; For Social Democracy), Patria para Todos (PPT; Homeland for All), Partido Comunista de Venezuela (PCV; Communist Party of Venezuela), and Movimiento Electoral del Pueblo (MEP; People's Electoral Movement)—refused to merge into the PSUV. The PCV, Movimiento Electoral Popular (MEP; Popular Electoral Movement), and a few of the small parties that initially contemplated fusion, including Unidad Popular Venezolana (UVP; Popular Venezuelan Unity) and the Tupamaros, named after the Peruvian indigenous leader Tupac Amaru and the Uruguayan urban guerrillas of the 1960s, chose to remain in the coalition but retain their party name. In the end, just a few of the much smaller regional parties obeyed Chávez's order, with some receiving generous returns. Fernando Soto Rojas, one of the most important leaders of Liga Socialista (LS; Socialist League), a small party that won just 0.5 percent of Chávez's votes in 2006, was elected the president of the National Assembly in 2011. Francisco Arias Cárdenas, leader of Partido Unión (PU; Union Party), was appointed ambassador to the UN and was Chávez's candidate for governor of Zulia in 2012. José Gregorio Briceño (dubbed El Gato, the cat), leader of the regional based Movimiento Independiente Ganamos Todos (MIGATO; Independent Movement We All Win), was reelected member as the governor of Monagas in 2008. Nonetheless, in general terms, the creation of the PSUV weakened the pro-Chávez coalition. Chávez won loyalty and discipline of his rank-and-file followers, but lost electoral support and some crucial political activists. Seeking to restore a broader coalition to face the 2012 presidential elections, Chávez created the Gran Polo Patriótico (GPP; Great Patriotic Pole), but it is simply the alliance of the majority party with the minority satellite communist PCV and multiple small social organizations (table 12.2).

Table 12.2.   Chávez's Vote Share by Parties in the 2006 Presidential Election and Their
Reactions to Chávez's Order to Merge into the PSUV

	Vote share (%)	Initial reaction	Final decision
Chavista total	62.18		
Movimiento Quinta República (MVR)	41.66	Acquiesce	Merge
Por la Democracia Social (PODEMOS)	6.53	Dissent	Split-up
Patria Para Todos (PPT)	5.13	Dissent	Split-up
Partido Comunista de Venezuela (PCV)	2.94	Dissent	Merge
Movimiento Electoral del Pueblo (MEP)	0.81	Dissent	Coalesce
Movimiento Independiente Ganamos Todos (MIGATO)	0.75	Acquiesce	Merge
Unidad Popular Venezolana (UPV)	0.68	Dissent	Coalesce
Clase Media Revolucionaria (CMR)	0.59	Acquiesce	Merge
Tupamaros	0.59	Dissent	Coalesce
Liga Socialista (LS)	0.50	Acquiesce	Merge
Movimiento por la Democracia Directa (MDD)	0.35	Acquiesce	Merge
Gente Emergente	0.25	Dissent	Split-up
Unión	0.25	Acquiesce	Merge
Movimiento Cívico Militante (MCM)	0.25	Acquiesce	Merge
Others (10 regional and local organizations)	1.31	NA	NA

Sources: Author's calculations based on official electoral data available from the CNE (www.cne.gov.ve).

    The pro-Chávez coalition faced fewer coordination problems than the opposition. The charismatic leadership of Hugo Chávez was crucial for the electoral success of the incumbent government: he controlled access to the ballots, the nomination of candidates, and the tickets for governorships, mayoralties, seats in regional and local legislatures, and even party bureaus. Chávez's control of his party was institutionalized by a 2010 reform of the political party law, which required that legislators vote along party lines or risk impeachment. By contrast, the anti-Chávez coalition makes decisions through far more complex and time-consuming negotiations, and also lacks a mechanism to enforce agreements.

The opposition is divided along three axes. One is ideological, the second is organizational, and the third corresponds to regional fragmentation. Opposition parties are spread all over the ideological space. On the Left they range from the radical Left, such as Bandera Roja (BR; Red Flag), to the Movimiento Humanista (MH; Humanist Movement) of the former guerrilla leader Douglas Bravo, and the PPT that formed part of the Chavista coalition until September 2010. On the Right members include the promarket, right-wing Proyecto Venezuela (PROVE; Venezuela Project), the traditionally conservative COPEI, plus a long list of center-right and center-left parties and individual leaders. The large majority of the Chavista voters (73 percent) considered themselves "socialist," whereas the opposition voters spread across three different doctrine positions. They describe themselves as Social-Democrats (41 percent), Christian-Democrats (23 percent), or Liberals (16 percent) (fig. 12.2).

The opposition is not only ideologically diverse, but also more electorally fragmented than the government party. At the national level, the pro-Chávez coalition is formed by five national parties (PSUV, PCV, UPV, Tupamaros, and MEP) and numerous other regional and local organizations. Yet, the effective number of pro-Chávez parties at the national level is one. Non-PSUV coalition members are little more than satellites that mobilize either extremely radicalized activists (such as the PCV, UPV, and Tupamaros), who consider themselves ideologically purer than the PSUV members, and minority local parties (MEP). The opposition coalition MUD, by contrast, is formed of twenty-nine political organizations and

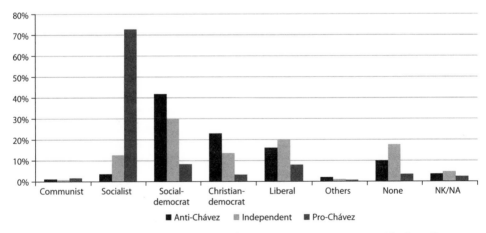

Figure 12.2. Ideological Fragmentation of Venezuelan Voters in 2011. Alfredo Keller y Asociados, *Encuesta trimestral*, Caracas, August 2011

Table 12.3.   National and Intra-Coalition
Fragmentation in Venezuelan Electorate According to 2010 Legislative
Elections

Coalitions/Parties	Vote share (%)	Effective No. of Parties
PSUV and allies	48.1	1.1
PPT	3.1	1
MUD	47.8	8.1
Total	100.0	2.1

Source: Author's calculations based on official electoral data available from the
CNE (www.cne.gov.ve).

based on the September 26, 2010, electoral results, there are eight effective opposition parties at the national level (table 12.3).

The PSUV won 94 percent of the pro-Chávez coalition vote in 2010, while
there is no such prominent member in the opposition field. Only four of the most
voted opposition parties gained two-digit vote shares: Un Nuevo Tiempo (UNT;
A New Time), Primero Justicia (MPJ; Justice First), Acción Democrática (AD;
Democratic Action), and Comité de Organización Política Electoral Independiente or Partido Social Cristiano de Venezuela (COPEI; Social Christian Party of
Venezuela). The three most successful parties obtained similar shares of the vote
(between 17 and 19 percent of the total national vote). One party (COPEI) won 10
percent of votes, while three parties gained between 4 and 6 percent. The remaining opposition parties received 2 percent or less of the votes (table 12.4).

Coordinating a coalition of many satellite miniparties and one big centralized
party, shaped and managed by a charismatic leader, is a far simpler task than har-
monizing a more pluralistic opposition. The opposition has been more successful
in the largest states, where it is also less fragmented, such as in Zulia, Táchira,
and Miranda. Nonetheless, the real problem of coordination is present at the
national level and is faced by the leaders of the so-called "group of seven," comprised of the seven parties with seats in the legislature plus the secretary general
of the coalition, Ramón Guillermo Aveledo.

The anti-Chávez coalition is also less nationalized than the PSUV, as evidenced
by the party nationalization scores (table 12.5) (Jones and Mainwaring 2003). The
party nationalization score for the MUD indicates that the coalition as a whole is
nationalized, but the majority of its members are not. AD is the single opposition
party with a relatively high score, and even in this case its individual score is lower
than the figure for the whole coalition. AD was also the third highest opposition

Table 12.4.   Opposition Parties' Vote Share in 2010 Legislative Elections

Political party	Vote share (%)	Political party	Vote share (%)
UNT	18.67	Cuentas Claras	0.92
MPJ	17.82	UNPARVE	0.67
AD	17.49	GE	0.54
COPEI	10.13	GERADIVU	0.43
PROVE	5.77	OPINA	0.39
PODEMOS	5.11	VP	0.36
MIN-UNIDAD	3.86	DALE	0.27
LA CAUSA R	1.96	FRUTOS	0.21
ABP	1.70	OFM	0.14
PROYECTO CARABOBO	1.40	Electores de Bolívar	0.11
BR	1.27	GOYOVA	0.02
MR	1.13	Others	8.67
MAS	0.97		

Source: Author's calculations based on official electoral data available from the CNE (www.cne.gov.ve)

party in 2011. The second highest party, MPJ, has a score larger than 0.5, but lower than AD, and much lower than the ruling PSUV. The highest opposition party, UNT, can be considered a regional party; it won 65 percent of its total national vote from one state (Zulia). COPEI, which used to be the second national party from 1958 to 1993, is currently a regional party of the Venezuelan Andes, specifically from Táchira (fig. 12.3, tables 12.5 and 12.6).

Ideological coherence, fragmentation, and nationalization make important differences in the efficiency of the two main political coalitions. Venezuela's opposition is much more ideologically diverse, hence programmatically incoherent, more regionally fragmented, and more regionalized than Chávez's coalition. Therefore, problems of coordination within the pro-Chávez coalition were easier to overcome, not only because of the former president's strong leadership, but also for institutional and ideological reasons.

Nonetheless, since the creation of the MUD, the opposition parties have found an institutional way to deal with their coordination problems in an increasingly efficient way. The first product of efficient coordination leads to the results of the 2010 legislative elections, in which the very heterogeneous opposition agreed on a unique national list and nominated the same candidates in plurality districts. For the first time since 2007, the opposition parties and the dissident PPT won the majority of the popular votes (49 percent and 3 percent, respectively). However, due to last-minute gerrymandering, the government was able to control the

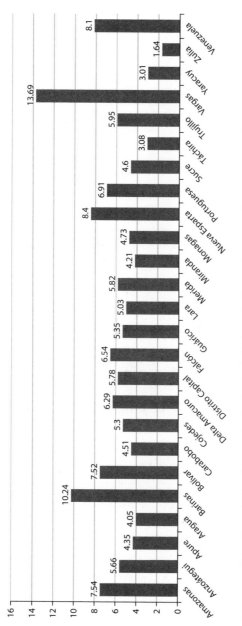

Figure 12.3. Number of Effective Parties in the Anti-Chávez Coalition, State Level, 2010. Author's calculation based on official electoral data available from the CNE, www.cne.gov.ve.

Table 12.5.   Nationalization of Venezuelan
Party System in 2010

Coalitions	Gini index	PN score
PSUV	0.09	0.91
PPT	0.74	0.26
MUD	0.16	0.84

Source: Author's calculations based on official electoral
data available from the CNE (www.cne.gov.ve).

Table 12.6.   Opposition Parties' Regionalization
at the State Level in 2010

Most voted opposition parties	Gini	PN score
AD	0.25	0.75
PJ	0.40	0.60
PODEMOS	0.42	0.58
COPEI	0.43	0.57
ABP	0.43	0.57
UNT	0.49	0.51
MIN-UNIDAD	0.52	0.48
PROVE	0.72	0.28
LA CAUSA R	0.69	0.31

vast majority of seats (60 percent, or 96 seats out of 163). Most of the opposition candidates to the legislature were appointed based on rules agreed by the parties. The rules essentially allocated candidacies among opposition parties on the basis of the results of the 2009 local and state elections. Each party employed different mechanisms to select their candidates including, in some cases, party primaries. In fifteen districts, where agreement was impossible, the rules mandated the organization of open primary elections. The PSUV organized closed primaries for all one hundred seats. The rest (sixty-five seats) were appointed by Chávez and top party leaders.

The second product of the coordination effort made by MUD was the 2012 open presidential primary, which involved six candidates from different political parties. Three of them were party leaders: Henrique Capriles from MPJ; Pablo Pérez from UNT; and Leopoldo López from Voluntad Popular (VP; Will of the People), and three others (María Corina Machado, Diego Arria, and Pablo

Medina) ran as independent candidates. Traditional parties (AD, COPEI, and MAS) supported Pérez, whereas smaller left-wing parties (PPT, PODEMOS, Causa R, and others) backed Capriles. The winner (Capriles) and the second runner up (Pérez) were governors of the largest states (Miranda and Zulia, respectively). They obtained 94 percent of the total vote cast (64 percent and 30 percent respectively, out of three million votes).

The turnout of 2012 primary elections exceeded any expectation. The elections highlighted the learning process undergone by the opposition. First, all the candidates accepted the results and enthusiastically supported Capriles. Second, in accordance with the primary rules established by the CNE, all regional electoral commissions of the MUD destroyed the list of voters in the election, despite a Supreme Court order that they be preserved by the military forces (the so-called Plan República, which regularly provides logistic support to the national electoral authority). According to the opposition leaders, the records were burned to ensure confidentiality and avoid the use of a new list to discriminate against and intimidate opposition supporters. These two facts revealed a level of political discipline and coordination that the opposition had not exhibited in the past. Yet, during and after the 2012 electoral campaign, recurring conflicts between MPJ and AD hampered political coordination and weakened the coalition.

Electoral Game: Un-Free but Meaningful Elections

In the Chávez regime, elections were unfair, but paradoxically they also were a crucial part of the story. From 1958 to 1998, nine national elections were held in Venezuela, whereas between 1999 and 2011, Venezuelans were mobilized to vote in fifteen increasingly un-free, but not meaningless, national elections (table 12.7).

The government has manipulated electoral and campaign laws to win the majority of seats with a minority of popular votes and has a strong influence on the CNE. Yet, elections are not blatantly fraudulent, and the opposition has been able to defeat the government though mostly in local and regional elections.

The opposition parties won the 2007 referendum, and in 2009 they won the most populated states of the country, one-third of the mayoral offices (including some in populated urban areas, such as Caracas and Maracaibo), and since 2011, they have controlled the presidency in four of the fifteen permanent committees of the National Assembly, as well as the vice presidency in four others. In 2008, the pro-Chávez coalition maintained control over the majority of governorships and mayoralties, winning sixteen states to the opposition's seven (table 12.8).

Table 12.7. Coalitions' Vote Shares (percentages of valid vote cast) and Turnout (as a percentage of total registered voters) in Venezuelan National Elections and Referendums, 1998–2009

Date	Election/Referendum	Pro-Chávez coalition	Anti-Chávez coalition	Others	Turnout
November 8, 1998	Congress (Lower House) election	33.8[1]	54.6[2]	11.6	52.4
December 6, 1998	Presidential election	62.5	31.5	6.0	66.5
April 25, 1999	Consultative referendum on constitutional reform				
	Question 1 (on calling a constituent assembly)	87.7	12.3		39.6
	Question 2 (on the electoral rules proposed by Chávez)	86.1	13.9		39.6
July 25, 1999	National Constituent Assembly election[3]	62.1	24.2	13.7	53.8
December 15, 1999	Constitutional approval referendum	92.2	7.8		44.4
July 30, 2000	Presidential election	59.76	37.52	2.72	56.3
July 30, 2000	National Assembly election (Lower House closed list PR seats)	61.11	37.67	1.22	44.4
December 3, 2000	Consultative referendum on labor-unions reform	69.4	30.6		23.5
August 15, 2004	Presidential recall referendum	59.25	40.74		69.9
December 4, 2005	National Assembly election[4]	100			24.9
December 3, 2006	Presidential election	62.96	36.98	0.06	74.7
December 2, 2007	Consultative referendum on constitutional reform[5]				
	Set A of yes/no questions	49.3	50.7		55.1
	Set B of yes/no questions	49.9	51.1		55.1
February 15, 2009	Constitutional amendment referendum	54.9	45.1		70.3
September 26, 2010	National Assembly election	48.2	47.2	3.14	66.4
October 7, 2012	Presidential election	55.1	44.3	0.6	80.5

Source: Author's elaboration based on electoral data available from the CNE (www.cne.gov.ve).

[1] Patriotic Pole (MVR, MAS, PPT).

[2] Anti-Chávez parties (AD, COPEI, PROVE, CONVERGENCIA). They did not formally join an electoral coalition, but in Congress they agreed on oppose Chávez's government and supported Herique Salas Römer's presidential candidacy.

[3] Owing to the electoral rules (plurality districts) the ruling coalition controlled 94.53% of seats (120 out of 131 seats).

[4] Anti-Chávez parties did not compete in an attempt to boycott the election.

[5] The CEN has neglected to report official results of the 2007 referendum.

Table 12.8. Coalitions' Vote Shares in 2008 Venezuelan Gubernatorial Elections

	Ruling coalition	Defector from ruling coalition	Opposition coalition	Defector from opposition coalition	Other	Electoral population (% of the total)
Caracas (DC)	44.94		52.42		2.64	13.09
Zulia	45.26		53.34		1.40	12.16
Miranda	46.10		53.11		0.79	10.14
Carabobo	44.52	6.56[a]	47.50		7.98	7.63
Lara	73.52		14.58		11.90	6.14
Aragua	58.92		39.81		1.27	5.95
Anzoátegui	55.09		40.59	3.34[b]	4.33	5.05
Bolívar	47.38		30.69	14.80[c]	21.93	4.72
Táchira	48.12		49.46		2.42	4.15
Falcón	55.36		44.40		0.24	3.22
Sucre	56.51	0.58[d]	42.21		1.28	3.20
Merida	55.04		44.70		0.26	3.00
Monagas	64.86	16.00[e]	15.02		20.02	2.92
Portuguesa	58.22	14.49[f]	26.93		14.85	2.87
Barinas	50.48	43.95[g]	4.93		5.57	2.55
Trujillo	59.96	13.22[h]	26.30		0.52	2.53
Guárico	52.54	33.20[i]	13.42		0.84	2.44
Yaracuy	57.83		28.91	12.01	1.25	2.05
Nueva Esparta	41.80		57.53		0.67	1.64
Apure	56.97		26.43		16.60	1.49
Vargas	61.57		32.19		6.24	1.37
Cojedes	52.44		39.59		7.97	1.11
Delta Amacuro	55.80		2.30	14.45	27.45	0.59

Source: CNE.

Note: The defector candidates are as follows: (*a*) General Luis Acosta Carles (multiple regional parties); (*b*) Benjamin Rausseo (PIEDRA); (*c*) Antonio Rojas Suarez (MPJ, PROVE, others); (*d*) Armiche Padrón (PCV); (*e*) Ramón Fuentes; (*f*) Bella Petricio (PPT); (*g*) Julio Cesar Reyes (multiple regional parties); (*h*) Octavio Mejía (PCV, PPT, others); and (*i*) Lenny Manuit.

At the local level in 2008, the PSUV won 269 mayoralties (about 82 percent of the total), the opposition won fifty-five (17 percent), and other parties (including the PPT) won a mere five (1 percent). While some mayoralties held elections in 2010, distribution of power between coalitions remained unchanged. Despite the overwhelming victory of the PSUV, the opposition won the metropolitan mayoralties of Caracas and the governorships of three of the five most populated states (Zulia, Miranda, and Carabobo). The former pro-Chávez and currently dissident governor of Lara, Henri Falcón, was reelected with an impressive 74 percent of the vote. While he received the support of the PSUV, he was not endorsed by Chávez, and since his reelection, the conflict between the president and the governor escalated. In the 2010 legislative election, Falcón left the PSUV and joined the PPT, which ran in the election against the Chávez coalition. After the legislative election, Falcón and the PPT adopted a clear oppositionist stance. The traditional anti-Chávez coalition also won in two smaller states (Táchira and Nueva Esparta). In total, 56 percent of Venezuelan voters were represented in the National Assembly by an anti-Chávez political organization or coalition (table 12.9).

A similar pattern can be observed in the 2010 election results. The PSUV won 48.2 percent of votes, leaving the opposition 47.2 percent, yet the opposition won the majority of votes and closed list seats in the Capital District and three most populated states. As a consequence of distortions in the electoral system and gerrymandering tactics, the governing coalition remained overrepresented in the National Assembly. Yet, the opposition won two more seats than the government. The government controlled 48 percent of seats, the MUD won 50 percent, and the PPT (formally pro-Chávez but now oppositionist) won a single seat in the legislature. This indicator suggests that, if all seats were proportionally allocated, due to the opposition predominance in the largest electoral districts, the opposition coalition would have probably controlled the majority of the legislature. Despite this unfairness, elections in Venezuela have been a peaceful mechanism to manage the extremely polarized political conflict.

A critical feature of the electoral politics in Venezuela is the lack of independence of the CNE. It has a five-member board, of which four members clearly favor Chávez's party, while one member is pro-opposition. The lack of autonomy of the CNE has been manifested in crucial decisions, such as the enforcement of the constitutional ban on public funding for electoral campaigns (Álvarez 2009). Despite constitutional prohibition, the government continually abuses state-owned mass media and other public resources. Government propaganda has included pictures of the president permanently posted on government vehicles, the Caracas metro system, street walls, billboards, and state buildings. Another important distortion of Venezuelan elections stems from the campaign funding system. The constitution bans public funding for politics, however independent NGOs have denounced the use of public resources to finance the ruling party's electoral campaigns.[3] The lack of an unbiased and transparent campaign financing system generates political inequities and corruption. Yet the National Assembly has not reformed the obsolete and inefficient regulatory framework of electoral campaigns

Table 12.9. Electoral Population, Ruling Coalition Vote and PR Seat Shares, and Most Voted Party by State in the 2010 Legislative Elections

State	Total electoral population		Ruling coalition		Most voted party	Most voted party share of votes (%)	Most voted opposition party
	Million	%	Votes (%)	Seats			
Zulia	2.19	12.6	44.4	3	UNT	54.8	UNT
Miranda	1.83	10.5	41.4	6	MPJ	57.1	MPJ
DC	1.55	8.9	47.7	7	MPJ	47.8	MPJ
Carabobo	1.39	8.0	43.2	6	PROVE	53.5	PRVZL
Lara	1.11	6.4	40.8	6	PSUV	40.8	AD
Aragua	1.09	6.3	50.3	5	PSUV	50.3	MPJ
Anzoátegui	0.94	5.4	45.0	1	AD	52.2	AD
Bolívar	0.86	4.9	45.6	6	PSUV	50.3	MPJ
Táchira	0.75	4.3	42.1	4	COPEI	56.4	COPEI
Sucre	0.59	3.4	51.4	3	PSUV	51.4	AD
Falcón	0.58	3.3	52.3	4	PSUV	52.3	AD
Merida	0.54	3.1	48.7	4	AD	50	AD
Monagas	0.53	3.1	58.7	5	PSUV	58.7	AD
Portuguesa	0.52	3.0	63.1	5	PSUV	63.1	AD
Barinas	0.47	2.7	56.3	5	PSUV	56.3	AD
Guárico	0.45	2.6	58.3	4	PSUV	58.3	AD
Trujillo	0.46	2.6	62.7	4	PSUV	54.6	CONVER
Yaracuy	0.38	2.2	54.6	4	AD	58	AD
Nueva Esparta	0.30	1.7	40.8	1	PSUV	60.5	AD
Apure	0.28	1.6	60.5	4	PSUV	54.8	AD
Vargas	0.25	1.4	54.8	3	PSUV	63.9	AD
Cojedes	0.20	1.2	63.9	3	PSUV	42.2	PPT
Amazonas	0.09	0.5	42.2	1	PSUV	71.5	AD
Delta Amacuro	0.01	0.1	71.5	4	PSUV	62.7	AD
Venezuela	17.36	100	48.2	98	PSUV		UNT

Source: Author's calculations based on official data available from the CNE (www.cne.gov.ve).

(Álvarez 1997), nor has the CNE enforced disclosure rules and mandatory monitoring of party and candidate finances.

The lack of the CNE's independence creates a dilemma for opposition parties. They face a tradeoff between participating in unfair elections, which legitimize the authoritarian rule but give them opportunities to gain seats, resources, and information, and boycotting the election to delegitimize the regime, but losing the opportunity to obtain partial victories against the government. This dilemma has resulted in erratic behavior—such as denouncing electoral fraud or corruption and, almost simultaneously, arguing that elections are the only game in town—and this has been a disincentive for opposition voter turnout. While NGOs, such as the influential Súmate, have criticized the CNE's impartiality (Súmate 2010b), there is a possibility that the critique may have reinforced the perception of electoral futility among some opposition voters.

Nonetheless, since 2006, despite blatant bias and unfairness, trust in elections has increased, probably because of the failure of other strategies such as strikes, demonstration, civil disobedience, and civic-military rebellion, along with some improvement of the electoral process.

The 2012 presidential campaign was business as usual. Chávez's was illegally financed with government money. State institutions, including the CNE, PDVSA, and the public media system, were blatantly biased against Capriles and the opposition parties. The opposition had no option but to denounce unfairness and corruption without any expectation of positive reactions from the CNE or the government.

Conclusions

The main obstacle to democratic governance in Venezuela is the nature of the political regime. President Chávez shaped politics as a revolutionary process, placing public policies, accountability, efficiency, and general governance in a secondary position. As a result, the main objectives of the government were to accumulate power, consolidate the institutional protection for the revolution, and maintain Chávez's position. In the opposition field, national policies were subordinated to an anti-Chávez strategy. The opposition's primary goal was to defeat Chávez, which explains in part why such heterogeneous parties can coalesce.

This chapter has characterized Venezuelan politics as a three-level game, and elections are the arena in which politicians compete for regime change and deal with coalition coordination. At the regime level, elections are instrumental in restricting political rights and civil liberties. At the political coordination level of the game, each politician attempts to solve the dilemmas of coordination within the coalition. These dilemmas emerge as a consequence of politicians' electoral ambitions, but also have the effect of political and ideological divergences on the pace of the revolution's radicalization (in the case of the pro-Chávez coalition) and the strategies to hamper the revolution (in the case of opposition parties). The main instrument of coordination in the progovernment coalition was Chávez's centralization of discipline enforcement and candidate nominations. The opposition has coped with coordination problems by multiparty pacts, supraparty organizations (CD and MUD), and multiparty primaries. And in the electoral game, politicians compete for votes and seats, but as elections are not the only game in Venezuela, the electoral competition is shaped by politicians' movements within the regime and political coordination games. This chapter has addressed the dilemmas faced by both pro-Chávez and anti-Chávez coalitions at each level of the game.

Venezuela not only faces political problems. Other important social and economic problems also hinder democratic governance. Among the most evident in the economic field are inflation and economic growth. Venezuela has the highest inflation rate in Latin America, hovering around 30 percent for over a decade. At the same time, it has one of the lowest economic growth rates in the region. In the social realm, Venezuela faces two important challenges. The government is dealing with an increasing eruption of social protest. From 2000 to 2011, the number of antigovernment demonstrations grew from 1,414 to 4,543 with at least thirty-three people killed in riots (Acosta 2012). Venezuela also has to cope with one the highest crime rates in the region. From 2003 to 2008, the homicide rate per 100,000 inhabitants grew from thirty-seven to forty-seven.[4] Three years later, the same indicator skyrocketed to sixty-seven homicides per 100,000 (Observatorio Venezolano de la Violencia 2011). Nonetheless, and despite the importance of these three issues, the most important challenge for democratic governance in Venezuela has been, and will likely remain, the nature of the political regime. Governance in Venezuela will become impossible without a healthy electoral democracy, which implies not only rule of law and independence of the electoral body, but also a much more cohesive democratic opposition.

NOTES

1. The Governor of Táchira, César Pérez Vivas, said that Chávez was leading the country to dictatorship ("Pérez Vivas" 2009). Armando Durán, a well-known politician and journalist, claimed that Chávez was a dictator (Durán 2010). The former communist and nowadays moderate Social-Democrat leader and newspaper editor, Teodoro Petkoff, recently said that Chavez was on the way to a dictatorship (Petkoff 2010). It should be stressed that Petkoff previously said on many occasions that Venezuelan democracy was threatened by authoritarian trends, but it was possible to speak out without fear.

2. Chávez, in a public speech in 2005, gave an order to "bury" the Tascón List, but he also recognized that the list was a necessary weapon to fight the "coup-monger opposition." In practice, the list is still regularly used by the government. See Hsieh et al. 2011.

3. See reports of the NGO *Monitoreo Ciudadano.* www.monitoreociudadano.org/; Súmate 2010a. www.sumate.org/Noticias/NPS/2010/343.htm.
4. See United Nations Office on Drugs and Crime. International Homicide Data. UNdata at http://data.un.org/.

REFERENCES

Acosta, Yorelis. 2012. "Análisis psicosocial de la protesta en Venezuela: 1999–2011." *Revista de la Escuela de Psicología.* Caracas: Universidad Central de Venezuela.

Álvarez, Ángel E. 1997. *Los dineros de la política: Competencia electoral en el mercado político e intervención del Estado.* Caracas: Universidad Central de Venezuela.

———. 2009. "El Consejo Nacional Electoral y los Dilemas de la Competencia Electoral en Venezuela." *América Latina Hoy* (Universidad de Salamanca) 51:61–76.

Brewer-Carías, A. R. 1998. *Poder constituyente originario y asamblea nacional constituyente.* Caracas: Editorial Jurídica Venezolana.

"Cabello: El único que garantiza la paz en Venezuela se llama Hugo Chávez." 2012. *El Universal,* March 10. www.eluniversal.com/nacional-y-politica/salud-presidencial/120 310/cabello-el-unico-que-garantiza-la-paz-en-venezuela-se-llama-hugo-chavez.

"CD Presentará Mañana Primer Informe sobre el Fraude." 2004. *El Universal,* September 7. www.eluniversal.com/2004/09/07/.

"Chávez insta a los cadetes a defender la revolución." 2010. *Noticiero Digital,* September 3. www.youtube.com/watch?v=I6KoElJ-jXQ.

Durán, Armando. 2010. "¿Dictadura o democracia?" *El Nacional,* June 21.

Freedom House. 2012. *Freedom in the World.* www.freedomhouse.org/report-types/free dom-world.

Hsieh, C. -T., M. Edward, D. Ortega, and F. Rodríguez. 2011. "The Price of Political Opposition: Evidence from Venezuela's Maisanta." *American Economic Journal: Applied Economics* 3 (2): 196–214.

Jones, Mark P., and Scott Mainwaring. 2003. "The Nationalization of Parties and Party Systems: An Empirical Measure and an Application to the Americas." Working paper, no. 304. Notre Dame: Kellogg Institute for International Studies.

Monitoreo Ciudadano. 2011. *Alerta Electoral #2: Un candidato compite contra el Estado (informe).* July 17. www.monitoreociudadano.org/.

"Observatorio Venezolano de la violencia: Informe homicidios." 2011. December 29. Caracas. www.observatoriodeviolencia.org.ve.

"Pérez Vivas: Chávez lleva al país por el camino de la dictadura." 2009. *El Universal,* June 16.

Petkoff, Teodoro. 2010. "Camino a la dictadura." *Tal Cual,* December 15. www.talcual digital.com/note/visor.aspx?id-45707.

Rodríguez, Francisco. 2008. "Venezuela's Revolution in Decline: Beware of the Wounded Tiger." *World Policy Journal* (Spring): 45–58.

Súmate. 2010a. "CNE debe evitar uso de recursos del Estado a favor de una parcialidad Participación de funcionarios públicos en campaña electoral es una violación a la constitución y leyes." Accessed September 9, 2010. www.sumate.org/Noticias/NPS /2010/343.htm.

Súmate. 2010b. *Independencia de los poderes públicos: ¿Está el poder electoral controlado por el poder ejecutivo?* Accessed February 11, 2010. http://infovenezuela.org/democ racy/cap1_es_3.htm.

United Nations Office on Drugs and Crime. 2011. International Homicide Data. Accessed February 15, 2011. UNdata at http://data.un.org/.

World Bank Group. 2011. "The Worldwide Governance Indicators (WGI) Project." http://info.worldbank.org/governance/wgi/sc_chart.asp.

Conclusion

*Early Twenty-first Century Democratic
Governance in Latin America*

Jorge I. Domínguez

By the start of the second decade of the twenty-first century, most Latin Americans lived under constitutional democratic regimes. Most elections were free, fair, and closely contested under universal suffrage. The opposition in most countries had a reasonable chance of winning a national election, and thus the outcome of elections was often uncertain, which is exactly as it should be in constitutional democracies. Basic freedoms of speech, mass media, assembly, and organization characterized politics and society in most countries, enabling candidates, political parties, nongovernmental organizations, and social movements to shape the public arena.[1]

One reason for this outcome is that most Latin Americans live in Brazil and Mexico where, early in the century's first decade, national elections crossed key thresholds in the evolving story of democratic transition and consolidation. Each of these elections highlighted important political themes in each country. Consider the cases.[2]

Rabble-rouser. Radical. Left-winger. Threat to prosperity. Dangerous socialist. These and other adjectives were used to describe Luiz Inácio "Lula" da Silva, from his first appearance in the late 1970s on Brazil's national political stage as a labor union leader, until his first election as president of Brazil in 2002. During the 2002 presidential campaign, domestic and international markets quaked because they continued to view Lula as a grave threat to the market economy. Interest rates spiked; there was also exchange-rate turmoil as Brazil's currency, the *real*, fell sharply relative to other currencies (Martínez and Santiso 2003, 363–88). By the end of his two terms as Brazilian president in 2010, however, as David Samuels shows in his chapter, Lula had become a highly successful president who had worked to lead Brazil to high rates of economic growth through market-conforming policies. He helped to build democracy and the market economy simultaneously.

In retrospect, Brazil's 2002 presidential election was a watershed in the history of democratic and market consolidation in Brazil. It demonstrated the effectiveness of Brazil's constitutional order through the public formulation and expression of opposing views and the fair and effective operation of its electoral institutions under the rule of law. It featured the role of parties, civil society, and a free mass media.

- It was the first time in forty years that one popularly elected Brazilian president, Fernando Henrique Cardoso, passed the sash of office to another, Lula.
- It transferred political power from the governing party to the opposition party.
- The election was hotly contested, with free, vigorous mass media coverage, and broad and deep engagement from civil society and political parties.
- Lula signaled transparently during his 2002 campaign that he and his party had changed their views and would henceforth "hug" the political center including the market economy.[3]
- Lula and his party went on to fulfill the promises made during the campaign, including significant continuity, with plausible adjustments, of his predecessor's successful market-oriented economic policies and social policies.
- By the end of the decade, significant progress had been made to incorporate all Brazilian social classes into the political process.

Brazilian citizens and their leaders constructed the country's democratic transition and consolidation. International factors were secondary, but not insignificant, however. During the 2002 presidential campaign, the Brazilian government required support from the International Monetary Fund (IMF) to stabilize the economy and calm international bond and exchange-rate markets. During the campaign, Lula publicly endorsed the IMF economic stabilization plan and promised to implement it upon his election as president; this was part of his strategy to signal credibly that he had changed his policy preferences. The US government, under President George W. Bush, supported the agreement between the IMF and Brazil. Indeed, it is no hyperbole that the IMF and the Bush administration contributed to Lula's election as president of Brazil and, in that way, to the consolidation of Brazil's democracy and prosperity. Democratic politics is always built at home, but it is easier to build with a supportive international community.

Now, consider Mexico.[4] It was 11 p.m. on July 2, 2000. The television networks, broadcasting from the Federal Electoral Institute (IFE), turned their cameras on the Institute's president, who was about to give the preliminary results of Mexico's 2000 presidential election. Speaking in a rushed monotone, he reported on the "quick counts" and other technical means of verifying the voting in advance of the complete count. He referred to statistical significance, or the lack thereof, of these tests, making the dramatic appear dull; he concluded on the cautious note that Vicente Fox, the candidate of an opposition party, Partido Acción Nacional (PAN; National Action Party), seemed ahead.

With a break that lasted only seconds, the television networks turned their cameras on President Ernesto Zedillo at his presidential office in Los Pinos. Zedillo, dressed formally for this occasion, wore the tricolor presidential sash across his chest. Behind him were two icons of republican Mexico. One was a gigantic flag of Mexico. The other was a portrait of the nineteenth-century president Benito Juárez. Zedillo spoke deliberately, pausing for effect and clear public understanding. Without hesitation, he boldly congratulated Vicente Fox on his election as president of Mexico and pledged that his administration would cooperate fully during the upcoming five-month transition period. He called upon his party, the Partido Revolucionario Institucional (PRI; Revolutionary Institutional Party), to be proud of a long record of accomplishment in the transformation of Mexico—under various names and formulations, the same party had ruled for seventy-one years—and, in that spirit, to support the election outcome.

Again with a short break lasting only seconds, the television cameras next turned their lights on the PRI headquarters and on the party's presidential candidate, Francisco Labastida. PRI leaders looked stunned. Some in the crowd shed tears. Then someone was inspired to start singing the national anthem, and others joined in. The special broadcast in its three parts lasted about ten minutes. It would be followed with images of Fox supporters celebrating in downtown Mexico City and elsewhere as the evening wore on. This account illustrates five changes in Mexican national politics that have endured.

- Television and radio were the means to communicate the remarkable transfer of political power that had just occurred.
- The constitutional reorganization of Mexico's electoral institutions proved essential to permit and enact a free election.
- Free, professional public opinion polling, and the associated technical work of academics, was an important instrument for this transition.
- The leadership of the outgoing president was also essential to impart confidence that the election outcome would be respected.
- Both the long-ruling PRI and the long-lived opposition PAN had changed to make a free, fair, hotly contested election possible.

In Mexico in 2000 as in Brazil in 2002, citizens and their leaders constructed democratization, yet international factors played a supportive role. In Mexico, Wall Street, London, Hong Kong, the Clinton administration, and other international actors conveyed the same message: let the election be free and fair—a good election was more important than the victory of a particular candidate.

Mexico's 2000 presidential election, as had been the case in its 1994 and 1997 national elections, featured a significant number of international and especially domestic civil society observers. Domestic and transnational civil society as well as election observation contributed to democratic practice.

The construction of Mexico's democratic transition also required that opposition leaders and their supporters shed the self-paralyzing expectation that the long-ruling party would commit electoral fraud and abuse. Parties must believe in the possibility of winning in order to be able to win.

The slow process of political transition in Mexico during the 1990s and in Brazil in the 1980s facilitated and contributed to democratic consolidation in both countries in the 2000s. As Shannon O'Neil's chapter on Mexico shows, the challenges of democratic governance remain formidable, especially in the area of security from criminal violence. Yet, most Latin Americans, living in Brazil and Mexico, experience democratic governance, market-oriented economic policies, more effective social policies, open political party contestation, opportunities to participate in civil society organizations, and freer mass media (see Taylor Boas's chapter for scope and limitations). The principal story in the respective processes of democratization was written at home, though in each case a benign international environment helped.

Latin America's Four Transitions

In the 1960s and 1970s, military coups overthrew constitutional democracies across South America except for Colombia and Venezuela, and in the 1970s, civil war and international intervention marked the experiences of many countries in Central and South America. In 1978, a transition to constitutional democracy began in the Dominican Republic when international intervention prevented election fraud to extend President Joaquín Balaguer's twelve years in office. Soon thereafter Ecuador and Peru held free elections won by the candidates most opposed to military rule. During the 1980s, civilian presidents would replace all of South America's military rulers. In early 1990, General Augusto Pinochet, who had governed Chile since a 1973 military coup, stepped down as president of Chile; his bid to extend his rule had been defeated in a plebiscite held in 1988. Since 1990, no military officer on active duty has served as president of any Latin American country. This process marked a double transition, therefore. One is the shift from an authoritarian to a democratic regime; the other is a change in the role of the military and other security forces in Latin American countries.

Starting in Chile in the 1980s, and spreading throughout the region during decades that followed, there were also significant economic transitions. Latin America suffered from a catastrophic economic crisis in the early 1980s. The region's performance during that decade was the worst since the worldwide economic depression of the 1930s. In response, Latin American governments shifted toward more market-conforming economic policies. Financial panics recurred, however, though often focused on specific countries (Mexico 1994, Brazil 1999, and Argentina 2001, among others). During the first decade of the twenty-first century, market-conforming economic policies continued to prevail in most Latin American countries, but the results of a widespread economic boom that stemmed from rising worldwide commodity prices raised considerable revenues for states. Some designed new social policies; others, new forms of state intervention in the economy, as argued in Sebastián Mazzuca's chapter.

To these various regimes, military, and economic transitions was added a fourth transition—cross-country and intertemporal variability in presidential tenure. On the one hand, military coup attempts had become much less common. Since the mid-1970s, only twice—Ecuador in 2000 and Honduras in 2009—did military coups overthrow an elected civilian president, albeit to install a different civilian as president, and additionally, only in Venezuela in 2002 was the president removed from office for a few hours until he regained his office. On the other hand, since 1990 a constitutional presidency has been interrupted short of a military coup or insurrection in ten of the eighteen Latin American countries (Brazil, six of the nine Spanish-speaking South American countries, the Dominican Republic, Guatemala, and Honduras). Presidential resignation under threat of constitutional impeachment or comparable parliamentary action occurred in Brazil 1992, Venezuela 1993, Ecuador 1997, 2000, and 2005, Paraguay 1999, Peru 2000, Argentina 2001, and Bolivia 2003 and 2005.[5]

Under the impact of the worldwide commodity boom, however, since the mid-2000s a president has been forced out only in Honduras in 2009, as one component of a military coup. The institutional foundations of presidentialist constitutional democracy were shaken during difficult economic times, even though the military for the most part remained firmly in the barracks, but the widespread commodity boom prosperity protected most incumbents across the ideological spectrum.

Civil-Military Relations

The transition from authoritarian rule would in the end render military coups a much less important route to political power than they had been in Latin America's past. Since 1990, however, three military leaders of coup attempts would eventually be elected civilian president of their respective countries. Hugo Chávez and Ollanta Humala led failed coup attempts in 1992 and 2000 but were subsequently elected president of Venezuela in 1998 and Peru in 2011, respectively. Lucio Gutiérrez was one of the leaders of the successful overthrow of Ecuador's president in 2000 and was elected president in 2002.

There is little variation in the incidence of military coups in Latin America: they are rare. There is greater variation, however, with regard to military influence. The most dramatic increase in military influence occurred in Venezuela, as highlighted in the chapter by Ángel Álvarez. President Chávez made military involvement in society and economy a hallmark of his rule.

The most noteworthy resurgence of civilian control over the military occurred in Chile. The turning point was the arrest of former dictator Augusto Pinochet in London in 1998. Subsequent actions of the Chilean Supreme Court and other Chilean courts revealed abuses and corruption during the Pinochet years, impelling the armed forces and the political parties that once had supported Pinochet to distance themselves from many aspects of his rule. The highly professional Chilean armed forces became subordinate to civilian authorities and cooperated with investigations of human rights abuses and political killings. In 2005, Chile's constitutional reforms abolished most elements of the privileged position of the military, discussed in Siavelis's chapter, and terminated all the hitherto constitutionally mandated authoritarian enclaves, except for the still privileged access of the military to earnings from international copper exports for weapons purchases. The Chilean military still plays a disproportionate role in setting its own budget and designing and overseeing the training of the officer corps, but the trajectory over the quarter century since the end of Pinochet's rule has been positive.

Also significant was the reduction of military influence in Peru. In 1992, the military backed President Alberto Fujimori's coup against the Congress and courts. The military played an influential role in the successful battle against the Sendero Luminoso (Shining Path) insurgency, which Peru had suffered since 1980. As a result, the military remained influential until President Fujimori's resignation in 2000. Interim President Valentín Paniagua dismissed the upper echelon of the armed forces and thus contributed powerfully to the proper subordination of the armed forces to civilian authority.

What explains these broad trends? In the first edition of this book, Jeanne Kinney Giraldo and I identified two factors to account for the changed role of the military, which was essential for democratic transitions and consolidation and for the decline in the incidence of successful military coups. The "supply" of coup efforts dried up. The military governments engaged in human rights abuses, repressed public liberties, and also mismanaged the economy and fell prey to corruption, damaging the military in the process. Military officers did not want to repeat those experiences.

The "demand" for coups also fell. Except for General Pinochet's government in Chile and, thanks to the oil boom, Ecuador's military government in the 1970s, long-term economic growth and sound management did not characterize military rule. Most dictators presided over declining living standards, and some committed acts of cruelty. Neither political parties nor business elites would think of military rule as a good solution to the problems of governance; instead, business elites turned to center or center-right parties, which have performed well in elections in Brazil, Colombia, and Central America, won two consecutive presidential elections in Mexico since 2000, and won the 2010 presidential election in Chile. Even during Argentina's economic collapse in 2000–2001, the demand for military coups dropped everywhere and, outside of Ecuador, Honduras, and Venezuela, it has disappeared in most countries. This pattern of decline in the "demand" for military coups, moreover, is part of a worldwide trend. The end of the Cold War deprived would-be coup makers of anticommunist "national security" rationales and US government support for coups. International action to prevent or halt coups, through the Organization of American States or the concerted actions of neighboring governments, also became more effective.

Explanations that highlight international factors or the decline in the demand for coups are fairly constant across countries; therefore, they cannot explain the variation in the frequency of coup attempts or in military influence over politics short of coups. Nor does variation in professionalism explain variation in military influence. A highly professional military has much influence in Chile but not in Argentina; a much less professional military has much influence in Peru (before as well as under the Humala presidency) but not in Mexico.

It is the variation in civilian demand for military influence in politics that explains the variation in such influence. Civilian demand for military influence dropped in Chile, Colombia, and Peru, and so did such influence. Civilian demand for military influence in politics remained high in Ecuador, Paraguay, and northern Central America, and so did such influence. President Chávez deliberately politicized the Venezuelan military, as Álvarez argues in his chapter, and so its influence increased. Only in Venezuela did demand for military influence increase, and this increase in Venezuela may be traced directly to President Chávez. In general, therefore, the assertion of civilian supremacy over the armed forces is the prevailing pattern, albeit with the noted important exceptions.

Responsible and Reliable Parties

Parties are the most effective instruments to articulate and aggregate social, economic, and political demands; set priorities; and respond to those demands and challenges. Parties organize parliamentary politics to support or oppose the executive. Bargaining between parties may reduce the level of conflict and creates the political space for the rise and consolidation of "arbiter" institutions such as the courts. Parties are heroes in the important stories in Brazil and Mexico that open this chapter. A key story across Latin America early in the twenty-first century has been that parties and politicians have honored their promises to the electorate—and in this respect there has been an impressive change over the last quarter century.

A half-century ago, Anthony Downs identified two traits of democratic parties: reliability and responsibility. "A party is reliable," he wrote, "if its policy statements at the beginning of an election period—including those in its pre-election campaign—can be used to make accurate predictions of its behavior." That is why, in this chapter's opening, I highlighted Lula's public transparency during the 2002 presidential election campaign. Downs also argued that a "party is responsible if its policies in one period are consistent with its actions (or statements) in the preceding period" (Downs 1957, 104–5). Mexico's PAN turned out to be a responsible party under its two different presidents between 2000 and 2012. Partisan reliability and responsibility are at the core of democratic politics. Democracy rests on the promise that parties do not intend to deceive the voters and that their candidates expect to govern within the broad parameters of their preelection promises. Voters should want more than just this from politicians and parties, but they must want at least this much from them.

By those standards, many parties in Latin American countries were unreliable and irresponsible in the late 1980s and early 1990s. There was a very wide gap between a presidential candidate's campaign promises and the policy choices as president (Stokes 2001, chap. 2). Thus parties were not reliable. The presidential campaigns of Carlos Andrés Pérez in Venezuela and Carlos Menem in Argentina, both in 1989, or of Alberto Fujimori in Peru in 1990, gave no hint of the strong market orientation of their economic policies once elected to the presidency. There was also a deep discrepancy between administrations of the same political party. Venezuela's successive Acción Democrática (AD; Democratic Action) administrations of Jaime Lusinchi and Carlos Andrés Pérez followed dramatically different policies before and after the 1998 presidential election. Mexico's PRI followed policies that differed just as markedly before and after the 1982 presidential election when Miguel de la Madrid replaced José López Portillo. Their parties were not "responsible."

Much has changed. Of the fifteen presidential elections held between 1988 and 1991 in fifteen Latin American countries, seven featured a dramatic switch between what parties promised during the campaign and what the candidates did once in office. Between 1992 and 1995, however, only three out of fourteen presidential elections featured such a dramatic switch (Stokes 2001, table 1.2). Employing the same criteria for the same countries after 1995, outside Ecuador none of the many presidential elections was followed by such a drastic change from campaign promises to implementation, and incumbent presidents were accountable on election day for their records in office.

Since 2000, reliability and responsibility have remained high. On the Left, Hugo Chávez was an exemplar of both traits. He ran against the Venezuelan establishment. His goals were public; he ran successfully for reelection on his record. He has showed that politicians who act to increase the state's role in the economy may also be reliable and responsible. On the Right, Álvaro Uribe is also an exemplar of both traits. He promised to tackle the problems of violence in Colombia and dedicated his two terms as president to this successful endeavor, as discussed in Eduardo Posada-Carbó's chapter. So too has been the case in Bolivia. Gonzalo Sánchez de Lozada won the presidency for the second time, after one term out of office; he promised and delivered on a continuation of the policies of his previous term—an obduracy that would contribute to his forced resignation in the face of mass protests. Comparably reliable and responsible was his sharp opponent and eventual successor, Evo Morales, elected president in 2005; over time, in campaigns and as president, Morales has acted as he has promised, as shown in George Gray Molina's chapter.

Downs's partisan responsibility was especially noteworthy in the 1990s and 2000s in El Salvador and Chile between successive administrations of four consecutive presidents, respectively, from El Salvador's Alianza Republicana Nacionalista (ARENA; Nationalist Republican Alliance) and Chile's Concertación coalition between Christian Democrats and Socialists. In both countries, the level of partisan responsibility and reliability was evident as well for the opposition parties, El Salvador's Frente Farabundo Martí para la Liberación Nacional (FMLN; Farabundo Martí National Liberation Front) and the alliance between Chile's parties of the Right, notwithstanding coalition name changes, discussed in Siavelis's chapter. In the 2000s, there was comparable partisan responsibility in economic policy between the successive PAN administrations of Vicente Fox and Felipe Calderón, treated in O'Neil's chapter. Equally responsible was Mexico's leading opposition party on the Left, the Partido de la Revolución Democrática (PRD; Party of the Democratic Revolution). Every Mexican president since the first seriously contested presidential election in 1988 has also been reliable; his campaign foreshadowed the new administration.

Partisan reliability and responsibility presumes, alas, that there are real political parties. Where parties and party systems are weak, the personalist supporters of individual politicians simply back the leader no matter what is said and done. Ecuador has had weak and mainly personalist political parties; therefore, it has been an exemplar of partisan unreliability. Only two presidents—Jamil Mahuad (1998–2000) and Rafael Correa since his first election in 2006—have shown Downsian reliability, that is, once elected they acted as they had promised during their campaigns that they would act. Parties have also been extremely weak in Peru, as discussed in Steven Levitsky's chapter. Thus it is not surprising that Alberto Fujimori had been one of the exemplars of partisan unreliability in 1990, nor that Alejandro Toledo, Alan García, and Ollanta Humala ran slightly left-of-center campaigns in 2001, 2006, and 2011 respectively, but each edged toward the center-right once elected president.

As noted at the start of this chapter, Lula's 2002 election as Brazil's president is a very good example of partisan reliability, but it poses a question regarding partisan responsibility. As his long-time supporters and opponents clamored, the 2002 campaign broke with various aspects of the PT's long-standing program. Yet, this break was done not in stealth but openly and transparently during the campaign. Moreover, Lula's administration, as Samuels shows in his chapter, sustained and expanded the social policies inherited from the Cardoso administration, in particular the successful conditional cash transfer program (renamed Bolsa Família under Lula), which has had a significant impact on the reduction of poverty in Brazil. In this respect, Lula demonstrated Downsian responsibility as well in terms of his own and the PT's history.

The resignation of President Fernando de la Rúa in late 2001, in the midst of a devastating economic crisis, permitted the Peronists (PJ; Partido Justicialista) to reemerge as the country's dominant party, as Calvo and Murillo explain in their chapter. The Peronists fragmented, however, in the run-up to the 2003 presidential election. Two Peronists, former President Carlos Menem and incoming President Néstor Kirchner, had been the top two candidates. Menem withdrew prior to the election's "second round" (mandated whenever no candidate wins a large enough share of the vote in the first round); Menem had run on his prior record of embracing the market economy. Kirchner ran as a center-left Peronist, tethered to the Peronist Movement's long-term commitment to greater state intervention in the economy, where he and his successor, his wife, President Cristina Fernández de Kirchner, would reanchor the Peronists and the policies of their governments. Because economic growth marked the Menem, Kirchner, and Fernández presidencies, each was able to win elections and hold onto the Peronist core constituencies, albeit in different ways. Kirchner and Fernández could claim accurately that they had been reliable—they acted as they said they would—and Downsian-responsible between their presidencies, and also because their economic policies echoed those that the Peronists had advocated before 1990.

What explains the varying trends in partisan reliability and responsibility? As Javier Corrales argued in the second edition of this book, those who were elected president in the late 1980s and early 1990s believed that they had no other choice but to betray their campaign promises and the records of their parties in order to enact policies that they deemed essential but for which there was little political support (Corrales 2003). International market forces edged presidents toward the political center, especially if their countries needed significant international financing, which most did. Opportunistically, presidents ran on the Left to get elected; they moved to the center or the Right to govern, often in response to a combination of domestic and international constraints. Incumbent parties were compelled to run on their records in office, however. In the 1990s, many incumbent parties succeeded in turning the economy around and making other improvements.[6] In the 2000s, an international commodity boom bolstered economic outcomes across nearly all Latin American countries, as Mazzuca's chapter shows. Success followed this superbly favorable international context, thus enabling politicians to become more reliable and responsible.

In the 1990s, incumbent parties succeeded in winning at least two consecutive elections in Argentina, Brazil, Chile, Colombia, El Salvador, Mexico, Paraguay, and Peru. Since 2000, incumbent parties also won at least two consecutive elections in that same list of countries (except Peru) but adding Bolivia, Costa Rica, the Dominican Republic, Ecuador, Nicaragua, Uruguay, and Venezuela. Just as importantly for democratic politics, even former-incumbent parties that lost elections since 2000 remained important contenders—Brazil's Partido da Social Democracia Brasileira (PSDB; Brazilian Social Democratic Party), the Liberal Party in Colombia, the PRI in Mexico, and the Liberals in Nicaragua. Propelled by an international commodity boom, economic growth made partisan reliability and responsibility electorally viable and valuable, and this is the key explanation for changing trends from the 1980s to the 2010s.

Since 2000, the question of partisan responsibility was posed sharply, albeit in different ways, in Brazil and Argentina. In both countries, in 2002 and 2003 respectively, the incoming presidents addressed the changes they were proposing forthrightly. The PT and the PJ repositioned themselves under the public glare. That Lula's administration hugged the political center just slightly to its left, and that Néstor Kirchner governed on the center-left, should have surprised no one. Public partisan reidentification absolves the PJ and the PT from the charge of partisan irresponsibility, even if some of their followers may remain unhappy with the turn of events.

Since 2000, only in Peru have politician and partisan unreliability remained high. Partisan irresponsibility was evident comparing Alan García's administrations in the 1980s (on the Left) and in the 2000s (on the Right). Levitsky's chapter explains why. High electoral volatility and the virtual disappearance of political careers make partisan responsibility across time almost impossible. The presence of multiple parties in the national legislature with easy and frequent defections makes partisan coordination nearly impossible. In turn, the lack of interpartisan coordination and weak state capacity make partisan reliability unlikely: if elected, the new incumbent finds it difficult to deliver on campaign promises because fellow partisans have broken away, legislative alliances reform and deform, and the state is incapable of implementing many policies. These mutually reinforcing behaviors render Peruvian parties irresponsible and unreliable.

In short, Latin American politicians and parties became more reliable and responsible since the mid-1990s. This trend toward democratic accountability is normatively laudable. It coexists with the long-sustained presence of ideological diversity and thus political pluralism within countries: there are strong parties or party coalitions with firmly held, albeit different, views in Chile, El Salvador, and Mexico, for example. There are significant differences between parties and blocs of voters in Brazil, Costa Rica, and the Dominican Republic, and between blocs of voters in Bolivia, Ecuador, and Venezuela.

Yet, too much virtue is also problematic in politics. The interaction between higher partisan reliability and responsibility, on the one hand, with sustained ideological differentiation, on the other, has contributed to political polarization. Politicians and parties honor the promises made to voters and, as a result, become less willing to compromise with other parties. Evo Morales, Hugo Chávez, and Álvaro Uribe have all been exemplary Downsians, but as a consequence they were also highly polarizing presidents. Uncompromising politicians pose risks for democratic institutions and practices because of their belief that their adversaries deserve no quarter, no tolerance, and at the extreme no dignity. In the early 2010s, these problems seemed most acute in Ecuador and Bolivia. The functioning of democratic politics wants politicians to be reliable and responsible, but it also wants politicians to bargain in order to govern. These compelling virtues highlight contrasting traits, not easily reconcilable as norms or in actual practice.

Party System Collapse, Dealignment, or Realignment

The story of political parties in Latin America is more complex than the preceding section implies. In the 1990s, several long-established and once powerful political parties collapsed. In Venezuela, these were Acción Democrática (AD; Democratic Action) and the Comité de Organización Política Electoral Independiente (COPEI; Social Christian Party), which had alternated in supplying the winner of every Venezuelan presidential election from 1958 to 1988 and between them had typically held four-fifths of the seats in Congress, as shown in Álvarez's chapter.[7] These two parties had weakened substantially before Hugo Chávez defeated them in 1998. In December 2005, hoping to discredit the election, AD and COPEI boycotted the national legislative elections; as a result, they had no seats in the new legislature and became even less effective at opposing President Chávez. In Peru, the Alianza Popular Revolucionaria Americana (APRA; American Popular Revolutionary Alliance), which had been Peru's largest political party since the 1920s, collapsed in the early 1990s following its disastrous term under President Alan García (1985–1990).

Both Peru and Venezuela evolved toward a no-party system. As Álvarez's chapter shows, Chávez politics was highly personalist, not subject to or dependent on a political party. Peru's parties decomposed before Fujimori's victory in 1990, as Levitsky shows.

Other parties have collapsed, though not to the same extent as in other party systems. In their chapter, Calvo and Murillo argue that the Argentine party system has undergone a process of voter dealignment, in particular among non-Peronist voters. Since 2000, Argentina's Unión Cívica Radical (UCR; Radical Civic Union), which elected its first president in 1916 and its most recent in 1999, also decomposed. As Calvo and Murillo show, Radical factions align with Peronist factions or with minor parties to retain electoral influence and win some subnational posts, but this UCR is a pale shadow of a once-vibrant centenarian party.[8] An array of small and sometimes transient parties competes for the political space that the UCR once occupied, but they have failed to create a significant non-Peronist party or a stable partisan realignment.

In Brazil, there has been no significant party collapse. However, the PT's three successive presidential election victories, the commodity boom and its translation into effective social policies, and the penchant of Brazilian democratic governments to govern with oversized coalitions to ensure legislative victories in Congress have the effect of weakening the effective capacity of the opposition to challenge the PT government. There is no sinister process at work, but Brazilian democratic politics would remain vigorous provided the opposition so remains.

A substantively different process may be under way in Bolivia and Colombia and, after a long pause (marked by party system collapse), perhaps also in Venezuela. This is party system realignment, not dealignment or party system collapse.[9] At first, the process of change resembled party system collapse. Bolivia's three main political parties during the 1980s and 1990s, each of which had elected a Bolivian president at least once in those years, weakened markedly; their voters scattered. In December 2005, Evo Morales was elected president with an absolute majority of the votes for his Movimiento al Socialismo (MAS; Movement toward Socialism), and he was reelected by a wider margin in December 2009. The MAS grew out of the coca growers' union and had a grass-roots structure beyond Morales's personal popularity. Instead of sustained party system collapse, however, Morales's government faced party system realignment, especially following the 2009 election. In his chapter, Gray Molina argues that territorial cleavages emerged in opposition. Some of these challenges are from indigenous communities, which have focused on specific policy decisions, not yet affecting partisan alignments. Other territorial cleavages, however, have fueled partisan realignment, with voters in Santa Cruz, Tarija, Beni, and Pando having become disproportionately more likely to support politicians and parties (independent of their names) that oppose Morales. This makes for party system realignment.

In Colombia, too, there was a significant partisan realignment at the century's start and, as Posada's chapter shows, not a party or party system collapse. The Liberal Party lost support during the Ernesto Samper presidency (1994–1998), which was tainted by allegations of undue influence from drug traffickers. Andrés Pastrana's presidency (1998–2002) lost support for his Conservative Party because the level of criminal and political violence remained extremely high. In 2002, Álvaro Uribe ran as a self-proclaimed political outsider under a party banner that he invented (commonly known just as U, which stood for Unity but mainly for Uribe); Colombians voted against the Liberals and the Conservatives. During the Uribe presidency (2002–2010), and especially in the 2010 presidential election won by Juan Manuel Santos, the U remained the president's party, the Conservatives and the Liberals regained strength (the Liberals gaining also in the 2011 municipal elections), while the Cambio Radical and the Polo Democrático Alternativo emerged as significant center-left parties in Congress—party system realignment indeed, even if this political process is still evolving.[10]

What explains the collapse or realignment of party systems? In the first edition of this book, Giraldo and I offered explanations for the breakdown of AD, the COPEI, and APRA in the 1990s that help as well to explain the realignments in Bolivia and Colombia in the 1990s. We argued, first, that AD and APRA had suffered from retrospective voter punishment, that is, voters assessed their performance in government and pronounced it dismal. Similarly, the implosion of Argentina's UCR in the early 2000s illustrates retrospective voter punishment of UCR President de la Rúa's economic stewardship, which was blamed for the economic catastrophe in 2001–2002. The same phenomenon was evident in Colombia blaming the Samper and Pastrana presidencies for the rise of violent insecurity (a phenomenon that is treated in Lucía Dammert's chapter on issues of violence and insecurity) and the downturn of the economy in the one South American country with the most sustained long-term good economic performance in the second half of the twentieth century. In Bolivia, the combination of economic recessions in its neighboring markets (Brazil in 1999, Argentina in 2001–2002) and sustained social protest associated with coca growers, indigenous movements, and other social movements, punctured by political violence and state repression in 2003, led to the resignation of President Sánchez de Lozada (see also Corrales' chapter). Because Sánchez de Lozada had been supported by a broad multiparty coalition, the big parties, not just his, were all blamed for the bad outcomes. (Corruption allegations were also pervasive in these and nearly all other cases, which is why corruption does not distinguish effectively between cases of party system continuity and cases of party system change.)

A second explanation for party system change, Giraldo and I argued, draws from Michael Coppedge's work (1994). Long-established political parties that have seemingly colluded to create an oligopoly of power and employ the electoral laws and the resources of incumbency to sustain their grip on public office, defying shifts in popular preferences, are vulnerable to voter revolt. Coppedge developed the concept of partyarchy to explain what had ailed AD and the COPEI. Colombia had long been an example of coalescent behavior between two allegedly rival parties—South America's most enduring formal duopoly. In Bolivia, the three biggest parties of the 1980s and 1990s had been both adversaries and allies according to the circumstances—a classic example of oligopoly collusion or "pacted democracy," as covered in Gray Molina's chapter, that led to the repudiation of the old parties in the 2005 and subsequent elections.

Party collusion may serve important political purposes at times. In Venezuela, partisan collusion at the end of the 1950s served to lay the groundwork for a successful transition to democratic politics. Also at the end of the 1950s, party collusion helped Colombia to end a long period of political violence. In the mid-1980s, party collusion in Bolivia was a key to braking hyperinflation and stabilizing the economy. What was good for a specific juncture would not serve the country's politics for all time, however.

Collusion alone had not, of course, unraveled the Bolivian, Colombian, or Venezuelan party systems in the past. Nor had "hard times" alone destroyed political parties during the 1980s, a terrible time for economic performance. The interaction of partisan collusion with retrospective voter punishment for "hard times," however, explains the difference between the defeat of a party in just one election and a more general collapse or realignment. In the 1990s and the 2000s in

Bolivia, Colombia, and Venezuela, the interaction between hard times and perceived interpartisan collusion killed the old party systems, which is the outcome common to both party system collapse and realignment.

A third explanation for party system change pertained to Peru and Venezuela, namely, the incumbent president's systematic and deliberate attempt to weaken political parties, at times including his own (this also means that the collapse of Venezuela's party system resulted from a cascade of converging calamities). In the 1990s, Peru's president Alberto Fujimori sought to undermine and disorganize the already feeble opposition parties, and he would go on to undermine even those parties he would create or that became his allies. Fujimori preferred personalist rule. In Venezuela, similarly, President Hugo Chávez sought to pulverize the already weak opposition. He endeavored to constrain their access to mass media (see Boas chapter), make difficult partisan organization, impede the development of independent sources of partisan funding, and inhibit the normal functioning of opposition parties. Chávez's own Movimiento Quinta República (MVR; Fifth Republic Movement) had been a highly powerful and electorally effective but also a rather personalist political machine (Merolla and Zechmeister 2011, 28–54). Civil society organizations were characteristically extensions of this personal machine (Hawkins and Hansen 2006, 102–32). In 2007, Chávez disbanded the MVR and compelled its merger with several smaller parties into the Partido Socialista Unido de Venezuela (PSUV; Venezuela's United Socialist Party), which created a more heterogeneous coalition quite dependent on him (see Álvarez's chapter). Parties and the party system collapsed in Peru and Venezuela, therefore, because two presidents, each of whom served at least a decade in power, made every effort to undercut opposition parties that were already suffering voter punishment. More remarkably, each of these two presidents prevented the institutionalization of his own party.

Why the difference, however, between party system breakdown and realignment? Breakdown and realignment proceed through a similar pathway that involves retrospective voting against hard times and typically blames a partisan oligopoly. What next requires explaining is not the defeat of old parties, which is common to both paths, but the reemergence of a party system in some countries but not in others. In the 2000s, Bolivia and Colombia (realignment) and Peru and Venezuela (party system collapse) differed in their respective political regimes. Levitsky and Way call certain regimes "competitive authoritarian" in order to signal the incumbent president's abuse of state power, notwithstanding the continuation of competitive-enough elections and a modicum of political liberties (2010). It is exceedingly difficult to construct new viable and stable opposition parties when the incumbent president systematically undercuts them. In Bolivia and Colombia, vigorous democratic contestation endured; incumbent presidents have had enough setbacks to prevent a slide to "authoritarianism." The story was different in Peru and Venezuela in the 1990s and 2000s. In 1992, incumbent President Fujimori staged a "self-coup" against the Congress, the Supreme Court, and the established political parties; notwithstanding some subsequent constraints on his power, he governed autocratically for the remainder of the 1990s. Chávez did not stage a self-coup but he used the power of the state to govern autocratically as well.

By the end of Chávez's first decade as president, however, the Venezuelan opposition showed signs of reemergence, overcoming party system collapse. Venezuela was a clear case of party system collapse approximately between 1990 and 2008. Chávez had weakened and disorganized the opposition, which was at times its own worst enemy; in 2005 the opposition parties had boycotted the national legislative elections and thus lost all representation in the national assembly. In 2006, Chávez trounced the opposition parties. Chávez followed this reelection with a much more active program of state intervention in economy and society and greater attempts to monopolize political power. In response to Chávez's intense decisiveness, the opposition began to come together. In 2008, most significant opposition parties formed a coalition to field a joint slate of candidates to contest the 2010 national legislative election. Assisted by appreciably weaker economic performance following the drop of the world price of petroleum in 2009, the opposition coalition tied Chávez's PSUV on election day 2010, winning a significant number of seats. President Chávez's illness (two well-publicized surgical interventions in 2011 and 2012 to remove malignant tumors) created a new political opportunity in time for the 2012 presidential election. In February 2012, State of Miranda Governor Henrique Capriles won an all-opposition primary election decisively; other opposition candidates agreed to support Capriles against Chávez. Tellingly, in this opposition primary Acción Democrática and COPEI backed a losing candidate. The new pro- versus anti-Chávez electoral split indicates the prospects for a party system realignment, not the rebirth of the old parties. Even following his reelection in October 2012, Chávez had been weakened by the economy's poor performance, his autocratic proclivities, and his health; his death in early 2013 widened the space for Venezuela to shift from two decades of party collapse toward partisan realignment.

Bolivia, Colombia, and possibly Venezuela illustrate the paths that either prevent partisan collapse in order to permit party system realignment, or may permit the emergence of a realigned party system following a prolonged collapse:

- The old parties remain strong enough to survive (Liberals and Conservatives in Colombia);
- Incumbent president's decisions create opportunities for opposition to reorganize (Bolivia and, belatedly, Venezuela), activating social cleavages (territorial in Bolivia), or creating a political cleavage (pro- versus anti-incumbent in Venezuela; Chile following the 1988 plebiscite).

Peru stands, therefore, as the sole example of sustained party system collapse for over two decades, principally for the reasons that Levitsky's chapter explains and that have been echoed above. This comparative analysis sheds light on the reasons why partisan realignment has yet to characterize Peru's politics. Fujimori's reluctance to create his own political party, Toledo's inability to launch one, and García's distancing from APRA party rebuilding in his second term all illustrate a failure to build the incumbent president's party (in contrast to Uribe's U and Morales's MAS). Moreover, Fujimori's government unraveled from within and did not require the prior establishment of a newly unified opposition party—unlike the processes to oppose Chávez in Venezuela or that sustained the opposition to Uribe in Colombia. The economic policies of Peruvian presidents, and the worldwide commodity boom from which the Peruvian economy benefited, outlined in Mazzuca's chapter, weakened the intensity of the opposition to the incumbent president; the Peruvian economic boom favored citizens unequally, creating the social-class ambience that elected Ollanta Humala president, but absent newly vibrant societal cleavages or felt anger evident in other instances of putative partisan realignment such as Bolivia or Venezuela in the late 2000s or in the late 1980s Chile, as argued in Siavelis's chapter.

The Challenges to Governing Institutions

Latin America's institutional challenges are highlighted by two key observations. First, since 2000 the natural resources export boom strengthened the state of nearly every country. In some, especially Bolivia, Ecuador, Venezuela, and, to varying degrees, Argentina, this commodity boom strengthened presidents who sought autocratic powers via plebiscitary legitimation (see Mazzuca's chapter). Such presidents wielded their new capacities against the opposition and also against the press (see Boas's chapter).

Second, even in Brazil and Mexico—whose trajectories in democratic politics are celebrated at the start of this chapter—the practice and outcomes of constitutional democratic governance raise grave questions about the quality of democracy.[11] In Brazil, the massive corruption scandals that came to light in 2005 were intimately connected to Lula's governing tactics. The executive governed thanks to its reliance on corruption to obtain support among members of Congress— monthly cash payments, or *mensalão*. This scandal forced out from office Lula's chief of staff, the finance minister, and the PT party president, but corruption scandals continued to tarnish Brazilian federal ministers under the Lula and Dilma Rousseff PT presidencies (see Samuels's chapter). In Mexico, the devastation from violence and other crimes associated but not limited to drug trafficking is widespread. Violence spiked in the second half of the 2000s. The key institutions of the Mexican state—the courts and the police—have proven woefully inadequate to fulfill the fundamental obligation of any state, namely, public order. Indeed, in many instances high-ranking police officials have been part of the criminal gangs that engage in widespread violence, as mentioned in O'Neil's chapter.

The problem of violence and insecurity is at the heart of Dammert's chapter. The problem of political violence, she notes, was once pervasive in the hemisphere, but it is now circumscribed to Colombia, where it has also been significantly reduced since 2000. The problem of criminal violence, however, has worsened. It has become severe in parts of northern Mexico and in the northernmost Central American countries, but it is a scourge throughout the continent. The manifold failures of the state are a common problem throughout Latin America, especially in countries where the state historically had been barely capable to perform basic tasks. Dammert also calls attention to the damage to civil liberties from a specific approach to combat crime, namely, increased severity in sentencing and the higher risk of arbitrary police behavior. These police and judicial practices give the appearance of combating crime while having little effect on its incidence, yet at the cost of breaching constitutional rights.

Even a long, sustained period of democratic governance, such as Argentina has experienced since the early 1980s, has not improved state institutions much. Power has remained concentrated in the executive at the expense of Congress and the courts. Important policies have been enacted by presidential decree, not legislation, and this practice has been common to presidents of quite varied ideological characteristics. Policy volatility comes to resemble policy capriciousness. Institutional instability was noteworthy with regard to the regulation of public utilities, which suffered from both rapid change and selective enforcement. It was especially alarming in the decisions of Presidents Kirchner and Fernández to compel the national statistics office to issue false statistics about inflation in order to court political favor (see Calvo and Murillo chapter).

Stronger Latin American states, even those that benefited from the commodity boom since 2000, have been unable to address the problems of public order; in some instances, they have used their new capacities to abuse power through corruption or autocratic governance. Criminal violence has spiked in Caracas as well, notwithstanding the vast resources that the Venezuelan petro-state received since worldwide petroleum prices rose after 2000. Mazzuca's chapter highlights the threat of abusive autocracies, and the concern about this threat is the key motivation for Corrales' chapter. Corrales examines cases of constitutional reform across Latin America over two decades and focuses on the likelihood that executive powers would be strengthened or weakened. He argues that, when both incumbents and opposition forces enjoy comparable levels of power, constituent assemblies are more likely to yield constitutions that curtail presidential powers; yet, when the opposition is politically weak, assemblies will instead expand presidential powers.

Stronger states may also yield good outcomes, however. Corrales, Mazzuca, and other authors do offer the prospect that sometimes the results of commodity booms and redefined constitutions may be for the better; they explain the good outcomes principally as the result of preexisting political, civic, and state institutions. In countries where good evolving political processes were in place prior to the commodity boom, the boom propelled further good outcomes. In countries where constitutionalism had been weak (Bolivia, Ecuador, Venezuela, and to a certain extent Argentina), the commodity boom strengthened the presidency at the expense of democratic constitutionalism.

Chile's constitutional reforms of 2005, for example, were a significant democratic advance that dismantled the authoritarian enclaves of the 1980 constitution. This reform occurred already under the commodity boom, which may have facilitated it. Economic booms strengthen all rulers (Mazzuca's argument)—even good ones, as Siavelis's chapter demonstrates for Chile.

Similarly, starting with the Pastrana presidency and continuing especially under the Uribe presidency, there were deliberate policies to strengthen the Colombian state and at the same time to modify key elements of its democratic regime. A more capable state fielded more effective military and police institutions that significantly lowered levels of political and criminal violence after 2000, enabling the reappearance of economic growth. Constitutional and legislative changes also improved the likelihood of political representation, as evident by partisan realignment. The Santos presidency built on this institutional upgrading through more consensual policies toward similar ends (see Posada-Carbo's chapter).

Brazil also significantly improved performance thanks as well to the commodity boom, as argued in Samuels's chapter. Building on the Cardoso presidency, the Lula presidency greatly expanded the state's investment in social policies, markedly reducing poverty rates, and significantly increasing education and health care engagement rates. Inequality rates fell as well. Voters rewarded the PT electorally but, unlike in Brazil's clientelist past, this was voter support for policies that had been well crafted, transparently discussed, and appropriately implemented.

Conclusions

Democratic politics is about contestation and representation. Democratic political regimes work more effectively, of course, when states have the capacity to implement the policies voted upon by the people's elective representatives and ensure compliance with the rule of law. Latin American countries thus entered the second decade of the twenty-first century somewhat bifurcated. Nearly all Latin American states had more resources at their disposal than they had enjoyed in decades. Some rulers used these resources to perpetuate personalist powers—most so in Venezuela but also in Bolivia, Ecuador, and Nicaragua (which benefited from Venezuelan assistance)—and these edged toward authoritarian traits while still retaining competitive-enough elections.[12] Yet, most Latin Americans lived in countries where the state sought to honor democratic elections and serve public purposes, adopting and executing policies that served well a much larger number of citizens than in the past.

Military coups have become less likely. Unreliable and irresponsible politicians and parties (in Downsian terms) had become less common. Party system breakdown endured in Peru but party system realignment may be under way in Bolivia, Colombia, and Venezuela, improving the prospects of representative democratic politics.[13]

The challenges to effective democratic governance remain severe. Deficits persist in representation, although they are fewer than in decades past. Coup attempts take place, though they now rarely succeed. The interaction between reliable and responsible parties, and partisan ideological cohesion has deepened polarization in several countries. Supreme courts and constitutional courts have become more effective and decisive in various countries, perhaps most so in Colombia. Deadlocks between executive and legislature became less common in the twenty-first century's second decade, and even where presidents lacked a parliamentary majority (Brazil, Mexico), there was sufficient accommodation for effective constitutional governance. A criminal violence pandemic threatens many cities and regions, and several whole countries in Central America, and this may be the most serious unresolved problem that states in the region face, regardless of whether their rulers have democratic or autocratic predilections.

The final chapter of this book's previous edition had a good ending, for that time and for now as well. Notwithstanding the serious difficulties, "in the long view, Latin Americans live today in freer more democratic countries than they did in the 1970s and 1980s. Latin American citizens are better educated and possess longer life expectancies; poverty rates have dropped. . . . Nearly all Latin American economies have resumed a growth path . . . even if much of this growth responds mainly to benign exogenous international price increases for the commodities that they export. In general, therefore . . . most Latin American governments have governed more effectively than their predecessors did a generation ago."[14]

NOTES

1. This chapter is the successor to Domínguez and Giraldo 1996. I remain very grateful to Jeanne Kinney Giraldo for her superb work on that chapter. The current chapter is also a successor to Domínguez 2003 and Domínguez 2008. Ideas and passages from those earlier versions appear in this fourth edition. This chapter, like its predecessors, is not a freestanding chapter. Instead, it calls attention to, and to some degree summarizes, themes that emerge in the preceding chapters of this book and in the earlier editions. There are textual references to the other chapters, but my debt to the authors in this book and its predecessors is much greater than these citations suggest. The views expressed here are mine alone, however. The Inter-American Dialogue and the authors are free to claim that this chapter's errors are all mine and all the insights are theirs.

2. Some of these passages were presented before US Senate, Committee on Foreign Relations, Subcommittee on Western Hemisphere, Peace Corps, and Global Narcotics Affairs, at Hearings regarding "The State of Democracy in the Americas," June 30, 2011.

3. For strong evidence of support of many features of the market economy in Brazil, including freer international trade, see Baker 2009, chaps. 6–8.

4. These passages on Mexico draw from Domínguez 2012.

5. See also Hochstetler and Samuels 2011, 127–46.

6. See for the 1990s and 2000s Weyland 1998, 539–68; Benton 2005, 417–42; Hunter 2007, 1–30; and Domínguez 2012.

7. See also Lupu 2010, 7–32; Heath 2009, 467–79; and Morgan 2007, 78–98.

8. For a more hopeful reading of the prospects for the UCR, see Lupu and Stokes 2010, 91–104.

9. This distinction and general formulation differs from the analysis in the book's third edition. See Domínguez 2008.

10. For different views of the Colombian party system see Moreno 2005, 485–509; and Dargent and Muñoz 2011, 43–71.

11. For more general discussion, see Levine and Molina 2011.

12. For general discussion, see Levitsky and Way 2010.

13. For studies of party systems, see also Kitschelt et al. 2010; and Levitsky and Roberts 2011.

14. Domínguez 2008.

REFERENCES

Baker, Andy. 2009. *The Market and the Masses: Policy Reform and Consumption in Liberalizing Economies.* New York: Cambridge University Press.

Benton, Allyson Lucinda. 2005. "Dissatisfied Democrats or Retrospective Voters? Economic Hardship, Political Institutions, and Voting Behavior in Latin America." *Comparative Political Studies* 38 (4): 417–42.

Coppedge, Michael. 1994. *Strong Parties and Lame Ducks: Presidential Partyarchy and Factionalism in Venezuela.* Stanford: Stanford University Press.

Corrales, Javier. 2003. "Market Reforms." In *Constructing Democratic Governance in Latin America,* edited by Jorge I. Domínguez and Michael Shifter, 74–99. 2nd ed. Baltimore: Johns Hopkins University Press.

Dargent, Eduardo, and Paula Muñoz. 2011. "Democracy against Parties? Party System Deinstitutionalization in Colombia." *Journal of Politics in Latin America* 3 (2): 43–71.

Domínguez, Jorge I. 2003. "Constructing Democratic Governance in Latin America: Taking Stock of the 1990s." In *Constructing Democratic Governance in Latin America,* edited by Jorge I. Domínguez and Michael Shifter, 351–81. 2nd ed. Baltimore: Johns Hopkins University Press.

———. 2008. "Three Decades since the Start of the Democratic Transitions." In *Constructing Democratic Governance in Latin America,* edited by Jorge I. Domínguez and Michael Shifter, 323–52. 3rd ed. Baltimore: Johns Hopkins University Press.

———. 2012. "Mexico's Campaigns and the Benchmark Elections of 2000 and 2006." In *The Oxford Handbook of Mexican Politics,* edited by Roderic Ai Camp, 523–44. New York: Oxford University Press.

Domínguez, Jorge I., and Jeanne Kinney Giraldo. 1996. "Conclusions: Parties, Institutions, and Market Reforms in Constructing Democracies." In *Constructing Democratic Governance in Latin America and the Caribbean in the 1990s,* edited by Jorge I. Domínguez and Abraham F. Lowenthal, 3–41. Baltimore: Johns Hopkins University Press.

Downs, Anthony. 1957. *An Economic Theory of Democracy.* New York: Harper and Row.

Hawkins, Kirk A., and David R. Hansen. 2006. "Dependent Civil Society: The *Círculos Bolivarianos* in Venezuela." *Latin American Research Review* 1 (4): 102–32.

Heath, Oliver. 2009. "Economic Crisis, Party System Change, and the Dynamics of Class Voting in Venezuela, 1973–2003." *Electoral Studies* 28:467–79.

Hochstetler, Kathryn, and David Samuels. 2011. "Crisis and Reequilibration: The Consequences of Presidential Challenge and Failure in Latin America." *Comparative Politics* 43 (2): 127–46.

Hunter, Wendy. 2007. "Rewarding Lula: Executive Power, Social Policy, and the Brazilian Elections of 2006." *Latin American Politics and Society* 49 (1): 1–30.

Kitschelt, Herbert, Kirk A. Hawkins, Juan Pablo Luna, Guillermo Rosas, and Elizabeth Zeichmeister. 2010. *Latin American Party Systems.* New York: Cambridge University Press.

Levine, Daniel H., and José E. Molina, eds. 2011. *The Quality of Democracy in Latin America*. Boulder, CO: Lynne Rienner.

Levitsky, Steven, and Kenneth M. Roberts, eds. 2011. *The Resurgence of the Latin American Left*. Baltimore: Johns Hopkins University Press.

Levitsky, Steven, and Lucan A. Way. 2010. *Competitive Authoritarianism: Hybrid Regimes after the Cold War*. New York: Cambridge University Press.

Lupu, Noam. 2010. "Who Votes for *Chavismo*? Class Voting in Hugo Chávez's Venezuela." *Latin American Research Review* 45 (1): 7–32.

Lupu, Noam, and Susan Stokes. 2010. "Democracy, Interrupted: Regime Change and Partisanship in Twentieth-century Argentina." *Electoral Studies* 29:91–104.

Martínez, Juan, and Javier Santiso. 2003. "Financial Markets and Politics: The Confidence Game in Latin American Emerging Economies," *International Political Science Review* 24 (3): 363–88.

Merolla, Jennifer L., and Elizabeth J. Zechmeister. 2011. "The Nature, Determinants, and Consequences of Chávez's Charisma: Evidence from a Study of Venezuelan Public Opinion." *Comparative Political Studies* 44 (1): 28–54.

Moreno, Erika. 2005. "Whither the Colombian Two-Party System? An Assessment of Political Reforms and their Limit." *Electoral Studies* 24:485–509.

Morgan, Jana. 2007. "Partisanship during the Collapse of Venezuela's Party System." *Latin American Research Review* 42 (1): 78–98.

Stokes, Susan. 2001. *Mandates and Democracy: Neoliberalism by Surprise in Latin America*. Cambridge: Cambridge University Press.

Weyland, Kurt. 1998. "Swallowing the Bitter Pill: Sources of Popular Support for Neoliberal Reform in Latin America." *Comparative Political Studies* 31 (5): 539–68.

Index

Page numbers in *italics* refer to tables and figures.